EUROPE AND THE WAR IN UKRAINE

The **Foundation for European Progressive Studies (FEPS)** is the think tank of the progressive political family at EU level. Our mission is to develop innovative research, policy advice, training and debates to inspire and inform progressive politics and policies across Europe. We operate as hub for thinking to facilitate the emergence of progressive answers to the challenges that Europe faces today.

FEPS works in close partnership with its members and partners, forging connections and boosting coherence among stakeholders from the world of politics, academia and civil society at local, regional, national, European and global levels.

Today FEPS benefits from a solid network of 68 member organisations. Among these, 43 are full members, 20 have observer status and 5 are ex-officio members. In addition to this network of organisations that are active in the promotion of progressive values, FEPS also has an extensive network of partners, including renowned universities, scholars, policymakers and activists.

Our ambition is to undertake intellectual reflection for the benefit of the progressive movement, and to promote the founding principles of the EU – freedom, equality, solidarity, democracy, respect of human rights, fundamental freedoms and human dignity, and respect of the rule of law.

This book has been published in cooperation with:

Amicus Europae Foundation
Aleja Przyjaciół 8,
00-565 Warszawa, Poland
https://fae.pl/

Fondation Jean-Jaurès
12 Cité Malesherbes,
75009 Paris, France
https://www.jean-jaures.org/

Foundation Max van der Stoel (FMS)
Leeghwaterplein 45, 5de verdieping, Den Haag, Zuid-Holland 2521DB, Netherlands
https://foundationmaxvanderstoel.nl/

Friedrich-Ebert-Stiftung Ukraine
Borysohlibska Str. 15A,
Kyiv 04070, Ukraine
https://www.fes.de/

Kalevi Sorsa Foundation
Siltasaarenkatu 18, 18-20 C, 6.krs,
Helsinki, Uusimaa 00530, Finland
https://www.sorsafoundation.fi/

Karl Renner Institute
Karl Popper Strasse 8,
A-1100 Vienna, Austria
https://renner-institut.at/

EUROPE AND THE WAR IN UKRAINE

FROM RUSSIAN AGGRESSION TO A NEW EASTERN POLICY

Edited by László Andor and Uwe Optenhögel

Book published in May 2023 by the Foundation for European Progressive Studies in association with London Publishing Partnership

FOUNDATION FOR EUROPEAN PROGRESSIVE STUDIES (FEPS)

Avenue des Arts 46 – 1000 Brussels, Belgium
www.feps-europe.eu
@FEPS_Europe

Supervision: Hedwig Giusto
Layout and editing: T&T Productions Ltd, London; Steve Anthony
Cover photographs: Adobe Stock

This book was published with the financial support of the European Parliament. It does not represent the view of the European Parliament.

ISBN: 978-1-913019-88-4 (pbk)
ISBN: 978-1-913019-89-1 (ePDF)
ISBN: 978-1-913019-90-7 (ePUB)

Table of contents

Foreword

The Russian aggression against Ukraine defined politics and life in Europe in 2022 and will continue to do so in 2023. Although it is primarily the people of Ukraine who are suffering the impact of Vladimir Putin's war, the indirect effects have been felt worldwide. Putin's invasion and its inherent potential to provoke chaos in the international system show that wars involving great powers can no longer be contained regionally in a globalised world.

Whenever this war eventually ends, it has already unleashed dynamics with far-reaching global implications. It is reinforcing the deglobalisation tendencies observable since the financial crisis of 2008–2009 and accelerated by the Covid-19 pandemic. In geopolitical terms, new centres of power are emerging, while geo-economically, a reconfiguration of energy, production, distribution and financial systems is under way.

For Europeans the Russian invasion triggered a reassessment and reconsideration of Eastern policies, going back not only to the previous chapters of the Russo-Ukrainian conflict but to the postcommunist transition as a whole. In regard to the transformation in Russia, it should be remembered that until 1998 developments in Russia were already taking the wrong path economically, and since about 2008 they have also taken the wrong path politically.

Already prior to the Ukraine war, the European Union had been living in a security paradox. The demand for security provided by Europe increased due to a growing arc of instability in the European neighbourhood and an increasingly distracted United States. The corresponding supply, however, was hardly to be found. Whereas the Union was making some progress institutionally, capacities were not available and – even more crucially – there was no political will to act. The concept of "strategic autonomy" was far from matching the security and military demands generated by the war. Into this European gap between high security demand and low security supply burst the Russian attack on Ukraine.

While Washington and London reacted decisively and NATO was revitalised as the main defence for Europeans, the EU particularly struggled with the military aspect of the conflict, which brought the reality of a major interstate war back to the European continent. The war put a definitive end to the post-Cold War European security architecture anchored in the Paris Charter (1990), following the global political earthquake of the fall of the Berlin Wall.

It is worth recalling the situation in Europe in 1989, just one year after the recognition of the existence of the European Community by the Soviet Union. In fact, throughout that year, a series of signs had suggested that the Soviet bloc was a pressure cooker about to blow. The borders of the Soviet Union had been defined by Joseph Stalin at Yalta and Potsdam, where he had imposed his map of Central and Eastern Europe with a traditional imperial political and military logic, according to which "whoever occupies a territory also imposes on it his own social system [...] as far as his army can reach. It cannot be otherwise." As soon as the Soviet Empire imploded, the European peoples under its rule strived for their own way. Estonia, Latvia, Lithuania, Poland, Hungary, the Czech Republic, Slovakia, Romania and Bulgaria all in turn became member states of the newly created European Union – a simultaneous process of joining a united Europe while escaping from a classical empire. Ukraine remained in the grey zone: was it a frontier or a buffer state?

It is becoming increasingly clear that Europe is paying a high price for not having sufficiently striven towards a common and proactive Russia policy. Putin led Russia back into international politics based on the claim of being a military world power. And he underpinned his increasingly aggressive foreign policy by relying on conservative, anticommunist and nationalist thinkers combining pan-Slavic ideas with anti-Western, neoimperialist Russian nationalism. These thinkers call for a "Russian world" (*Russkiy mir*) that relativises existing state borders and explicitly includes the diaspora, a comprehensive concept that addresses ideological, political, cultural, geopolitical and identity issues. This approach is supported by the Russian Orthodox Church, which wants to make the "Russian world" an outpost of Christian civilisation once more. The concept of *Russkiy mir* has already been employed by Putin to legitimise Russia's annexation of Crimea. Could it be that the ultimate aim is to build a new Holy Russian Empire?

Unfortunately, it seems that the West failed to take either this doctrine or security concerns about Russia seriously up until the outbreak of the Ukraine war. Against this background, the question of whether security on the European continent can be organised only with Russia or only against Russia gains a wholly different meaning. Peaceful coexistence with Putin's Russian world is currently hard to imagine. What is emerging is an existential confrontation between looking to the past and building the future.

However, we need to admit that not only has study and strategy on Russia been lacking but so too has appreciation of the complexity of Ukraine as a country and a nation. The fragility of the Ukrainian state and the general weaknesses of the Ukrainian economy should have been assessed more seriously.

Nevertheless, since the initial shock one year ago, European leaders have acted with remarkable unity, determination and speed. Up to now the conflict has been highly dynamic, both militarily and politically. Ambitions, objectives and achievements have been as dynamic as the policies of the stakeholders involved. While not a military player at the beginning of the conflict, the EU has emerged as a significant actor by aiding the Ukrainian war effort, supporting refugees, sanctioning Russia and turning Ukraine into a candidate for EU membership. What continues to be a major challenge is to reconcile the open-ended war effort with the economic and social dynamics and interests of, and within, the EU itself.

The European strategy in response to the Russian invasion has been aimed at encouraging Ukraine and mobilising Western support, but it has not come without risks. Many EU leaders started to overstate the chances of Ukraine joining the Union, raising expectations that made Ukrainians believe their country could somehow naturally fit into EU structures as we know them today. When speaking publicly with Ukrainian politicians about the chances of EU accession, populist narratives frequently popped up suggesting that the speed of accession depends on the bureaucratic performance in Brussels, and not on the country in question matching EU standards and rules, without being rebutted by EU officials.

At the same time, when speaking to EU citizens, EU leaders constantly downplayed the expected costs of economic warfare. No wonder Europeans were disappointed when the sanctions imposed on Russia did not help force the aggressor to end its campaign and leave Ukraine alone, and even more so when the continent slid back into inflation and economic recession and started to face a long-term fall in growth potential and living standards.

Europe nevertheless ended the year 2022 remarkably united in its unwavering support for Ukraine. A new financial aid package was even adopted, together with another round of sanctions against Russian officials, as well as business and media figures. On the other hand, European views remained diverse regarding expectations about how the war should end, what kind of postwar security architecture should be built, and how much room would remain for restarting economic cooperation with Russia once the war is over.

It is clear that, at least in the first year of the war, social democrats have not been rewarded for fighting at the vanguard of solidarity with Ukraine. However, progressive forces have distinguished themselves in this difficult year by going beyond the necessary international solidarity and reconciling it with two further objectives: fair distribution of the costs of war within our societies; and avoidance of unnecessary escalation, in tandem with simultaneous preparations for peace and reconstruction. No other political force seems concerned with this broader responsibility, which remains a distinctive characteristic of social democrats.

The eventual reconstruction of Ukraine will provide the opportunity for a second transition. In this process, it will be absolutely vital to learn from the grave errors of neoliberal transition in the post-Soviet societies. Social democrats can be self-confident in this regard and promote a way forward "for the many, not the few". This time reconstruction must go far beyond liberal market capitalism. It needs a proactive, enabling state pursuing social, industrial and technological policies, respecting decentralisation and regionalism, and showing a commitment to sustainability.

In this sense, FEPS's contribution to the debate, already important before, is particularly important now during the war in Ukraine. This book represents a continuation of this work. It offers an initial comprehensive picture of the war and its repercussions in Europe and may serve as a stimulus for informed debate about Ukraine's future in Europe.

Enrique Barón Crespo

André W. M. Gerrits

1 | The ideological and philosophical context of the war

We should take Vladimir Putin's philosophical and ideological concerns seriously. They define his world outlook; they drive his policies; and they revolve around Ukraine. The hegemony over Ukraine is the key link between Russia's regional sphere of influence and its global power. And in Putin's eyes, Russia is a global power, or Russia is not – literally. In Putin's perception, the war in Ukraine is a war for the survival of Russia.

The war in Ukraine is the biggest threat to peace and stability in Europe since World War II. What inspired Russian President Vladimir Putin to plunge his country into such an uncertain conflict? How does he justify and legitimise the war, or the "special military operation" in the new-speak that is now mandatory in Russia? What are Putin's philosophical or ideological drivers, and how have they developed over the course of the war?

The first thing that arises in response to these questions is a counter-question: what does it matter? Should we attach any real significance to Putin's philosophical justification of the war in Ukraine? Given the rambling, sometimes incoherent and contradictory nature of his reflections, both their philosophical and ideological significance must be considered low. And this does not seem particularly problematic, given the fact that a politician should be primarily judged by his actions, not his ideas. But even the political significance of Putin's narrative is not obvious. It is mainly a matter of interpretation. We cannot be sure whether the Russian president is driven by the ideas that he presents, or whether his public statements mainly serve to *legitimise* his political actions. In other words, does Putin believe in the narrative he presents, or is it mere window-dressing, a justification to the public of geopolitical aggression and the strengthening of his own power? The honest answer is we do not know. There are a multitude of reasons behind the war against Ukraine, including what one may recognise as Putin's political "philosophy", his worldview. And the importance of this becomes greater if the little information we have of the decision-making process leading up to the invasion (or actually the re-invasion) of Ukraine turns out to be correct. The decision to assault Ukraine was allegedly made in very small circles, if not by Putin personally.[1]

There seems ample reason to take Putin's more philosophical and ideational statements seriously. They may be inconsistent and contradictory at times, and they are not fixed (nor can they be, because they are partly determined by a geopolitical context over which the Russian leader has limited influence), but they are largely consistent. And let's not forget: we have often been surprised by the extent to which authoritarian rulers believed in the ideological webs they spun themselves.

Despite the ubiquity of official rhetoric (in the press, on talk shows, in education, in other state-run agitprop and in the church) and the tightened censorship and repression, dissenting – even critical – voices on the war in Ukraine can also be heard in Moscow. Generally, these are radical voices, who believe that the war is being fought incompetently or at least not forcefully enough. Military bloggers, Chechen leader Ramzan Kadyrov, the alleged founder of the paramilitary Wagner group Yevgeny Prigozhin, a series of conservative *klubs* and individual, radical geopolitical thinkers such as Alexander Prokhanov and Alexander Dugin make dissident noises, but they do not fundamentally deviate from the official political discourse, defined by Putin himself.

In this contribution I limit myself to what can credibly be considered to be Putin's political philosophy. Putin's thoughts are distilled from his most important public "appearances" shortly before and during the war: a 6,000-word article "On the historical unity of Russians and Ukrainians" (a piece on the relationship between Russia and Ukraine that he published in July 2021, and which has been plausibly characterised as "Putin's ideological treatise behind the invasion");[2] Putin's two pre-invasion speeches,

---

1   Myth and reality may not be far apart here. In 2015 Putin confirmed in an official documentary that the decision to annex Crimea had been taken by himself, on the eve of the ending of the Sochi Olympics, after overnight deliberation in the company of four confidants, including three (former) KGB officers. Putin has not commented on the decision-making process surrounding the invasion in March 2022, but it is widely assumed that things have not been much different, with the exception perhaps that even fewer individuals were involved.

2   Kuzio, T. (2022) "Imperial nationalism as the driver behind Russia's invasion of Ukraine". *Nations and Nationalism*, 29(1): 30–38. DOI: 10.1111/nana.12875

on 21 and 24 February; his speech after the signing of the treaties on the accession of Donetsk, Luhansk and the Zaporizha and Kherson regions to Russia (30 September);[3] and the talk he delivered at the annual international Valdai conference on 27 October 2022.

Putin's worldview

Russia watchers have reported Putin's alleged "conservative turn" more than a decade ago, following his comeback as president (2012) and the annexation of Crimea (2014). Putin's conservative ideas have frequently been interpreted as mainly instrumental. They seem to play well with the Russian majority and with the right-wing and populist political forces in Europe and the US. Putin's conservatism certainly has instrumental traits. Both the timing of his conservative spin and the themes that he put forward can be well explained by the political legitimacy crisis in the wake of the tandem spectacle that took the authoritarian regime by surprise (massive street demonstrations in Moscow and tens of other Russian cities in 2012) and by the populist advance in Central and Western Europe. Putin's diatribes against the militant multiculturalism, secularism and liberalism of a disconnected, transnational elite are also doing well outside Russia. Yet there is little reason to suppose that Putin's conservatism is not also a matter of conviction. The consistency and the persistence of his arguments are too strong to neglect. Putin *has* a conservative worldview.

Judging from his public appearances, Putin's view of the world, including his understanding of Russia–Ukraine relations, seems to be influenced mainly by a group of conservative, anticommunist, mostly religiously inspired thinkers: "White" counter-revolutionaries from the early days of the Bolshevik regime such as Ivan Ilyin (1883–1954), Nikolai Berdyaev (1874–1948) and Vladimir Solovyov (1853–1900); dissidents from the Soviet era, in particular Alexander Solzhenitsyn (1918–2008) and Alexander Zinoviev (1922–2006), both of whom were forced to leave the Soviet Union; and the ethnocultural and Eurasianist ideas of Soviet scholars such as Lev Gumilov (1912–1992) and his distant ideological relative Alexander Dugin (born 1962). What does this motley crew of thinkers have in common? First and foremost, they stress that Russia and the West (including the democratic part

---

3 "Signing of treaties on accession of Donetsk and Lugansk people's republics and Zaporozhye and Kherson regions to Russia". Press release, President of Russia website, 30 September 2022. URL: http://en.kremlin.ru/events/president/news/69465.

of Europe) are deeply different civilisations – a notion popularised by the 19th-century philosopher Nikolay Danilevsky (1822–1885). They emphasise the unique nature of Russia, defined by a combination of history, religion (orthodoxy), political culture (autocracy) and geography (space). They highlight the threat that Western Marxism and liberalism pose to the spiritual unity and distinctiveness of the Russian civilisation. And they are committed to the shared historical mission of the Eurasian peoples, led by Russia, and in this context they question or dismiss the historical or future statehood of Ukraine (and, on occasion, Belarus and Kazakhstan). State and church are the main institutional pillars of this conservative, nationalist tradition. Today the Orthodox Church seems to have regained its traditional position again: prominently present in official discourse, yet firmly subordinate to the state. If there are significant dissidents within the Orthodox Church in relation to the war in Ukraine, they have yet to come forward.

A side note on the concept of influence. First, Putin refers to the above-mentioned thinkers with some regularity in his public appearances, but he mentions others too. Moreover, Putin refers approvingly to some aspects of their thinking while he ignores others. And most importantly, Putin may share several of the core thoughts of these intellectuals, but he draws his own *political* conclusions. The idea that Putin has been ideologically hijacked by a bunch of long-deceased conservative Russian thinkers is nonsense. Putin's actual political decisions, including the decision to re-invade Ukraine, are driven by a series of considerations, some of an ideational, some of a more practical nature (practical, but misguided) – as I argue below. Still, Putin stands in a strong intellectual tradition, and he seems to appreciate it. He is evidently attracted not only by the deep-rooted distrust these conservative thinkers harbour towards the West, but also by the counterbalance that a "gathering of the Russian lands",[4] a "Russian Union" (Solzhenitsyn) of Russia, Ukraine, Belarus and the northern part of Kazakhstan could offer against it. When

---

4   Should the invasion of Ukraine also be seen as a final attempt by Putin to assert himself as one of Russia's great leaders? There is little evidence for this. In June 2022, relaxedly reclining in a designer chair in front of a group of attentively listening young people, Putin drew a parallel between his "special military operation" and the "Great Northern War" (1700–1721) between Peter the Great's army and the Swedes. The similarity was that both military endeavours were not aimed at conquest, Putin emphasised, but rather at reclaiming territory historically belonging to Russia. ("Putin and Peter the Great: Russian leader likens himself to 18th century tsar". *BBC News*, 10 June 2022. URL: https://www .bbc.com/news/world-europe-61767191.)

Solzhenitsyn developed the concept of a "Russian Union", he was building on ideas that were popular in White émigré circles, and he preluded what Putin now considers the East Slavic core of his "Greater Eurasia". It is a fine irony of history: one of the most vilified dissidents of Soviet times became a source of political inspiration for the former KGB officer who is now running Russia.

Putin's worldview cannot be seen as anything other than a break with Russia's recent communist history (and a reconnection with an earlier past). For someone who lamented the collapse of the Soviet Union as a "major geopolitical disaster", Putin is remarkably disparaging of the communist superstate. He is particularly critical of the nationality politics of the early Soviet leaders (Lenin in particular), especially towards Ukraine. After the October Revolution, the Bolsheviks created a new Ukrainian political entity based on an artificial national identity, Putin wrote in his article in July 2021. "Modern Ukraine is entirely the product of the Soviet era," he argues. "We know and remember well that it was shaped – for a significant part – on the lands of historical Russia." With the collapse of the Soviet Union, Russia's rulers facilitated the de facto independence of the pseudo-state Ukraine – Putin argues – without caring about the loss of these "ancient Russian lands", including Crimea, and its inhabitants. This historical interpretation is not without significance; it implies that Putin does not feel in any way politically bound by what was agreed with Ukraine during Soviet times. In his television speeches on the eve of the invasion, Putin also recalled the role of Lenin and his essentially confederate state plans. "Why was it necessary to appease the nationalists," he wondered. "What was the point of transferring to the newly, often arbitrarily formed administrative units [...] vast territories that had nothing to do with them?" Lenin's ideas about state-building in the Soviet Union were not a "mistake", Putin asserts; "they were worse than a mistake". And he adds menacingly: "Today the 'grateful progeny' has overturned monuments to Lenin in Ukraine. They call it decommunization. You want decommunization? Very well, this suits us just fine. But why stop halfway? We are ready to show what real decommunization would mean for Ukraine."

History is never far away in Putin's public appearances on Ukraine, especially and predictably the Great Patriotic War. Much of his televised speech on 24 February Putin devotes to the aggressive, expansionist policies of the West, with the United States in the lead. "What next," he asks. "What are we to expect?" And he makes a comparison with Russia on the eve of World War II. "In 1940 and early 1941 the Soviet Union went to great lengths to prevent war or at least to delay its outbreak. To this end, the USSR sought not to provoke the potential aggressor until the very end by refraining or postponing the most urgent and obvious preparations [...] When it finally acted, it was too late," Putin concluded. "The country stopped the enemy and went on to defeat it, but it came at a tremendous cost." In one passage, Putin compares the United States to Nazi Germany; he criticises Stalin; and he defends the attack on Ukraine as a defensive, preemptive strike – a truly inventive use of history.

The invasion: two explanations

There are two clusters of explanations for Russia's invasion of Ukraine: a security-policy explanation, which puts the war in the context of post-Cold War relations between Russia and the West, and a cultural-historical one, in which the invasion is seen as the result of Putin's specifically imperialist and revanchist interpretation of relations between Russia and Ukraine.

In the security explanation the Russian aggression is expounded on the basis of a typical "realist" doctrine, the security dilemma: where one state (or alliance) takes measures to strengthen its security, the other state may perceive this as affecting its own security, and act accordingly, which is then considered by the first party as security threat, and so on. NATO's eastward expansion and Russia's response could be considered as such a security dilemma. The cultural-historical explanation on the other hand seeks the cause of the war mainly in Putin's views on Ukraine and the historical relationship between Ukraine and Russia. In this explanation the war is essentially the result of an unfinished decolonisation process and Russia's deep-seated imperialist mindset.

In the debate among Western observers of the war the two explanations are generally opposed. "Realist" observers tend to follow the security-policy explanation, where the Russian invasion is deemed to have been triggered to a greater or lesser extent by NATO expansion. They do not consider the belief that NATO never had aggressive intentions towards Russia to be particularly relevant, as the security dilemma is primarily a matter of perception. Many "liberal" observers share the cultural-historical explanation, denying that the West ever posed a serious threat, and they look for reasons in the vindictive, violent nationalism of the Putin clique. Liberals also see the war in Ukraine as a struggle between democracy and dictatorship, while realists believe that Russia is acting primarily as a great power. They point out that powerful democracies (the United States in particular) do not behave substantially differently from authoritarian regimes once they believe their essential interests are at stake.

The idea that Putin would have feared a democratic Ukraine because it could lead to political contamination of Russia is not particularly convincing. For few Russians, independent Ukraine (democratic but weaker, poorer and more unstable than Russia) was a shining example. Putin fears a democratic Ukraine mainly because it is an independent Ukraine.

I have never understood the rigour of choosing either the security or the historical-cultural explanation. The Russian invasion of Ukraine is several things at once: an attempted backlash against the expansion of Western institutions, the subjugation of Ukraine, the entrenchment of Russia's global position and the consolidation of Putin's personal power. Moreover, the two explanations are not mutually exclusive. On the contrary, my argument is that Putin's ideational and security considerations are closely intertwined. It is unlikely that geopolitical considerations alone explain Putin's war against Ukraine, but it is perfectly probable that they contributed to the radicalisation of his increasingly derogative and aggressive views on Ukraine and its relationship with Russia. National identity, national interests and national security are social constructs, and they are subject to constant change, as is the political strategy derived from them. Most realists and liberals will agree that the "incompatible logics of sovereignty (Ukraine's) and imperialism (Russia's)"[5] underlie the war, only they interpret both the causes and consequences of these "incompatible logics" differently.

In Putin's public appearances both the security-political and cultural-historical motive for the invasion are emphasised, albeit not always to the same extent and with the same arguments. The essence of Putin's cultural-historical justification of the war is the denial of Ukrainian national identity and statehood. Putin repeatedly confirms his belief in the deep-rooted unity of the Eastern Slavs, which he defines as the eternal association of Great Russians, Little Russians (Ukrainians) and White Russians (Belarusians), from the medieval commonwealth of Kyiv Rus to today, and tomorrow. Russia, Ukraine and Belarus share an identity *and* a destiny. Ukraine can therefore only exist in close alliance with Russia, Putin emphasises. Any other interpretation of mutual relations is

---

5   Mälksoo, M. (2022) "The postcolonial moment in Russia's war against Ukraine". *Journal of Genocide Research*, 11 May, p. 1. DOI: 10.1080/14623528.2022.2074947

part of an "anti-Russian project". The same logic also seems to apply to the other Slavic "nations" in the former Soviet Union, Belarus and parts of Kazakhstan. On several occasions in 2014 Putin publicly noted that Kazakhstan had never been a state before 1991 and that it owed its sovereign status entirely to Russia. It was Putin's way of putting the tense relations between Kazakhstan – then under the leadership of Nursultan Nazarbayev – and Russia during the aftermath of the annexation of the Crimea in the right historical perspective.[6]

Putin has consistently argued that the conflict between Russia and Ukraine is in fact a civil war, not between Russians and Ukrainians, after all "one people", but between the "junta" in Kyiv and the larger part of the Ukrainian population. Final responsibility for the conflict however lies with the "West", which has always tried to drive a wedge between Ukrainians and Russians. As the war dragged on and the extent and the importance of Western military assistance to Ukraine became obvious, Putin increasingly shifted his rhetoric, from a Russo-Ukrainian 'civil war' to a confrontation between Russia and NATO – decades in the making, as he adds. The West played a vital role in what Putin perceives as the ill-fated "Ukrainification" of Ukraine. After the annexation of the Crimea and the armed conflict in the Donbas and strongly supported by an increasingly wide-ranging economic, political and military cooperation with the EU and with NATO and its member states, Ukraine drifted ever further westward, away from Russia and its self-declared zone of privileged interest.

On the eve of the invasion of Ukraine Putin gave two televised speeches, on 21 and 24 February. As in his article on the "historical unity" of Russians and Ukrainians (12 July 2021), his 21 February speech is mainly about the historical closeness of Ukrainians and Russians and only then about the responsibility of the West. Putin even accuses Kyiv of trying to blackmail the West. The Ukrainian leaders have used the perceived threat of Russia as a bargaining chip for its relations with the West. In his speech of 24 February, in which he announced to the Russian people that he has ordered the "special military operation" in Ukraine, he shifts his attention to the responsibility of the West. He blames the West for its support of Kyiv's genocidal politics in the Donbas, targeted against "the millions of people who live there and who pinned their hopes on Russia, on all of us". (Earlier, in his July 2021

---

6   "Putin downplays Kazakh independence, sparks angry reaction". *Radio Liberty/Radio Free Europe*, 3 September 2014. URL: https://www.rferl.org/a/kazakhstan-putin-history -reaction-nation/26565141.html.

article, Putin compared Kyiv's forced assimilation policy to the use of weapons of mass destruction against Russia.) Apparently, Putin believed that the argument of the threat from the West would do better with both his own subjects and international public opinion than the alleged connection between Russians and Ukrainians or the artificiality of the Ukrainian state and nation.[7] Half a year later, in Putin's speech to the Valdai conference, the crimes against the people in the Donbas were hardly mentioned at all anymore. The war was now almost entirely blamed on the aggressiveness of the West, or at least of a part of the West, as we will see below. Russia is waging a defensive, civilisational war, in the name of the entire non-Western world, to defend its sovereignty and its freedom against the incorrigible tradition of Western arrogance and interference, as Putin argues.

A sober analysis of the actual circumstances of the invasion indicates how crucial Putin's cultural-historical motivations have been. However heavily the NATO threat was felt, it did not deter Russia from launching a full-scale military operation against Ukraine. Apparently, neither the risk of a military confrontation with the West nor the chance of significant resistance by the Ukrainian military was considered particularly high. These were dramatic mistakes, with far-reaching consequences, and very much inspired by the misguided rhetoric of the Kremlin leadership. Putin was misled by his own belief in the indissoluble bond between Ukrainians and Russians, in Ukraine's weak national identity and its shaky statehood. And recent history had already suggested otherwise. In a 1991 referendum, Ukraine's independence from the Soviet Union was supported by 92.3% of voters (the percentages in the Russian-speaking regions of eastern Ukraine were barely lower, except for Crimea). The "fascist junta" that Putin thought he would oust with a military lightning raid on Kyiv was led by a president elected three years earlier with 73% of the popular vote, again with comparable figures in the East. The Kremlin believed it could subjugate a country

---

7   In August 2022, six months into the war, in an ever more repressive Russia, a poll by the Levada Center showed that 68% of the Russian respondents (down from 83% in October a year earlier) still had a positive opinion of Ukrainians. ("Attitude towards countries and their citizens", 16 September 2022.) Incidentally, from another poll a few weeks before, Levada reported that 76% of respondents still supported the actions of the Russian armed forces in Ukraine (46% fully and 30% more yes than no). ("Conflict with Ukraine: August 2022", 14 September 2022).

of 43 million people, larger than France, with a military force of about 175,000 troops![8]

And finally, the security- and the history-related explanations for Russian intervention in Ukraine have different implications for the West. The security-policy account provides the West with some leeway towards Russia, possibly even with some influence. After all, in this explanation Russia largely responds to the enlargement strategies of NATO and the European Union. The cultural-historical argument, which emphasises deeply rooted ideational sentiments and ambitions, offers far fewer options (other than fierce resistance or granting Russia a geopolitical licence).

Eurasia and "Fortress Russia"

The war in Ukraine is both a strategic conflict with the West and a late-colonial act of aggression by the Kremlin. Indeed, the essence is the same in both cases: the Russian pursuit of hegemony over Ukraine. Russia's rulers reject an independent, sovereign Ukraine because it undermines their *Weltanschauung*, it thwarts their geopolitical ambitions (hegemony in the Eurasian part of the world) and it jeopardises their economic and political interests. The geopolitical notion of Eurasia is key to Russia, and Ukraine is key to Eurasia.

Like other aspects of how Putin perceives Russia's place in the world, the notion of "Eurasianism" was developed by émigré White Russian thinkers in the interwar period. Alexander Dugin is Russia's foremost Eurasianism ideologue today.[9] His ideas are an intriguing mixture of the classical geopolitical, the rabidly nationalist, the blatantly aggressive and the confusingly mystical. Is Putin a "Eurasianist"? If so, he is probably not of the Dugin-type. To the best of my knowledge, Putin never defined himself as an Eurasianist, which would also presuppose that there is a generally accepted definition of Eurasianism, and there is none. Putin

---

8   The underestimation of the risks of the military operation against Ukraine also seems to have been influenced by the social surveys conducted across Ukraine in February 2022 and commissioned by the Ninth Directorate of the Fifth Service of Russia's Federal Security Service (FSB). While the FSB surveys apparently indicated that large parts of the Ukrainian population would resist a Russian invasion and that any expectation that Russian forces would be greeted as liberators was unfounded, it apparently continued to provide the Kremlin with rosy estimates about the chances of quick results from the military operation. (Reynolds, N., and J. Watling (2022) "Ukraine through Russia's eyes". Royal United Services Institute website, 25 February.)

9   Dugin's *Foundations of Geopolitics* (*Osnovy geopolitiki: geopoliticheskoe budushschee Rossii*, Moscow: Arktogeya, 1997) was required reading at military academies in Russia.

---

does not refer to Eurasianism as such, the ideology, but rather to Eurasia, the geopolitical bloc. He values Eurasia as a largely self-sufficient and powerful territorial and political counterweight to expansive Atlanticism. Although there is little reason to believe that Dugin is a particularly influential individual in the Kremlin today, Putin seems to share the more rational core of his ideas, as does the greater part of the Russian political elite today. Putin's rhetoric is a moderate, more geopolitical than ideological variant of the anti-Western ideology of the conservative thinkers I mentioned earlier, including Dugin.

There are practical and to some extent also ideational aspects to Putin's international strategy that relate to Eurasianism. This is not just about Putin's still rather unsuccessful ambition to strengthen and institutionalise cooperation with states in Eurasia (whose centrepiece is the Eurasian Economic Union), but also about his efforts to epitomise Russia as a distinctive, a unique civilisation. Russia has never considered and does not consider itself an enemy of the West, Putin told his audience at the Valdai conference in October. Russia is not locked in conflict with the West, but only with a certain "part" of the West. For Putin, there are two "Wests": the aggressive neoliberal, neocolonial and cosmopolitan West and the traditional, Christian, freedom-loving and patriotic West. With the latter West, Russia feels an affinity, he assured his audience at Valdai; with the former, Russia will never reconcile. The current civilisational discourse is not exclusive to Russia, and as elsewhere (China most prominently) it has a long though interrupted pedigree and a distinctly anti-Western connotation. Russia under Putin comes close to what the British scholar Christopher Coker identifies as a "civilisational state", a political entity that combines the attributes of a state and a civilisation.[10]

And Russia is a civilisation under pressure. Putin repeatedly uses the image of a "beleaguered Russia". To cope with that siege, Russia has opted for a combination of expansion (Putin's "Greater Eurasia") *and* isolation ("Fortress Russia"). These are two long-standing strategic reflexes that we frequently encounter in Russian history. They are as classic as their Western counterparts – namely, containment, to rein in Russia's expansion, and the ambition to transform Russia in our image.

Putin's "Greater Eurasia" includes both his aspiration to reintegrate Russia and the post-Soviet space, and to establish closer geopolitical

---

10   Coker, C. (2019) *The Rise of the Civilizational State* (Cambridge: Polity). In Coker's view the civilisational state is ideologically defensive rather than offensive (the notion of sovereignty is key); it is eminently nonuniversalist and claims its own civilisational space; it is locked into a struggle with eternal enemies; and it is by nature authoritarian.

relations with China and with other non-Western powers, including Turkey, Iran and India. In this sense it combines Russia's main foreign policy ambitions: a multipolar global order with a Russia-dominated Eurasia as one of its major poles. Regional and global realignment are closely linked in Putin's worldview. Regional hegemony is a prerequisite for global multipolarity. And multipolarity appears in every major Russian foreign policy document since the Cold War, as does the professed stubborn refusal by the West to accept this emerging reality. In the Russian view, a multipolar world is a world of great powers and large spaces (spheres of influence). Putin has very specific ideas about what superpower status means. Great powers "rule" the world. Only great powers enjoy true sovereignty. The sovereignty of smaller powers is negotiable. Only a strong and self-confident Russia, the core of a reintegrated Eurasia, can be a pole in a new international order, a real alternative to Western domination of the international system. Even regime-loyal analysts[11] admit that Russia still has a long way to go. "Russia throughout the entire post-Soviet period has played an economically huge but politically disproportionally small role in the life of the former Soviet republics," noted one of them recently. "The countries of the region will be forced to correct this anomaly. Politics must be brought into balance with economics and geography." I have rarely come across a more straightforward rationalisation of the war against Ukraine.

For Putin, Russia is a great power, or Russia is *not* — literally. And Ukraine is crucial for Russia's status as a great power and thus, as Putin has repeatedly and logically pointed out, for Russia's survival. For Ukraine sovereignty is possible only "in partnership with Russia", as Putin explained in his July 2021 article. "For our country, it is a matter of life and death, a matter of our historical future as a nation," he told the Russian people in his televised speech on February 24. A Ukraine that severs its links with Russia "is not only a very real threat to our interests but to the very existence of our state and to its sovereignty". In the eyes of Putin, the war against Ukraine is a war for survival.[12]

---

11   Sutyrin, V. (2022) "The future of Russia's Eurasian project in the context of growing geopolitical risks". Valdai Discussion Club, "Expert opinions", 28 November. URL: https://valdaiclub.com/a/highlights/the-future-of-russia-s-eurasian-project.

12   I am not sure if Putin's reference to "a matter of life and death" is meant hyperbolically, but it is entirely in line with what "realist" observers noted decades back, including Zbigniew Brzezinksi, former security adviser to President Carter: "Without Ukraine, Russia ceases to be an empire, but with Ukraine suborned and then subordinated, Russia automatically becomes an empire." ("The premature partnership" (1994). *Foreign Affairs*, 73(2): 80.)

Russia is a big, but also a "lonely" power, Lilia Shevtsova (2010) wrote a decade back.[13] Postcommunist Russia may be a lonely power, but it has never been an isolationist one. And that also seems to be changing now, at least with regard to the "West", including "Europe". Not only has the war in Ukraine isolated Russia from the West, and perhaps from a larger part of the world if the war continues, but increasingly this is being presented as a choice, as a strategy of self-isolation. Russia faces a hundred years of "strategic solitude" (or two hundred, or three hundred), Vladislav Surkov – former adviser to President Putin – noted some time ago.[14] This is the idea of "Island Russia" or "Fortress Russia". It is a controversial notion but, since the invasion of Ukraine, one increasingly in vogue in Moscow. Even moderate foreign policy thinkers[15] use it to advocate a policy of cultural distance, of "indifference" to Europe (or in a broad sense to the "globalist project" or the "collective West") – not hostility, but distance and noninterference. This is a modern interpretation of ideas which Danilevsky popularised in his *Russia and Europe* (1869), but which in fact go back much further. They are key aspects of what has come to be known as the Russian Tradition, the expression of the belief that Russia has experienced its own unique development, through adherence to shared cultural values and political practices – a trajectory independent from and worth defending against the "West".

As with Eurasianism, Putin publicly advocates a moderate version of this strategy of indifference. He does not tire of emphasising that protecting Russia's sovereignty and unique identity are among the main drivers of his foreign policy, but while he appreciates the Eurasian bloc's self-sufficiency, he also stresses that this has nothing to do with isolation or autarky. And like the moderate "isolationists", Putin makes virtually no mention of the European Union. The EU seems to have all but disappeared from Russia's geopolitical considerations.

---

13   Shevtsova, L. (2010) *Lonely Power: Why Russia Has Failed to Become the West and the West Is Weary of Russia* (Washington, DC: Carnegie Endowment for International Peace).

14   Surkov, V. (2018) "Odinochestvo polukrovki (14+)". *Rossiya v Globalnoi Politike*, 9 April. URL: https://globalaffairs.ru/articles/odinochestvo-polukrovki-14/.

15   Mezhuev, B. V. (2022) "Can Russia keep up cultural distancing in relations with Europe?" *Russia in Global Affairs*, October/December.

Conclusion

This contribution starts from the assumption that we should take Russian President Vladimir Putin's philosophical and ideological motivations seriously. While Putin was initially widely seen as a rather pragmatic political leader, whose politics were driven by a realistic assessment of Russia's interests and capabilities, since his return as president in 2012 his *ideological* motivations are increasingly recognised and emphasised: conservatism, aversion to liberalism and universalism, and an ever-stronger emphasis on Russia's civilisational identity and uniqueness. Putin's references to the thinkers who inspire him, a bunch of mostly conservative, anticommunist and Russian-nationalist thinkers, are too consistent and too convincing not to take them seriously. Putin *has* a conservative, Russian-nationalist worldview.

Putin's ideological drives are reflected in his Ukraine policy. Ukraine is a core part of Putin's views on Russia's role in the region and globally. Putin probably made the decision to invade Ukraine himself, or in very limited company. In doing so he was guided by two clusters of considerations: security policy and cultural-historical arguments. Putin believes that Ukraine will have to conform to Russia's geopolitical interests, that Ukraine has a right to exist only in an alliance with Russia, and that such a hegemonic relationship is vital for Russia. Ukraine occupies a key place in Russia's concept of a regional power, without which it cannot be a global power, without which it cannot survive.

Putin, as more and more Russian intellectuals are inclined to do, links Russia's position in the world to its unique civilisation. Crucially, the borders of the Russian state and its civilisation, and population, are not congruent. The "Russian world" goes beyond the Russian state. The Russia world is the core of Eurasia, Russia's "space" or "pole" in Putin's much desired multipolar global order. The notion of the civilisational state has expansive and defensive aspects. It is largely inward-looking in its relations with the West, hence its emphasis on sovereignty, on noninterference, on Fortress Russia. However, it is eminently expansive towards Russia's immediate neighbourhood, towards the countries that make up Eurasia, where Russia claims a hegemonic role. In Putin's view, a strong state, a regional sphere of influence and global clout are directly intertwined. And hegemony over Ukraine is an indissoluble part of this. The war combines a reaction to the expansion of Western influence deep into Russia's sphere of influence and a massive, ideologically driven post-colonial convulsion. But most of all, the war is a pivotal moment in the political debate that was initiated with the demise of the Soviet Union: what is Russia, and what will it be, an empire or a nation-state? It is too early to tell if Putin's answer – Russia as empire – will survive the war.

Further reading

Götz, E., and J. Staun (2022) "Why Russia attacked Ukraine: strategic culture and radicalized narratives". *Contemporary Security* Policy, 43(3): 482–497.

Kuzio, T. (2022) "Imperial nationalism as the driver behind Russia's invasion of Ukraine". *Nations and Nationalism*, 29(1): 30–38. DOI: 10.1111/nana.12875

Mälksoo, M. (2022) "The postcolonial moment in Russia's war against Ukraine". *Journal of Genocide Research*, 11 May, p. 1. DOI: 10.1080/14623528.2022 .2074947

Mankoff, J. (2022) "Russia's war in Ukraine: identity, history, and conflict". Report, CSIS, Washington, DC, April.

Mezhuev, B. V. (2022) "Can Russia keep up cultural distancing in relations with Europe?" *Russia in Global Affairs*, October/December.

Putin, V. (2021) "On the historical unity of Russians and Ukrainians". President of Russia website, 7 December. URL: http://en.kremlin.ru/events/president/ news/66181.

Putin, V. (2022) "Address by the President of the Russian Federation". President of Russia website, 21 February. URL: http://en.kremlin.ru/events/president/ news/67828.

Putin, V. (2022) "Address by the President of the Russian Federation". President of Russia website, 24 February. URL: http://en.kremlin.ru/events/president/ news/67843.

Reynolds, N., and J. Watling (2022) "Ukraine through Russia's eyes". Royal United Services Institute website, 25 February. URL: https://rusi.org/explore-our -research/publications/commentary/ukraine-through-russias-eyes.

Roberts, K. (2017) "Understanding Putin". *International Journal* 72(1): 28–55.

Shevtsova, L. (2010) *Lonely Power: Why Russia Has Failed to Become the West and the West Is Weary of Russia* (Washington, DC: Carnegie Endowment for International Peace).

Surkov, V. (2018) "Odinochestvo polukrovki (14+)". *Rossiya v Globalnoi Politike*, 9 April. URL: https://globalaffairs.ru/articles/odinochestvo-polukrovki-14/.

Sutyrin, V. (2022) "The future of Russia's Eurasian project in the context of grow-ing geopolitical risks". Valdai Discussion Club, "Expert opinions", 28 Novem-ber. URL: https://valdaiclub.com/a/highlights/the-future-of-russia-s-eurasian -project.

Jack Thompson

2 | Inconsistent power: US strategy in the Ukraine war and beyond

The United States' strategy in the Ukraine war is designed to provide Kyiv with enough support to ensure that the conflict ends in a strategic defeat for Moscow. This approach typifies the Biden administration's move towards a global strategy that is more multilateral, less focused on kinetic operations and more reliant on allies and proxies. While Europeans should welcome this shift in US strategy, big questions remain about its long-term viability, both in Ukraine and at the global level.

US policymakers have been candid about their primary goal in the Ukraine war. In April 2022 US Secretary of Defense Lloyd Austin told reporters:

> We want to see Russia weakened to the degree that it can't do the kinds of things that it has done in invading Ukraine. So it has already lost a lot of military capability and a lot of its troops, quite frankly. And we want to see them not have the capability to very quickly reproduce that capability.

A few days later, another official more succinctly summarised American thinking, saying that Washington wants "to make this invasion a strategic failure for Russia".

In seeking to impose a strategic failure on Russia in Ukraine, the US is heralding a departure from its post-1990 strategy of liberal hegemony. The current administration of President Joe Biden views "strategic competition" between major democracies and autocracies as the primary dynamic shaping international security, and its approach to the Ukraine war serves as a first step towards the formulation of a new grand strategy – at least the version favoured by US multilateralists. Such a strategy would more accurately reflect the position of the US in the international system: it remains the most powerful actor, but with diminished influence, and needs to invest more resources at home.[1]

Ukraine can be seen as the template for a strategy in which the US remains engaged and seeks to lead but attempts to outsource more responsibility to allies and proxies and is more dependent upon multilateral institutions. This approach allows Washington to husband its military strength in case it is needed in the Indo-Pacific, but to also remain an integral part of the European security architecture. Although not an embrace of more austere options such as offshore balancing or restraint, Biden's approach signifies a prudent retreat from the hubris inherent in liberal hegemony.[2]

While Biden's attempt to shift US strategy in a more multilateral, more collaborative and less militarised direction is likely welcome from the European perspective, a number of questions remain about the long-term viability of this approach. The US has a history of inconsistent policy and rhetoric regarding Ukrainian security, especially when it comes to NATO membership, so there is no guarantee that US aid will remain at current levels. Indeed, though support for aid to Ukraine among the public and policymakers remains strong, a significant minority – mostly on the right, but also some on the left – would like to reduce or end aid to Ukraine and impose a negotiated peace on the country. At this point, such an agreement would be on terms favourable to Russia.

When it comes to US grand strategy at the regional and global level, there is an inclination in both major parties to prioritise security in the Indo-Pacific – and competition with China – over Europe. However, multilateralists will be more likely to view European security as worthy of US attention and resources than nationalists. In addition, political dysfunction will likely remain a significant factor in the evolution of US strategy. In particular, the resurgence of nationalism on the US right, and its scepticism about the European project, collective security and multilateral institutions, will influence the ability and willingness of subsequent administrations to sustain Biden's policies.

---

1   Key members of Biden's foreign policy team such as National Security Advisor Jake Sullivan essentially called for this approach even before he took office. See, for instance, Ahmed, S., and R. Engel (eds) (2022) "Making US foreign policy work better for the middle class". Report, Carnegie Endowment for International Peace, September. URL: https://carnegieendowment.org/2020/09/23/making-u.s.-foreign-policy-work-better-for-middle-class-pub-82728.

2   Mearsheimer, J. J., and S. M. Walt (2016) "The case for offshore balancing: a superior U.S. grand strategy", *Foreign Affairs*, 95(4): 70–83; Posen, B. R. (2014) *Restraint: A New Foundation for U.S. Grand Strategy* (Ithaca, NY: Cornell University Press).

Rethinking US grand strategy

Between 1990 and the early 2010s the US leveraged its military primacy and global influence in an often unsuccessful effort to spread democracy, free markets and liberal values. Considering the profound changes in international security in recent years, this strategy of liberal hegemony is outdated. The US is no longer a lone superpower. It confronts China, a powerful rival with global aspirations, and several regional challengers, foremost among them Russia. In addition, US military and economic power has receded from the relative peak of the 1990s, with unsuccessful wars in Afghanistan and Iraq highlighting the limits of US influence. The international economy remains deeply interconnected, but there is pressure in most Western states to limit their exposure to economic globalisation, both for security and domestic political reasons.

Faced with this daunting international environment, most policymakers recognise the need to rethink key tenets of US foreign policy. However, there is no consensus on what a revamped grand strategy should entail, other than that China should be a central focus. The Trump administration endeavoured to implement a nationalist vision designed to reduce US involvement in alliances and multilateral institutions. It also sought to respond to the concerns of alienated, mostly white Americans about globalisation by reducing immigration and extracting trade concessions from other states. Though a majority of Americans regard this approach with scepticism, "America First" remains influential on the right.

Biden mostly rejects his predecessor's nationalism. Instead, his administration hopes to retain the beneficial aspects of liberal hegemony while acknowledging the limits imposed by US decline and the downsides of the globalised economy. According to the Biden administration, the foremost factor shaping the international system is strategic competition between the major democratic and autocratic powers to "shape what comes after" the era of liberal hegemony. It believes that engagement and leadership remain essential, but that the US can only succeed by working closely with allies and via functional multilateral institutions. According to the Biden administration, the two most potent threats confronting the Americans and their allies are China and Russia.[3]

---

3 "National Security Strategy", October 2022 (www.whitehouse.gov/wp-content/uploads/2022/10/Biden-Harris-Administrations-National-Security-Strategy-10.2022.pdf); Brands, H. (2021) "The emerging Biden doctrine: democracy, autocracy, and the defining clash of our time", *Foreign Affairs* 29 June (https://fam.ag/3zliLFb).

The US identifies China as the only state with both the intent and capabilities to fundamentally alter the international system, and consequently has prioritised the Indo-Pacific region for years. Hindered by strategic limitations, Russia is a lesser threat, but it can harm the international system – and especially Europe – if left unchecked. As a consequence, US policymakers still consider European security a matter of national interest, though a large minority of GOP nationalists are sceptical about the benefits of engagement in the region, and the Indo-Pacific will take priority over Europe in strategic planning.

US strategy in the Ukraine war

Current US strategy in the Ukraine war is unambiguous: the Biden administration intends to provide sufficient support so that Kyiv can prevent a Russian victory, and in doing so inflict a crippling blow on Moscow in the broader US–Russia strategic competition. Since the Russian invasion, US support for Ukraine has been substantial, if slower and less forthcoming than Kyiv would prefer. However, to get to this current strong level of assistance, the US travelled a long, inconsistent and – from Ukraine's perspective – not always constructive path.

For years after the end of the Cold War, Washington allowed Ukraine to aspire to NATO membership without doing much to facilitate its accession to the Alliance, or to communicate honestly about the difficulties such a process would entail. This unhelpful combination of encouraging rhetoric and insufficient action culminated in the 2008 Bucharest Summit, at which Ukraine and Georgia were promised NATO membership at some undefined point in the future, without being given the requisite Membership Action Plans (MAPs) to facilitate the process. The George W. Bush administration wanted to provide MAPs but decided not to do so in the face of reluctance from some European allies.[4]

After the Russian annexation of Crimea and intervention in the Donbas region in 2014, the US and NATO in effect adopted a messy compromise. They sought to help Ukraine in the face of Russia aggression – and helped enough to fuel Russian paranoia – but were constantly afraid of helping so much that they would spark a direct conflict between NATO and Russia. By offering some but not enough assistance, and rhetorical support for NATO membership at some undefined point, they unfairly encouraged

---

4   Charap, S. (2022) "NATO honesty on Ukraine could avert conflict with Russia". *Financial Times*, 13 January. URL: https://on.ft.com/42YpxhF.

Ukrainian hopes at the same time as they alarmed Moscow, which had long warned that Ukrainian membership was a red line.

This uneasy balancing act provided the backdrop for US strategy at the outset of the Russian invasion, and the – possibly apocryphal – offer to evacuate Ukrainian President Volodymyr Zelenskyy. On the eve of the war, US intelligence estimated that Ukrainian resistance would collapse in the face of superior Russian firepower. In making this – in retrospect, alarmist – assessment, Washington was influenced by the precipitous collapse of the Afghan army in 2021. With such a pessimistic mindset guiding its prewar thinking, Washington had three objectives, more or less in this order: avoid a direct military conflict with Russia; meet its commitments to NATO allies; and help Ukraine avoid a battlefield defeat. Aid to Kyiv in the early days was correspondingly modest, consisting mainly of defensive weapons, ammunition and body armour. The administration hesitated to go further, fearing that Moscow would retaliate in reaction to the delivery of advanced weaponry and that US ordnance could be captured or diverted to the black market.[5]

When Russian forces failed to take Kyiv in early April 2022 and the conflict moved to eastern and southeastern Ukraine, US thinking shifted. Washington began to provide more advanced armaments, such as M777 howitzer artillery, along with the training to operate it. As the impact of this weaponry became clear, the US felt empowered to go further – for instance, by providing High Mobility Artillery Rocket Systems (HIMARS), which can strike targets at a greater distance and with more accuracy. At a meeting on 26 April, Secretary of Defense Austin told US allies: "Ukraine clearly believes that it can win, and so does everyone here."

There has been a discernible shift in US thinking away from concern about Russian red lines and towards an emphasis on the extent to which Ukrainian success could serve US interests. One policymaker compared the gradual increase of aid and lack of Russian retaliation to the proverbial amphibian in water: "Russia was the frog, and we boiled the water slowly, and Russia got used to it." Biden administration officials recognise that by inflicting tens of thousands of casualties on Russian forces, the Ukrainians are in the process of neutralising the conventional military threat posed by Moscow for the foreseeable future. At a cost of slightly

---

5   Cooper, H., and D. E. Sanger (2022) "U.S. warns of grim toll if Putin pursues full invasion of Ukraine". *New York Times*, 5 February. URL: https://nyti.ms/3nKW5f9.

less than $80 billion in 2022 – or about 5% of total US defence spending – this is a shrewd use of resources.[6]

There are limits to what the US can and will provide, however. For instance, it has hesitated to deliver ATACMS surface-to-surface missiles that could directly target Russia. In addition, because some weapons – such as NASAMS ground-based air defence systems – are in short supply and because the West lacks the industrial capacity to manufacture large numbers of some weapon systems quickly, Ukraine will continue to face shortages. Perhaps most frustratingly for Ukraine, the Americans and their allies have been slow to deliver systems that would increase the lethality and effectiveness of the Ukrainian army, such as modern battle tanks and fighter jets.[7]

Despite shortcomings such as the slow provision of weapons, the trajectory of US thinking has been encouraging. Indeed, it could herald a new approach to conflicts, in which Washington avoids direct military intervention and instead sends weapons and aid only to peoples and states that demonstrate the will and capacity to fight their own battles. This would dovetail with a broader global strategy designed to account for reduced US power and influence and more reliance on allies and partners.[8]

While military aid has been the most visible aspect of US efforts intended to help Ukraine defeat Russia, economic measures have also inflicted considerable damage on Moscow's war effort. There are several components of the US economic strategy. These include a price cap on Russian oil – an ambitious but potentially unwieldy step intended to reduce income from Moscow's top export. Western governments have also frozen $300 billion in Russian state assets and billions more in private assets. The US has imposed export controls to limit access to microchips and other key technologies essential to the Russian war effort. Finally, through the imposition of sanctions, the US has sought to discourage state and other actors from providing political or economic support to the Russian campaign. As a result of these

6   Ash, T. (2022) "It's costing peanuts for the US to defeat Russia". Center for European Policy Analysis website, 18 November. URL: https://cepa.org/article/its-costing-peanuts -for-the-us-to-defeat-russia.

7   Yaffa, J. (2022) "Inside the U.S. effort to arm Ukraine", *New Yorker*, 17 October (www .newyorker.com/magazine/2022/10/24/inside-the-us-effort-to-arm-ukraine); Rathbone, J. P., S. Pfeifer and S. Chávez (2022) "Military briefing: Ukraine war exposes 'hard reality' of West's weapons capacity", *Financial Times*, 2 December (https://on.ft.com/42NZKIU).

8   O'Brien, P. P. (2022) "The future of American warfare is unfolding in Ukraine". *The Atlantic*, 25 November. URL: https://www.theatlantic.com/ideas/archive/2022/11/us -military-intervention-afghanistan-ukraine-war/672265/.

efforts, the Russian economy was forecast to contract by at least 3% in 2022 and the long-term prognosis is dire: a recent study released by Yale University economists suggests that, as long as Western sanctions remain in place, there is "no path out of economic oblivion" for the Russian economy.[9]

The impact of Western economic measures can also be seen on the battlefield. Much of the equipment Russia has sent into battle has been outdated or improperly maintained. These problems have been exacerbated by pervasive corruption. And now Russia faces the daunting task of replacing massive amounts of materiel lost in conflict. The technology in that equipment is usually sourced from the West and – because of sanctions – Russia will struggle to replace it. Microchips represent a case in point. There is evidence that Russia has been forced to cannibalise consumer goods such as dishwashers for their microchips, amid reports of Russian shortages of missiles and hypersonic weapons.[10]

US strategy in the Ukraine war has been imperfect, as it is still bearing too much of the burden in providing Kyiv with military and other types of support. The US has provided €64.8 billion in aid and the Biden administration has asked Congress for an additional €35.9 billion, bringing total US commitments to €100 billion. In contrast, European countries and the EU together have provided just over €52 billion in total aid and commitments. Although a sensible investment by the Biden administration, US largesse is exacerbating the imbalance in sharing the transatlantic security burden at a time when the gap should be shrinking.[11]

---

9   "Treasury imposes swift and severe costs on Russia for Putin's purported annexation of regions of Ukraine", press release, US Department of the Treasury, 30 September 2022 (https://home.treasury.gov/news/press-releases/jy0981); Mosolova, D. (2022) "Russia's economy enters recession with 4% contraction", *Financial Times*, 16 November (https://on.ft.com/3ntqGhf).

10   Johnson, J. (2022) "Russian attempts to restock its military may be doomed to failure", *Breaking Defense*, 19 May (https://bit.ly/3TZYfUb); Johnson, R. (2022) "As Ukraine counterattacks, Russia's military facing steep artillery, resupply challenges", *Breaking Defense*, 11 September (https://bit.ly/40mwBmF); Whalen, J. (2022) "Sanctions forcing Russia to use appliance parts in military gear, U.S. says", *Washington Post*, 11 May (https://wapo.st/3JTUURI); Sheftalovich, Z., and L. Cerulus (2022) "The chips are down: Putin scrambles for high-tech parts as his arsenal goes up in smoke", *Politico*, 5 September (https://politi.co/3KdLmm0).

11   Cancian, M. F. (2022) "Aid to Ukraine explained in six charts", Center for Strategic and International Studies website, 18 November 2022 (www.csis.org/analysis/aid-ukraine -explained-six-charts); "Ukraine Support Tracker", Kiel Institute for the World Economy website (www.ifw-kiel.de/topics/war-against-ukraine/ukraine-support-tracker/).

The US has been too slow to provide Kyiv with the type of advanced weaponry that it needs. The time for caution has passed with respect to provoking Russia – at least when it comes to conventional military responses – or as regards weapons reaching the black market. The Ukrainians have demonstrated that they will use effectively whatever weapons and assistance the Americans and their allies provide. The more the Ukrainians have to work with, the faster they will be able to degrade Russian military capabilities.

Domestic opposition to US strategy in Ukraine

Despite widespread public support for Ukraine, a bipartisan minority of Americans – 26% according to a January 2023 poll – would like to reduce aid.[12] On the right, this sentiment is fuelled by two sets of ideas. One is a growing tendency towards nationalism and unilateralism in foreign policy and a belief that Europeans should be obliged to solve problems in their own backyard. Opposition to aid for Ukraine has become a way for Republicans to express broader ambivalence about NATO and European security. Regarding the $40 billion aid package to Ukraine in May 2022, Josh Hawley, a Republican senator, argued that it was "more than three times what all of Europe has spent combined" and hence "allows Europe to freeload" on US security spending. In the previous Congress, this opposition was essentially symbolic. But in the new Congress, right-wing populists will wield considerable influence in the House of Representatives and have promised to challenge the current funding levels for the Ukrainian war effort.[13]

The other impulse driving opposition to Ukraine is sympathy for Russian President Vladimir Putin. A small but passionate subset on the right views Putin as an ally in a global effort to preserve culturally conservative values. The Russian leader's embrace of white Christian nationalism appeals to Americans worried about perceived threats to traditional racial, sexual or gender values. Though disavowed by most elected Republican officials, there is ample support for Putinism on the Christian right; at the

---

12   Dunn, A. (2023) "As Russian invasion nears one-year mark, partisans grow further apart on U.S. support for Ukraine", Pew Research Center website, 31 January. URL: https://pewrsr.ch/3JU9id3.

13   Satter, S. (2022) "GOP faction signals tougher fight for Ukraine aid ahead". *Roll Call*, 17 November. URL: https://rollcall.com/2022/11/17/gop-faction-signals-tougher-fight-for-ukraine-aid-ahead/.

2022 America First Political Action Conference, many in the crowd could be heard shouting approvingly "Putin! Putin!"[14]

Support among congressional Democrats for aid to Ukraine is relatively solid – even a staunch progressive such as Bernie Sanders believes that the Russian invasion "has to be resisted" – but there is unease on the party's left wing. Candidates on the campaign trail have encountered criticism from voters worried about the shaky state of the US economy and the possibility of nuclear war, and influential leftist publications such as *Jacobin* have warned about the growing "potential for disaster and escalation" and urged Washington to seek a negotiated settlement. These views formed the backdrop against which 30 members of the Congressional Progressive Caucus sent a letter to President Biden in October 2022 calling for a negotiated ceasefire. Though the letter was withdrawn amid widespread criticism, the longer the war lasts, the more such sentiment will influence Democratic legislators.[15]

Implications for international security and for Europe

Europeans should welcome Biden's attempt to craft a US grand strategy less reliant on direct military intervention and more reliant on allies and multilateral institutions. While far from perfect, this approach has mostly been productive as it relates to the Ukraine war. But Europeans should be wary about the sustainability of this approach, both as it applies to Ukraine and as it relates to long-term European security.

A negotiated settlement to the Ukraine war looks unlikely for now, and continued US aid over the medium to long term is uncertain, given unease about the conflict on the mainstream right and the left wing of the Democratic Party. Until Washington develops a consensus about

14   Olmos, S. (2022) "'Key to white survival': how Putin has morphed into a far-right saviour", *The Guardian*, 5 March (www.theguardian.com/us-news/2022/mar/05/putin-ukraine-invasion-white-nationalists-far-right); Moreton, B. (2022) "The bond that explains why some on the Christian right support Putin's war", *Washington Post*, 5 March (https://wapo.st/3nlni7L).

15   Weigel, D. (2022) "Bernie Sanders: House progressives were wrong on Ukraine", *Semafor*, 25 October (www.semafor.com/article/10/25/2022/bernie-sanders-the-house-progressive-caucus-ukraine-letter-was-wrong); Marcetic, B. (2022) "The Biden administration is in no rush to help Ukraine negotiate an end to the war", *Jacobin*, 30 May (https://jacobin.com/2022/05/peace-talks-diplomacy-negotiations-ukraine-russia-war-biden-johnson); Marcetic, B. (2022) "What are the chances for a negotiated end to the Ukraine war? It's complicated", *Jacobin*, 25 August (https://jacobin.com/2022/08/ukraine-war-russia-zelensky-putin-settlement-diplomacy).

Ukraine's future in NATO – and no such consensus will form in the near future[16] – it should be explicit about the fact that membership will not be possible for now. NATO's other member states, who are also divided, should do the same.

When it comes to the likely direction of the US grand strategy in the coming years, especially as it relates to Europe, three scenarios are plausible.

One potential path is an *engaged* strategy. This approach would entail maintaining many of the policies crafted by the Biden administration. It would mean a more multilateral, less militarised foreign policy, more reliant on allies and proxies. An engaged US would approach strategic competition with China with at least a degree of deliberation and in partnership with allies in Europe and the Indo-Pacific. This should lessen the likelihood of direct conflict with Beijing. The growing degree of political dysfunction plaguing the US would stabilise – though significant improvement is unlikely – and democratic institutions would recover somewhat from the current bout of backsliding. In this scenario, the US retains sympathy for and an – albeit secondary – interest in European security. The engaged scenario would be the most conducive to European interests, even if it would still entail occasional frictions, including bouts of unilateralism and protectionism. It would also be the best-case scenario for Ukraine and the worst for Russia. But an engaged approach will be difficult to maintain consistently, given the depth of dysfunction now endemic in the US political system and the likelihood that the increasingly nationalist, illiberal Republican Party will usually control at least one chamber of Congress, and that it will likely retake the White House by 2028.

A second plausible trajectory for the US in the coming years would be a *nationalist* strategy. This variant would consistently follow the path first blazed by Donald Trump in an erratic fashion during his presidency but now embraced, at least to a degree, by most Republicans. It would include some combination of scepticism about or even hostility towards multilateral institutions, the European Union and European security, ambivalence about cooperative security, including NATO, and a conviction that the US can successfully compete with China on a unilateral basis. In this scenario, military confrontation with China is somewhat more likely. A nationalist US strategy would demand the support of European and other allies on occasion, but would have little use for genuine partnership. The

---

16   Desiderio, A., C. Gijs and N. Vu (2022) "Lawmakers split on Ukraine's new NATO bid". *Politico*, 30 September. URL: https://politi.co/3TNwe26.

willingness and ability of a nationalist US to act constructively abroad would be further undermined by intensifying political dysfunction and further democratic backsliding, as the illiberal tendencies in the Republican Party overwhelm US institutions. This is the worst-case scenario from the European perspective, and for Ukraine, but a full-blown nationalist US strategy may be averted. Given the strength of public support for NATO, added to the fact that Democrats have enjoyed a clear if narrow advantage in presidential elections since the early 1990s, nationalism, though likely influencing US strategy, will not dominate it.

This leaves a third, *inconsistent* approach as the most likely US strategy in the coming years. In this scenario, the US would follow neither the path of engagement nor the path of nationalism consistently, but would instead oscillate between the two and, sometimes, exhibit elements of both. This would be characterised by cycles of constructive security partnership with Europe giving way to a more unilateralist and hostile approach. It would mean China remaining the foremost priority for strategic planning, but also a shift in the US approach from a more collaborative approach to addressing China's most troubling economic and military behaviour and a more unilateralist approach in which Washington demands European support but shows little interest in genuine consultation. In this scenario it is unclear to what extent the US would continue to provide substantial aid to Ukraine, but at a minimum the additional uncertainty would make the conflict even more challenging for Kyiv.

Further reading

Moreton, B. (forthcoming) *Slouching Towards Moscow: American Conservatives and the Romance of Russia* (Cambridge, MA: Harvard University Press).

O'Brien, P. P. (2022) "The future of American warfare is unfolding in Ukraine". *The Atlantic*, 25 November. URL: https://www.theatlantic.com/ideas/archive/2022/11/us-military-intervention-afghanistan-ukraine-war/672265/.

Stent, A. E. (2015) *The Limits of Partnership: U.S.–Russian Relations in the Twenty-First Century* (Princeton, NJ: Princeton University Press).

Walt, S. M. (2018) *The Hell of Good Intentions: America's Foreign Policy Elite and the Decline of U.S. Primacy* (New York: Farrar, Straus and Giroux).

Yaffa, J. (2022) "Inside the U.S. effort to arm Ukraine". *New Yorker*, 17 October. URL: https://www.newyorker.com/magazine/2022/10/24/inside-the-us-effort-to-arm-ukraine.

Reinhard Krumm

3 | The legacy of Europe's Eastern policy: insufficient engagement or influence

Russia's war of aggression against Ukraine is a serious violation of the Paris Char-
ter. In November 1990, signatory states agreed on common security, to recognise
the territorial integrity of states and to settle conflicts without resorting to arms.
Given what has occurred in Ukraine, this chapter examines the premises and
objectives on which the EU's policy approaches have been based and looks at
where these clearly failed, while also analysing the limitations of the West's policy
towards Russia.

Mistakes and limitations in Eastern policy

If a European security policy approach leads to war rather than helping
to create security, then either the situation was hopeless anyway, and
the available options limited, or the chosen approach was wrong. In the
view of Germany, but also of the EU, Russia's war of aggression against
Ukraine is a serious violation of the Charter of Paris for a New Europe. In
November 1990, the signatory states agreed on recognition of the territorial integrity of states, on the settlement of conflicts without resorting
to arms, and on common security. Given the striking difference between
this agreement and what has occurred since, this chapter examines the
premises and objectives on which the EU's policy approaches have been
based until now and looks at where these approaches clearly failed to
take adequate account of a parting of ways. This also includes an analysis of the limitations of the West's policy towards Russia.

It is unfortunately the case that foreign policy failures are not uncommon, nor are they limited to the EU or the US. Such examples can be
found not only in recent political events in Europe (the Yugoslav wars,
the Armenia–Azerbaijan conflict), but also in the Middle East (the wars in

Iraq, Libya and Syria) and central Asia (Afghanistan). In addition, there are armed confrontations – such as the Israel–Palestine conflict – that no longer count as full-scale wars, yet remain a constant source of unrest. It is undoubtedly the case that sociopolitical and security developments in a region are shaped by the actors on the ground, some of whom have greater influence (Russia), some less so (the EU), and others with only very limited power to shape outcomes (Georgia, Ukraine). In general, smaller states are rarely able to successfully influence other countries, particularly larger ones. Ukraine's war against Russia might yet prove an exception.

Germany has no coherent Eastern policy, and the EU also lacks a coordinated approach to the East. Experts have voiced the need for such a strategy and have proposed initiatives to bring one about. For example, in 2019 a position paper of the Social Democratic Party of Germany (SPD) parliamentary group on détente policy formulated this intention: "Our goal is a European policy on Russia." The reality was very different: in Germany, in the EU, and even within the Euro-Atlantic framework, politicians and even academics were unable to unite behind a set of common interests with regard to Russia, and states even worked against each other. At the same time, Russia increasingly refused to engage in constructive dialogue because it was pursuing other interests.

The features that influence Germany's policy on Russia's war of aggression against Ukraine are Russia's geographical proximity and the degree of emotion associated with the two countries' shared history. For Germany and also the EU, this is more than just a war. Above all, it symbolises the failure to sustainably integrate Russia into a European framework for peace, which was seen as a quite realistic prospect for some years following the collapse of the USSR. However, it also symbolises the failure to peacefully integrate the neighbouring states of Eastern Europe – the "Eastern neighbourhood" – and lay the foundations for stability and prosperity. Moreover, Berlin had repeatedly stressed Germany's particular responsibility for Eastern Europe, given the atrocities committed during World War II and their consequences.

For the countries of Eastern Central Europe such as Poland, the Czech Republic and the three Baltic states, Russia's unprovoked military assault on Ukraine is seen as a clear indication of history repeating itself. In their view, Russia – the largest country in the world, with a mostly imperial history, where constitutional institutions, pluralism and democracy were only belatedly introduced – should be engaged with only to the minimum extent possible, while always maintaining strong defences. In an EU of bridge-builders versus barricade-builders vis-à-vis Russia, therefore, neither analyses nor policy options could be reconciled.

Another factor was the realisation that the 1990s – which were very successful from the German and European perspectives, including as they did the enlargement of the EU, democratic and economic transformation in the states of Eastern Central Europe, and an end to ideological antagonisms – were the exception rather than the beginning of a new normality in security policy. What had been fêted as the "end of history" turned out to be simply its continuation. The tremendous upheavals that took place in Russia had only lessened the rivalries, not eliminated them. In what Russia itself terms "times of turmoil", it was possible for the West to support reforms in the states of Eastern Central Europe and at the same time even support the six states of the Eastern Partnership (Armenia, Azerbaijan, Belarus, Georgia, Moldova and Ukraine) in their attempts to implement reforms. Nevertheless, building sustainable relations with Russia in order to ensure that Moscow did not undermine this policy was successful only in Eastern Central Europe, and not in Eastern Europe, in countries such as Belarus, Moldova and Ukraine. With the exception of the third Strategic Arms Reduction Treaty (START III), all attempts to achieve any further major reductions in the conventional and nuclear arsenal met with failure.

Historians, who always want to place developments into periods, could therefore declare 2022 to be the end of the 20th century, rather than 1989, as had hitherto generally been considered the case. One argument for this is that the centrality of the Cold War and its aftermath, with the emerging superiority of the West, has finally come to an end. This much was made clear by the UN vote in March 2022 to condemn the Russian war of aggression. The 35 states that abstained were pursuing their own interests, rather than being united against Russia or in support of the West, meaning the EU and the US. For instance, China and India are now influential enough to represent their own centres of power alongside Russia, the EU and the US – or, to put it another way, to demand multipolarity. Consequently, Russia now has alternatives to its historically needed European partners.

If we wish to analyse the failures of European and German security policy, we thus need to focus on the objectives that Germany and the EU have defined and pursued with regard to Russia and the states of the Eastern neighbourhood in recent years, then examine the premises underlying them.

Two political objectives of Germany towards Russia and Eastern Europe

First objective: establishing a security community within the framework of the Organization for Security and Co-operation in Europe

An agreement on such a community, based on the Paris Charter of some 20 years earlier, was reached at the summit of the Organization for Security and Co-operation in Europe (OSCE) in the Kazakh capital Astana in December 2010. The declaration was also signed by the Russian Federation, which is somewhat surprising given that it followed Russian President Vladimir Putin's aggressive speech at the Munich Security Conference (2007), the war in Georgia (2008), and the NATO summit in Bucharest (2008), at which the US broached the subject of NATO membership for Georgia and Ukraine.

An updated security agreement had initially seemed an attainable prospect under Russian President Dmitry Medvedev (2008–2012). The EU's initiative for a partnership for modernisation with Russia took place during this period, as well as the US reset with Russia, which led to the disarmament treaty START III. The same period, however, also witnessed the war in Georgia, which spurred Washington's initiative – rejected by Germany and France – to offer Ukraine and Georgia the NATO Membership Action Plan. It is still unclear whether Ukraine was ready to pursue that ambitious plan of joining NATO.

There was, however, little in the way of investment in shared European security arrangements with Russia and the countries of Eastern Europe. Medvedev's plan for a new security architecture was rejected and the situation in Russia – the "tandem" domestic power-sharing relationship between Prime Minister Putin and President Medvedev, the crackdown on the demonstrations that followed, and other examples of domestic repression – led to the EU and the US keeping their distance. The annexation of Crimea in 2014 made any form of strategic partnership with Russia impossible. The two sides shared no common interests that could have been actively promoted.

The relationship was increasingly dominated by sanctions, mutual accusations of political interference, a Russian-initiated armed conflict in the Donbas region, Russia's military support for the Syrian dictator Bashar al-Assad and the absence of influential Russian advisers with an interest in a constructive exchange with the West. As a result, countries such as Poland or the Baltic states no longer saw any point in trying. The minimum objective was now nothing more than to maintain the status quo of European security.

Second objective: establishing a secure, stable and prosperous Eastern neighbourhood as the basis for a peaceful Europe

The EU's neighbours became increasingly important for the EU following the social upheavals led by those wanting a final break with the legacy of the USSR. The events in Georgia (the 2003 Rose Revolution) and Ukraine (the 2004 Orange Revolution) stand out in this regard, although many of the reform processes got stuck in a labyrinth of oligarchy and corruption. Moscow declared these efforts to be externally directed, and as such a security risk to Russia, and it did everything it could to passively destabilise those states (for instance, by recognising the Georgian republics of Abkhazia and South Ossetia as independent states).

Moscow also interfered in Moldova through the Russian-affiliated Republic of Transnistria, as well as in the conflict between Armenia and Azerbaijan, which were at war with each other over the province of Nagorno-Karabakh. Moscow's aim was both to prevent further rapprochement with NATO and to make it impossible for those neighbouring states to enjoy democratically and economically successful governments.

The Eastern Partnership initiative was an EU response to the Georgian war and had very mixed results. As with the first objective, there was no consensus in Germany or the EU on how to achieve a stable, secure and prosperous Eastern neighbourhood when it was adjacent to a country prepared to escalate tensions. The question of whether it is possible to decouple Europe's security from that of Russia is one that still has not been decisively answered.

The German government advocated "intensive collaboration on the path to prosperity, security and democracy",[1] but it remained unclear how this programme was to be contextualised in relation to a policy on Russia. The best example of this was the construction of the Nord Stream 2 pipeline, which was intended to allow cheap gas to be imported into the EU while simultaneously promoting security through interdependence. The countries of Eastern Central Europe were vehemently opposed to

---

1   Motion of the parliamentary groups of the SPD and of the Christian Democratic Union (CDU) and Christian Social Union (CSU), document 19/9916, 7 May 2018.

its construction, as they considered interdependence to be a weakness in security policy. The counter-argument, now refuted in practice, was that it was precisely such interdependence that would lead to greater international security.

Despite the Association Agreements (AAs) signed with the EU by Georgia, Moldova and Ukraine (while Armenia signed a Comprehensive and Enhanced Partnership Agreement (CEPA), a slimmed-down version of an AA), the all-important external security of the first three of those states (with Armenia putting its faith entirely in Russia) remained unclear. The squaring of the circle – meaning a prosperous future for the six states of the Eastern Partnership, with simultaneous security from or with Russia – did not succeed. The possibility that the Russian government would ignore all the negative political and economic consequences and deploy actual military force to achieve its objectives was completely underestimated. Any political solution currently seems out of reach.

Five premises of the European security policy approach towards Russia and Eastern Europe that have proven problematic

1. European security was seen as a given

Despite Russia's annexation of Crimea, the armed conflict in the Donbas, the erosion of the system of disarmament and the political upheavals in the US, European politics failed to prioritise security policy in recent years. On the one hand, Russia's security concerns were dismissed as unjustified, while on the other hand, Russia's desire and ability to escalate conflicts was underestimated. The results of surveys revealing that populations in various European countries, including Russia, were dissatisfied with their position in international politics did not prompt the EU to take security threats seriously enough to stimulate any discourse about them. This reluctance was criticised by a senior German diplomat as a "comfort zone of bad relations".

The situation in the states of Eastern Central Europe and Eastern Europe, the latter including the countries of the Eastern Partnership and Russia, was often similar. Whether in Tallinn, Warsaw, Tbilisi or Kyiv, the Russian threat was always in the foreground due to these states' geographical proximity to Russia, their past history and their assumption that Russia was path-dependent and would thus continue to be an aggressive, imperial state. In those capitals, the hardening of the Russian position was taken as a clear sign that talks as instruments of détente had become useless. In other words, there was no longer any point to the dual approach – détente and deterrence – that had been formulated as a strategy in the Harmel Report at the time of the Cold War. Détente had become pointless; deterrence remained the only option. NATO's Forward Presence in the Baltic countries and Poland was the logical answer to the need for more security, but it was followed by no further policy approaches. The West and Russia perceived each other only in terms of potential threats.

The region that was actually insecure was further east, in the countries of the Eastern Partnership. The possibility of NATO membership for Georgia and Ukraine was initially thought to be the solution for a more secure EU Eastern neighbourhood. When that failed, association agreements with the EU were offered. The desire for protection from Russia remained the ultimate goal, yet neither country had any plans to engage in serious talks with Russia, partly because there were no clear signs from Moscow to engage, and partly because its proposals were not in line with international treaties. Alternatives to NATO membership, such as neutrality, were strongly rejected, particularly by experts in the field but also by politicians, as the feeling was that Russian aggression should not be rewarded by bowing to Russia's demand not to expand the Alliance.

2. Europe's Eastern policy was not considered a priority

Russia's annexation of Crimea increased the desire for a European Eastern policy, particularly in Germany. Heiko Maas, the former German foreign minister, announced an initiative in this regard, but no details followed and his diplomats were given no instructions. There were plenty of reasons to think beyond the confines of the EU's current policy on Russia, and strategic planners in the EU states did indeed do so. However, the rapid pace of developments in foreign and security policy, along with Moscow's increasing hostility (encapsulated in Putin's statement: "As long as the EU sanctions us, we don't concern ourselves with Western policy"), caused every idea to fall by the wayside.

There was also the problem that interests among the EU diverged considerably, with member states evaluating threats differently and not sharing the same objectives. This made it difficult for the EU, without a common set of interests, to negotiate with Russia over future European security. Likewise, there was no consensus on the fundamental questions involved. Which states should an Eastern policy focus on: the countries in the Eastern neighbourhood, Russia or the region as a whole? Or should there be a single, comprehensive package? And, if so, should that policy include, exclude or oppose Russia? Should it aim for some kind of coexistence, containment or forced regime change?

The OSCE, which was founded to promote discussions on European security, has also been unable to develop approaches to détente, due to a lack of interest among its member states in finding islands of cooperation as first steps towards solutions, vested interests preventing attainment of a consensus, and a hardening of the positions of individual participating states (the US and Russia). Only a few countries (Switzerland, Germany and Austria) that have assumed the annual OSCE chair over the last decade have actively engaged in the process and sought out new approaches – but without success.

3. The Eastern Partnership states were thought to be of little significance to European security

Following the eastward enlargement of NATO, Europe seemed well prepared for a Russian attack, not that any such aggression was anticipated at that time. What was overlooked was the fact that, even during the Cold War, one of the most difficult challenges had been to reconcile the security interests of the then Soviet Union with those of the countries of Eastern Europe, such as Poland and Czechoslovakia. What now need to be considered are the interests of Russia and the new Eastern Europe, meaning the states of the South Caucasus, as well as Belarus, Moldova and Ukraine.

Ukraine, the largest country in this region, stands out in this regard, in part because its size, population and location make it an important country for any alliance, in both economic and security policy terms, and also because Russia is only prepared to acknowledge Ukraine as an independent state if it toes the Kremlin's foreign policy line.

All six Eastern Partnership countries lie geographically between the EU and Russia and are of interest to both – for Russia, either as part of its sphere of influence or even as part of its own territory. The EU of course recognises these sovereign states as such, acknowledging that there are those that wish to increasingly align themselves with the West (Georgia, Moldova and Ukraine) in order to finally achieve prosperity and stability within the framework of the EU after many years of reforms. The EU also acknowledges those taking other paths (Azerbaijan and Belarus), as well as Armenia, which is attempting to find a balance between the EU and Russia.

The EU underestimated the potential for conflict in the precarious security situation in Ukraine in 2014 because it interpreted Russia's security interests with regard to Ukraine as concerned only with the latter's democratic transformation, while simultaneously failing to consider the worst of all scenarios – namely, a military escalation on the Russian side based on security concerns, but also nonrecognition of the independence and sovereignty of Ukraine. There was a failure to put a convincing deterrent in place, or a somewhat compelling détente. This does, however, beg the question of how either of these approaches could have been defined and translated into a convincing policy.

4. It was thought to be only a matter of time before Russia began to pursue a Western path

Although most expert analyses expected Russia to have serious problems, it continues to function despite seven packages of sanctions imposed by the EU, sanctions by the US and the ostracism it has endured in many countries. Despite being viewed by the West as a "regional power" (as former US President Barack Obama commented disdainfully), as an economic weakling or as a corrupt and failing state, the world's biggest country is capable of sustaining a war against the second largest country in Europe, Ukraine. World Bank analyses of Russia prior to the recent military aggression found plenty to criticise, but they also praised its fiscal policy and degree of economic modernisation. Given Russia's current economic resources, the EU and the US still underestimate the actions, atrocities and escalations of which this vast land remains capable. Sanctions after the annexation of Crimea certainly had an effect, but their impact was not as quick or severe as anticipated. Compared with the 1990s, Russia had built up reserves and its economy was sufficiently strong to weather the storm.

Moreover, Russia had also undertaken several reforms to its security policy, which, to some degree at least, had strengthened its military. In 2017, for example, the yearbook *The Military Balance* from the International Institute for Strategic Studies, a British think tank, stated that "Russia is ready and able to deploy its armed forces", particularly in the event of its political leadership believing geopolitical losses were otherwise unavoidable.

These developments should reduce confidence in the assertion that the EU or the US can put Russia on the right track, as was assumed in the 1990s, particularly as the majority of its population do not see this as a solution to their myriad problems. While Russia was at least interested in following the Western example until at least the mid-1990s, even if only in economic terms by turning its back on the planned economy during that period, it has been clear even since the time of Boris Yeltsin that Russia and the West have fundamentally different ideas about European security. Russia's rejection of the West's narrative led to the end of Medvedev's term in office, a tightening of the thumbscrews in Russia itself and the increasingly frequent discrediting of the Western model as misguided.

Given the growing lack of opportunity for serious conversations between Russian and EU politicians, civil society in Russia was seen by the West as taking on a key role in breaking the deadlock, but without the EU and the US understanding that it was precisely the politically engaged members of Russian society whom the state suspected of working against it. The colour revolutions served as justification for these suspicions, leading to increasingly repressive measures that culminated in Russia's "foreign agent" law, designed to harass those working with foreign states or NGOs. The authoritarian regime could not envision any benefit for itself from a civil society that it saw as working to overthrow it and as following a model of development that the Russian state no longer had any desire to emulate.

5. Europe believed itself to be Russia's primary interest

Germany and the EU have invoked history in their relations with Russia. Without a developed Europe as a partner, which today comes in the shape of the EU, Russia is felt to be incapable of reform and therefore of economic survival. In the 1990s in particular, this resulted in the conclusion that pressure on Russia would need to be increased to bring about political change.

Moreover, Brussels failed to take into account Moscow's efforts to establish additional partners alongside the EU, which itself is doubtless of great economic importance for Russia. The EU was, of course, well aware that Russia was not sufficiently powerful at the time to be a superpower in its own right. Even so, Russia was not isolated and dependent on its Western neighbours. First, there were its partners in the BRICS cooperation: Brazil, India, China and South Africa – all states that abstained in the UN vote in March 2022 from condemning Russia's attack on Ukraine. In addition, there was the fact that Russia and China were drawing increasingly closer. Russia now tops China's list of special relationships, being accorded a degree of importance far exceeding, for example, that of Germany. In other words, Russia now has options, unlike during the Cold War. Russia's centuries-long slavish imitation of the West, with its constant attempts to catch up and modernise, is no longer without alternatives. The assumption that the EU has unlimited, unrivalled and powerful instruments that can exert influence over Russia is thus no longer correct.

Conclusion

An analysis of the objectives of German and EU Eastern policy and the premises behind these objectives clearly shows that decision-makers underestimated how badly relations with Russia were deteriorating and the volatile situation of the Eastern European countries. European security had already become very fragile by 2014. While Russia escalated in word and deed, the states of Eastern Europe – Georgia and Ukraine in particular – saw a narrow window of opportunity to draw as close to the West as possible.

They did so because they were encouraged by the EU and the US, which – with their military and economic power – considered themselves obviously superior to Russia. However, the EU and the US overlooked the limited options available to Western centres of power in a world where the West and Russia are no longer the only players, and they failed to consider the growing international influence of countries such as China, Brazil, India and Turkey. Despite its very long European history, Russia also has options in the Asian continent, where much of Russia itself is situated.

The EU and the US were unable to forestall Russia's war of aggression against Ukraine because they lacked sufficient commitment to do so. Nevertheless, it may be that even such a commitment would not have been enough, and the attack launched by Russia on 24 February 2022 shows that opportunities for influencing Russia are now even more limited than before. Whether we will be able to change this reality is highly doubtful, but the possibility remains. We all have to try harder.

Further reading

High Representative of the Union for Foreign Affairs and Security Policy (2015) "Review of the European Neighbourhood Policy". Joint Communication, European Commission, 18 November. URL: https://neighbourhood-enlargement .ec.europa.eu/system/files/2019-01/151118_joint-communication_review -of-the-enp_en.pdf.

Kluter, A., and R. Krumm (2016) "For a European progressive Eastern policy". Report, Friedrich Ebert Foundation. URL: https://library.fes.de/pdf-files/id-moe/12270.pdf.

Kofman, M., and A. Kendall-Taylor (2021) "The myth of Russian decline: why Moscow will be a persistent power". *Foreign Affairs*, November/December. URL: https://fam.ag/42GjOx3.

RAND Corporation (2019) *A Consensus Proposal for a Revised Regional Order in Post-Soviet Europe and Eurasia* (Santa Monica, CA: RAND Corporation). URL: https://www.rand.org/content/dam/rand/pubs/conf_proceedings/CF400/CF410/RAND_CF410.pdf.

Remnick, D. (2022) "A Ukrainian diplomat on the future of Russian aggression". Interview in the *New Yorker*, 29 April. URL: https://www.newyorker.com/podcast/the-new-yorker-radio-hour/a-ukrainian-diplomat-on-the-future-of-russian-aggression.

Rumer, E., and A. S. Weiss (2021) "Back to basics on Russia policy". Carnegie Endowment for International Peace website, 9 March. URL: https://carnegieendowment.org/2021/03/09/back-to-basics-on-russia-policy-pub-84016.

Trenin, D. (2021) "What Putin really wants in Ukraine". *Foreign Affairs*, 28 December. URL: https://fam.ag/3JRkaZ9.

Christos Katsioulis

4 | The end of strategic autonomy as we know it

The Russian war against Ukraine is a shock for the EU, and a reminder of its limits in security policy. However, this shock has also helped clarify the aspirations of European strategic autonomy. It has become clear that the more ambitious level of reaching independence in security and defence is currently not achievable; nor does any member state still aim in this direction. The Russian aggression has introduced a healthy dose of pragmatism into the European debate, helping to focus efforts on realistic and necessary aims. However, hard choices still lie ahead for the EU and avoiding them further is not an option. There is a need to find common ground about what kind of European security order the EU aspires to, and how existing institutions and processes such as enlargement fit into it.

European security is in tatters and the European Union is (again) struggling to find its role. This might sum up the situation after Russia's invasion of Ukraine brought the reality of a major interstate war back to Europe. The first impression was clear: a major blow to the hope that the EU might be able to achieve "strategic autonomy" – or strategic sovereignty as some call it – and align its status as an economic superpower with more robust capabilities in the realm of security and defence. While Washington and London reacted decisively and NATO was revitalised as the main defence for Europeans, the EU struggled. The institutional order of European security has thus changed to the detriment of the EU. Strategic autonomy for the EU is still on the cards in the wake of Russia's attack on Ukraine – but under new conditions, and with obstacles to overcome.

To examine these obstacles we must first look at the concept of strategic autonomy and the situation of the EU in security and defence before the outbreak of the Russian war against Ukraine. The second part of this chapter will concentrate on the changes the war has triggered and delve into the possible repercussions for a strategically sovereign EU after the war.[1]

The concept of strategic autonomy

The idea of being autonomous or acting autonomously has been used in a rather excessive manner throughout Europe in recent years. From the issue of defence – building a European army – to the more broadly defined issue of supply chains in a postpandemic world,[2] strategic autonomy would seem to be the way forward. Frédéric Mauro describes it as an "obscure object of desire", indicating the vagueness of the term.[3]

To make strategic autonomy a political guideline, there needs to be a definition of its ambition in terms of what it should aspire to achieve in security and defence. Looking at the development of the strategic debate in Europe, three levels of European strategic autonomy need to be differentiated.[4] First, there is the ambition to provide international crisis management, which lies at the heart of the Common Security and Defence Policy and denotes the EU's aim to deal with crises in its vicinity autonomously. This describes the lowest level of ambition. Second, there is strategic autonomy in the sense of military independence. This is a later definition of the concept, which was introduced into the strategic debate in the past decade and found its way into the EU's Global Strategy.[5] It aims at providing security inside and outside the EU, as well as an autonomous and competitive technological and industrial base for European defence. Politically the latter concept was directed – at least by some – against the United States, aiming for a more autonomous EU separate

---

1   It should be noted at this point that the text of this chapter was finished in December 2022. Developments since that date cannot be taken into account, although they might have an important influence on how the EU develops.

2   Fabry, E., and A. Veskoukis (2021) "Strategic autonomy in post-Covid trade policy: how far should we politicise supply chains?" Report, Istituto Affari Internazionali, July.

3   Mauro, F. (2021) "Europe's strategic autonomy: that obscure object of desire". Analysis no. 13, French Institute for International and Strategic Affairs, October. URL: https://www .iris-france.org/wp-content/uploads/2021/10/EN-ANALYSIS-13-EUROPE%E2%80%99S-STRATEGIC-AUTONOMY-October-2021.pdf.

4   For all three aspects, see ibid.

5   European External Action Service (2016) "Shared vision, common action: a stronger Europe – a global strategy for the European Union's foreign and security policy". Strategy document, EEAS, June. URL: https://www.eeas.europa.eu/sites/default/files/eugs_review _web_0.pdf.

---

from the US and NATO.[6] Third, the latest and broadest understanding of strategic autonomy is a rather indiscriminately used concept of autonomy in the broader sense, applying to a wider range of issues including trade, finance and investment. Josep Borrell, the EU's foreign policy chief, has indicated that this may be unhelpful and has tried to redirect the debate to the narrower sense of security: "Strategic autonomy has been widened to new subjects of an economic and technological nature, as revealed by the Covid-19 pandemic. However, the security dimension remains predominant and sensitive."[7] While this priority seems sensible, it cannot be overlooked that security in general, but defence more specifically, has been the EU's weak point not only at the institutional level but also in relations among member states.

Nonetheless, there is a pattern in EU security policy – which also applies to defence – whereby the institutional framework is built up with speed and diligence while the capabilities of member states lag behind and political will seems scarce. The preconditions for a more clearly defined political direction, such as mutual trust between member states and a sense of shared destiny, have never really been fulfilled. Both have clashed with two issues that have been redefined since 24 February 2022: on the one hand, differing perceptions of the relationship with NATO and the US; and on the other, the question of how to deal with Russia.[8]

This has not prevented the EU from implementing a series of international missions.[9] But despite the aim for "a stable world and a safer Europe",[10] the world at large, but especially the European neighbourhood, has become increasingly unstable with the emergence of a more autonomous Europe. The wars in Georgia, Ukraine, Armenia and Azerbaijan, the ongoing conflict in Syria with the active participation of Russia and Turkey, and conflict zones in the Middle East and below the Sahel all bear witness to this worsening situation. Even before the Russian war against

6   Borrell, J. (2020) "Why European strategic autonomy matters". Blog post, European External Action Service, 3 December. URL: https://www.eeas.europa.eu/eeas/why-euro pean-strategic-autonomy-matters_en.

7   Ibid.

8   Mauro, F. (2021) "Europe's strategic autonomy", p. 5; Retter, L., et al. (2021) "European strategic autonomy in defence: transatlantic visions and implications for NATO, US and EU relations". Report, RAND Europe, p. 3. URL: https://www.rand.org/content/dam/rand/ pubs/research_reports/RRA1300/RRA1319-1/RAND_RRA1319-1.pdf.

9   For a full overview of EU missions, see the webpage of the European External Action Service "Missions and operations: working for a stable world and a safer Europe" (www .eeas.europa.eu/eeas/missions-and-operations_en).

10   Ibid.

Ukraine these would have been important drivers for an intensified effort towards European strategic autonomy.

To summarise, once the idea of strategic autonomy for the EU arose, a paradox developed. The demand for security provided by Europe grew due to the worsening security situation in the European neighbourhood and an increasingly distracted or absent United States. But the supply was nowhere to be found. Whereas the EU was making considerable progress institutionally, capacities were not available, and – even more crucially – there was no political will to act. And into this European gap between high security demand and low security supply came the Russian attack on Ukraine.

Strategic autonomy in light of the Russian war against Ukraine

The unprovoked Russian War against Ukraine is a turning point in European history, or a "*Zeitenwende*" as German Chancellor Olaf Scholz described it a few days after the beginning of the war in a seminal speech to the Bundestag.[11] It thus also has significant repercussions for the EU, changing the context in which its security policy needs to develop, the urgency of addressing issues of inadequate capabilities, and the rationale concerning partners. Some of the determining factors in strengthening European strategic autonomy have considerably changed since the Russian war against Ukraine.[12]

First, on the political level, the war has brought perceptions of threat among EU member states closer together. With Russia as the aggressor blatantly violating international law, threat perceptions that were previously diverse – especially between the eastern and western members of the EU[13] – have converged considerably and will converge further. This could already be observed when the question of sanctions against Russia was put on the table. Never before did the EU decide so swiftly on a sanctions regime that would have a significant impact not only on

---

11   Scholz, O. (2022) "Regierungserklärung von Bundeskanzler Olaf Scholz am 27. Februar 2022". Federal Government of Germany website, 27 February. URL: https://www.bundesregierung.de/breg-de/suche/regierungserklaerung-von-bundeskanzler-olaf-scholz-am-27-februar-2022-2008356.

12   Retter, L., et al. (2021) "European strategic autonomy in defence", p. iv.

13   Katsioulis, C., et al. (2022) "Navigating the disarray of European security". Security Radar 2022, Friedrich Ebert Foundation, February. URL: https://library.fes.de/pdf-files/bueros/wien/18980-20220310.pdf.

Russia but on European societies as a whole. The common conviction that there needed to be a clear signal towards Moscow prevailed and helped overcome political differences. Second, the perennial apple of discord – namely, the rivalry between the EU and NATO – could be set aside, at least in the medium term. This discord has long stood in the way of political unity within the EU, hindering progress in decision-making as well as capacity building.[14] The war has revitalised the Atlantic Alliance and made clear that it serves a specific and very necessary purpose in Europe: territorial defence still relies on NATO, and thus on the support of the US.

There is a third political change that the war has brought, strengthening both the EU and NATO considerably. The Danish population voted in a referendum to opt in to the EU's Common Security and Defence Policy, ending its outsider status going back decades. This shows that popular opinion on EU security policy may have changed after the Russian attack and that traditional political stances can change. The same applies to NATO, with Sweden and Finland – two traditionally neutral countries – joining the Alliance in light of their revised perceptions of threat. Last, but not least, cooperation between EU member states and the UK has improved. Although Brexit and the ensuing debates have poisoned the waters between London and the EU for some years, the war has shown the need for cooperation and introduced a sense of shared destiny, at least in light of a common adversary.

The EU's Strategic Compass reflects at least the first two of the above-mentioned changes. Changing the original timeline, which foresaw presentation of the Compass in November 2021, the EU included the main lessons from the Russian attack. There is a common understanding about the threat Russia poses to the EU and the kind of international order the latter represents. The Compass also frames the strategic environment of the EU as a field of fierce competition not only with Russia, but also with China and other potential adversaries. By acknowledging NATO as the foundation of collective defence for its members and the complementarity between the EU and NATO, it opens a path to constructively strengthening both institutions towards a common purpose. It also outlines concrete ideas about how to increase cooperation between the two institutions sustainably.

---

14 Von Ondarza, N., and M. Overhaus (2022) "Rethinking strategic sovereignty: narratives and priorities for Europe after Russia's attack on Ukraine". SWP Comment no. 31, Stiftung Wissenschaft und Politik, April, p. 5. URL: https://www.swp-berlin.org/publications/products/comments/2022C31_Strategic_Sovereignty.pdf.

At an institutional level, however, the war has revealed the Janus-headed principle of the EU's decision-making process. As discussed above, the EU was able to swiftly impose sanctions on Russia when the political momentum was opportune and all member states agreed. This was even more impressive as the Russian government clearly did not anticipate such a decision being supported by all member states. However, once the initial shock over the aggression had subsided and political considerations resurfaced, problems of unanimity once again came to the fore. As long as individual member states are able to bend decisions their way to serve short-term political aims or even influence electoral deliberations, the EU will not be an international force to be reckoned with. Though this is hardly a new insight, the need to change this has become far more pressing. The German government, for example, has renewed its aim to introduce qualified majority voting into the security policy of the EU, and others support this. This still seems unrealistic, bearing in mind the importance of the veto, especially for smaller EU member states. But it could lead to a renewed effort to build a group inside the EU that shares not only threat perceptions but also a vision for how to move forward from them, perhaps in the form of Permanent Structured Cooperation (PESCO). This would be at the vanguard of a more integrated European security policy, sidelining the unanimity principle. The political pressure of the war could thus lead to differentiated levels of integration in the EU according to overlapping strategic cultures, following the example of the EUFOR Crisis Response Operation Core.[15]

The war has also brought change on the level of capabilities. Since the shock at a war on the EU's border brought the focus back on national defence capabilities, some major decisions have been taken. What stands out is the decision of the German government to invest €100 billion in its defence budget over the coming years and permanently spend more than 2% of GDP for that purpose.[16] Although the German defence budget was already raised after 2014, this injection of major resources will make the country the biggest defence spender in Europe by a considerable margin. Other member states have also decided to invest more in armaments. This will allow EU member states to shoulder more responsibility within NATO and provide more capabilities for the EU in the foreseeable future.

15 Biscop, S. (2022) "Strategic autonomy: not without integration". FEPS Policy Brief, Strategic Autonomy Series, January, p. 9. URL: https://feps-europe.eu/wp-content/uploads/downloads/publications/220113%20strategic_autonomy_sven_biscop.pdf.

16 Scholz, O. (2022) "Regierungserklärung".

However, the more profound change this investment initiative will bring about is stronger integration of European armies. With investment decisions taken at a similar time, there is a chance to align at least the procurement of more costly material and thus make use of economies of scale for the benefit of budgets all over Europe. At the same time, many European member states have emptied their depots of older weapon systems to support the Ukrainian army. Taken together, this offers the opportunity to build interoperability into the various European armies from the outset by procuring systems together, by making use of new financial instruments the EU is providing for defence, and by ending the existing structure of a multitude of arms systems being used by different European armies, which has made cooperation and joint operations nearly impossible. With these efforts, combined with the enhanced role of the European Commission in defence, the opportunity exists for consolidation and integration of European defence in the coming years.[17]

The German government has already pledged to use the additional spending to enhance the European dimension. This has been clear from the very inception, with the chancellor outlining in his initial speech that the funds would be used to buy not only American weapon systems such as the F-35 but also the Future Combat Air System, a European platform. This was further underlined in the following months[18] and could be the seed to enable the EU to act autonomously in future.

A promising new way for the EU to deal with upcoming challenges is the example of the European Peace Facility (EPF). An instrument originally designed to finance activities with military implications and support armies of member states and partner countries with infrastructure, training and equipment, the EPF has been instrumental in providing quick and unbureaucratic support to Ukraine in times of need. Although the EPF had funding of approximately €6 billion for seven years, the EU has made quick use of nearly half of these funds to supply Ukraine with military equipment. The EPF thus shows how adaptable and flexible the EU can be when needed.

Apart from changes at the political, institutional and capability levels, the war has also helped clarifying the aspirations of European strategic

---

17 Puglierin, J. (2022) "Der Strategische Kompass: Ein Fahrplan für die Europäische Union als sicherheitspolitische Akteurin". BAKS-Arbeitspapier Sicherheitspolitik 7/22, Federal Academy for Security Policy, p. 5. URL: https://www.baks.bund.de/sites/baks010/files/arbeitspapier_sicherheitspolitik_2022_7.pdf.

18 "Ministerin Lambrecht: Die Europäer müssen selbst wirksamer abschrecken". Federal Ministry of Defence website, June. URL: https://www.bmvg.de/de/aktuelles/ministerin-europaeer-muessen-selber-wirksamer-abschrecken-5450158.

autonomy. It has become clear that the more ambitious level of reaching independence in security and defence is currently not achievable; nor does any member state still aim in this direction. The Russian aggression has introduced a healthy dose of pragmatism into the European debate, focusing efforts on realistic and necessary aims. The sometimes ideological debate over the EU and/or NATO is over. The real question seems now to be: how much room is there for Europe in NATO? This takes into account the necessary strengthening of European capabilities, as well as the pivot towards the Pacific that is happening in the US, despite the current war in Europe. However, there remain a number of synergies between NATO and the EU that are yet to be exploited sufficiently. The EU's Strategic Compass is revealing this as a direction towards a more flexible, effective and nimble EU.[19]

The EU and the broader picture of European security after February 2022

The Russo-Ukrainian War has raised not only a series of questions regarding the internal structure of EU security policy but also broader issues regarding its position in a not yet visible postwar European security order. The war has practically ended an era in which the Paris Charter had actual meaning for the participating states of the OSCE. While the 1990 charter declared the end of an era of confrontation and division and the beginning of a new time of cooperation and respect,[20] the Russian war may act as a caesura similar to the fall of the Berlin Wall, heralding another new era. The EU therefore needs to reach a common understanding about the kind of security order it seeks. Here, internal divisions will again emerge over whether such an order should be confrontational and directed against Russia in a kind of Cold War 2.0 or whether it should allow for a potential Russian return into common European arrangements in future, thus preserving cooperative elements.

Related to this overarching issue is the question of the EU's relationship with the OSCE. As the institution born out of the Commission on Security and Cooperation in Europe and the Paris Charter, it embodies the idea of cooperative security. This is why it has become sidelined in the wake of this war between two participating states. The EU could continue to use the OSCE, as it did in 2022 under the Polish presidency, to signal

---

19   Puglierin, J. (2022) "Der Strategische Kompass", p. 4.

20   OSCE (1990) "Charter of Paris for a New Europe". Paris, 19–21 November. URL: https://www.osce.org/files/f/documents/0/6/39516.pdf.

its opposition to the Russian war. However, this would likely provoke (and already has provoked) reciprocal moves from Russia and deprive the OSCE even more of its capacity to act, impacting its manifold and effective field missions all over Europe, specifically in the Western Balkans. If the EU instead concludes that the OSCE in itself is worth preserving, it could also try to use the Vienna-based institution as one of the few platforms where Russia and EU members sit regularly around the same table to explore opportunities for the Russian government to participate in solving planetary challenges such as the climate crisis, food and water safety, or nuclear proliferation. Such an approach would require a paradoxical mixture of confrontation and cooperation, which might stretch the EU's ability to find common positions among its 27 member states when implementing a common strategy in Vienna.

Other parts of the puzzle of European security are open questions regarding the countries of the Western Balkans, Georgia, Moldova and Ukraine. The Balkan countries have been in the EU waiting room for years, joined recently by Moldova and Ukraine. The politics of enlargement and broader geopolitical issues thus start (again) to become intertwined. The EU needs to clarify – first and foremost for itself – what logic will dominate in dealing with these countries' aspirations to join the club; otherwise, a mix of domestic factors, questions over decision-making effectiveness and crisis-driven geopolitics will further muddy the profile of EU security policy. As the current offer of EU membership towards Ukraine and Moldova is clearly driven by the aim of bringing these countries into the European camp, the same logic should also be applied to the countries of the Western Balkans. There, Russia is also trying to act as a spoiler and to use existing ethnic divisions to obscure reform agendas.[21] This would again force the EU to take a leap and reach a decision that has long been procrastinated over or buried in bureaucratic logic.

In both cases – the handling of the OSCE and enlargement policy – the Russian war against Ukraine forces the EU to confront issues that have been neglected for too long. However, the avoidance of hard choices cannot be the way the EU conducts its security policy in future. A common understanding must thus be reached about what kind of European security order the EU aspires to, and how existing institutions and processes such as enlargement fit into it.

---

21 Stronski, P. (2022) "Russia in the Balkans after Ukraine: a troubling actor". *Politika*, Carnegie Endowment for International Peace, 20 September. URL: https://carnegieendowment.org/politika/87959.

Conclusion

In conclusion, it is clear that Russia's war against Ukraine has not only shattered fundamental security assumptions in Europe but also challenged the EU to sharpen and deliver on its ambitions regarding strategic autonomy. Politically, common threat perceptions must be complemented by a common vision of Europe's security order, guiding future political decisions over enlargement in particular.

On the matter of hard security and defence, the security ambitions of the EU before 2022 consisted of a highly ambitious institutional setup that was lacking political will and especially the means to act on these aspirations. Current decisions by a number of European governments will allow many of the capability gaps to be closed in the coming years. The way these investments are implemented will be the first litmus test of Europe's ability to get its act together militarily. Should the chance be seized and the EU helps its member states integrate their militaries more effectively, the Union will be in a far better position to act in security policy. The level of ambition has been lowered and is now more achievable. First, the need to shoulder a heavier burden inside NATO will put the European pillar to its next test. While nobody expects Europeans to fully replace the US, especially their nuclear umbrella over the Alliance, Washington will expect a bigger European footprint in conventional forces. This goes for the current US administration, and even more so should there be a change in government after the next presidential elections in 2024. Second, Europe will need to deal with crisis management in its neighbourhood for the foreseeable future without much US support. While the current war overshadows this issue, the many hotspots surrounding the EU need attention and possibly even stabilisation.[22] Third, this war caught many European countries unprepared and unable to organise territorial defence on their own. The EU therefore has a key role to play in enabling member states to overcome this challenge and prepare for a new era in Europe during which military means will be an important factor in ensuring the safety of European citizens.

An EU able to fulfil these ambitions would finally put flesh on the bones of strategic autonomy, a promise now nearing 25 years of age. The world has changed radically in this time – and with it the meaning of this sometimes blurry, politically contested concept. But what hasn't changed is the need for the EU to supplement its economic weight with

---

22   For the upcoming challenges, see Haass, R. (2022) "The dangerous decade: a foreign policy for a world in crisis". *Foreign Affairs*, September/October.

an accordingly heavy footprint in security policy. The Russian war is just the latest reminder to the EU that the much-cited mismatch between its status as an economic giant and a military dwarf, which is otherwise constantly distracted by internal infighting, is still a reality and needs fixing. If the EU cannot gain the ability to act in an increasingly chaotic and confrontational environment, it risks becoming the playing field for other actors – and that would be the opposite of strategic autonomy.

Further reading

Biscop, S. (2022) "Strategic autonomy: not without integration". FEPS Policy Brief, Strategic Autonomy Series, January. URL: https://feps-europe.eu/wp-content/uploads/downloads/publications/220113%20strategic_autonomy_sven_biscop.pdf.

Borrell, J. (2020) "Why European strategic autonomy matters". Blog post, European External Action Service, 3 December. URL: https://www.eeas.europa.eu/eeas/why-european-strategic-autonomy-matters_en.

European Council (1999) "European Council declaration on strengthening the Common European Policy on Security and Defence". Cologne, 3–4 June. URL: https://www.europarl.europa.eu/summits/kol2_en.htm.

European External Action Service (2016) "Shared vision, common action: a stronger Europe – a global strategy for the European Union's foreign and security policy". Strategy document, EEAS. URL: https://www.eeas.europa.eu/sites/default/files/eugs_review_web_0.pdf.

European External Action Service (2019) "EU Battlegroups". Fact sheet, EEAS, 5 October. URL: https://www.eeas.europa.eu/sites/default/files/factsheet_battlegroups.pdf.

Fabry, E., and A. Veskoukis (2021) "Strategic autonomy in post-Covid trade policy: how far should we politicise supply chains?" Report, Istituto Affari Internazionali, July.

Grevi, G. (1999) "Strategic autonomy for European choices: the key to Europe's shaping power". Discussion Paper, European Policy Centre, July. URL: https://www.epc.eu/content/PDF/2019/190719_Strategicautonomy_GG.pdf.

Haass, R. (2022) "The dangerous decade: a foreign policy for a world in crisis". *Foreign Affairs*, September/October.

Kaminski, T. (2022) "Don't look at Trump: the EU needs strategic autonomy". Review no. 16, 4liberty.eu, pp. 34–47. URL: http://4liberty.eu/wp-content/files/TOMASZ_KAMISKI_DONT_LOOK_AT_TRUMP_THE_EU_NEEDS_STRATEGIC_AUTONOMY.pdf.

Katsioulis, C., et al. (2022) "Navigating the disarray of European security". Security Radar 2022, Friedrich Ebert Foundation, February. URL: https://library.fes.de/pdf-files/bueros/wien/18980-20220310.pdf.

Mauro, F. (2021) "Europe's strategic autonomy: that obscure object of desire". Analysis no. 13, French Institute for International and Strategic Affairs, October. URL: https://www.iris-france.org/wp-content/uploads/2021/10/EN-ANALYSIS-13-EUROPE%E2%80%99S-STRATEGIC-AUTONOMY-October-2021.pdf.

OSCE (1990) "Charter of Paris for a New Europe". Paris, 19–21 November. URL: https://www.osce.org/files/f/documents/0/6/39516.pdf.

Puglierin, J. (2022) "Der Strategische Kompass: Ein Fahrplan für die Europäische Union als sicherheitspolitische Akteurin". BAKS-Arbeitspapier Sicherheitspolitik 7/22, Federal Academy for Security Policy. URL: https://www.baks.bund.de/sites/baks010/files/arbeitspapier_sicherheitspolitik_2022_7.pdf.

Retter, L., et al. (2021) "European strategic autonomy in defence: transatlantic visions and implications for NATO, US and EU relations". Report, RAND Europe. URL: https://www.rand.org/content/dam/rand/pubs/research_reports/RRA1300/RRA1319-1/RAND_RRA1319-1.pdf.

Scholz, O. (2022) "Regierungserklärung von Bundeskanzler Olaf Scholz am 27. Februar 2022". Federal Government of Germany website, 27 February. URL: https://www.bundesregierung.de/breg-de/suche/regierungserklaerung-von-bundeskanzler-olaf-scholz-am-27-februar-2022-2008356.

Stronski, P. (2022) "Russia in the Balkans after Ukraine: a troubling actor". *Politika*, Carnegie Endowment for International Peace, 20 September. URL: https://carnegieendowment.org/politika/87959.

Von Ondarza, N., and M. Overhaus (2022) "Rethinking strategic sovereignty: narratives and priorities for Europe after Russia's attack on Ukraine". SWP Comment no. 31, Stiftung Wissenschaft und Politik, April. URL: https://www.swp-berlin.org/publications/products/comments/2022C31_Strategic_Sovereignty.pdf.

Kersten Lahl

5 | Western weapons for Ukraine: road to escalation or end of the war?

Arms supplies to Ukraine are legal, legitimate and indispensable. They have prevented the extinction of the state, and in future they will play a decisive role in enforcing a diplomatic solution. Moreover, not to stand up forcefully against Putin's ambitions would be extremely risky for future international cooperation and global stability.

The strategic military situation

Russia's war against Ukraine, which began in 2014 with the annexation of Crimea and the fighting in Donbas, entered its decisive phase at the start of 2022. Rather than being a "special military operation", as Moscow claims, it was a scripted attack on a sovereign neighbouring state. On 24 February, Russian troops marched into Ukrainian territory from the east, north and south with overwhelming force. During this phase, few analysts thought Ukraine would have any real chance of withstanding the supposedly overwhelming superiority of the aggressor, and yet the Kremlin's goal of a lightning victory failed to materialise.

While Russia was initially able to achieve considerable territorial gains in the south, its progress in the east stagnated. In the north, its attack on Kyiv – obviously its key objective with the expectation of a quick victory within a couple of days – went disastrously wrong. Serious, unexpected shortcomings in Russia's conduct of the war became apparent: from inept operations to poor logistics to poor military morale, which stands in stark contrast to that of the Ukrainian defenders. Of the factors that military theorist Carl von Clausewitz considered decisive in war, the Russians possess only "superiority in numbers", and none of the "moral forces" such as bravery or the element of surprise in the conduct of operations. The extended duration of the stalled attack and its partial repulsion has increasingly transferred momentum to the defenders. The Russian withdrawal from Kyiv, the sinking of the *Moskva*, the counteroffensive at Kharkiv and, most recently, the liberation of Kherson are clear indications that the "culminating point" is now within reach for Ukraine. Russia's shift in its current attacks more and more to civilian targets underlines this assessment.

This was the situation at the end of 2022. Forecasting further military progress is difficult. On the one hand, the balance is clearly tilting more towards Ukraine, which is now ever more frequently taking the initiative. Some analysts are even predicting that it is only a matter of time before they manage to liberate their entire territory, including Donbas and Crimea, despite Russia's desperate further mobilisation efforts. Nonetheless, a grinding war of attrition and a fragile cementing of the status quo are also possibilities, as the Ukrainian defenders also appear to be exhausted. A particularly disastrous scenario, however, would be an escalation including nuclear weapons and/or an extension of combat operations beyond the theatre of war in Ukraine.

Necessary and legitimate arms supplies

Against this backdrop, the question arises as to whether the West possesses any meaningful strategic response. Military support for Ukraine is generally regarded as an indispensable step in the search for a solution – as a prerequisite for its continued existence as a sovereign state with its own national territory, citizenry and authorities. It is beyond doubt that Ukraine would have fallen long ago had it not been for arms supplies from the West. The West's approach is, of course, not without controversy, as it carries with it the risk of unintentional and uncontrollable escalation, a fact that its critics often point out.

Russia is guilty of violating the prohibition on the use of force under Article 2 of the United Nations Charter. Ukraine's right to defend itself against Russian aggression to an extent that is necessary and proportionate is therefore undisputed for as long as the UN Security Council fails to fulfil its responsibility of maintaining world peace, or while its capacity to act is obstructed from within. Whether it is permissible to provide military support to the defender that extends beyond collective self-defence, however, remains something of a moot point. Some commentators argue that there would be a requirement to stay neutral, but there are more convincing arguments that consider external aid to be perfectly permissible without violating the principle of noninterference.

The UN General Assembly's clear attribution of aggression invalidates the duty of impartiality for third states – in fact it rather makes the opposite case. In any event, it excludes an appeal to the classical law of neutrality, which would ultimately entail treating the attacker and defender equally. The law is also clear on the question of whether a third country becomes an official combatant by virtue of its assistance to a state under attack: the answer is no, as long as its armed forces do not intervene on the territory of one of the warring parties, or provided it does not formally declare war.

Disputable, however, is the question of which arms supplies are to be considered and how they are to be delivered. In reality, the formal legal position is of less importance than how such supplies are regarded by the Russian leadership. Ultimately it is Russian President Vladimir Putin who decides how he interprets specific arms supplies and whom he considers an adversary. This unpalatable fact forces us to examine any support given to Ukraine not only for its legality but also for its practical consequences.

The purpose, rather than the weapon itself, is decisive

Germany's security policy has traditionally placed particular importance on such issues. The simple principle used to be that no weapons would be supplied to conflict zones (with narrowly defined exceptions). Russia's aggression forced an abrupt abandonment of this position – as part of a postulated "turning point" (*Zeitenwende*). Since then, it has seemed neither wise nor opportune to refuse military aid to a European country in existential distress – even in the absence of a formal obligation to assist. In principle, the debate is no longer about whether Ukraine should be supported at all, but rather about how precisely this support should materialise. There is, of course, an obvious dilemma in maintaining Ukraine's chances of survival on the one hand and limiting the danger of escalation on the other. In practical terms, it is therefore necessary to assess which weapons should be supplied without hesitation and which only with reservations, or not at all.

When searching for answers, the terms "offensive versus defensive" or "light versus heavy weapons" are often mentioned, but this is venturing into unsafe territory. First it depends on the level being discussed. A weapon used tactically in an "aggressive" manner may serve a strategic defence purpose. Self-defence without the ability to counterattack at the local level, let alone organise counteroffensives, is ultimately doomed to failure. From the aggressor's viewpoint, any invasion in which the defender lacks any chance of reclaiming lost territory would be comparatively risk-free and therefore attractive. Consequently, strategic defence without the means to launch offensives is not an option in practice. Conversely, weapons systems that serve essentially "defensive" purposes can also be perceived as offensive. A classic yet extreme example is a missile defence system, which threatens the opponent's nuclear second-strike capability and thus the strategic balance. Even supposedly defensive weapons could potentially trigger what is known as a "security dilemma" and, under certain conditions, set in motion a cascade of bilateral rearmament. The conclusion we can draw from these considerations is that weapons are not in principle offensive or defensive by nature. How they are viewed depends on the purposes to which they are put and how the opponent interprets those purposes.

Similar considerations lead to questioning the distinction between "light" and "heavy" weaponry. First, there are no clear criteria for the designation "heavy", although aspects such as weight, size, ammunition type, calibre or number of operators could serve as an approximate benchmark. The term "heavy" is most often used in relation to six categories: battle tanks, infantry vehicles, artillery, combat helicopters, combat aircraft and warships. Anything else would therefore be "light". However, this gives only a rough indication of the potential impact on escalation risks. For example, antitank mines – light weapons by the above definition – have a similar destructive capability to a heavy tank. This is also the case for shoulder-supported antiaircraft missiles and their lethal effect against aircraft or helicopters. Artillery reconnaissance systems and ammunition transporters are just as important in a destructive firefight as heavy howitzers. A Marder infantry fighting vehicle with its rather weak 20 mm gun is not that much more of a decisive threat than kitting out its dismounted crew with bazookas they can fire from outside the vehicle in the battlefield. And finally, modern weapons such as artificial-intelligence-based drones and cyber-devices do not easily fit into the categories "light" or "heavy", despite their devastating potential.

This means that it is not the supposed nature of individual weapons that determines undesirable escalations, but rather how the opponent calculates their complex effect on the course of the war. This realisation, which forces an analysis not only of the available military options but also of how the opponent will perceive them, makes decision-making particularly difficult. In this grey area, one must be careful not to fall victim to enemy narratives that deliberately inflame fears of hybrid warfare. Under

President Biden, the US has therefore signalled clearly and publicly that it is ready to support Ukraine for the long haul without simultaneously wishing to engage in a direct conflict between Russia and the West. Behind it is a targeted de-escalating signal to Putin: Russia's territorial security will remain intact.

The military impact of arms supplies

The current situation in the Ukrainian war zone is fragile. With all due caution, it can be described as follows: Russia's attack has ground to a halt. Its troops continue to occupy significant amounts of Ukrainian territory, but in many places – such as was recently the case in Kherson – it is no longer able or is struggling to hold onto it. Its current approach is more one of strategic defence on enemy territory. Ukraine, on the other hand, is increasingly taking the initiative on the ground, admittedly without any realistic chance of achieving its ultimate objectives of regaining access to the Sea of Azov, the Donbas and Crimea. At present, there are signs of a very fragile breathing space in which the Russian side is trying to buy time and wear down Kyiv with terror attacks on civilian targets. This would seem to pave the way for an attempt at finding a diplomatic solution to the conflict, but there is no will to do so: the Ukrainian side is, quite understandably, unwilling to even consider any formal cession of territory, while the Russian side has yet to meet any of its obvious war objectives, nor the whipped-up expectations of its population. There is therefore much to be said for the assumption that a military stalemate could continue and claim many victims on both sides.

The status quo would, however, change if the Ukrainian armed forces were given the means to ramp up the effectiveness of their counteroffensive and thus achieve a truly decisive turnaround in the war. They have the operational skills but lack the necessary resilient armoured forces that combine firepower with high manoeuvrability. Without these means, they risk being pushed back step by step once their opponent has had time to replenish and reorganise its forces. Conversely, it would likely be in Russia's interests to play for time now, to consolidate remaining gains and expand them once it has built up its forces, or even to completely subjugate its opponent. This means that it is vital for Ukraine to use the current window of opportunity to achieve military success before it closes again.

The approach of giving the Ukrainian armed forces the possibility of making a decisive move requires full-blooded commitment on our part.

Delivering a few hundred armoured infantry vehicles or even main battle tanks will not suffice. The prerequisites for modern joint and combined warfare are much more exacting and require a complex framework of measures, ranging from intensive training and an efficient logistical base to the synergistic integration of various types of weaponry into an effective operational concept. There is also the need to put in place an effective defence against Russian drones and long-range missiles, which are directed less against military targets than against the civilian population and critical infrastructure. This requires an ambitious, coordinated master plan, which cannot be realised in the short term. It goes without saying that the later this is started, the harder it becomes to implement. Delayed, sporadic aid to Ukraine does not significantly improve its situation on the battlefield and thus undermines the political objective of ending the war while preserving the sovereignty of the invaded state. Hesitancy will therefore only reduce military opportunities and result in increased losses.

Political classification of arms supplies

What is the significance from a security perspective of supplying arms to Ukraine in an attempt to turn the tide of Russia's war in favour of the defenders? Some analysts point to the risks of an escalation spiral that becomes uncontrollable, resulting in the Kremlin crossing the nuclear threshold and/or NATO becoming directly involved in the war. Neither can be completely ruled out a priori, a fact the Kremlin likes to use for propaganda purposes and one that sometimes finds fertile ground in the post-heroic societies of Western democracies – for example, by claiming Moscow's allegedly greater ability to escalate the conflict. Nevertheless, as long as all sides' actions are driven by rational, interest-driven thinking, neither of these two scenarios is particularly likely. In reality, resorting to such moves would not improve the situation for Russia – rather the opposite, in fact. Besides, if Putin were seriously considering such options, he would have already resorted to them in the wake of past military failures. It therefore seems that deterrence works, at least so far.

One thing remains true, however: since the end of the Cold War, Europe has never been as close to the precipice of a full-scale war as it is today. The situation today is somewhat reminiscent of the great debate surrounding NATO's Double-Track Decision in the 1980s, which was also marked by strategic rationality on the one hand and grave fears on the other, particularly in Germany. This therefore acts as an incentive for the Kremlin to employ targeted propaganda and disinformation to engender a social split in the West and quasi-impotent backtracking in the face of Russian threats.

Looking more closely, we should question the aforementioned theory of Putin's unilateral greater ability to escalate the conflict, which critics constantly use to call for a diplomatic solution that allegedly "reconciles interests". In conventional terms, the war is already pushing the Russian army to its limits, particularly in terms of the land forces that are crucial for holding on to conquered territory. For geostrategic reasons, Putin cannot afford to focus all of his resources on Ukraine alone. Russia's borders are too extensive, and its domestic and neighbourhood problems too severe. Moscow therefore has no choice but to deploy its resources carefully. Its attempts to terrorise the Ukrainian people with long-distance rocket and drone attacks, with the aim of forcing them to surrender, will in all probability fail and have little to no impact on the situation as regards combat on the ground. The opposite perspective is more plausible: normally it is only the aggressor who has the option to de-escalate, who is in a position to pause or even halt their offensive. The defender, however, has only the choice of either responding to the challenge or surrendering. The Kremlin's dominant position therefore gives it the power to de-escalate the situation. Putin has the ability to initiate a process to resolve the conflict. He alone can end the war if — and this is what matters — it suits his interests better than continuing to pursue his military ambitions in the face of heavy losses.

We therefore need to ask what political impact Western arms supplies are having on Putin's calculations — in other words, how they are affecting his key objectives. One thing is clear: if the Kremlin really is worried about Russia's vital and legitimate security interests and believes it can uphold them only by invading its neighbour, any assistance given to Ukraine will inevitably mean an escalation that results in Moscow responding even more robustly. This would not necessarily mean that a solution acceptable to all sides could not be achieved at the diplomatic level, though it would require some creativity. Corresponding proposals have already been put forward. However, if Putin's real objectives are far more ambitious and directed in essence towards the renaissance of some kind of Russian empire and the division of Europe, any sort of negotiated solution based on compromise would be rendered impossible unless we were ready to disregard the fundamental principles of the international order. On the contrary, it is clear under this assumption that Putin would not end his attacks until the political costs to him threatened to significantly exceed the attainable military benefits.

Putin's overall objectives have not been in doubt since the beginning of 2022 at the very latest. His motives for pursuing war are neoimperial expansion and consolidation of power, rather than acting preemptively to ensure the national security of Russia. For him, this means eliminating the idea of an independent Ukrainian nation and the attractiveness of its Western-oriented social model to the Russian people. Given this assumption, we can posit that arms deliveries to Ukraine serve to de-escalate rather than escalate. Only such deliveries can create an opportunity to end the conflict by making plain the ultimate futility of the aspiration for a Greater Russia. In the longer term as well, destroying Putin's ambitions is an invaluable condition for European and even global peace. It is the only way to expunge the threat of a return to the aggressive methods of the past. It is a prerequisite to enabling close international cooperation and a successful return to far more important issues such as better climate protection, arms control and fair development policy. Above all, however, it will act to reinforce what is essential to the stability of the global order: the authority of international law.

Conclusion

Arms supplies to Ukraine have played a decisive role in this war in preventing the violent extinction of Ukraine and preserving it as a state. Looking to the future, they can also force a change in military strategy, prepare a viable basis for diplomatic solutions and thus open up opportunities for ending the war under conditions that accord with international law. This strategy is by no means without risk and requires both consistency and moderation. In addition to providing the help that Ukraine needs, it is also in the interests of the West to prevent the war from inadvertently spreading and escalating uncontrollably. Rather than speaking in terms of victory or defeat, it is therefore useful to sum up the objective by means of the following formula: Russia must not win, and Ukraine must not lose. This idea signifies something of a balancing act in terms of deciding which arms supplies are necessary, both in quantitative and qualitative terms – what is sufficient and what is less advisable. Even so, this assessment does not change the fact that carefully calibrated arms supplies are an indispensable instrument in pursuit of a peace deal. No other option currently looks as promising.

Further reading

Hobe, S. (2020) *Einführung in das Völkerrecht*, 11th edition (Tübingen: UTB GmbH).

Lahl, K., and J. Varwick (2022) *Sicherheitspolitik verstehen*, 3rd edition (Frankfurt am Main: Wochenschau Verlag).

Sasse, G. (2022) *Der Krieg gegen die Ukraine* (Munich: C. H. Beck).

Talmon, S. (2022) "Waffenlieferungen an die Ukraine als Ausdruck eines wertebasierten Völkerrechts". Blog post, *Verfassungsblog*, 9 March.

Von Clausewitz, C (2010) [1832/1834] *On War [Vom Kriege]* (Scotts Valley, CA: CreateSpace).

Hans-Peter Bartels

6 | Europe needs an operational Bundeswehr

Following Germany's reunification in 1990 the country's armed forces were reduced with each passing year. Their mission became only to take part in multinational out-of-area missions. Since Russia's attack on Ukraine, however, it is obvious that their main task must once again become collective defence. This has consequences for their budget, equipment, personnel and structure. The Scholz government is working on appropriate reforms.

A turning point in defence policy

A government statement by German Chancellor Olaf Scholz in the Bundestag on 27 February 2022 stated: "We need planes that fly, ships that set sail and soldiers who are optimally equipped for their missions."[1] The fact that Scholz explicitly addressed something that should actually be a given, albeit in a slightly ironic manner, marked a paradigm shift in defence policy and a further departure from the era of his predecessor Angela Merkel. For 16 years, the CDU chancellor, who had emergency command and control over the armed forces from 2005 to 2021, was indifferent to whether they were operationally ready.

However, Putin's attack on Ukraine has made defence a top priority in Germany, as it was during the Cold War under the chancellorships of Willy Brandt and Helmut Schmidt. In order to restore Germany's capability to fulfil its military obligations to NATO in full, SPD Chancellor Scholz is striving to achieve a long-ignored standard when it comes to Germany's armaments, noting: "This is of course achievable for a country of our

---

1   Scholz, O. (2022) "Regierungserklärung von Bundeskonzler Olaf Scholz". Cabinet of Germany website, 14 December. URL: https://www.bundesregierung.de/breg-de/service/bulletin/regierungserklaerung-von-bundeskanzler-olaf-scholz-2153850.

size and significance in Europe." As regards its size and significance, Germany is the fourth largest economy in the world after the US, China and Japan, the second biggest NATO nation, the second largest contributor to the United Nations and, objectively, Europe's most populous and richest country.

Spending 2% of GDP annually on defence would in no way be beyond Germany's means; even 3% or 4% (as in the US) is possible, if needs be. In 1984, for example, the proportion of GDP spent on the defence of the Federal Republic was 3.5% – and West Germany was not impoverished at that time, nor had it succumbed to militarism.

Reached in November 2021, the coalition agreement between the three governing parties – the SPD, the Greens and the Free Democratic Party (FDP) – gave the new government the green light to pursue the 2% quota agreed within the Atlantic Alliance. The agreement specifies the objective of spending 3% of GDP on "international affairs" – a compromise formula originally put forward by Wolfgang Ischinger, the long-standing chairman of the Munich Security Conference. This would enable development aid (requirement: 0.7% of GDP) and diplomacy to be adequately financed, while at the same time fulfilling the NATO defence commitment (2% by 2024).

If there had been no war, this would likely have remained a theoretical commitment or would have remained on the back burner, certainly not to be reached before 2024 and perhaps much later than that – if indeed at all. But with the planned allocation from a €100 billion "special fund" approved by the Bundestag, the 2% target could theoretically be realised immediately, in 2022 – a solid basis for fully provisioning and modernising the Bundeswehr.

Nevertheless, the regular defence part of the federal budget would need to grow year by year to maintain the 2% line in six or seven years, once these "special assets" have been exhausted. It will, after all, still be necessary to finance cost increases in the areas of personnel and operations (at a time when inflation is high), as well as the maintenance of newly acquired weapons and equipment. Freezing the "normal" €50 billion defence budget for the next few years – as envisaged in the Federal Government's medium-term financial planning, in order to comply with the constitutional "debt brake" and avoid the need to make cuts elsewhere in the budget – is not a good idea. It would represent the exact opposite of planning: closing our eyes and burying our heads in the sand!

As far as the political superstructure is concerned, in an article for the *Frankfurter Allgemeine Zeitung* (dated 21 March 2022), former constitutional judge Udo Di Fabio sets out the perfect correlation between restoration of military strength on the one hand and the red–green–liberal coalition's aspiration for a rules-based world order on the other. A values-based foreign policy approach alone is not enough, argues Di Fabio. He writes of the "necessity of diplomatic negotiating power being backed up by power politics" as essential in the "geopolitical self-assertion of democracies", concluding: "If Western democracies wish to assert themselves in the face of open military aggression, they must extend the concept of sustainability from the realm of ecology, in which it remains eminently important, to the context of power politics."

This is something that Germany is now doing. Hard power has become decisive, and a new way of thinking is taking hold. Scholz used the term "turning point" three times in his government statement. Not all traditional thinking in terms of foreign and security policy is wrong: continuing to strive for European sovereignty is still the right approach, for example. Nonetheless, a lot needs to change, and our democracy must become more resilient if we wish to preserve our freedom in the long term. Incidentally, the very last word of Scholz's historic speech – probably not coincidentally – stands as a kind of political imperative for the age in which we now find ourselves: "defend".

Where should extra money for the Bundeswehr come from?

The €100 billion armaments fund, which has now been incorporated into constitutional law, should speed up procurement planning at the Federal Ministry of Defence, decision-making processes in parliament and bidding for tenders on the part of the armaments industry. It only took a few days for the Düsseldorf-based Rheinmetall Group to notify the ministry of more than €40 billion worth of deliverable military equipment, ranging from tanks to new types of artillery shells. A fourth tranche of Eurofighters worth €5 billion for the German defence division in Munich is already under contract with Airbus, while a substantial order is being placed with Israeli companies for state-of-the-art missile defence technology.

Planning what to do with the additional €100 billion does not seem to be a problem: the planning will continue to be based on the Bundeswehr's Capability Profile, published in 2018, which provided for investments in armaments to the tune of €200 billion by 2031. The profile is clearly derived from the pledges that Germany made to NATO. At that time, however, this plan for the full provisioning of a ready-to-use Bundeswehr seemed financially unviable, at least initially. The proportion of the 2021 defence budget allocated to pure defence investments in the form of weapons and equipment was €8 billion, which is far too low a sum.

This amount is likely to more than triple for the foreseeable future due to annual transfers from the Bundeswehr's "special assets". This will mean that the Federal Ministry of Defence will have an annual budget of around €25 billion per year for purchases from now on. Scholz's speech was long-awaited and received as something of a political liberation.

However, the first big orders will go to American rather than German industry. The coalition agreement of the governing parties included not only included a political commitment to Germany's participation in the Atlantic Alliance's nuclear sharing agreement but also a voluntary under-taking to make a decision right at the start of the legislative term on the procurement of a suitable nuclear weapons delivery system to succeed the old European fighter bomber, the Tornado. That decision came out in favour of purchasing F-35 jets, which will cost €10 billion in total. A further 15 Eurofighters will also be procured for electronic combat.

Bundeswehr planners estimate that additional acquisitions from the US, which have been postponed several times due to funding issues, will cost in the region of €6–8 billion: to ensure the mobility of the German army, the Luftwaffe needs new heavy US transport helicopters as a replacement for decommissioned CH-53 helicopters.

The German navy is aiming to achieve a technological leap forward in these uncertain times by bringing forward its order for new air defence frigates, which will also – thanks to US technology – have missile defence capability.

All these things are important and will be implemented in one form or another. However, the prime focus must clearly be on fully equipping and modernising the army. In 2022 not one single brigade was fully equipped and immediately ready for action. Germany has promised NATO three divisions with eight to ten combat brigades (5,000–6,000 soldiers each). This is what the Alliance is counting on to defend its members in Europe. While additional allied air force and naval units can be moved eastward towards any crisis-like threat, what counts in terms of a deterrent are combat-ready, deployment-capable forces in Central Europe. A given sit-uation might well escalate dangerously by the time reinforcements arrive from across the Atlantic or from the UK, Italy or Spain.

Fully equipping our ground forces, which have been depleted over decades, can therefore no longer be postponed. They need modern command stations; functional armoured personnel carriers and combat helicopters; more artillery and drones; larger wheeled formations; digital telecommunications; full night-combat capability; portable bridges; and their own air defence capacities, logistics and medical staff.

While not all of this materiel can or should be supplied by German industry, the proportion produced in Germany and Europe as a whole will be very high. The domestic arms industry still sets international standards when it comes to ground systems, something that now sounds like reassuringly good news, unlike in the past where such exports were seen as a negative.

What should be clear is that the programme to restore the armed forces to full operational capacity can only succeed if the procurement system is reformed. However, the Bundeswehr Procurement Acceleration Act is not enough in this instance. Instead, the Koblenz Procurement Office (BAAINBw) should be relieved as quickly as possible of the maintenance role it was assigned in the last reform of the Bundeswehr in 2011, as this is something that each service of the armed forces must be able to carry out itself. In addition, responsibility for routine purchasing should be transferred to other parts of the Bundeswehr's administration, including individual units where appropriate. The Koblenz office's staffing might still not be enough, as many of its positions are still unfilled, but it would be in a better position to fulfil its core task, which remains unchanged: the procurement and ongoing modernisation of aircraft, tanks, ships, helicopters, missiles, ammunition and electronics.

However, even the finally agreed budget increase will not cover the costs of everything that has already been called for, planned and agreed.

Low-risk, quickly realised purchasing solutions therefore now have a certain priority over laborious joint programmes involving specific requests from three or more countries. A critical revision is still pending of the six Franco-German Macron–Merkel development projects agreed in 2017 (the Future Combat Air System, Main Ground Combat System tanks, Tiger III helicopters, Eurodrone, artillery, maritime reconnaissance aircraft), but it will need to be undertaken.

Industry before consolidation

When the main purpose of military procurement – gaining superior defence capability – returns to the fore as starkly as it has done now following the Russian attack on Ukraine, the ancillary objectives of procurement policy necessarily take a back seat. Such ancillary objectives include European cooperation, technological sovereignty and the share of value added by each country. Forcing competing arms companies together in the form of European multinational programmes, regardless of the cost, is something that governments will not be able to afford for much longer.

There is now a clear trend towards ordering commercially available, proven military equipment. Poland, for example, procures South Korean tanks and howitzers. Many NATO nations are no longer prepared to accept delays due to long delivery times or waiting for new developments. We are already in an emergency situation, and rapid growth in combat strength is designed to have a deterrent effect.

The declared EU target of investing 35% of all member states' arms expenditure in joint European programmes is thus increasingly being sidelined. In 2022 the European Defence Agency complained in its Coordinated Annual Review on Defence report that the rate has actually fallen slightly, from 19% to 18%. Recent emergency purchases due to the war in Ukraine are likely to reduce the share allocated to joint projects even further. The more than 60 projects that fall under the Permanent Structured Cooperation (PESCO), in which 25 of the 27 EU nations participate, have to date had little impact on that share. This is also the case for the large number of well-intentioned cooperation projects in NATO's parallel Framework Nations Concept.

The European pillar of the Atlantic Alliance is still characterised by a kind of "small-state mentality" when it comes to armaments policy. A total of 23 European states are simultaneously members of NATO and the EU (including Sweden and Finland), which is actually a rather impressive "Europe of defence" (*l'Europe de la défense*, as the French like to call it). However, their combined armies maintain 12 different types of battle tank, 16 types of combat aircraft, 55 different models of transport aircraft and 12 different types of submarine. This is the very opposite of effectiveness, and a greater degree of standardisation would be desirable to ensure military interoperability.

Although Central and Eastern European allies are now sending their old Soviet-era materiel to Ukraine (and having it replaced by decommissioned Bundeswehr materiel in a form of "circular exchange"), in objective terms the "turning point" favours the continuation of inherited diversity rather than consolidation, which would of course be desirable.

This is especially true of Europe's defence industry, which remains small in scale and predominantly national in nature. This has made the industry increasingly uncompetitive in comparison with far larger US contenders. Changing the structure of Europe's defence industry continues to be a task for European policy, and a European arms summit is needed to address the topic of mergers and the division of labour. This would then need to be followed by industrial policy initiatives.

Europe's extremely successful civil aviation industry only became truly European through political management, which started some 50 years ago. The industry had previously been hopelessly fragmented, and many at the time believed that it was doomed to near extinction. This example shows clearly that political leadership can and must make a difference!

Reforms the Bundeswehr now needs

Regardless of whatever additional long-awaited materiel the Bundeswehr acquires, its operational readiness will remain precarious if it fails to carry out structural reforms. However, this internal reform process has still not been initiated.

Until the fall of communism and German reunification in 1990, the task of the Bundeswehr was solely to defend the West German state within the structures of NATO's defences along the intra-German border. Following reunification, its primary purpose then became multinational crisis intervention outside the Alliance's boundaries. Since 2014, for the first time in its history, it has had to cope with two primary tasks simultaneously. It must continue to execute out-of-area operations (in the Balkans, Afghanistan, the Sahel, the Middle East, the Mediterranean and the Indian Ocean), while also deploying troops and resources to restore NATO's defence capabilities in Europe. The Federal Government's 2016 White Paper on Security Policy and the 2018 Bundeswehr Concept that fleshes it out, together with the military Capability Profile that operationalises NATO force planning for the Bundeswehr, explicitly take these new dual tasks into account. For some years now, additional funding has been allocated to the defence budget for additional personnel and materiel (€32 billion in 2014; €50 billion in 2022). The decline has been halted, and the military is now being expanded.

Russia's attack on Ukraine has made the task of "collective defence" ever more pressing. This fundamental change in position and mandate does, however, require structural reforms, which can also be used to correct the mistakes and shortcomings of the past. The lesson to be learned from previous Bundeswehr reforms is that disruptive talk of "bottom-up" change does little to resolve problems and instead contributes to uncertainty and sclerosis. Since to some degree everything is always undergoing a process of small-scale change (redeployment, disbandment, reorganisation, Europeanisation, new weapons systems, infrastructure constraints and so forth), framing changes in an "evolutionary" context is probably the best way to approach this. The changes should begin in areas where they will have the greatest impact. On balance, the best approach would probably be to maintain as much continuity as possible while implementing as much reform as necessary.

All previous attempts to systematically rectify materiel shortages through the use of special organisations, ad hoc working groups and additional staff commitments have only had a limited impact on the problem. Those involved – the official armaments sector, the armed forces, ministries and industry – may point the finger of blame at each other, but that leads nowhere. Centralisation, privatisation, juridification and diffusion of responsibility are the established principles of the present, the validity of which should now be thoroughly scrutinised.

The number of branches and organisational areas into which the German military is divided continued to grow during the years in which it was reduced in scale. The army, air force and navy were joined by the Joint Support Service, the Joint Medical Service and the Cyber and Information Domain Service, each of which was created out of previous structures. Such fragmentation makes operational collaboration between the various branches of the armed forces and their organisational areas a challenge. The fragmentation has also led to an increase in the number of commands and headquarters.

A review should therefore be conducted to establish whether it would be possible to reduce the number of organisational areas and streamline the remaining structures. The army, air force, navy and other surviving organisational areas should each have a command authority that is in charge of all their responsibilities and, where appropriate, an office responsible for supporting tasks such as training, planning, maintenance, development and other support tasks.

The future Bundeswehr structure is intended to reverse the decline by increasing troop numbers (at the expense of redundant staff structures) and creating sustainable organic units. The forces trained to undertake the most demanding main mission of defending the Alliance and Germany must also be able to undertake global crisis intervention missions. These dual missions require them to be fully equipped with materiel to ensure a high level of operational readiness at all times.

When it comes to defence of the Alliance, all of Germany's deployable army, air force and navy are subordinate to the NATO headquarters, which was established for this purpose. These forces include NATO operational units (Joint Force Commands), Component Commands, integrated Combined Air Operations Centres of the NATO command structure in the case of the Luftwaffe, and the NATO-assigned Multinational Corps of the NATO force structure in the case of the army. This means that there is no need for a national leadership organisation for collective defence. The only exception is the new national Territorial Command for Host Nation Support tasks ("the German hub") to support Allied troop movements and for the purposes of domestic German security.

The indivisible assumption of responsibility by a single command structure must be ensured at the appropriate level in each case. In practice, this means decentralisation wherever possible, and centralisation only where unavoidable.

The paradigm that has been in force for some 20 years whereby the armed forces are managed in a "process-oriented" and "economically efficient" manner is in need of a critical review. A business management approach cannot meet the criterion of high operational readiness (which requires stockpiling rather than a "just in time" approach). If a single command structure is to exercise ultimate authority, responsibility for materiel must be returned to the inspectors of each of the armed forces during the utilisation phase – that is, once the equipment has been put into service.

For many smaller partner nations, Germany plays the role of a "supportive power" in Europe, which means that German military structures must remain open to "docking" with other European armed forces, even in peacetime.

How severe is the demographic problem?

Only 1 in every 450 people in Germany is an active soldier in the Bundeswehr, or just 182,000 out of 83 million. Based on its current personnel structure and recruitment practices, the Bundeswehr needs to recruit at least 20,000 new soldiers and some 5,000 civilian employees each year just to maintain current staffing levels. Around 5,000–6,000 of that 20,000 will be new "voluntary conscripts" serving for 7–23 months, while 3,000 will be "rehires" and experienced lateral entrants, and thus considerably older than 18. Some 3,000 of the 20,000 new soldiers will leave within the first six months alone, for a variety of reasons. This is something that cannot be changed.

Taking all of the above into account, we are left with roughly 10,000 classic recruits from the cohort who have just turned 18, 19, 20, 21 or 22 years old who will actually remain in the Bundeswehr as regular soldiers. This annual figure of 10,000 – out of an average total cohort of 780,000 young men and women in Germany – represents a very low proportion, only 1 in 78. If the Bundeswehr were able to turn that one into two, it would soon reach its target of 200,000 personnel and could even reduce enlistment periods again in order to create younger and more "athletic" armed forces.

These are only theoretical calculations and are therefore particularly eye-catching, but they should stop us from becoming too downhearted with regard to demographics. There are enough young people out there and also plenty of motivated, fit, skilled and slightly older people.

The decisive factor in future will be how the Bundeswehr presents its offer of employment in the military: as a job that's almost as good as a civilian career or as something exceptional, which it really is. This is the case now to an even greater extent than in the past.

Many young Germans want to contribute to something meaningful: socially, ecologically, politically and for democracy. Today, more than ever, voluntary military service represents a contribution to the defence of our democracy. The important aspects in this regard are democracy, freedom, dignity, justice and international solidarity.

Germany is providing new answers to the current global crisis. In future, serving in the Bundeswehr will seem more meaningful to many people than before the war in Ukraine.

Further reading

Bartels, H.-P. (2019) *Germany and a Europe of Defence: Global Responsibility Requires the End of Small-State Particularism* (Bonn: Dietz).

Bartels, H.-P., A. M. Kellner and U. Optenhögel (eds) (2017) *Strategic Autonomy and the Defence of Europe: On the Road to a European Army?* (Bonn: Dietz).

"Mehr Fortschritt wagen" (2021). Coalition agreement 2021–2025 between the SPD, Alliance 90/The Greens and the FDP. URL: https://www.spd.de/file admin/Dokumente/Koalitionsvertrag/Koalitionsvertrag_2021-2025.pdf.

Scholz, O. (2022). "Regierungserklärung von Bundeskonzler Olaf Scholz". Federal Government of Germany website, 14 December. URL: https://www .bundesregierung.de/breg-de/service/bulletin/regierungserklaerung-von -bundeskanzler-olaf-scholz-2153850.

"Weißbuch der Bundesregierung zur Sicherheitspolitik und zur Zukunft der Bundeswehr" (2016). White paper, Federal Government of Germany. URL: https:// www.bundesregierung.de/resource/blob/975292/736102/64781348c12e 4a80948ab1bdf25cf057/weissbuch-zur-sicherheitspolitik-2016-download -data.pdf.

András Rácz, Ole Spillner and Guntram Wolff

7 | Sanctions and the Russian war economy

Since the annexation of Crimea in 2014 Russia has been under an EU sanctions regime. While sanctions were initially light, they were massively tightened after the attack on Ukraine in February 2022. This has served as a strong signal of the West's resolve to oppose Russia's war. Sanctions have significantly weakened Russia's ability to wage war. One year on, Russia is still in the process of shifting its economy to a war economy. We discuss Russia's economic adjustment with a specific focus on the shifting of resources to war purposes and the effect of sanctions on military production. Ukraine's allies should maintain, tighten and adapt sanctions to further weaken the military and economic power of the Putin regime.

In the public debate on the usefulness and effectiveness of sanctions, the reality of a continuing war is often used as a blanket argument for the ineffectiveness of existing sanctions. However, the effect of sanctions on autocrats' political behaviour is only a narrow definition of the target. Instead, sanctions also signal the unity of the sanctioning parties and exert their effect by weakening the economic, financial and military capacities of the adversary in the medium to long term. We discuss in a recent paper the effects of sanctions on Russia and highlight that they are indeed effective.[1] We also show that the assessment is not straightforward, given the large number of sanctions and the complex interactions with the war itself.

In this chapter we focus on the Russian economy in the war, on how sanctions affect military production and on how Russia is shifting its economy to a war economy to adapt to the sanctions and its need to boost military production to compensate for the losses inflicted by Ukraine.

---

1 Rácz, A., O. Spillner and G. B. Wolff (2023) "Why sanctions against Russia work". *Intereconomics*, 58(1): 52–55.

The Russian economy

The International Monetary Fund estimates that the Russian economy contracted by 3.4% in 2022; for 2023, a further contraction of 2.3% is forecast. However, ever since the beginning of the war, access to reliable data on the Russian economy has been severely limited and only embellished and highly selective economic data has been published. Consequently, an analysis must be based upon more unconventional data sources, such as high-frequency consumer data, information from Russian trading partners, or data mining of shipping figures. Based on such data, a group of researchers from Yale University's Chief Executive Leadership Institute paints a picture of Russia's economic situation that differs fundamentally from the Kremlin's official narrative. According to the Yale study, over 1,000 Western companies have announced their departure from Russia since the beginning of the invasion. In the long term, such a large-scale withdrawal means the loss of innovative forces. Likewise, the company exodus is accompanied by a brain drain. More than 500,000 Russians have already left the country, of which about half have a high level of education or worked as skilled workers in the tech industry, for example. Again, the effects of sanctions are not directly measurable, but their effect on the domestic quality of life is certainly a factor in emigration decisions.

Nevertheless, the Russian economy contracted much less than independent forecasts suggested in the first half of 2022. Important factors dampened the shock of the war and the effects of sanctions. First, the single most important revenue source for Russian firms and for the Russian state – fossil fuels – remained largely untouched by sanctions. In fact, despite a decline in production, some Russian data reveal that oil and gas revenues substantially increased during 2022. The data show that during January to October, oil and gas revenues amounted to 9.788 trillion roubles, or 44% of total revenue, a 34% increase compared with the corresponding period in 2021. The West thus avoided sanctioning the most important Russian revenue source during 2022. Second, the Russian government reacted to the recession by supporting companies and sectors that were particularly hard hit. Third, the longer the sanctions have lasted, the more Russia has managed to find ways of circumventing them. For example, although crude oil has been sanctioned from December 2022, and oil products from February 2023, the declining export volumes to Western Europe could be redirected to India and China, among others. Furthermore, Russia has relied on "grey imports" of sanctioned high technology via transit countries in Central Asia or Turkey, although these imports are more costly, time-intensive and less reliable. On the whole, sanction cooperation has nevertheless remained relatively stable and deviations and dropouts have been idiosyncratic rather than systematic.

Russia's war economy in a time of sanctions

Financing a war is expensive, and even more so if a country is under a sanctions regime. While official spending information on the war is classified, military expenditures in 2022 are estimated to exceed 5% of GDP, thus constituting the largest share of GDP since the end of the Soviet Union. Russian military spending could have amounted to around $90 billion during 2022.

Russia increasingly organises its budget towards serving its war machinery. Public information is again scattered and the quality of the data may be compromised. According to the *Financial Times*, classified budget spending has increased by more than 40% to $95 billion, compared with prewar planning of $54 billion. Russian foreign trade data have disappeared entirely. According to some public data, spending on defence, law and order was only 2.7 trillion roubles during January to October 2022. Yet in September 2022 the estimate for the entire Russian defence budget for that year was adjusted to 4.7 trillion roubles ($77.7 billion), and this change might not be the last. Prime Minister Mikhail Mishustin announced after the 2023 budget consultation in September: "The Head of State ordered us to take measures to meet the needs of our armed forces and military formations." Compared with the 2021 draft of the 2023 budget, the defence budget was thus increased by more than 40%, accumulating to $84 billion. Compared with the 2022 budget, spending on the military and security services will grow from 24% of budget spending to almost 33% – at the cost of other expenditures.

Beyond defence, spending on internal security and law enforcement is also increasing. Expenditure on national defence, internal security and law enforcement in 2023–2025 will average 5.7% of GDP, as indicated in the main instructions of the Ministry of Finance. Moreover, the Kremlin has further reduced local and regional powers and burdened regional budgets with buying military equipment, a process closely linked to the ongoing mobilisation. At the same time, as Boris Grozovski of the Wilson Center has reported, government agencies outside the defence and security sectors have been tasked with reducing spending by 10% to limit debt servicing costs and inflation pressures.

Russia had a budget deficit of around 2.3% of GDP in 2022 ($48 billion), compared with an originally planned surplus of 1%. This deficit was financed through various channels. First, the previous budget surplus was completely used up. Second, the National Welfare Fund was used to finance parts of the deficit. Third, oil and gas revenues were no longer saved in the National Welfare Fund but directly spent. Not only did the federal budget contain a deficit, but regional budgets also had deficits.

The 2023 budget law calculates on the basis of a 20% drop in fossil fuel revenues, inflation of 5% and a reduction of GDP by 1%. This forecast seems overly optimistic because it assumes an unlikely average oil price of $70 per barrel (while Urals oil was trading below $40 in January) and a reduced level of military mobilisation, and thus a lower reduction in manpower on the labour market. GDP could therefore decline even further and pose problems for Russia. Currently, the Russian Ministry of Finance expects a budget deficit of 2% of GDP for 2023, which seems likely to be financed by domestic borrowing. The liquid part of the National Welfare Fund will be used to finance some of the deficit. However, it is not an infinite and lasting source of deficit finance as it is expected to run out of money in three to four years. Moreover, large parts of the National Welfare Fund remain frozen in Western central bank accounts. In addition, the Central Bank of Russia (CBR) is indirectly printing money; or in other words, the government is issuing CBR-funded bonds to be bought by state-owned banks.

On the whole, Russia remains able to fund its military activities in the short term by refocusing its budget on military activities. However, the current means of financing its war comes at significant cost to other spending items.

Import sanctions

Import sanctions cause production losses due to a lack of materials, inputs and technology. According to the data of Russia's main trading partners, Russian imports decreased by up to 50% in the first half of 2022. Consequently, sanctions do not only affect sanctioning countries (who have seen their exports to Russia fall by 60%) but also nonsanctioning countries (exports down 40%). Many countries are reluctant to undermine sanctions and to thus suffer the consequences in far more important Western markets. These choices can be attributed to the existing asymmetrical dependencies between Russia and its trading partners:

while Russia imports a lot from a few trading partners, it is only one purchaser among many for these countries.

The crucial question for Russia is whether it will be able to substitute for the lack of imports from sanctioning countries in the medium term. Apart from China and India, all other countries among the top ten largest economies subscribed to the sanctions. Despite a few examples to the contrary, such as Turkey, Russian attempts to substitute for import shortfalls largely failed in the first months after the war began, as can be well seen in the examples of China and India. Chinese exports to Russia fell by an average of almost 15% from March to June compared with the same months of the previous year. India also saw a massive decline in exports to Russia, with a 22.7% drop in the first half of the year compared with the corresponding period of the previous year.

However, this trend will probably not persist in the medium term: since July, Chinese exports to Russia have been rising sharply again year-on-year. Overall Chinese exports to Russia in 2022 ultimately exceeded the previous year's by 12.8%. In India too, export shortfalls are becoming smaller and smaller compared with the respective months of the previous year. However, to date, Indian exports have remained below the previous year's.

Nonetheless, doubts persist over whether rising Chinese and Indian imports can fully replace critical technologies from sanctioning countries. Therefore, by weakening Russia's economic base and preventing access to critical technologies, the sanctions have proven impactful. The concrete industrial consequences of the sanctions and their consequences for Russia's war-waging capability can be observed particularly well in the vehicle and weapons industries.

Effects of import sanctions on Russia's military capabilities

Strict sanctions in the technology sector, combined with the withdrawal of Western high-tech companies, have had a concrete impact on the Russian armed forces. Russia is currently barely able to replace losses of military materiel with newly produced weapon systems. In addition, on a more structural level, the sanctions implemented back in 2014 have weakened the armed forces.[2]

---

2   We discuss this in Rácz, A., O. Spillner and G. B. Wolff (2023) "Why sanctions against Russia work".

Without the sanctions packages imposed in 2014, the course of the war against Ukraine would have played out differently. This can be illustrated by three examples: the delivery of French Mistral-class helicopter-carrying assault ships, cancelled by France in 2014; the development and production of 4+ generation Sukhoi Su-57 stealth fighters, which has significantly slowed down; and the PAK DA bomber, which could not yet be developed.

Since February 2022, sanctions against military and dual-use products have been significantly tightened. And despite repeated claims to be self-sufficient, the Russian defence industry remains heavily dependent on parts and components imported from the West. The T-72 tanks use French-made Thales thermal cameras and Japanese optics, but these are no longer available; production of several modern air defence weapons (9K37 Buk, 9K22 Tunguska) had to be stopped due to the lack of German-made electronics; and production of Kh-101 cruise missiles also suffers as Taiwanese, Dutch, US and Swiss components are no longer available. Russia's most advanced satellite-guided 300 mm Tornado missiles use US-made gyroscopes – and there are further examples. Although inventories were immense, Moscow's capabilities to conduct precision strikes have thus been weakened through sanctions. Vehicle production, including military vehicle production, has suffered greatly. The renowned truck manufacturer KAMAZ had to halt production of all its modern military-use platforms because the Bosch fuel injectors produced in Germany are no longer available. This affects the wheeled platforms of several Russian weapons, such as the Pantsir surface-to-air defence system, as well as heavy military trailers, supply trucks and many special vehicles.

The withdrawal of many Western high-tech companies has thus delivered a major, so far largely irreparable blow to the Russian defence industry. Consequently, since February 2022 Russia has been able to rely only on Western-made parts and components that it has stockpiled in advance, and these stocks are limited and depleting. Import substitutes cannot fully replace pre-2022 shipments of Western high-tech products.

Adaptive measures by the Russian defence industry

One year on, however, the Russian defence industry has shown a remarkable level of adaptability to the post-February 2022 sanctions regime, by employing various means of damage control.

First and foremost, Russia has developed and is operating several parallel channels to circumvent the high-tech sanctions by running imports via third countries that did not join the Western sanction regimes, such as China, Turkey and Kazakhstan. In this way Russia is still able to acquire microchips, semiconductors and other high-tech components, albeit not at the prewar amounts and levels of diversity, and not without substantial additional costs and delays.

Second, prewar stockpiles have probably not yet run out, although this is hard to fathom exactly from open sources. The result is nevertheless clear: despite the sanctions, Russia is still able to produce some of its high-tech precision weapons. A Conflict Armament Research investigation revealed that Russia fired Kh-101 cruise missiles at Kyiv in November that were manufactured in September–October 2022 – that is, months after the technological sanctions came into force.

At the same time, it needs to be noted that the number of modern missiles and cruise missiles used against Ukraine is decreasing from attack to attack. Hence, despite partially sustained manufacturing, Russia is apparently gradually running out of modern missiles. The fact that Moscow employs air defence and even antiship missiles against ground targets points in the same direction: namely, to decreasing stockpiles of precision weaponry.

Another way of reducing the effects of sanctions on arms manufacturing is to import weapons and components from countries that have not joined Western sanction regimes. Hence, Russia is importing attack drones from Iran, tanks and armoured vehicles from Belarus, and huge amounts of artillery ammunition from North Korea.

The fourth solution Russia is employing to reduce the effects of sanctions is to redesign its own weapon systems to decrease their dependence on Western technology and use domestically manufactured parts instead. This is the classic strategy of import substitution, which the Russian defence industry has been exercising at least since 2012, when Sergei Shoigu became minister of defence and ordered diminished reliance on Western technologies. However, substituting with domestically made products decreases the military capability of the weapons.

The fifth way is to deconserve and modernise ex-Soviet weapon systems such as T-62 tanks that did not yet rely on Western technologies at all, as they were still produced during the Cold War. The modernisation of outdated weapon systems is another indicator of the hardship Russia's defence industry is suffering in manufacturing modern weapons.

The sixth means is to significantly increase the speed of production. The move towards a war economy has permitted such acceleration via increased demand and more resources for the sector. As of January 2023, several Russian arms plants are already working in three shifts, six or seven days a week, and are offering competitive salaries to their employees. This, of course, does not help the problem of technological degradation, but it does help address battlefield losses.

Lastly, it should be stressed that Western sanctions do not affect the entirety of Russia's defence industry complex. Russia has long achieved full production autarchy in the manufacture of nuclear weapons and intercontinental ballistic missiles, as well as submarines, including nuclear-powered ones. Hence, while several branches of the conventional arms industry are suffering from sanctions, these problems leave the bulk of Russia's nuclear deterrence arsenal unaffected.

Conclusions

The EU is achieving a large part of its self-defined goals through sanctions. The Russian domestic economy has suffered massive damage and the sanctions have had an impact on the military capabilities of the Russian armed forces. However, Russia remains able to fund its military activities in the short term through a war economy and refocusing its budget on military activities. This way of financing its war comes at a significant cost to other spending items.

Regarding the defence industry, Russia has had to either halt or downgrade the manufacture of several high-tech weapon systems. Although not all production lines have completely come to a halt, production numbers have decreased even for the modern systems that Russia is still able to manufacture, as indicated by several measures taken to address apparent shortages.

Meanwhile, Russia still has many older, ex-Soviet weapon systems conserved and stockpiled. Reactivating these weapons and – following some modernisation – deploying them to Ukraine would still enable the Russian army to strengthen its defences there, thus concentrating the remaining modern weaponry on offensive operations.

All in all, Western sanctions are causing a lasting technological degradation of Russia's conventional armed forces. However, there is no collapse visible in any sectors of the defence industry. By accepting losses in technology levels and production numbers, Russia is still able to keep its military industry operational and provide its armed forces with the minimum necessary supplies for a considerable while more. Hence, sanctions are not going to stop Russia's military machine, although they are constantly weakening and downgrading it.

Western sanctions thus do reduce Russia's military capabilities. In light of various adaptive measures taken by Russia in response to sanctions, it is important to maintain and even strengthen sanctions where possible. Overall, sanctions can be an effective tool in dealing with military conflicts. Germany should maintain and tighten them with partners to continue supporting Ukraine.

Further reading

Belton, C. (2020) *Putin's People: How the KGB Took Back Russia and Then Took On the West* (New York: Farrar, Straus and Giroux).

Byrne, J., G. Somerville, J. Byrne et al. (2022) "Silicon lifeline: Western electronics at the heart of Russia's war machine". Report, Royal United Services Institute, August.

Chowdhry, S., J. Hinz, K. Kamin et al. (2022) "Brothers in arms: the value of coalitions in sanctions regimes". Kiel Working Paper 2234, Kiel Institute for the World Economy.

Itskhoki, O., and D. Mukhin (2022) "Sanctions and the exchange rate". *Intereconomics*, 57(3): 148–151.

Olsen, K. B., and S. F. Kjeldsen (2022) "Strict and uniform: improving EU sanctions enforcement". DGAP Policy Brief 29, German Council on Foreign Relations, 29 September.

Rácz, A., O. Spillner and G. B. Wolff (2023) "Why sanctions against Russia work". *Intereconomics*, 58(1): 52–55.

Sonnenfeld, J., S. Tian, F. Sokolowski et al. (2022) "Business retreats and sanctions are crippling the Russian economy". Working paper, Yale School of Management.

Yuliya Yurchenko

8 | Ukraine's economic and social losses: what future for the (postwar) country?

On 24 February 2022, when Russia once again invaded Ukraine, it was already one of the poorest and most indebted countries in Europe, at war since 2014. Its needs and losses have grown exponentially: dislocation of the labour force, destruction of infrastructure, ecological damage and more. In this chapter I highlight the types and scale of losses Ukraine has sustained so far[1] and elaborate on the conditions under which these can, if possible, be recovered. I argue the case for large-scale multifaceted international assistance, debt cancellation and "fiscal activism" as preconditions for (re)building a resilient, sustainable economy and making a Ukraine for which millions are fighting, dying and suffering a reality.

The current state of affairs and context

When Russia once again invaded Ukraine on 24 February 2022, it was already one of the poorest and most indebted countries in Europe, having weathered a "transition to market" and associated "unintended consequences", numerous economic crises, and nearly eight years of war with Russia and its proxies in the Donbas and Crimea. Budgetary expenditure on arms has grown exponentially, as have humanitarian and medical needs (of the wounded). The scale of GDP contraction in April was projected by the World Bank at 45%,[2] while the poverty rate projection for 2023 was a 58% year-on-year increase – and by now those figures will be higher. Money is and will be needed to reconstruct Ukraine's homes and

---

1   It is impossible to discuss all of these in this brief chapter; here I highlight some of the most evident and brutal, although none are unimportant even if they have not made it into the final draft. A more detailed discussion waits to be developed elsewhere.

2   This has been updated for a better projection since there are a few reasons for optimism.

infrastructure, and for cleaning up, demining and decontaminating cities and the countryside.

Currently some 20% of Ukraine is occupied; it is losing infrastructure and industrial and agricultural capacity, imports and exports are disrupted, and industries are leaking cadre due to displacement, refugee flows, impairment (physical and mental trauma) and death. The main culprit of the war – the Russian Federation – will have to pay for the ruination it has caused; but although proposals and actions are being discussed, the creation of repossession/reparation mechanisms, decisions on the destiny of frozen assets and more are unlikely to happen until Ukraine's victory. For now, therefore, I wish to focus on the losses Ukraine has sustained to date, set against the backdrop of the constraints and opportunities lying before Ukraine's governing institutions, and the potential and challenges for recovery set out in the postwar reconstruction plan presented in Lugano on 4–5 July 2022.[3]

Economic and social losses to date

The full scale of losses is unknown due to the ongoing shelling and the impossibility of carrying out calculations with any degree of precision in front-line areas, let alone those temporarily occupied. Only after the full withdrawal of Russian troops from Ukraine's constitutional borders will it be possible to make such assessments; even then, the most valuable losses will arguably be impossible to assess: the value of lives lost, futures ruined, childhoods stolen, bodies and minds injured, homes and heirlooms forever lost, and ecocidal damage done to the humans and nature of today and tomorrow. The deep essences of the concepts of "value" and "price" take on their most visceral forms when one is staring in the face of a genocidal war carried out by a death cult regime. And by the time I finish writing this sentence, someone, indeed many, will have died or sustained injury: humans, animals, irredeemable elements of complex ecosystems that have become arenas of senseless war.

The Ministry of Ecology and Natural Resources of Ukraine puts environmental damage at "an estimated $46 billion and still rising – [which] includes direct war damage to air, forests, soil and water; remnants and pollution from the use of weapons and military equipment; and contamination from the shelling of thousands of facilities holding toxic and

---

3 URLs: https://recovery.gov.ua/en, https://www.urc2022.com.

hazardous materials".[4] The long-term impact of losses to ecosystems is impossible to quantify, especially since Ukraine "contains habitats that are home to 35% of Europe's biodiversity, including 70,000 plant and animal species, many of them rare, relict, and endemic".[5]

*

The value of lives lost is indisputably difficult to measure, as beyond the body count there is all else that numbers cannot grasp. Since the annexation of Crimea in 2014, the Office of the UN High Commissioner for Human Rights (OHCHR) estimates the total number of conflict-related casualties in Ukraine from 14 April 2014 to 31 December 2021 to be 51,000–54,000: 14,200–14,400 killed (at least 3,404 civilians, an estimated 4,400 Ukrainian forces and an estimated 6,500 members of armed groups) and 37,000–39,000 injured (7,000–9,000 civilians, 13,800–14,200 Ukrainian forces and 15,800–16,200 members of armed groups).[6]

From 24 February 2022 to 12 February 2023, the OHCHR recorded 18,955 civilian casualties in the country.[7] This included

- a total of 7,199 killed (2,888 men, 1,941 women, 226 boys and 180 girls, as well as 32 children and 1,932 adults whose sex is not yet known);
- a total of 11,756 injured (2,616 men, 1,856 women, 341 boys and 253 girls, as well as 260 children and 6,430 adults whose sex is not yet known).

Of this total, 10,167 casualties were in the Donetsk and Luhansk regions (4,189 killed and 5,978 injured):

---

4   Zhou. J., and I. Anthony (2023) "Environmental accountability, justice and reconstruction in the Russian war on Ukraine". Stockholm International Peace Research Institute website, 25 January. URL: https://www.sipri.org/commentary/topical-backgrounder/2023/environmental-accountability-justice-and-reconstruction-russian-war-ukraine.

5   "Assessing the environmental impacts of the war in Ukraine". WWF website. URL: https://wwfcee.org/our-offices/ukraine/assessing-the-environmental-impacts-of-the-war-in-ukraine.

6   OHCHR (2022) "Conflict-related civilian casualties in Ukraine". Report, OHCHR, 27 January. URL: https://bit.ly/3IKlK7b.

7   OHCHR (2023) "Ukraine: civilian casualty update 13 February 2023". OCHR website. URL: https://www.ohchr.org/en/news/2023/02/ukraine-civilian-casualty-update-13-february-2023.

- on government-controlled territory, 7,946 casualties (3,679 killed and 4,267 injured);
- on territory controlled by Russian armed forces and affiliated armed groups, 2,221 casualties (510 killed and 1,711 injured).

The OHCHR cautions that the actual figures will be "considerably higher, as the receipt of information from some locations where intense hostilities have been going on has been delayed and many reports are still pending corroboration".[8] Numerous reports of rape, torture, intimidation, forced deportation and genocidal violence in both freed and occupied territories against people of all ages are being collated daily.[9]

Ukraine does not publish combat losses

Care for the traumatised population and the displaced with medical needs, as well as recovery of the wounded, requires increasing cash and medication flows, a lot of it coming in as donations from home and abroad, including free psychological helplines and resources. The efforts of healthcare workers and volunteers alike cannot be overestimated. Still, in 2022, the UN Office for the Coordination of Humanitarian Affairs (UNO-CHA) reported that of the $4.3 billion in emergency humanitarian funding needed or pledged by various countries, $3.4 billion or 80% had been raised. Bilateral assistance from the US, the EU, the UK and other states plays a vital role, as do direct individual donations; some $1 billion was collected via the 20 largest foundations, such as the Prytula, United24 and Come Back Alive funds.[10]

While the generosity is overwhelming, it is already petering out, as declining donations indicate. Ukraine will need reliable sources of funds. Healthcare system reforms launched in 2017 tried to fix the problems lingering from Soviet days, aggravated by commercialisation, underfunding and poor pharmaceutical sector regulation (especially in terms of quality and prices), yet they led to inadequate regionalised provision and uneven access to care, which all came out in the wash under Covid-19 pandemic

---

8   Ibid.

9   "Allegations of genocide under the Convention on the Prevention and Punishment of the Crime of Genocide (Ukraine v. Russian Federation)". International Court of Justice website. URL: https://www.icj-cij.org/en/case/182.

10   URL: https://forbes.ua/news/ukraintsi-ta-inozemtsi-zadonatili-mayzhe-1-mlrd-u-nay bilshi-fondi-z-pochatku-viyni-23012023-11234.

mismanagement, and now war.[11] Residual centralised elements in the system allowed the flow of wounded and those in need of inpatient care to be managed to an extent, while leaving a lot of lessons to be learned regarding what does or does not work in the country's healthcare system – issues that will need to be addressed via (post)war policies.

Given a difficult macroeconomic situation and massive spending on defence, Ukraine needs external aid of roughly $4 billion per month to support the war effort and sustain essential public services. The Ukrainian government has put the need for budgetary support for 2023 at $38 billion.[12] The damage is so severe that even usual advocates of market solutions to both market and nonmarket problems are calling for some unconventional measures. In a report, and later a book, published by the CEPR, Barry Eichengreen and Vladyslav Rashkovan advocate for grants and debt relief.[13]

*

By the end of 2022 the total amount of documented damage to Ukraine's infrastructure was estimated at $137.8 billion (at replacement cost).[14] Since autumn 2022 all thermal and hydropower stations have been damaged, and by February 2023 about a third of all power generation and distribution capacity had been lost; "at least twice during these attacks, Ukrainian nuclear power plants lost connection to the grid, posing nuclear safety risks".[15] Now Russia is draining the Kakhovka water reservoir,

---

11   Slobodyan, O. (2023) "European integration for healthcare: between European recommendations and Ukrainian realities". *Commons*, 2 February. URL: https://commons .com.ua/en/yevrointegraciya-ta-ohorona-zdorovya-v-ukrayini/.

12   See, for example, Becker, T., et al. (eds) (2022) *A Blueprint for the Reconstruction of Ukraine* (London: Centre for Economic Policy Research). URL: https://cepr.org/ publications/books-and-reports/blueprint-reconstruction-ukraine.

13   Gorodnichenko, Y., I. Sologoub and B. W. di Mauro (eds) (2022) *Rebuilding Ukraine: Principles and Policies* (London: Centre for Economic Policy Research). URL: https://cepr .org/publications/books-and-reports/rebuilding-ukraine-principles-and-policies.

14   At the time of writing, the figures listed are the most up-to-date. ("The total amount of damage caused to Ukraine's infrastructure due to the war has increased to almost $138 billion". Kyiv School of Economics website. URL: https://kse.ua/about-the-school/ news/the-total-amount-of-damage-caused-to-ukraine-s-infrastructure-due-to-the-war -has-increased-to-almost-138-billion/.)

15   Prokip, A. (2023) "Ukraine quarterly digest: October–December 2022". *Focus Ukraine*, Kennan Institute, Wilson Center, 18 January. URL: https://www.wilsoncenter.org/blog -post/ukraine-quarterly-digest-october-december-2022.

---

which is used to cool the largest nuclear plant in Europe at Zaporizhzhia, putting its safety at risk and compromising the functioning of the adjacent hydropower plant.[16]

Being a major global grain exporter, the loss of 40% of production in 2022[17] is and will be felt in Ukraine and abroad, especially in low-income countries. Decreases in rural household food production of 25–38% (depending on proximity to front lines), normally responsible for 25% of total national output, are also being felt in reductions in supply and price inflation.[18] In the early days of the invasion in 2022, the "Russia must pay" project was launched to document war damage to the Ukrainian economy; the results and analysis are published on the damaged.in.ua website and are updated regularly.[19] The data is collected to be used

(1) to document war crimes and human rights violations; (2) for the formation of claims against the Russian Federation in international courts for compensation for damage caused: lawsuits for international courts require aggregate evidence and a register of damaged objects in accordance with the methodology of estimating; (3) for individual compensation; (4) to receive war reparations and compensations for damage from the aggressor for the reconstruction of Ukraine.[20]

Ukrainian postwar rebuilding tasks run up against the challenges of uncertain financial, demographic and institutional capacity. Further

16   Brumfiel, G., C. H. Jin, J. Fenton et al. (2023) "Russia is draining a massive Ukrainian reservoir, endangering a nuclear plant". *National Public Radio*, 10 February. URL: https://n.pr/3ZmoSUk.

17   Food and Agriculture Organization of the United Nations (2022) "Ukraine: strategic priorities for 2023 – restoring food systems and protecting food security". Report, FAO, December. URL: https://www.fao.org/3/cc3385en/cc3385en.pdf.

18   This includes "approximately 85 percent of fruit and vegetable production, 81 percent of milk and around half of livestock production" (ibid., p. 1).

19   "The assessment is the result of the joint work of the KSE Institute, government bodies under the leadership of the Ministry of Reintegration, the Ministry of Regions and the Ministry of Infrastructure in cooperation with other ministries and partner organizations within the framework of the National Council for the Recovery of Ukraine from the Consequences of War." The scope of damage is analysed by KSE Institute analysts and volunteers from partner organisations: the Center for Economic Strategy, Dragon Capital, the Anti-Corruption Headquarters, the Institute of Analytics and Advocacy, Transparency International Ukraine, Prozorro.Prodazhi, Prozorro, the Ukrainian Council of Shopping Centers, CoST Ukraine, VkursiAgro, TVIS Ukraine and the Association of Retailers of Ukraine. URL: https://damaged.in.ua.

20   URL: https://kse.ua/russia-will-pay/.

Table 8.1. Total damages in monetary terms (December 2022–January 2023, at replacement cost; $bln).

Housing stock	54.0	Culture, sport, tourism	2.2
Infrastructure	35.6	Healthcare	1.7
Assets of enterprises	13.0	Administrative buildings	0.8
Education	8.6	Electronic communications	0.6
Energy (open source data calculation, to be corrected in future)	6.8	Social sphere	0.2
Agriculture and land resources	6.6	Financial sphere	0.1
Transport	2.9	Demining	–
Trade	2.4	Ecology (emissions damage, not direct to any assets)	14.0
Utilities	2.3		
Total: 137.8			

Source: KSE (2023).

complications arise when we assess the "externalities" of the war alongside the "unintended consequences" of the market reform Ukraine has been through since 1991 (corruption and oligarchs being part and parcel of this, but not the only ill), which it is still implementing now and plans to take further after the war (see the Lugano plan and labour reform below). In the process of its "transition to market" since 1991, Ukraine has suffered large scale de-development, meaning that its foundational economy, public services and infrastructure have deteriorated and suffered from systemic and chronic underfunding. This has led, among other things, to socialisation and individualisation of the costs of meeting needs previously catered for by those state-funded services, and/or those services altogether lacking or being of reduced supply with notable regional variations. Discursive normalisation of those changes and responsibilisation of the populace for this combination of state and market failures has become an additional ideological stumbling block in the way of efforts by a growingly agitated civil society to address the symptomatic results of those failures, such as demands for full private healthcare provision instead of a fully deployed state-funded system.

Some of this has to do with mismanagement, corruption and embezzlement, yet a lot of it also has to do with a combination of the "costs" of the EU rapprochement reform, budgetary constraints, the conditionality of International Monetary Fund (IMF) structural adjustment loans and similar limitations on fiscal policy choices that straightjacket even the most well-meaning state administrators.

*

It is hard to be precise about social losses and damages, not unlike the economic ones, albeit for different reasons. The war is some nine years old, but the refugees and displaced people of pre-2022-invasion Ukraine, numbering over 2 million, received much less attention than those of 2022.[21] Many went to Russia, but 1.7 million were internally displaced persons (IDPs) inside Ukraine by the end of 2021.[22] The invasion of 2022 led to 7.7 million IDPs already by mid-spring, and this number keeps changing. According to a recent International Organization for Migration report, as of 23 January 2023, "5.4 million IDPs are displaced across Ukraine. This represents a decrease compared to 5.9 million as of 5 December 2022. The estimated number of IDPs in Ukraine has been steadily declining since August 2022." Among those, "58% of all IDPs have been displaced for six months or more. However, the crisis remains dynamic with 12 per cent of IDPs (equivalent to 640,000 people) becoming displaced in the past two months."[23]

According to the UNHCR, the UN Refugee Agency, 8,054,405 refugees from Ukraine were recorded across Europe as of 7 February 2023, of which 4,830,738 were Ukrainian refugees registered for Temporary Protection or similar national protection schemes in Europe.

In addition, 2,872,068 refugees were recorded in the Russian Federation and Belarus, comprising 2,852,395 and 19,673, respectively. These

---

21 Cincurova, S. (2015) "Ukraine: Europe's forgotten refugees", *Open Democracy* 10 November (www.opendemocracy.net/en/can-europe-make-it/ukraine-europes-forgotten-refugees/); B. Mitchneck, B., J. Zavisca and T. P. Gerber (2016) "Europe's forgotten refugees: the humanitarian crisis in Ukraine", *Foreign Affairs*, 24 August (https://fam .ag/3KkHCiT).

22 Internal Displacement Monitoring Centre: https://www.internal-displacement.org/countries/ukraine.

23 International Organization for Migration (2023) "Ukraine internal displacement report: general population survey – round 12". Report, IOM, 23 January. URL: https://dtm .iom.int/reports/ukraine-internal-displacement-report-general-population-survey-round -12-16-23-january-2023.

---

figures are estimates and are difficult to verify, while potential further movement of persons was not possible to factor in at the time of writing, according to the UNHCR.[24]

According to the office of Ombudsman Dmytro Lubinets, hundreds of thousands of Ukrainian children were forcibly taken to Russia, while accurate information about their location, names and numbers is unknown.[25] So far, the identity of only 13,000 of these children has been established.[26]

Many figures, depending on the location and method of tracking used, are not fully accurate, especially in the case of IDPs who do not register as such. Many displaced people stay with friends, family or in the private rental sector, while many move back to cities freed from Russians. Many do so as they cannot afford to be away any longer (for financial reasons, or due to care and other needs), even when the dangers of warfare remain near their homes. Dislocations come with loss/decimation of income, support networks, access to goods and medication, and more. Women who flee to Poland and require an abortion, for example, have to face a local near-ban on such procedures, while LGBTQI persons who end up in Russia face discrimination and a lack of access to the care they may require.[27]

---

24   "The Regional Refugee Response Plan brings together UN, NGO and other relevant partners and focuses on supporting host country governments to ensure safe access to territory for refugees and third-country nationals fleeing from Ukraine, in line with international standards. It also prioritises the provision of critical protection services and humanitarian assistance." The Refugee Response Plan covers Bulgaria, the Czech Republic, Hungary, Poland, the Republic of Moldova, Romania and Slovakia, where a total of 2,380,365 refugees are recorded, of which 2,369,955 are registered for Temporary Protection or similar national schemes. In other European countries, various national schemes or Temporary Protection schemes are utilised. Overwhelmingly Poland and Germany (over 1 million persons), then the Czech Republic (nearly 0.5 million), followed by Italy, Spain, the UK, Bulgaria and France (over 100,000 but less than 200,000) are primary target countries of the refugee flows (UNHCR 2023).

25   "Ombudsman: hundreds of thousands of Ukrainian children could be deported to Russia". *Ukrinform*, 22 December 2022. URL: https://www.ukrinform.net/rubric-society/ 3639037-ombudsman-hundreds-of-thousands-of-ukrainian-children-could-be-deported -to-russia.html.

26   "Operational data portal: Ukraine refugee situation". UNHCR website. URL: https:// data.unhcr.org/en/situations/ukraine.

27   Welch, H. (2022) "Women this week: UN says Ukrainian refugees in Poland need abortion access", Council on Foreign Relations, 20 May (www.cfr.org/blog/women-week -un-says-ukrainian-refugees-poland-need-abortion-access); "LGBTI people affected by the war in Ukraine need protection", statement by the Commissioner for Human Rights, Council of Europe website, 17 May 2022 (www.coe.int/en/web/commissioner/-/lgbti -people-affected-by-the-war-in-ukraine-need-protection).

Capitalist and patriarchal reproductive inequalities have been exacerbated by displacement – for refugees and IDPs alike, albeit with impacts varying in their severity. Fleeing the war during martial law has in most cases led to enforced single parenthood as men of conscription age (18–60 years) – and women in certain professions obliged to serve in the military – are not allowed to leave the country unless exempt (for medical grounds, for having three or more children or vulnerable dependants, or for other reasons).[28] The structures of inequality rooted in the conditions of women and families prior to fleeing the country intersect with those where they end up staying, with respect to the material conditions for women, the support they get from Ukraine and in their target location, access to networks, language and professional skills, and so on. According to a study by the Razumkov Centre,

> 14% of Ukrainian refugees [...] had difficulties in securing children's education, and 13.5% in securing their leisure and after-school activities. Not only schools' and nurseries' operating hours, but also those of bureaucratic institutions, shops, pharmacies, etc. often overlap with working hours, so a single mother cannot secure her household's needs, look after the children, and keep a job.[29]

Moreover,

> almost 60% of [refugees] only have enough resources to buy food and basic inexpensive clothing and housing items, and another 12% can barely make ends meet, compared to 11% and 2% respectively back in Ukraine; 42% of respondents had problems finding a job, 32% housing for rent, with a further 21.5% lacking any housing, and 15% claiming uncomfortable housing conditions.[30]

Internally displaced persons experience similar problems, albeit in their own cultural and linguistic environment, since familiarity with institutions and processes is a key difference and helps adaptation to an extent. Here too, the gender dimension is pronounced, though less so than with refugees, with 25.4% being adult males and 32% adult females

---

28   For the full list of exemptions, see the website of Ukrainian Ministry of Defence: https://www.mil.gov.ua/news/2022/03/15/vidpovidi-na-najposhirenishi-pitannya-pro-mobilizacziyu-v-umovah-voennogo-stanu-vid-ganni-malyar/.

29   Ryabchuk, A. (2023) "Who will stay and who will return? Divergent trajectories of Ukrainian war refugees in the EU". *LeftEast*, 17 January. URL: https://lefteast.org/divergent-trajectories-of-ukrainian-war-refugees-in-the-eu/.

30   Ibid.

(aged 18–59; 1,357,000 and 1,715,000 respectively), though they face similar inequalities imposed by the conditions of patriarchal capitalism.[31] Adequate resources (including cash), as well as suitable and stable housing, are acute issues for IDPs (even if they remain in their homes), not least as 79% of households consist of IDPs only (not mixed with hosts), of which 73% have at least one vulnerable member.

Real estate and particularly rental markets are poorly regulated, while rental prices in cities considered relatively safe have magnified overnight while availability is low. Social housing or policies as such are nonexistent and "would work better if they were developed in peacetime", but instead "the main efforts of the authorities are not aimed at providing affordable housing to as many citizens as possible, but to support construction [companies]".[32] This leads to an institutional inability to adequately respond with viable solutions to IDPs' housing needs. For example, by 2020 some 70% of IDPs from the 2014 war still had their housing needs unmet, relating to three forms of displacement: "displacement caused by the dangers of war, displacement caused by destruction of homes, and displacement caused by the rent market itself".[33]

The bombing of schools and kindergartens and the disruption of education and care for children present extreme challenges that are made worse by preexisting problems in those sectors, from chronic underfunding and understaffing to low wages of employees and to parents struggling financially, especially in single-parent (mainly maternal) households, in terms of available time and resources to provide care and meet needs.[34]

A comprehensive state-funded housing programme is vital in the immediate, short and long term if the needs of IDPs and returning refugees are to be addressed. For this, new policies need to be developed, which may be tricky if the role and function of the state in the National

31   International Organization for Migration (2023) "Ukraine internal displacement report".

32   Liasheva, A. (2022) "Without shelter: housing policy in wartime". *Commons*, 2 April. URL: https://commons.com.ua/en/zhitlova-politika-pid-chas-vijni/.

33   Liasheva, A. (2022), "52 apartments for IDPs: the gap between housing policy and the shocks of war". *Commons*, 23 September. URL: https://commons.com.ua/en/zhitlo-ta-vijna-v-ukrayini/.

34   Dutchak, O., O. Tkalich and O. Strelnyk (2020) "Who cares? Kindergartens in the context of gender inequality". *Commons*, 15 December. URL: https://commons.com.ua/en/hto-poturbuyetsya-ditsadki-v-konteksti-gendernoyi-nerivnosti/.

Recovery Plan (see below) is not reimagined.[35] Most Ukrainians cannot afford properties on the inflated mortgage and rental markets, nor to upgrade the old Soviet stock that was depleted by three decades of poor municipal investment and the recent wars; nor should they have to pay for what is a basic human need: a roof over one's head.

The situation with regard to employment, wages and income amid displacement, shelling and inflation is too challenging. Accurate data is lacking, as with many other indicators. What is clear is that employment problems, which were already plentiful before the war and made worse by the Covid-19 pandemic, have been further exacerbated. Blinov and Djankov (2022) used wage payments data from one of Ukraine's largest commercial banks to get a picture: "Since the start of the war, nominal wages have managed modest growth, amounting to 3% by end-October. However, wages dropped 11% in real terms over the January to October period and their decline has accelerated to 18% in the past month."[36] Moreover, they add, "13% of hired employees have lost their job since the start of the war and there is evidence of increasing job losses". This comes amid year-on-year inflation in 2022 alone rising to 26.6%, from 10% at the end of 2021; in prepandemic 2019, it was 4%.[37] To top it all, instead of protecting the rights of people in wartime, a bonfire of workers' rights was made via the adoption of anti-labour laws in mid-2022 which stripped some 70% of workers of labour code protection. According to Vitaliy Dudin, a labour lawyer and leader of the Sotsialnyi Rukh (Social Movement) organisation,[38] the changes "affect workplaces with hundreds of workers, including public sector jobs at risk of austerity policies, such as hospitals, railway depots, post offices and infrastructure maintenance".[39]

Jobs are being lost, savings depleted, credit cards maxed out; many struggle to service their debts, and even more will struggle to gain access to credit finance now and in future due to access criteria/costs and

35   Bobrova, A. (2022) "The war in Ukraine has caused a housing crisis: here's how to combat it". Cedos website, 6 May. URL: https://cedos.org.ua/en/the-war-in-ukraine-has-caused-a-housing-crisis-heres-how-to-combat-it/.

36   Blinov, O., and S. Djankov (2022) "Ukraine's wages and job loss trends during the war". *VoxEU*, Centre for Economic Policy Research, 17 November. URL: https://cepr.org/voxeu/columns/ukraines-wages-and-job-loss-trends-during-war.

37   "Inflation report: January 2023". National Bank of Ukraine. URL: https://bank.gov.ua/admin_uploads/article/IR_2023-Q1_en.pdf?v=4.

38   URL: https://rev.org.ua/english/.

39   Rowley, T., and S. Guz (2022) "Ukraine uses Russian invasion to pass laws wrecking workers' rights". *Open Democracy*, 20 July. URL: https://www.opendemocracy.net/en/odr/ukraine-draft-law-5371-workers-rights-war-russia/.

availability alike. Never mind the unfairness of household debt accumulation, this is why this debt must be written off as part of the (post)war recovery approach,[40] since an economy cannot run on a mix of the good will of increasingly poor friends/relatives and sporadic local and foreign donations to supplies of food, medication and clothes. A set of comprehensive policies must be developed, with a complete overhaul of the response to problems that existed before the 2014 and 2022 invasions, which exacerbated those problems but did not create them.

Debt politics amid socioeconomic upheaval and erosion of sovereignty

Chaotic borrowing and debt explosion in Ukraine over the years was partly a result of oligarchic state capture and kleptocracy. Loans from international financial institutions were issued under conditions of social spending cuts, economising on vital needs and funding of key parts of the economy. The country's debt demand context was characterised by the loss of a real economic base at a rate disproportionate to the growth required to maintain the health of the economy or honour debts, state or private. As a result, a double squeeze on the economy was produced due to the ongoing need for loaned capital (state, commercial and consumer), complicated by the inability to repay even the interest. Debt increased by up to five times (denominated in Ukrainian hryvnia), due to – among other things – dollarisation, euroisation and dependency on imports of high value-added goods. Until the summer of 2022, Ukraine adhered to its debt obligations. From 24 February to 2 October 2022, "the amount of funds paid by the government for the repayment of domestic debt instruments exceeds by UAH 54,093.9 million the amount of funds raised in the state budget at auctions for the sale of government domestic loan bonds".[41] Clearly, an alternative form of financing is needed and it must come in the form of grants, not more loans concealed as aid.

A temporary suspension of debt servicing was agreed between Ukraine, the Paris Club and the G7 on 20 July 2022 and signed on 14 September 2022, for one year dating from 1 August 2022, with a

---

40 "Ukraine household debt". CEIC Data website. URL: https://www.ceicdata.com/en/indicator/ukraine/household-debt.

41 "Payments on government bond repayments since beginning of war exceed borrowing by UAH 54.1 billion". *Ukrainian News*, 4 October 2022. URL: https://ukranews.com/en/news/885992-payments-on-government-bond-repayments-since-beginning-of-war-exceed-borrowing-by-uah-54-1-billion.

possible extension for one more year (a decision affecting about 75% of all foreign debt).[42] Although a glowing result of multipartite international civil society campaigning,[43] this remains insufficient, not least since IMF debt conditionality is firmly in place and debt surcharges are still to be paid.[44]

In Ukraine's case, historically conditional relationships with EU/Western partners and Russia (mainly), both economic and geopolitical, add extra dimensions of simultaneous complexity and fragility, via debt, trade arrears and import/export dependencies. Debt as an instrument of external control and expropriation of national wealth, combined with the modern system of taxation and trade regimes, is a powerful diluter of the decision-making autonomy fundamental to any meaningful exercise of political sovereignty. Debt leads to "alienation of the state"[45] – that is, the national state ceases to be an autonomous agent of authority that is representative of its people. Ukraine had to engage in sales of war bonds and utilise numerous rapid financing mechanisms available internationally to fund the war effort where aid was insufficient, each coming with its own conditions and more constraints and hurdles for the country to overcome in the future.

The Lugano Principles: whither recovery?

In Lugano, Switzerland, on 4–5 July 2022, the Ukraine Recovery Conference (URC2022) was cohosted by the governments of Switzerland and Ukraine. Initially planned as the Fifth Ukraine Reform Conference, the aim was changed due to the Russian invasion of Ukraine.[46] Discussions revolved around (1) the institutional architecture for smart recovery, (2) recovery of infrastructure, (3) the economy, (4) the environment and (5) society. Seven principles on which the above are to rest were agreed and reflected in a document to be treated as "live" and evolving:

---

42 "Ukraine signs Memorandum of Understanding on official debt payments suspension with international partners in the G7 and Paris Club". Ministry of Finance, Government of Ukraine website, 14 September 2022. URL: https://bit.ly/3K1JnjB.

43 "Ukraine to suspend foreign debt repayments", press release, Debt Justice, 20 July 2022 (https://debtjustice.org.uk/press-release/ukraine-to-suspend-foreign-debt-repayments); see also: https://rev.org.ua/pidsumki-2022/.

44 "Ukraine: projected payments to the IMF as of February 28, 2023". IMF website. URL: https://bit.ly/3FUhNTU.

45 Karl Marx, *Das Kapital,* Volume 1, Chapter 31.

46 URL: https://www.urc-international.com/urc-2022.

(1) partnership; (2) reform focus; (3) transparency, accountability and rule of law; (4) democratic participation; (5) multistakeholder engagement; (6) gender equality and inclusion; and (7) sustainability.[47]

The above sounds promising, but upon deeper examination it appears the aims will be hard to achieve with the means chosen; in other words, the state will struggle to finance or attract enough private investment, or direct it where it is most needed – the whole $750 billion of it so far[48] (I will leave governance structures aside due to the space limitations of this chapter). At the same time, the State Property Fund of Ukraine[49] has largely become an auction platform selling off to the highest bidder the remaining and often mismanaged state property, instead of investing in it. The last nearly nine years of war, global pandemic and economic slowdown have significantly undermined Ukraine's investment attractiveness and devalued its currency, and the sale of assets generates little value for the state budget. Moreover, wouldn't passing these objects into the ownership of local communities or employees and making cheap financing available to them be a more reasonable and economically beneficial option?

The reconstruction plan and EU prospects: what can make it a success?

A lot of discussion about the reconstruction plan revolves around its having been modelled on the Marshall Plan. What is often forgotten is some of the key aspects of what made the latter a success. A lot of the support came in the form of cash grants (Ukraine will need many more of them) or loans ($11.8 billion at the then dollar value).[50] European countries often used this money to buy essential goods such as wheat and oil and to reconstruct factories and housing.[51] A similar plan for Ukraine would

---

47   URL: https://recovery.gov.ua/en.

48   "Ukraine estimates cost of reconstruction at $750 billion". *Euractiv*, 5 July 2022. URL: https://www.euractiv.com/section/europe-s-east/news/ukraine-estimates-cost-of -reconstruction-at-750-billion/.

49   The name of its website – https://privatization.gov.ua/ – offers great insight into the ideological makeup of the people in charge of it.

50   There is a separate discussion to be had about the role and appropriateness of concrete elements of loan conditionality that is beyond the size and scope of this chapter.

51   Eichengreen, B. (2010) "Lessons from the Marshall Plan". World Development Report 2011 Background Papers, World Bank. URL: https://openknowledge.worldbank.org/ handle/10986/27506.

need to be (re)designed and executed in alignment with the best practice and standards of EU labour rights, public services and environmental protection; for that to happen, a number of changes need to occur, which I outline below.

Ukraine's extraordinary situation presents a case for large-scale, multifaceted international assistance, state (and household) debt cancellation and conditionality rewriting to facilitate "*fiscal activism*"; in other words, measures aimed at stabilising business cycles via discretionary use of fiscal policy. The austerity that Ukraine is practicing with the neoliberal economic thinking that took root among its politicians and a basic lack of funds – wartime or not – is uneconomical and unecological; what is needed is full state-funded redevelopment and financing of public services and the care economy – *with a radical internalisation of positive externalities into assessment of state investment returns* – which must become mainstream political discourse in Ukraine and among its international partners. The state in Ukraine, unlike its stereotypical perception, is not bloated; on the contrary, "the share of national income that is distributed through taxation and budgeting in Ukraine is much less than in developed European countries".[52] The state was the key agent in rebuilding much of Europe, Japan and South Korea after World War II, when the "developmental state" was elaborated as a concept, and now is the time to return to it as "free" markets have failed. The principles of the European Green Deal and beyond, with the state at the centre of recovery, are what are now needed.

The IMF and other creditors are needed as sources of financing. But it is state institutions that carry out the recovery and should have "ownership of the reconstruction process".[53] Moreover, the key role of civil society (NGOs and trade unions), delivering where state and markets alike have failed since 2014, must be acknowledged, scaffolded and financed by the state instead of international crowdfunders: this polycentric form of the state as institutional network can deliver the rebuilding Ukrainians

52 Kravchuk, A. (2022) "To help Ukraine, cancel its foreign debt: an interview with Alexander Kravchuk", by D. Broder. *Jacobin*, 8 March. URL: https://jacobin.com/2022/03/ukraine-cancel-foreign-debt-imf-economic-conditions.

53 Gorodnichenko, Y., and I. Sologoub (2022) "The reconstruction of Ukraine should start today: the first step is Ukraine's safety". *Focus Ukraine*, Kennan Institute, Wilson Center, June 1. URL: https://www.wilsoncenter.org/blog-post/reconstruction-ukraine-should-start-today-first-step-ukraines-safety.

envisage.[54] Local enterprises should have priority access to public investment. The economic policy consensus has shifted globally to favour the
(post-)Keynesian vision of state-led investment in economies to boost
confidence and kickstart the multiplier effect. While structural adjustment programmes (SAPs) have been criticised by the IMF's own research
as limiting macroeconomic growth, de facto relationships with the fund's
borrowers have not changed; other than being renamed loan "conditionalities", in essence the terms have not become less rigid, but in fact more
so. This is why it is so important that these debts are cancelled and the
conditionalities abandoned.

Ukraine will need green/low-carbon job creation (in the care economy,
arts, education, environmental preservation and sustainable research and
development), a just transition and energy democracy which will maximise opportunities for its economic self-sufficiency and reduce the import
dependency of key industries. Job creation is vital as millions of Ukrainians work abroad seasonally, while more now have left the country. By
2017 some 7-9 million had left the country to work abroad, 3.3 million in
2011-2021 alone, "while their families remained in Ukraine. The inflow of
remittances to Ukraine in 2020 reached $12.1 billion."[55] While those trans-
actions support Ukraine's economy, they are hardly an indicator of good
quality of life for average citizens whose lives are destabilised. In 2021
alone, 660,302 persons left the country amid the challenges exacerbated
by the Covid-19 pandemic. Vast numbers have fled the country since the
invasion of 24 February 2022. Conditions must be created for people to be
able to return and will need to range from infrastructure and (social) housing (re)building (including whole towns in some cases) and sustainable job

---

54   The principles of polycentricity, as laid out in Elinor and Vincent Ostrom's Nobel prize-
winning framework (1990): the latter calls for abandoning state–market dualism, instead
opening space for (self-)management via the relative autonomy of agents of various ranks
in a system of negotiations, balancing and monitoring collective governance. See Ostrom,
E. (1990) *Governing the Commons: The Evolution of Institutions for Collective Action*
(Cambridge University Press), DOI: 10.1017/CBO9780511807763; (1994) "Neither market
nor state: governance of common-pool resources in the twenty-first century", conference
paper, International Food Policy Research Institute, Washington, DC, June 2; (2010)
"Polycentric systems for coping with collective action and global environmental change",
Global Environmental Change, 20(4): 550–557, DOI: 10.1016/j.gloenvcha.2010.07.004.

55   URL: https://opendatabot.ua/analytics/migration-2021.

creation across Ukraine. Surveys,[56] multiple journalistic articles, reports and anecdotal evidence all point to Ukrainians' will to return to Ukraine (1) once it is safe and (2) once they have somewhere to go back to. Many return even without the promise of a job or survival guarantees (with reasons ranging from a lack of funds, to nostalgia, to being subject to xenophobia abroad).

EU integration can become a saving grace for Ukraine's economy or it can become a force for further de-development and peripheralisation. Lessons from the experiences of other economically weaker and newer member states are of key importance here, and it has been observed that integration processes are a "game that has long been rigged against all the countries of the periphery".[57] Ukraine's situation is extraordinary not least due to its membership path laid through the debris of a genocidal war for which rapprochement with the EU and NATO was used as a pretext. Moreover, from the outset the demographic, economic, institutional and ecological tasks at hand are enormous, even judged by the standards of an advanced peacetime economy. This sets the context for an equally extraordinary arrangement of the rules of engagement of which many are already under way; yet big and progressive aims are not matched by the means proposed to achieve those. For recovery to become what was outlined in Lugano, a fundamental rewriting of the global regime of debt and policy conditionality is required, while the "black holes" of offshore tax avoidance and evasion, including transfer pricing,[58] must disappear. Furthermore, a proposal can be made for a potential blueprint or example to follow in construction for similar economies globally. We need to think beyond Ukraine, we need to think of Ukraine as part of the global economy, and we need to think about alternative economic systems altogether, built by and for noospheric societies[59] – societies of the era of reason, in which wars, poverty and ecocide are made impossible by design.

---

56 "The polling group Rating, which surveyed Ukrainian refugees on the subject of when they would return home, said that 24 percent of respondents want to return, but will wait for a certain time; 48 percent will return, but after the end of the war; and 8 percent said that they would not return home." Odarchenko, K. (2022) "Will Ukrainian refugees return home?" *Focus Ukraine*, Kennan Institute, Wilson Center, 19 August. URL: https://ukraine.wilsoncenter.org/blog-post/will-ukrainian-refugees-return-home.

57 Dooley, N. (2015) "The real political economy of Ireland". SPERI Comment, Sheffield Political Economy Research Institute, 1 September.

58 Yurchenko, Y. (2013) "'Black holes' in the political economy of Ukraine: the neoliberalisation of Europe's 'Wild East'". *Debatte: Journal of Contemporary Central and Eastern Europe*, 20(2–3): 125–149. DOI: 10.1080/0965156X.2013.777516

59 Yurchenko, Y. (2021) "Humans, nature and dialectical materialism". *Capital and Class*, 45(1): 33–43. DOI: 10.1177/0309816820929123

Further reading

Bojcun, M. (2021) *Towards a Political Economy of Ukraine: Selected Essays, 1990–2015* (Stuttgart: Ibidem).

Dalton, D. (2023) *The Ukrainian Oligarchy After the Euromaidan* (Stuttgart: Ibidem).

Laplat, F., and C. Ford (eds) (2023) *Ukraine: Voices of Resistance and Solidarity* (London: Resistance Books).

Mykhnenko, V. (2020) "Causes and consequences of the war in eastern Ukraine: an economic geography perspective". *Europe-Asia Studies* 72(3): 528–560. DOI: 10.1080/09668136.2019.1684447

Velychenko, S., J. Ruane and L. Hrynevych (eds) (2023) *Ireland and Ukraine: Studies in Comparative Imperial and National Histories* (Stuttgart: Ibidem).

Yurchenko, Y. (2018) *Ukraine and the Empire of Capital: From Marketisation to Armed Conflict* (Pluto Press: London).

Andriy Korniychuk

9 | A nation in transition: the impact of war on Ukraine's politics and society

Full-scale war marks a pivotal moment in Ukraine's nation-building process, prompting its society to finally break free of Russia's centuries-old (neo)imperialist grip – politically, mentally, culturally and economically. The survival and resilience of the Ukrainian democratic project will determine whether renewed imperialist expansionism in wider Europe succeeds or meets its ultimate demise.

(Re)discovering Ukraine's ethnic and cultural identity

Russia's full-scale invasion of Ukraine in 2022 has brought unfathomable pain and suffering. Its consequences will be felt across generations, stretching far beyond Ukraine's borders. The fierce, brave and successful resistance of the Ukrainian people against an unprovoked aggression has made the world (re)discover this Eastern European country as a sovereign nation with a rich history and unique ethnocultural code. An external threat of such unprecedented magnitude has led to a process of profound, previously unseen introspection and self-reflection in Ukrainian society. For Ukraine to become an EU member, it must be rebuilt as a modern, prosperous, resilient democracy. The ongoing societal changes therefore warrant a closer look. I have chosen to focus on two equally important angles: the symbolic (identity and nation-building processes) and the practical (the socioeconomic and demographic realms). The war has already had a profound impact on both, and trends and processes observable in these contexts will define Ukrainian society once the war ends.

Peter Pomerantsev accurately observes that Ukraine is "a country where very different stories of the past play out simultaneously, but where the question of what Europe means is now contested most fiercely and existentially".[1] While he concludes that "more developed countries have breakdowns about how to balance their identity with the fluctuations and instabilities of globalization", Ukraine's complex path to nation-building and identity formation positions it well to emerge in the avant-garde of modernity. In part, this is why I argue for the importance of Ukraine's status as "a non-linear nation [...] which resists straight lines and a space that breaks all the old, limited models of identity"[2] in order to be fully embraced and comprehensively understood. Such an exercise would make an important contribution to the restoration of historical justice for its people. And yet, it needs to be added that a society which has (re)discovered itself can no longer be understood through outdated theoretical concepts and methodological approaches (for example, the dichotomy between pro-Russian eastern regions of Ukraine and pro-Western western regions of the country). For this process to succeed, it is equally important that discussions of Ukraine's past and future no longer bypass the perspective of its society. Against this challenging background, the following chapter aims to spark further reflections on how to support a nation in the process of formation under the extreme conditions of an ongoing war.

Grassroots Ukrainisation: a (political) nation in the making

The societal demand to articulate nation-building elements more visibly in the public sphere has noticeably grown since Ukraine gained independence. Even under Russia's nagging geopolitical shadow and regular interference in domestic affairs, Ukrainian society has slowly but steadily (re)discovered its identity (or identities). The war with Russia, which began in 2014 and escalated into a full-scale conflict in 2022, became the moment for Ukrainian identity to be vividly proclaimed in the public sphere and to take deeper roots on the local level. Such a development was enabled primarily due to a paradigm shift in how the process was perceived, and how it progresses.

Top-down, centrally driven attempts at nation-building prior to 2022 – most notably by former president Viktor Yushchenko soon after the Orange Revolution of 2004 – failed due to a lack of societal ownership

---

1   Yermolenko, V. (ed.) (2019) *Ukraine in Histories and Stories: Essays by Ukrainian Intellectuals* (Kyiv: Internews Ukraine, UkraineWorld), p. 12.

2   Ibid.

of the process and of national consolidation around its rationale. Prior to the full-scale Russian invasion, demand for Ukraine's own path, separate from Russia, had already been growing. In 2019, when facing Volodymyr Zelenskyy in a presidential run-off, Petro Poroshenko organised his campaign around the slogan "Army, Language, Faith", with billboards that featured him facing Russian President Vladimir Putin – the primary threat to all three. Zelenskyy ultimately enjoyed a landslide victory in the second round, and yet Poroshenko's followers (often referred to as "the 25%", reflecting his electoral result) had already formed a vocal group of supporters of more pronounced "Ukrainisation". At that time, the scale of such demands did not yet allow one to talk about a nationwide consolidation, but I use this example to signal an important societal trend. Accounting for only a sparse number of traditionally defined ideological parties in Ukraine, political projects (such as Svoboda, the "Freedom" party) that attempted to trumpet nationalistic values gained only modest electoral support. Only three years ago, when the war was still mainly concentrated in two eastern regions of the country, no nationwide consensus existed with respect to the speed or shape of Ukrainisation. There was a growing understanding about the importance of promoting Ukrainian language and culture, while the autocephaly of the Orthodox Church of Ukraine was hailed as an important step towards remedying historical injustice. However, heated debates continued over how, and in what way, Ukraine should proceed with de-Sovietisation and how it should approach the presence of the *Russkiy mir* (Russian world) on its territory. The invasion in 2022, with the atrocities and destruction it has brought, has profoundly impacted the described processes, resulting in what Olexiy Haran – Ukraine's leading political scientist and academic – refers to as "grassroots Ukrainization", which foresees "national values not being imposed by the government or political elites, but spread within and between people".[3]

From a progressive standpoint, several additional aspects of the process are worth highlighting. While constituting a majority in numbers, for decades Ukrainians were a de facto minority in their own land in terms of declared identity and cultural presence. Russian ideological, cultural and religious dominance were profound, far-reaching and often repressive. In this context, the experience of victimisation in society must not

---

3   Haran, O. (2022) "Interview with Olexiy Haran: 'What we are seeing now in Ukrainian society is grassroots Ukrainization'", by O. Kushnir. *Forum for Ukrainian Studies*, 15 November. URL: https://ukrainian-studies.ca/2022/11/15/interview-with-olexiy-haran-what-we-are-seeing-now-in-ukrainian-society-is-grassroots-ukrainization/.

be allowed to develop after the war into a culture of oppression, with retaliation as the only tool. Being united in diversity – maintaining a genuinely inclusive society that respects and protects vulnerable groups and minorities once the war ends – is challenging because "historically Ukraine has never had common rules for everyone that were acceptable, discussed and supported by all".[4] Furthermore, in light of the gravity of the atrocities committed since the start of the 2022 Russian invasion, it is important that "anti-Russia" should not become a defining feature of Ukraine's identity and/or occupy the centre of its further nation-building process. I do not question the importance of transitional justice in the context of Russia's aggression as it offers instruments that can help a nation in pain move on, while victims can find at least some solace and relief. Nevertheless, to successfully complete its democratic transition Ukraine should pave its own unique way. One important task for the EU will be to support Ukraine in defining itself in positive terms (what it is, and what it can achieve), as opposed to negative ones (what it is not, and what it cannot achieve). The latter process should recognise that Russia, in whatever form it persists in, will continue to be an important factor in Ukraine's future. At the same time, arguably for the first time in Ukrainian history, an unprecedented national consolidation around common values creates the conditions for society to free itself from Russian shackles.

Ukraine's democracy tested by war

The strength and resilience of Ukraine's democracy lies in its society: horizontal social ties, decentralised governance, vibrant civic networks and an agile private sector.[5] This is why decentralisation and civic engagement have produced such impressive results, not least in the context of Ukraine's successful resistance against an aggressor in possession of superior military resources.[6] At the same time, Ukrainian writer Andriy Kurkov uses the term "democratic anarchy matrix" to describe the following paradox: "Ukrainians are willing to participate in elections, and they fight for the victory of their candidate only to start fighting against him

---

4   Yermolenko, V. (ed.) (2019) *Ukraine in Histories and Stories*, p. 172.

5   Lutsevych, O. (2022) "Immediate recovery funding is key to Ukraine's security". Chatham House website, 18 July. URL: https://www.chathamhouse.org/2022/07/immediate -recovery-funding-key-ukraines-security.

6   Romanova, V. (2022) "Ukraine's resilience to Russia's military invasion in the context of the decentralisation reform". Report, Batory Foundation. URL: https://www.batory.org .pl/wp-content/uploads/2022/05/Ukraines-resilience-to-Russias-military-invasion.pdf.

or her several days later."[7] These processes have long historical roots in the hetman-Cossack system, which rejected any form of monarchy and also led to pronounced reservations regarding (political) power in general. The Soviet regime in Ukraine, which forced collectivist behaviour and adoration of the Communist Party onto Ukrainians, only exacerbated this distrust towards the power of political elites. The democratic anarchy matrix returned as soon as the Soviet Union collapsed. It has become vividly manifest in the Russo-Ukrainian War, which is essentially a direct confrontation of opposing values. And yet, in the discussed context, it should not be surprising that Ukrainians have continued to distrust public authorities even since the war with Russia started in 2014, while placing their confidence in institutions with a distinct social component – the armed forces, the church, civil society and voluntary organisations.[8] In the lead-up to the most recent presidential elections in 2019, pollster Gallup reported that for two consecutive years Ukrainians had a world-low level of trust (9%) in their national government.[9]

On the one hand, a confrontational, antagonistic relationship between the government and the people may safeguard society against authoritarianism and usurpation of power. Some commentators ironically remark that revolutions could be described as Ukraine's export commodity, referring to a number of successful mass protests in its modern history – the Revolution on Granite in 1991, the Orange Revolution in 2004, and the Revolution of Dignity, also known as Euromaidan, in 2013. On the other hand, the success and effectiveness of postwar recovery and modernisation of the Ukrainian state will depend on a strong social contract. Therefore, it is of paramount importance that society develops more confidence in its (national) institutions. The latter requires a systemic, bottom-up process that prioritises the quality of democratic processes over the speed of their implementation. Assessments of the effectiveness of the Ukrainian

---

7   Yermolenko, V. (ed.) (2019) *Ukraine in Histories and Stories*, p. 94.

8   Among social institutions, Ukrainians have the most trust in the armed forces (96% trusting them completely or to some extent), the president of Ukraine (82%), humanitarian and charitable organisations (78%), the church (70%), universities (62%), women's organisations (59.5%), state institutions (55%), the police (55%) and environmental organisations (54%). Data from the Razumkov Centre, "Citizens' assessment of the situation in the country, trust in social institutions, political and ideological orientations of Ukrainian citizens under the conditions of Russian aggression (September–October 2022)" (in Ukrainian). URL: https://bit.ly/3JWIito.

9   Bichus, Z. (2019) "World-low 9% of Ukrainians confident in government". Gallup website, 21 March. URL: https://news.gallup.com/poll/247976/world-low-ukrainians -confident-government.aspx.

state seem to have improved significantly since the start of the full-scale invasion.[10] Public opinion surveys indicate that Ukrainians showed more interest in politics in 2022, while confidence in their ability to impact political decisions has also grown. Even so, state institutions continue to suffer the highest negative ranking among surveyed citizens. While the available data may indicate a general positive trend,[11] the extent to which Ukrainian society projects the image of the state onto the successful and effective conduct of its army still requires comprehensive research. Furthermore, the factor of "uniting under the flag" also needs to be taken into account, as a feature not uncommon for a country that has to resist an external enemy.

In the context discussed above, militarisation and securitisation of Ukraine's society warrant additional attention. Martial law, an inevitable step for a country facing an aggressor, entails centralisation of power and curtails basic rights and freedoms. In essence, the longer the war drags on, the more it will test the strongholds of Ukraine's democracy. At the same time, a high level of state security is increasingly seen in society as an important condition for Ukraine's reconstruction to succeed and for its democracy to survive. Russia's conduct of war, which targets and intimidates civilians extensively and deliberately, has already had an impact on the perception of security in Ukrainian society. Since the invasion, the number of people in favour of firearm ownership has doubled.[12] The brutality of war, witnessed and felt by a substantial number of citizens, will have a long-term societal impact. While the need to prioritise security is legitimate, Ukraine will require safeguards against a number of overarching challenges that arise with the militarisation of democracy and securitisation of the public sphere. Ukrainian experts warn that in the worst-case postwar scenario of weaker institutions and/or further

---

10   According to the Rating Group, at the end of 2021 only 5% of interviewed respondents believed that the central government coped well with all of its responsibilities. In May 2022 this number had increased to 54%. The Razumkov Centre presented similar conclusions, based on a survey conducted in October 2022: while in 2020 35% of citizens trusted state institutions, this figure had grown to 55% in 2022.

11   "Trust in the state: how to save national unity for the victory". Democratic Initiatives Foundation website, 20 September 2022. URL: https://dif.org.ua/en/article/trust-in-the-state-how-to-save-national-unity-for-the-victory.

12   "Eleventh national poll: personal freedoms, security, and weapons". Rating Group website, 23 May 2022. URL: https://ratinggroup.ua/en/research/ukraine/odinnadcatyy_obschenacionalnyy_opros_lichnaya_svoboda_bezopasnost_i_voprosy_oruzhiya.html.

distrust in the government and the judicial branch, (para)military groups could well end up becoming judge, jury and executioner.[13]

Ukraine's recovery and modernisation, possibly even its path to EU accession, are very likely to be security-driven (or security-dependent). One of the biggest mistakes that Brussels and/or EU member states could make is to allow this process to end up in radicalisation and polarisation of Ukrainian society. It is no coincidence that Timothy Snyder chose the word "bloodlands" to characterise Ukraine's turbulent past. To paraphrase contemporary Ukrainian philosopher Volodymyr Yermolenko, Ukraine as a nation was born – and is now coming of age – amid violence and traumas. The concept of "building back better", widely incorporated into current discussions and thinking about Ukraine's future, should include mechanisms and instruments to help its people address their traumatic experiences, deeply rooted in both past and present. This requires a distinctly progressive mindset and a strong social contract with the post-war Ukrainian state that enables it to take care of society in an inclusive manner, addressing the needs of vulnerable and minority groups. It needs a comprehensive and effective system of rehabilitation covering both mental and physical health, as well as instruments that allow for dialogue and nonviolent communication to be developed as essential elements of societal resilience. The Ukrainian democratic project will prove fragile and incomplete if these aspects are neglected or discounted.

Society on the move: socioeconomic consequences of the Russo-Ukrainian War

Back in 2016–2017, while I was travelling around Ukraine researching the needs of internally displaced persons (IDPs), meeting and talking to those who had mostly lost their homes in Crimea and two eastern regions of Ukraine (Luhansk and Donetsk oblasts), I vividly recall a statement with which they emphasised their hope for a brighter future: "Ukraine is its people." In mentioning this, it is not my intention to start a conversation about the possibility of concessions regarding the territorial integrity of Ukraine. The latter, rightfully, is very likely to remain off the (negotiation) table in the foreseeable future, unless the war takes an unfortunate turn for Ukraine. I wish instead to use this observation to discuss the impact the war has had on the socioeconomic

---

13   Pekar, V. (2022) "Ukraine and the EU: scenarios of European integration". *New Eastern Europe*, 18 November. URL: https://neweasterneurope.eu/2022/11/18/ukraine-and-the -eu-scenarios-of-european-integration/.

and demographic situation in the country. Human capital represents one of the pillars of any successful postwar recovery. The generation of Ukrainians born on the brink of the country's independence (1991) will recall a famous TV advertisement proudly stating: "We are 52 million." In three decades since, the demographic situation has become dire as the population has rapidly shrunk (to approximately 38 million by the time of the invasion). A low birth rate, an ageing society and emigration, together with a high death rate that the war only exacerbates, are among the most worrying trends mentioned by the UN Human Development Index. Russia's full-scale invasion has not only significantly aggravated existing demographic challenges but begun to change the structure of the population as well.

Despite successful advances by the Ukrainian army in autumn 2022, facilitating the liberation of significant portions of the occupied territories, the mobility of the population remains extremely challenging for the government to manage. Things could be further complicated by ongoing, focused Russian attacks on Ukraine's critical infrastructure. Prior to the full-scale invasion in 2022, international organisations reported approximately 700,000 individuals who were considered internally displaced in Ukraine. In its most recent assessment in October 2022, the International Organization for Migration speaks of a staggering number of 6.2 million internally displaced,[14] mainly people from eastern and southern regions fleeing to Ukraine's west. While the problems that the community of IDPs faces are not entirely new, their scale is unprecedented. A few important observations can be drawn from the experience of assisting IDPs since the start of the war in 2014. While many Ukrainians have shown solidarity in hosting their compatriots during this difficult time (as have many other Europeans), it is clear that the government will need long-term housing and community-building strategies[15] at a time when the demographic composition of localities in the east and west of the country remains uncertain and will continue to undergo rapid and deep structural change. The authorities struggled to find a comprehensive approach to these challenging issues even when the number of IDPs was much lower (in 2013–2021).

---

14 International Organization for Migration (2022) "Regional Ukraine crisis response: situation report". Report, IOM, 27 October. URL: bit.ly/40tG4sw.

15 Bobrova, A., V. Lazarenko, Y. Khassai et al. (2022) "Social, temporary and crisis housing: what Ukraine had when it faced the full-scale war". Report, Cedos, 13 October. URL: https://cedos.org.ua/en/researches/social-temporary-crisis-housing/.

On top of internal displacement, the UNHCR – the UN Refugee Agency – estimates that 7.8 million Ukrainians already left the country in 2022.[16] Women, children and the elderly constitute the majority of those who were forced to leave the country at the start of the full-scale invasion. For Ukraine not to end up with "a lost generation", an education policy[17] targeted at children residing both at home and abroad should become an important Europe-wide priority. This is chiefly because early assessments indicate that children (and their education in particular) may be viewed as the main reason for those who moved away from Ukraine to remain abroad.[18] And with the above situation in mind, gender-attuned policymaking and support activities for Ukraine are no longer a progressive recommendation but an existential necessity. Last but definitely not least, the Ukrainian diasporic community has proven to be a substantial, impactful contributor to the country's development. Taking into account its diversity and local peculiarities across different countries, it should be seen by the EU as a key stakeholder with strong agency to participate in Ukraine's reconstruction and modernisation.

The loss of human capital reflects a general pattern of unprecedented stress that the war has exerted on Ukraine's economy. While reliable data pertaining to unemployment is scarce or absent in 2022, it is clear that economic activity in the eastern and southern regions of Ukraine has shrunk significantly or stopped completely due to damage or destruction of local infrastructure. Complete or partial loss of income among IDPs is prevalent, since for the majority remote work remains inaccessible or simply impossible. Although ongoing migration trends (for example, the low number of applications for refugee status in the EU) suggest that many of those who stay abroad are likely to return in future, it should be expected that labour shortages and brain drains will emerge as substantial challenges for Ukraine's economy.

In the context presented above, the social security of the working population and protection of its labour rights will play a key role in

---

16   "Operational data portal: Ukraine refugee situation". UNHCR website. URL: https://data.unhcr.org/en/situations/ukraine. (Accessed 30 November 2022.)

17   Nazarenko, Y. (2022) "Education of Ukrainian refugees abroad (February 24–June 20, 2022)". Report, Cedos, 29 June. URL: https://cedos.org.ua/en/researches/education-of-ukrainian-refugees-abroad-february-24-june-20/.

18   "Attitudes and assessments of Ukrainian refugees returning to their homeland". Razumkov Centre, April–May 2022 (in Ukrainian). URL: https://razumkov.org.ua/napriamky/sotsiologichni-doslidzhennia/nastroi-ta-otsinky-ukrainskykh-bizhentsiv-shcho-povertaiutsia-na-batkivshchynu.

ensuring that there are enough hands and minds to rebuild Ukraine after the war. At the same time, labour relations have been characterised for decades by "informality" and a low level of social security. Prior to 2022, the International Labour Organization additionally mentioned youth inactivity due to skills mismatches, the low activity of women aged 25–39 and a large number of pensioners of working age as challenging areas in need of improvement. Due to Ukraine's incomplete and/or outdated legal solutions and widespread informal practices, systematic violations of labour rights and discrimination against disadvantaged groups remain commonplace. In the difficult context of a war economy, remote work and digitalisation might be considered as partial solutions. At the same time, the Covid-19 pandemic has shown that Ukraine's labour law (including its Soviet-era Labour Code) does not offer sufficient instruments to respond to modern labour trends. Furthermore, civil society, experts and trade unions warn that amendments to labour legislation that the current government continues to implement even during the invasion[19] are likely to have a further detrimental effect on employment and working conditions. These ongoing changes weaken social dialogue, undermine collective bargaining and diminish the role of trade unions. In this context, it is important that, despite the obvious limitations of the war economy, the social security of the population should not be undermined behind its back while citizens are fighting a war with the aggressor. Such a state of affairs will not benefit the critical need to strengthen the social contract mentioned earlier, nor will it bring Ukraine closer to EU membership. This is why instruments such as the European Pillar of Social Rights can become an important reference point in Ukraine's development and economic recovery. Ultimately, however, these types of challenges show that society already needs to make an ideological choice about the future governance model of the country its citizens are fighting for. Considering the peculiarities of Ukraine's democracy and its challenges, a progressive perspective merits considerable attention.

---

19   Under Law 2136-IX, "On the organization of labour relations during martial law", employers can increase maximum working hours, transfer employees to carry out tasks not listed in their contracts and fire employees while they are on vacation. With the rights of trade unions being curtailed, vulnerable groups of workers are in a particularly precarious position.

Further reading

Bobrova, A., V. Lazarenko, Y. Khassai et al. (2022) "Social, temporary and crisis housing: what Ukraine had when it faced the full-scale war". Report, Cedos, 13 October. URL: https://cedos.org.ua/en/researches/social-temporary-crisis -housing/.

Filipchuk, L., and E. Syrbu (2022) "Forced migration and war in Ukraine (March 24– June 10, 2022)". Report, Cedos, 27 June. URL: https://cedos.org.ua/en/ researches/forced-migration-and-war-in-ukraine-march-24-june-10-2022/.

Lutsevych, O. (2022) "Immediate recovery funding is key to Ukraine's security". Chatham House website, 18 July. URL: https://www.chathamhouse.org/ 2022/07/immediate-recovery-funding-key-ukraines-security.

Nazarenko, Y. (2022) "Education of Ukrainian refugees abroad (February 24– June 20, 2022)". Report, Cedos, 29 June. URL: https://cedos.org.ua/en/ researches/education-of-ukrainian-refugees-abroad-february-24-june-20/.

Pekar, V. (2022) "Ukraine and the EU: scenarios of European integration". *New Eastern Europe*, 18 November. URL: https://neweasterneurope.eu/2022/11/ 18/ukraine-and-the-eu-scenarios-of-european-integration/.

Romanova, V. (2022) "Ukraine's resilience to Russia's military invasion in the context of the decentralisation reform". Report, Batory Foundation. URL: https://www.batory.org.pl/wp-content/uploads/2022/05/Ukraines-resilience -to-Russias-military-invasion.pdf.

Yermolenko, V. (ed.) (2019) *Ukraine in Histories and Stories: Essays by Ukrainian Intellectuals* (Kyiv: Internews Ukraine, UkraineWorld).

Bohdan Ferens

10 | How the Russian war changed domestic politics in Ukraine

It seems useful to address the questions of how much domestic politics in Ukraine have changed since the beginning of the full-scale invasion. This also extends to the role played by Ukrainian President Volodymyr Zelenskyy and his supporters, whether the electoral preferences of Ukrainians have changed, what political forces may emerge in future and whether there will be demand for progressive politics in postwar Ukraine.

Some dates forever change our reality and leave their mark not only on the history of individual states but on the global community as a whole. Such a date becomes a kind of watershed for certain processes, reshaping life into "before" and "after". Undoubtedly, 24 February 2022, the day of the start of Russia's full-scale invasion of the territory of Ukraine, will forever remain such a date in the modern history of Ukraine. But the origins of the Russo-Ukrainian War appeared back in 2014, as a result of the illegal annexation of Crimea and the temporary occupation of part of the Donbas.

Russian President Vladimir Putin, with his decision to launch an unjustified aggression, not only undermined the European security system but also accelerated domestic political processes in Ukraine that are aimed at the final severing of political, economic, religious and cultural ties with Russia.

The prewar agenda

At the end of 2021, with each new message from Washington about Russia's impending full-scale invasion of Ukraine, anxiety was growing. However, President Zelenskyy focused in his New Year's address mainly on domestic issues: the celebration of the 30th anniversary of independence, economic recovery, vaccination, road construction, raising salaries for doctors and sporting achievements. Particular attention was paid to countering Russian aggression in the Donbas and consolidating Western support for Ukraine. The president endeavoured to radiate calmness and confidence that the coming year would definitely be better than the previous one. This, in fact, was the main message of his TV address.

The year 2022 began with a proposal, initiated by the US Democrats, to approve a package of sanctions on Putin if he decided to launch a full-scale invasion. Meanwhile, the political struggle in Ukraine only intensified. Ex-president Petro Poroshenko was accused of treason and aiding terrorism as part of an investigation into the illegal purchase of coal from occupied territories. A notorious pro-Russian politician close to Putin, Viktor Medvedchuk, was also accused in this case and placed under house arrest. Medvedchuk was an active negotiator between Kyiv and Moscow during the previous president's term, in particular on prisoner exchanges. He managed to significantly increase his financial and media assets thanks to the trade in Russian oil products during 2014–2018.

In opinion polls in January 2022, according to the Kyiv International Institute of Sociology,[1] the highest support was for Zelenskyy – whom 23.5% of those who declared a choice said they would vote for in a presidential election – followed by Poroshenko (20.9%).

A somewhat different situation was observed in the rating of political parties. The European Solidarity party, led by Poroshenko, began to overtake Zelenskyy's Servant of the People party, with the two parties gaining a respective 18.9% and 13.7% of support among respondents. About 10% of respondents said they were ready to support another opposition political force, the pro-Russian Opposition Platform for Life, one of the leaders of which was the above-mentioned Medvedchuk.

These electoral assessments prompted Zelenskyy and his supporters to engage in a more active political struggle, on the one hand to maintain primacy and on the other to prevent the weakening of the domestic political situation, which would make Ukraine more vulnerable in a confrontation with Russia.

The so-called "fight against the oligarchs" also resonated on the domestic agenda. The Law on Oligarchs[2] initiated by Zelenskyy entailed the creation of a register of oligarchs – a kind of blacklist that entailed

---

1   URL: https://www.kiis.com.ua/?lang=ukr&cat=reports&id=1090&page=1.

2   "On preventing threats to national security associated with excessive influence by persons who wield significant economic and political weight in public life (oligarchs)".

---

legal and financial consequences for those included on it. Decisions about whom to include on the list had to be approved by the National Security and Defence Council, headed by the president. In addition to possible reputational risks within the country, oligarchs potentially to be included on the list could face real business problems, in particular within the framework of cooperation with international creditors.

Such "unfriendly actions" from the president aggravated conflicts, in particular with one of the richest and most influential oligarchs from Donbas: Rinat Akhmetov. The latter's distinguishing characteristic was the ability to find a common language with the leader of any government, from the fugitive ex-president Viktor Yanukovych to Zelenskyy himself. Akhmetov readily responded to the request of the newly elected president in 2019 to either contribute to the purchase of ambulances or allocate significant amounts to fight Covid-19. In addition, his media empire systematically covered the activities of the president and representatives of his political party.

However, Akhmetov's desire to create his own group of influence in Ukraine's parliament, potentially including a number of people's deputies from the pro-Zelenskyy faction, spoiled relations with the president. Zelenskyy regarded this as a direct threat to his authority and an attempt to alter the political balance of power with an eye on future elections.

Nevertheless, with the growing threat of a full-scale invasion by the Russian Federation, the domestic political agenda gradually began to be replaced by the need to consolidate within the country, as well as to seek significant support, including military aid, from Western partners. Unfortunately, rounds of international negotiations and attempts by European leaders to reduce the level of geopolitical escalation did not yield the desired results. A new, harsh military reality was rapidly approaching Kyiv.

The Zelenskyy effect

For ordinary Ukrainian citizens as for Zelenskyy himself, it was painfully difficult to accept the new reality that shattered the lives of millions on the morning of 24 February 2022. Only two days before the full-scale invasion, the president had assured everyone that there was no reason for sleepless nights and that Ukraine had long been ready for anything. The belief that Putin's recognition of pseudo-republics in the Donbas might not lead to anything more significant was not just an assumption but most likely a common conviction of the president's team. Defence Minister Olexii Reznikov, in an interview with *Ukrainska Pravda* published exactly at the moment Russian cruise missiles were already falling on Kyiv, was convinced that "Putin will not risk bombing a second Jerusalem – Kyiv."[3]

Apparently, although the president and his entourage recognised precisely the signs of an impending catastrophe, the hope that everything would work out and the desire to maintain the illusion of ordinary life dominated to the last. Nobody wanted to accept the new reality, which subsequently changed literally everything, including Zelenskyy himself.

It is no secret that some Western leaders assumed Kyiv would be unable to resist the onslaught of Russian troops. Putin was also counting on this, and the Russians were probably expecting to encircle or capture Kyiv as quickly as possible. According to their assumptions, Zelenskyy would leave the capital and a so-called "interim government" consisting of Ukrainian politicians who previously fled to Russia was already being prepared.

But Kyiv resisted – and so did Zelenskyy. At the most critical moment in the recent history of Ukraine, he managed to gather himself internally and show his leadership abilities, first of all mobilising those directly responsible for the country's survival (the army, security services and government), while enlisting the support of political opponents and rallying Ukrainian citizens around him.

Zelenskyy showed resilience, determination and courage, staying in Kyiv at the most dangerous time for the country – and for himself personally – and refusing Polish President Andrzej Duda's proposal to organise a possible evacuation. This act, together with the successful repulsion of Russian attacks, contributed not only to raising the morale of the Ukrainian army, institutional resilience and the mobilisation of the population, but also to the willingness of Western leaders to effectively help Ukraine in its struggle for survival.

The Zelenskyy effect manifested itself for the second time in this way, but for a different reason. In casting their votes for his candidacy at the 2019 presidential election, the vast majority of voters were protesting against corrupt political elites. By contrast, with the beginning of full-scale hostilities, cohesion in society and support for the president was dictated, first of all, by the need for self-preservation and opposition to Russian aggression. Every repulsed enemy attack, every square metre of liberated Ukrainian land, every downed Russian missile and every visit of a Western leader to Kyiv contributed to the strengthening of national unity and the belief that Ukraine will survive.

---

3   URL: https://www.pravda.com.ua/articles/2022/02/24/7325213/.

On the one hand, the war finally destroyed the image of Zelenskyy as an inexperienced politician with an acting background. It was replaced by an image of a man who proved able, at the most critical moment, to effectively fulfil his constitutional duties, remaining the guarantor of the country's sovereignty and territorial integrity. The unprecedented support of the electorate (93% in March 2022) is clear confirmation of this, as is the formation of a pro-Western coalition of support for Ukraine. Even political opponents who criticised him in the past have recognised the president's resilience and suitability for his position.

On the other hand, Zelenskyy only reflects the civil resistance that has been growing with every day of confrontation, both on the front line stretching for hundreds of kilometres and in the hinter regions of Ukraine.

The narrowing scope of domestic politics

The new circumstances following the invasion radically altered domestic policy, as was especially evident in the first months of the war. Many internal processes were put on pause. There is an explanation for this. When the primary task for the state and its citizens is to survive and repulse a threat that has arisen, everything that happens in politics is subordinated to this goal. The wartime agenda mainly deals with issues related to the provision of the army, support for economic activity, guaranteeing social benefits, priority assistance to victims of military operations and restoration, where possible, of destroyed facilities and critical infrastructure. Everything else is of secondary importance.

Of course, this does not mean that nothing else is happening unrelated to the war. After all, there are still behind-the-scenes intrigues, personnel changes, corruption risks and the desire of certain unscrupulous politicians and managers to exploit the opportunity to pursue their own selfish interests. Especially when martial law is introduced – bringing restrictions on civil rights and freedoms and a noticeable simplification of certain rules – the circle of decision-makers narrows and public and parliamentary control weakens. This is a forced measure to which the majority agrees in order to make timely and effective decisions, as it is not always possible to achieve results using peacetime approaches and procedures.

Separately, it is necessary to consider state institutions, as the vital activity of the state always depends on their stability and interaction. After the full-scale invasion, the key state authorities managed to reorient themselves within a short time and respond as quickly as possible to emerging challenges. This was possible thanks to effective coordination, well-established digital support, and the dedication of civil servants at various levels. At the same time, there were also difficulties associated with the departure of part of the state apparatus to safer regions of Ukraine, or abroad.

Bankova Street, where the Office of the President is located, remains the centre for all important decision-making. In this regard, nothing has changed significantly in comparison with the prewar period. The president and his inner circle – including the head of his office, Andriy Yermak – retain their influence both on the government and the Verkhovna Rada, the Ukrainian parliament. Previously, it was more difficult to collect votes in the Rada for certain decisions. The loyalty of the pro-presidential Servant of the People faction was not always enough, so they had to cooperate with other factions. Gathering support has become much easier during wartime, especially when it is needed for votes on bills that relate to backing for the army, the economy and obligations relating to European integration.

However, sometimes other issues related to corruption scandals and the promotion of narrow interests seep into the agenda: for example, voting for the Urban Planning Law, which was promoted by the head of the president's party, Olena Shuliak. The Verkhovna Rada adopted the law on reform of urban planning in Ukraine on December 13 2022. According to its initiators, the new legislation provides for a significant change in the rules of the game in the construction market. The authors of the law – and there are more than a hundred of them – are convinced that this will reduce corruption risks in the industry and introduce transparent rules, effective state control and effective mechanisms of responsibility for violating urban planning legislation.

Critics, on the other hand, believe such legislative innovations will benefit large developers, reducing the role of local governments and contributing to chaotic and irresponsible development. It is noteworthy that this legislative initiative provoked a conflict within the presidential faction. Representatives of the pro-Russian Opposition Platform for Life, which since February 2022 has split into different groups, cast their votes in favour of the law.

This example illustrates that, despite the state of war and a significant narrowing of political processes, some resonant legislative initiatives are still being considered, requiring special attention from all interested stakeholders. This is particularly true in the absence of broadcasts of plenary sessions of the parliament, as well as opportunities for journalists to attend the discussion of issues.

The number of draft laws initiated by deputies has meanwhile generally decreased, as well as the share of proposals that are usually classified as lobbying.

Depoliticisation

The war has nullified many Ukrainian politicians, regardless of whether they belong to the older or younger generation, as they have been simply unable to find their place amid the reality that developed after 24 February. According to reports, Yulia Tymoshenko – the former prime minister of Ukraine, who leads her own faction in parliament – left the country at the beginning of the invasion of Russian troops and returned only when the situation became more secure. Although she is trying to demonstrate her political activity, it is not as effectual as before. In a similar situation are two former chairmen of the Verkhovna Rada: Volodymyr Groysman (once in the team of Petro Poroshenko) and Dmytro Razumkov, who went from being the first name on the national party list of the Servant of the People party to a political opponent of Zelenskyy and his entourage. Not so long ago Groysman and Razumkov had made no secret of their political ambitions and desire to bring their parties into the next parliament, but given the circumstances that have arisen, it will now be extremely difficult to do this.

The Opposition Platform for Life, which arose from the fragments of the former Party of Regions, found itself in the most unenviable situation. This political force was guided in its activities mainly by pro-Russian sentiment, and with the start of a full-scale invasion, public demand began to increase for its deputies to be stripped of parliamentary powers. The future of this reformatted political force is now extremely vague, as its association with the Kremlin's aggression is increasingly growing in the public consciousness.

Meanwhile, some former top politicians have joined the Armed Forces of Ukraine. It is possible that such a move will allow them to return to the top political league with an enhanced reputation once the war is over.

While the main opponent of the current government, Poroshenko, has not ceased his activity, it is now concentrated not on politics but more on helping the army. He is well aware that at any moment the charges brought against him earlier may be renewed. Therefore, it is extremely important for him and his political force to maintain electoral support, which would allow him to survive in the fight against Zelenskyy and his supporters.

One of the key problems faced by political leaders in opposition to the ruling party is the lack of normal political life during martial law and the opportunity to appear on TV.

Demediatisation

The monopoly right to control the broadcast media is now concentrated in the hands of the authorities, who justify this by citing the need to implement information delivery with one voice. While state broadcasting plays a role of strategic and practical importance, some journalists, public figures and foreign experts consider it a dangerous monopoly that may be exploited for political purposes.

After the Russian invasion, the country's main television channels began broadcasting the same content around the clock, dubbed the "United News telethon". Each TV channel has its own slot on air, broadcast simultaneously on all channels. Initially, United News was broadcast by five channels owned by various Ukrainian oligarchs, as well as state channels. It is noteworthy that three channels owned by former president Poroshenko did not receive slots and, therefore, do not participate in the preparation and broadcast of the telethon.

Deoligarchisation

The war has also significantly affected Ukraine's oligarchs. President Zelenskyy's commitment to deoligarchisation has not only survived the outbreak of a large-scale war, but has intensified under the pressure of new circumstances. The biggest losses have been suffered by Rinat Akhmetov, an oligarch from Donbas who for many years ranked as the richest person in Ukraine. He has proven the most unlucky during the war so far. The Russians have destroyed the key factories of Metinvest and are systematically destroying the electrical substations of the DTEK holding, with almost 80% of the land owned by one of its corporations occupied. Akhmetov has been forced to close his media empire[4] in order not to be placed on the register of oligarchs and to get rid of unprofitable assets, since the media have never been profitable in Ukraine. The preservation of Akhmetov's political influence also remains a big question.

---

4 "Law on oligarchs in action: Akhmetov leaves media business". *Ukrinform*, 11 July 2022. URL: https://www.ukrinform.net/rubric-society/3526756-law-on-oligarchs-in-action-akhmetov-leaves-media-business.html.

The losses of Akhmetov, according to *Forbes* estimates, are equivalent to those of the other members of the top ten oligarchs combined, totalling $9.3 billion. At the beginning of February 2022, his fortune was estimated at $13.7 billion, while today it totals $4.4 billion. Even so, it is too early to write off Akhmetov, as he hopes for a quick recovery after the war.

As for other oligarchs, their financial condition has also decreased since the start of the full-scale invasion:

- Victor Pinchuk: from $2.6 billion to $2 billion;
- Vadym Novinsky: from $3.5 billion to $1.3 billion;
- Gennadiy Bogolyubov: from $2 billion to $1.1 billion;
- Ihor Kolomoisky: from $1.8 billion to less than $1 billion;
- Petro Poroshenko: from $1.6 billion to $0.7 billion.

Another effective tool used by President Zelenskyy has been to deprive some oligarchs of citizenship. So far, the most famous of those who have lost their Ukrainian citizenship are Ihor Kolomoisky, the oligarch who owns the channel on which Zelenskyy worked for a long time; Hennadiy Korban, a former partner of Kolomoisky; and Vadym Rabinovich, a leader of the pro-Russian Opposition Platform for Life. The removal of citizenship from these odious figures has increased the general pressure on all oligarchs.

The next important step in deoligarchisation was taken on 6 November 2022, when the National Securities and Stock Market Commission implemented the decision of the headquarters of the Supreme Commander to seize the shares of large industrial companies belonging to some oligarchs. This was done because of, among other things, the importance of these enterprises for the conduct of the war, and in accordance with the Law of Ukraine "On the transfer, expropriation or seizure of property under the legal regime of war or a state of emergency", which calls for "expropriation into state ownership" of shares of strategically important enterprises. The takeover affected, in particular, five large industrial companies owned by oligarchs:[5]

- Ukrnafta (42% of the shares belonged to Kolomoisky);
- Ukrtatnafta (60% of the shares belonged to Kolomoisky and Bogolyubov);

---

5   Minakov, M. (2022) "The war has helped Ukraine rein in the oligarchs". *Focus Ukraine*, Kennan Institute, Wilson Center, 15 November.

- Motor Sich (Vyacheslav Boguslaev almost sold 56% of his shares to Chinese investors, but the deal was stopped by the Antimonopoly Committee, and Boguslaev is under arrest);
- AvtoKrAZ (owned by Konstantin Zhevago);
- Zaporizhtransformator (owned by Konstantin Grigorishin).

The confiscated shares are now considered military property under the jurisdiction of the Ukrainian Ministry of Defence. At the end of martial law, in accordance with the law, these shares will either be returned to their owners or the owners will be reimbursed their value.

All of these moves taken by the Zelenskyy administration show that deoligarchisation did not merely resume during the war but is now a much more radical process, changing the established balance of power in Ukraine. The ongoing war and the imposition of martial law have provided the government with the opportunity to significantly limit the influence of the oligarchs. It remains to be seen how much this opportunity can be exploited.

Local politics

The regional component has always played a key role in Ukrainians' political preferences. Voters from the southern and eastern regions (Odesa, Mykolaiv, Kherson, Dnipropetrovsk, Zaporizhzhia, Donetsk, Luhansk and Kharkiv) have often supported parties or individual politicians offering closer cooperation with the Russian Federation. By contrast, the support of the central and western regions has traditionally leant towards more pro-Western political forces proposing integration into the EU and NATO. The struggle for power in the first two decades of Ukraine's independence was dominated mainly by representatives of the industrial eastern regions, the so-called Dnipropetrovsk and Donetsk groups of influence. However, with the Orange Revolution in 2004 and the ascent to power of pro-Western President Viktor Yushchenko, the situation began to change.

This short digression into the past gives us an idea of how, even in peacetime, the struggle for the regions in Ukraine was not only an internal political competition, but also a geopolitical game in which the interests of Russia and the West clashed.

It has always been much easier for political opponents to divide the electorate on a regional basis, using language, religion, historical figures and the Soviet past as markers for influencing electoral preferences.

Political technologists, like their clientele, were guided first of all by their own narrow interests, thus dividing, not sewing together, the regions of the country. Such trends were observed even before the illegal annexation of Crimea and Russia's temporary occupation of parts of the Donetsk and Luhansk oblasts in 2014.

As a response to attempts to forcibly impose the concept of the "Russian world" on the southeast parts of Ukraine, the electoral pendulum began to swing rapidly towards pro-Ukrainian and pro-Western political leaders and forces. The election to the presidency of Poroshenko in 2014 and Zelenskyy in 2019 heralded a change in the electoral palette. Regional differences began to gradually blur. The emergence of a nationwide pro-Ukrainian superstructure began, displacing regional political features. Russia failed to take this new Ukrainian reality into account in its hostile desire to move deep into Ukraine to occupy the southeast regions in February 2022. The bridgehead, of course, had been prepared.

The Russians have been trying to expand their influence for decades by infiltrating local elites, providing political and financial support, spreading propaganda, and strengthening ties with the church and the criminal world. But the outcome that Russian troops hoped for in temporarily occupying Kherson and part of the Zaporizhzhia region in March 2022 did not occur. They were greeted not with flowers, but with Molotov cocktails and rallies of thousands of brave locals who stopped Russian tanks without weapons. It became obvious that the overwhelming majority of local citizens and elites alike refused to support Russia.

The occupiers had to quickly create pseudo-administrations and appoint previously mothballed collaborators, many of whom were part of the pro-Russian political party Opposition Platform for Life.

On 20 March 2022 Zelenskyy signed a decree prepared by the National Security and Defence Council of Ukraine to ban the activities of 11 pro-Russian political parties, including the Opposition Platform for Life and other parties identified as "socialist" or "left". This again confirmed the assumption that the left of Ukraine's political spectrum was predominantly represented by pseudo-socialist parties that were instruments of Russian influence.

Since Russia's full-scale aggression began, all regional policy has been aimed at ensuring that the regions endure under very harsh conditions. The regions were divided into the front line and the rear. Given daily Russian shelling and destruction, the first priority for the front-line areas was to survive. For the rear regions, it has been of paramount importance to maintain economic activity, help the Ukrainian army and receive internally displaced persons.

Local government is now practically nonexistent, since the conditions of war have changed the system of government, shifting power to the executive central authorities. Political processes on the ground have been put on a long pause. The loyalty of mayors to the central government corresponds to the growing popularity of Zelenskyy.

The autonomy of local government bodies, which has been strengthened with fairly effective decentralising reform, is a key component not only of European but even of Ukrainian politics. However, the threats associated with the Russo-Ukrainian War once again demonstrate the danger of collaborationist elements at the local level, which, under certain circumstances, may become a serious threat to the territorial integrity and sovereignty of the country.

Electoral shifts

It is customary to say that politics is impossible in time of war. But war is, in fact, a continuation of politics, especially if the conflict becomes protracted. Politics does not disappear, even during martial law. It just takes on a different form, as well as shifting the focus of the issues under consideration.

It is difficult now to predict when future elections will be possible in Ukraine. Most likely, no elections can be expected before the end of the war. Consequently, many political players remain in limbo, trying to maintain their voter base and adapt to the prevailing conditions.

It is logical that in wartime all power is concentrated in the hands of the president, under whom the vertical control structure is built. After all, decisions need to be made as quickly and efficiently as possible. At the same time, many are wondering how things will develop once peace is restored. Will Ukraine be able to return to a competitive political struggle between different political parties and leaders? So far, the vast majority of Ukrainians support the president and the Armed Forces of Ukraine, which is a key factor in countering Russian aggression. Future electoral preferences, however, will be determined by the duration and outcome of the Russo-Ukrainian War.

We can say with confidence that parties and politicians who promoted the pro-Russian agenda have lost their formerly monolithic voter base. These voters, predominantly from the southeast part of Ukraine, have suffered the most from the war. Pursuant to a presidential decree, the main parliamentary party that previously represented their interests, the Opposition Platform for Life, has been banned.

In addition, the banned party's representatives are accused of complicity in actions aimed at undermining the sovereignty and territorial integrity of Ukraine. Many political experts believe that these processes are already irreversible and there is practically no chance that pro-Russian politicians will enjoy a revival in future. However, we should not forget that similar assumptions were made after the Revolution of Dignity in 2014, when pro-Western political forces came to power. Parts of the pro-Russian Party of Regions, of which fugitive ex-president Yanukovych was formerly a member, still managed to get their faction into parliament. Of course, it is not entirely correct to compare this with the current situation, since the scale of Russian destruction is much more significant.

Despite all this, there remain significant numbers of people in the southeast of Ukraine, including internally displaced persons and pensioners nostalgic for the Soviet past, whose electoral preferences are now difficult to measure. Most of this electoral niche will presumably support President Zelenskyy and his revamped political party. At the same time, it is possible that new political projects with populist leaders will enter the vacant electoral field. Key topics for political debate will include further militarisation, the fight against corruption, economic recovery, the social model of postwar Ukraine (given the increasing burden of social spending on the budget), the fight against unemployment and regional inequality (where some front-line regions suffered much more than those in the rear), European integration, linguistic questions (given the significant segment of society that remains Russian-speaking), and religious and cultural characteristics.

It can be assumed that with regard to the emergence of new political forces, demand for a conditional "party of the military" and "party of volunteers" can be expected. The first political force could be represented by one of Ukraine's current generals, perhaps even General Valerii Zaluzhnyi. But for a volunteer political platform, there will be a serious struggle among various charitable foundations and public organisations. The most popular figure is Serhiy Prytula, who was previously involved in politics and, since the outbreak of the war, has managed to launch the biggest of the crowdfunding campaigns to help the Ukrainian army, including the acquisition of Turkish-made Bayraktar unmanned combat aerial vehicles and the lease of a satellite to track the movements of Russian troops.

Perhaps there will be a resurrection of certain politicians from the past who went to the front. The main political opponent of Zelenskyy, ex-president Poroshenko, will try to retain primacy with his fairly well-established voter base. However, many political projects launched before the war may not be able to recover and find their voters.

Prospects for a progressive recovery

The Russian war continues to bring devastation and grief to millions of Ukrainians. European countries are bracing for the possible next influx of refugees as, after systematic rocket attacks, critical infrastructure in Ukraine continues to collapse, leaving civilians to survive in harsh conditions without heat, electricity or water. Despite this, it is important to start preparing for the restoration of Ukraine with socially oriented targets.

Such reconstruction must provide for the involvement of the widest possible range of stakeholders: from public authorities to social movements, trade unions, international experts and the direct beneficiaries of reconstruction. In addition, social groups that have suffered the most from the war and remain the most vulnerable should be at the centre of rebuilding: veterans, working families, the elderly and the disabled. International assistance, education – both formal and informal – and legislation focused on social protection should become the basis for the institutional restructuring of Ukraine.

Many will want to start over with a clean slate after the end of hostilities. Public discourse may shift not to restoration, but to renewal. This should increase mass demand for new ideas and new political faces.

At the same time, many contradictions will likely remain, and some may even intensify. Maintaining the level of unity that was observed in the first months of the invasion will be extremely difficult in the postwar period, especially if the accumulated problems are not quickly resolved.

Ideological fragmentation will continue to be nominal. Leader-oriented political projects will compete for power, and populism will take on a more sophisticated form.

It is logical that progressive political forces could resist such tendencies. But influential social democratic parties in Ukraine do not yet exist. Consequently, the social agenda is being defended mainly by individual political movements, public organisations and weakened trade unions. Without substantial support from European social democrats, rebuilding Ukraine with a focus on inclusion, pluralism and justice will be extremely difficult.

Further reading

Minakov, M. (2022) "The war has helped Ukraine rein in the oligarchs". *Focus Ukraine*, Kennan Institute, Wilson Center, 15 November. URL: https://www.wilsoncenter.org/blog-post/war-has-helped-ukraine-rein-oligarchs.

Ireneusz Bil

11 | More than a neighbour in need: Polish and EU support to Ukraine

Russia's full-scale military aggression against Ukraine confirmed the worst fears of Polish policymakers and foreign policy thinkers about the course of events in Eastern Europe. Along with other EU member states and EU institutions, Poland launched an unprecedented effort to support Ukraine in the political, humanitarian, financial and military dimensions. The outcome of the war, together with postwar EU and national policies adopted for the reconstruction and integration of Ukraine and other aspiring Eastern EU members, will determine the long-term stability and prosperity of the whole region.

One of the principal factors that shaped Poland's Eastern policy was its decision in the early 1990s to pursue European Union and NATO membership. These were strategic decisions that enabled Warsaw to act on its foreign policy beyond its actual weight. After a period of uneasy and socially painful reforms, Poland quickly became a leader in the political and economic transition in Central and Eastern Europe. This in turn made Warsaw eligible to apply for NATO and EU membership. The pace of integration set much of the tone and content of Eastern policy. The success of the Polish transformation meant that many countries in the region closely watched what was happening in Poland. They began to attach more and more importance to relations with Warsaw, which quickly became a point of reference for countries undergoing transition.[1]

The concept of "strategic" or "privileged" relations emerged, primarily regarding contacts with Ukraine and Lithuania. This followed growing expectations among neighbouring nations, which were looking for an opportunity to follow Poland's path and embrace the process of European

1   The author writes more broadly on this topic in "Polish Eastern policy in the years 1989–2022", Friedrich-Ebert-Stiftung Warsaw, 2023 (submitted for publication).

integration. The Eastern countries saw in Poland an important intermediary in relations with the West, and Warsaw sought to use these structures to influence the Eastern policy of other EU member states.[2] Additionally, Poland skilfully took advantage of so-called enlargement fatigue among older EU members, among whom – with the exception of Germany and Austria – there was little interest in the East.

An even more significant factor strengthened Poland's credibility. This was the genuine conviction of the Polish political elite that the EU and NATO should not end at the Bug River but should extend to all European countries in the East that meet the right criteria and identify with the ideas of a common Europe. This belief was rooted in the sense of historical responsibility and shared fate. No less important was the pragmatic principle (also followed by Germany in the 1990s vis-à-vis Central Europe) about the need to export stability and prosperity to the east of its borders. The consequence of these attitudes was an attempt by Polish politicians to play the role of neighbourhood spokesman at various international meetings, emphasising the importance of countries such as Ukraine in European politics.

Greater criticism of this historically oriented Eastern policy appeared for the first time during the cohabitation period of 2005–2007 (the government of the Civic Platform and President Lech Kaczyński). The preceding policy was accused of ineffectiveness, of overestimating Poland's ability to influence events in the East, of excessive national ambitions, and finally of using international activity and historical policy for internal political purposes.

The government of Donald Tusk (2007–2015) therefore made greater use of the EU's potential to support transformation in the East. This is how the EU's Eastern Partnership (EaP) initiative, developed jointly with Sweden, was established. The EaP was to be the EU's second "external dimension", the first being the Union for the Mediterranean. The goal of the EaP was to support six former Soviet states (Ukraine, Belarus, Moldova, Georgia, Armenia and Azerbaijan) in the process of political, institutional and economic transformation. The principal legal instruments for the transition (to be negotiated and signed) were the Association Agreements (AAs) and the Deep and Comprehensive Free Trade Agreements (DCFTAs). It was significant that the EaP had become part of the

---

2   "Polish Eastern policy: a full record of the discussion organised by the Stefan Batory Foundation and the editorial office of *Tygodnik Powszechny* on 1 March 2001" (in Polish). URL: https://www.batory.org.pl/ftp/program/forum/ppw.pdf.

European Neighbourhood Policy (ENP), not enlargement policy as Poland had initially wanted.

During the rule of the Law and Justice (PiS) party in Poland (2015–present), foreign policy – and Eastern policy in particular – has fallen low on the list of priorities. Attention has been focused on internal affairs and the conflict with the EU over judicial reform. Poland has also not joined the Normandy Format, a grouping of states that worked out the Minsk agreements on the regulation of the Donbas conflict. To the disgust of the PiS government, the Minsk agreements facilitated the reorientation of Kyiv towards stronger EU countries like Germany and France. After Polish diplomatic withdrawal, the political vacuum in Kyiv was quickly filled by Lithuania, which took over the Polish position as the main "ambassador" of Eastern interests in the EU. The conflict between the Polish government and Brussels over the rule of law and Polish judicial reform led to a further weakening of Poland's position in the East. Countries seeking integration and funds from the EU preferred to stay away from the European "troublemaker".

This period of colder relations has been reflected in diplomatic activity. Prior to 2022, neither former prime minister Beata Szydło nor her successor Mateusz Morawiecki ever visited Kyiv or Tbilisi. Morawiecki first visited Kyiv only after the outbreak of war in February 2022, in the fifth year of his premiership. The activity of Polish President Andrzej Duda, meanwhile, has been similarly unimpressive, especially when compared with his predecessors. For example, he did not visit Ukraine at all during 2018 and 2019, and he has never visited Moldova during his presidency.

In the context discussed above, an important focus of the PiS government and President Duda has been on building another platform for cooperation, the so-called Three Seas Initiative. At its core, this is an interesting project with noteworthy potential. It is largely based on the earlier established Central European Initiative and involves the construction of multimodal transport corridors along the North–South axis, connecting the basins of the Baltic Sea, Black Sea and Adriatic Sea. This European corridor lacks infrastructure for the free exchange of goods, and the potential for mutual cooperation seems largely untapped. The original sin of the PiS initiative was to give it an unsaid political meaning: competitive, not compatible with the East–West axis, building a counterweight to Russia and also to Germany.

What is striking is that the initiative has not embraced the key Polish partners in the East – Ukraine and Moldova – despite all the opportunities arising from association with the EU. However, both countries were already oriented in their policies towards Brussels, Berlin and Paris, not on the mediation of Warsaw, which was at odds with the EU. Therefore, both countries were treated with reluctance by the Polish government, and until the outbreak of the war in 2022 they remained on the periphery of this initiative.

The invasion of Ukraine in 2022

The full-scale invasion of Ukraine by the Russian Federation on 24 February 2022 has become a turning point in European history. The phrase used by German Chancellor Olaf Scholz, "*Zeitenwende*", perfectly captures the groundbreaking nature of the conflict, the first large-scale land invasion in Europe since World War II. It is a war that is illegal according to international accords and treaties, and that was initiated by a permanent UN Security Council member, which under the UN Charter is particularly responsible for upholding peace and preventing armed conflicts.

Besides being groundbreaking in the legal, military and humanitarian sense, the war in the East has sent shock waves throughout the world of democratic nations. Post-1989 European politics was firmly anchored in the belief that such a large-scale, aggressive armed conflict would be impossible in Europe, as the fatalities of both World Wars are painfully engraved into the collective memory of societies and political elites. Russia, previously an important part of the anti-Hitler coalition and one of the countries that suffered the most during World War II, shared – in the eyes of most Westerners – the same determination that "never again" should an aggressive war return to the European continent. This belief was undermined, but not shattered, by the 2014 annexation of Crimea and the proxy war in Donbas. However, the February 2022 invasion made even the most profound believers in the peaceful and cooperative nature of the current regime in Russia cease to have any doubts about the flimsiness of their arguments.

Poland's historical caution and previous scepticism – or even (as some put it) "paranoia" – about developments in Russia allowed it to avoid many of the strategic mistakes that some other countries have made. First, Warsaw turned out to be better prepared to withstand the energy embargo that was introduced after the Russian invasion. Already in 2006, the Polish government announced the decision to build a liquefied natural gas (LNG) terminal on the Baltic Sea, which started operations in 2015.

In 2019, Warsaw declared its intention to cease long-term gas supply contracts with Russia.[3] Instead, Qatari and US gas was contracted via the LNG terminal in Świnoujście and via the new Baltic Pipe gas pipeline from Norway. In this way, by the eve of the Russian invasion of Ukraine, Poland and Russia had already gone through a process of gradual energy decoupling – costly in financial terms, but limiting the dangers of physical shortages. The process would be even more effective if the Polish government had not earlier blocked many opportunities for the development of renewable energy.

National and EU humanitarian responses

Poland is recognised today for its humanitarian response and assistance to millions of Ukrainian refugees who have flooded to Europe since 24 February 2022. According to the Polish Border Guard, over 8.213 million refugees from Ukraine crossed the Polish–Ukrainian border up until December 2022.[4] Currently officially registered under the Temporary Protection Directive are more than 1.5 million Ukrainian refugees, 93% of them women and children. Unofficially, over 3 million Ukrainians are either temporarily or more permanently residing in Poland. Significant numbers of refugees officially registered for temporary protection are also hosted by other EU member states: over 1 million in Germany, 460,000 in the Czech Republic, 165,000 in Italy, 146,000 in Bulgaria and 102,000 in Slovakia.

The relatively smooth influx and accommodation in Europe of millions of refugees would not have been possible without immediate organisational, legal and financial undertakings by the Polish government, Polish local councils and EU institutions alike. In the opening days of the refugee crisis, Warsaw greatly reduced the usual border formalities and allowed for entrance even without passports and personal ID cards. The Polish government issued a statement that every Ukrainian refugee would be welcomed and even allowed to bring their pets without the usual

---

3 On 15 November 2019, Polish energy company PGNiG issued a declaration of will to end the so-called Yamal Contract through which Poland buys gas from Russia. Similar moves have not been made by oil company PKN Orlen, although Russian oil deliveries to Poland contribute much more to the Russian budget than gas. See the PGNiG website, "Oświadczenie woli zakończenia Kontraktu Jamalskiego z dniem 31 grudnia 2022 roku". URL: https://pgnig.pl/aktualnosci/-/news-list/id/oswiadczenie-woli-zakonczenia -kontraktu-jamalskiego-z-dniem-31-grudnia-2022-roku/newsGroupId/10184.

4 "Ilu uchodźców z Ukrainy jest w Polsce?" URL: https://300gospodarka.pl/news/ uchodzcy-z-ukrainy-w-polsce-liczba.

veterinary documents and requirements. Assembly points for refugees opened in every district of Poland, the largest being in Warsaw, Rzeszów, Kraków and other big cities. Local authorities provided free accommodation, food and other necessary supplies for all those in need. In addition, a huge number of citizens and organisations voluntarily offered assistance, free accommodation and further help. Many information sites and webpages were set up in the Ukrainian language to facilitate access to services including relocation, healthcare and accommodation.

However, due to the sheer number of refugees, Poland quickly started to become overwhelmed by the organisational burden and logistical challenges. Immediate coordination of assistance at the EU level and the implementation of the EU's Temporary Protection Directive on 4 March 2022 helped address these challenges and institutionalise assistance to Ukrainian refugees. It alleviated pressure on national asylum systems and permitted displaced persons to enjoy harmonised rights across the EU. These rights include residence, access to the labour market and housing, medical assistance, social welfare assistance, and access to education for children. The temporary protection will last for at least one year (until 4 March 2023) and up to three years, depending on how the situation in Ukraine evolves.[5]

Besides the above, the EU has delivered a wide range of financial and other assistance, including humanitarian aid and civil protection support, as well as direct assistance to Poland and other countries hosting refugees through cohesion policy funds, home affairs funds, technical support, support for border management and the EU solidarity platform.

Parallel streams of support have been directed towards Ukraine. On 24 May 2022, the Council of the European Union adopted a regulation allowing for temporary trade liberalisation and other trade concessions with regard to certain Ukrainian products.[6] At the European Council of 30–31 May 2022, EU heads of state and government declared that the EU was ready to grant Ukraine new exceptional macrofinancial assistance of up to €9 billion in 2022. Of the total of €9 billion, the release of the first €1 billion was approved by the Council in July 2022. An additional

---

5   Additionally, the EU has allocated €523 million in humanitarian assistance to help civilians affected by the war in Ukraine. This includes €485 million for Ukraine and €38 million for Moldova. EU member states alone have mobilised over €957 million.

6   European Council (2022) "Ukraine: Council adopts temporary trade liberalisation with Ukraine". Press release, 24 May. URL: https://www.consilium.europa.eu/en/press/press-releases/2022/05/24/ukraine-council-adopts-temporary-trade-liberalisation-with-ukraine/.

€5 billion was released as a matter of urgency in September 2022. The assistance is designed to help strengthen the resilience of Ukraine and is provided in the form of highly concessional long-term loans.

Military-technical assistance

Poland's long-standing distrust of Russia and the current government's deep antipathy towards Moscow have also seen Warsaw adopt a different trajectory than common in Europe in the development of its armed forces. Polish military strategists have never believed that large-scale conventional warfare is a thing of the past. This attitude was reinforced by the fact that Poland is a "front-line state" of both NATO and the EU, and any potential European conflict might thus be fought predominantly on Polish territory. As a result, Poland has preserved a relatively large and heavily equipped army, comprising over 150,000 soldiers. Over 30,000 of these belong to the Territorial Defence Forces – light forces newly established in 2017 that incorporate weekend soldiers. After an initial 16 days of training, they conduct frequent exercises and prepare to carry out defence tasks in their own region. These units were established after internalising the lessons from the war in the Donbas, where the presence of even lightly trained and equipped but highly motivated and numerous forces proved its value. With the 2022 Russian invasion of Ukraine, the role such units played in the defence of Kyiv and the east of the country against technically superior yet less numerous forces proved the validity of this concept. Current plans foresee a further increase in the quantity of troops in the Polish armed forces, up to 300,000 by 2035.

Poland has also maintained the largest pool of heavy military equipment in Central and Eastern Europe. As a result, prior to the start of the war in February 2022, it had more main battle tanks than Germany, France and the United Kingdom combined. Similarly significant numbers of heavy artillery, infantry fighting vehicles (IFVs) and armoured personnel carriers (APCs) have also been kept in stock. Even though this is often outdated post-Soviet equipment, it has been maintained in good technical condition, and it is often modernised to improve its combat effectiveness.[7] Simultaneously, new pieces of modern gear have been gradually

---

7   A good example is the modernisation of the T-72M1 tank to the T-72M1R version. Despite being limited in scope, the vehicle now has greatly improved operational capabilities, including among other things a thermal imaging system better than that of most modern Russian tanks and new, encrypted communication devices.

---

introduced into the army over the past decade, including 155 mm Krab self-propelled howitzers (SPHs) and Rosomak 8x8 wheeled APCs.

The relatively high quantity of both older and more modern heavy equipment has allowed Poland to become one of the largest contributors of military hardware to Ukraine. Poland has donated over 240 T-72M1/T-72M1R main battle tanks, 18 155 mm Krab SPHs, and unspecified numbers of other heavy vehicles including BWP-1 IFVs, PT-91 Twardy tanks, S-125 Newa SC missile systems and 2S1 Gvozdika 122 mm SPHs. In addition, large quantities of smaller weapons such as Piorun MANPADS and Grot 5.56 mm automatic rifles were delivered to the Ukrainian army, along with huge stockpiles of various munitions. Poland also paid for over 11,700 (of a total 20,000) of Elon Musk's Starlink terminals for satellite internet access, essential to provide internet connections for Ukrainian military networks.[8]

Polish assistance was among the first to arrive in significant amounts early in the war, so its importance in upholding morale and helping repel the first wave of attacks cannot be underestimated. Due to its geographical location and developed infrastructure in the border regions (airports, highways and railways), Poland has also quickly become a logistical hub for the Ukraine assistance operation in both the humanitarian and military dimensions.

The aggression against Ukraine has also proved to be a testing time in the development of the EU's own defence institutions. As early as three days after the invasion, the EU announced that it would provide weapons to Ukraine through the European Peace Facility (EPF), operational since July 2021, marking the first time in its history that the bloc has provided lethal weaponry. Over the first six months, the EU provided €2.5 billion to Ukraine for arms and equipment via the EPF.[9] Through the EPF Committee and the clearing house hosted by the European External Action Service, member states can be reimbursed for equipment delivered to Ukraine. This applies to both lethal and nonlethal aid, such as bulletproof vests and helmets.[10] Poland is among the countries to use the facility

---

8   URL: https://gospodarka.dziennik.pl/news/artykuly/8569261,ukraina-terminale-star link-elon-musk-polska-gospodarka.html.

9   Trenkov-Wermuth, C., and J. Zack (2022) *"Ukraine: the EU's unprecedented provision of lethal aid is a good first step"*. United States Institute of Peace Website, 27 October. URL: https://www.usip.org/publications/2022/10/ukraine-eus-unprecedented-provision -lethal-aid-good-first-step.

10   Bilquin, B. (2022) "European Peace Facility: Ukraine and beyond". European Parliament Research Service website, 18 November. URL: https://epthinktank.eu/2022/11/18/ european-peace-facility-ukraine-and-beyond/.

most extensively, including financing the purchase of 54 155 mm Krab SPHs for the Ukrainian armed forces, to be produced and delivered in 2022–2023.

Conclusion and outlook

Assessing the prospects for ending the war, rebuilding and securing Ukraine, containing or normalising relations with Russia, and bringing stability to the region requires further conceptualisation of policies towards Ukraine and the broader Eastern European region. This applies both to member states (Germany's Ostpolitik being the most obvious example) and European political institutions. The need to reinforce the common denominator of EU Eastern policies is a lesson learned from the experiences of recent months. Managing the humanitarian crisis and then developing multifaceted assistance to Ukraine would not be so effective without synergies among the actions of member states and the opportunities offered by EU institutions and the *acquis communautaire*.

This context also applies to the Polish Eastern policy. Poland has been most successful when it has searched for a synergy between its European policy and Eastern policy; between its presence in the EU and NATO, and the formula of cooperation with its neighbours. In the previous decade, as in 2022, Warsaw effectively used EU institutions to wield political influence above its relative level of power. In contrast, when Polish policy drifted towards projects based on the idea of itself as a regional power – when it tried to test the loyalty of its neighbours, or build alternatives or competitors for proven forms of cooperation, relying on some imaginary ideas about Poland's role and national agenda – then the Polish position usually weakened and the gains from such policies were minor.

A paradigm shift will also need to take place in EU policies towards Ukraine. There is no doubt that the geopolitically exposed countries in the East (Ukraine, Moldova and Georgia), as well as in the Balkans, need to be anchored more strongly in the European project. The Eastern Partnership played a positive role in providing Ukraine with various forms of assistance through Multiannual Indicative Programmes (MIPs), revised milestones, action plans, and financing mechanisms and instruments. The EU role and horizontal contacts and relations between EU institutions and Ukraine/Moldova will now increase. Granting them candidate status signifies a recategorisation of these countries in the EU's policies, and ultimately embracing them through the instruments of the Enlargement Policy.

These intensified interactions cannot be just an acceleration of already established legal and institutional approaches, as the task of rebuilding, supporting and embracing Ukraine is hardly comparable to previous enlargement challenges. The EU should offer Ukraine a new "Partnership for Rebuilding and Enlargement". The EU's financial and technical assistance is indispensable for the rebuilding and recovery of the Ukrainian state. Special funds should be considered that would draw on the experiences of the NextGenerationEU reconstruction fund and be centred on common borrowing. This would need to be supported by loans from the World Bank and International Monetary Fund support to guarantee the liquidity of public finances.[11] After necessary accommodations and providing proof of its eligibility, Ukraine should also be offered the chance to go beyond the DCFTA+ and gain full access to the EU's single market.

Besides offering Ukraine and Moldova intensified and tangible cooperation, these countries should be simultaneously required to comply with the EU's fundamental principles: democracy, human rights, a free market economy, an independent judiciary and a rules-based order. External pressure to fulfil these obligations is essential to steer clear of the post-war dangers of authoritarianism and militarisation of Ukrainian politics and society.

Further reading

Auguff, P. (2022) "Na Ukrainie działa 20 tys. terminali Starlink. Ponad połowę kupiła Polska". Dziennik.pl, 17 October 2022. URL: https://gospodarka.dziennik .pl/news/artykuly/8569261,ukraina-terminale-starlink-elon-musk-polska -gospodarka.html.

Bilquin, B. (2022) "European Peace Facility: Ukraine and beyond". European Parliament Research Service website, 18 November. URL: https://epthinktank .eu/2022/11/18/european-peace-facility-ukraine-and-beyond/.

Buras, P., and K.-O. Lang (2022) "Partnership for Enlargement: a new way to integrate Ukraine and the EU's eastern neighbourhood". Policy brief, European Council on Foreign Relations, 17 June. URL: https://ecfr.eu/publication/ partnership-for-enlargement-a-new-way-to-integrate-ukraine-and-the-eus -eastern-neighbourhood/.

---

11   For a broader discussion on EU reconstruction and cooperation, see Buras, P., and K.-O. Lang (2022) "Partnership for Enlargement: a new way to integrate Ukraine and the EU's eastern neighbourhood". Policy brief, European Council on Foreign Relations, 17 June. URL: https://ecfr.eu/publication/partnership-for-enlargement-a-new-way-to-integrate-ukraine -and-the-eus-eastern-neighbourhood/.

European Council (2022) "Ukraine: Council adopts temporary trade liberalisation with Ukraine". Press release, 24 May. URL: https://www.consilium.europa.eu/en/press/press-releases/2022/05/24/ukraine-council-adopts-temporary-trade-liberalisation-with-ukraine/.

Trenkov-Wermuth, C., and J. Zack (2022) "Ukraine: the EU's unprecedented provision of lethal aid is a good first step". United States Institute of Peace Website, 27 October. URL: https://www.usip.org/publications/2022/10/ukraine-eus-unprecedented-provision-lethal-aid-good-first-step.

Mārtiņš Vargulis

12 | Baltic perspectives on the war in Ukraine

Russia's aggression in Ukraine continues to impact the Baltic defence system. The adaptation that began in 2014 now has an additional impetus, providing a wake-up call for Baltic politicians to strengthen defence capabilities. The purpose of this chapter is to identify the Baltic perspective on how Russia's aggression affects regional security, to analyse important decisions regarding the strengthening of Baltic military capabilities and to define still missing tasks to be carried out in the coming years.

Russia's aggression in Ukraine, which took on a new form on 24 February 2022, has continued to impact the Baltic defence system. The adaptation that began in 2014 now has an important additional impetus, providing another wake-up call for Baltic politicians and representatives of the defence sector to further strengthen defence capabilities. Important decisions have been made. First, in seeking solutions to Russia's ever-increasing aggression, the Baltic states have looked for ways to recruit more military personnel. Second, regional and international solutions have been sought to strengthen the air defence dimension, which has lagged behind for decades. Third, important decisions have been made with regard to missing elements of land forces, providing them with the necessary equipment. Fourth, there has been a continuation of investment in new technologies, enabling the armed forces to wage war in the context of electronic warfare. Finally, there has been political commitment across the Baltic states to increase defence budgets by spending more than 2% of GDP.

Several of these projects had already been planned before 24 February 2022, and the full-scale warfare launched by Russia has only strengthened them. It has also made it easier to implement several of the projects by attracting additional financial resources, which have had the unanimous support of ruling political elites in the Baltic countries. Despite the intensive implementation of military procurement, there are still several shortages in the Baltic region that could be exploited by the adversary in times of crisis or war. Significant deficiencies still affect the air and sea dimensions, where Russia has superiority in the Baltic region (not including Finland and Sweden, which are still not full-fledged NATO members). Therefore, the purpose of this chapter is to identify the Baltic perspective (mindset) on how Russia's aggression in Ukraine affects regional security, to analyse the most important decisions taken regarding the strengthening of Baltic military capabilities and to define still missing elements and tasks to be carried out in the coming years.

Shared threat perceptions and solidarity as preconditions for victory

From the perspective of the Baltic states, to display credible deterrence NATO needs to reinforce and demonstrate its ability to use its might if required. A demonstration of strength, which could be expressed via large-scale exercises or deployment of permanent Allied forces, is the best signal to any aggressor (especially Russia) that the defence of each country, and thus of the Alliance as a whole, is being seriously planned, tested and valued. Softening and reducing positions will be perceived as a point of weakness that Russia will exploit in its own interests. There-fore, in the current security environment, the measures adopted since 2014 and complemented in 2022, including in the Baltic region, form the (minimum) basis for further strengthening of NATO's common deter-rence and defence policy.

Solidarity and the desire to protect the country are highly valued ele-ments in the administration of Russian President Vladimir Putin. Accord-ing to the doctrine of General Valery Gerasimov, influencing public senti-ment in a way that provides a basis for military intervention is among the aspects at the core of any military operation. Accordingly, the strength (or weakness) of a state depends directly on society's willingness to protect its country as well as its allies, if this is required.

One essential element of resilience and solidarity is a common understanding of the level and classification of threats. Following Russia's invasion and annexation of Crimea, several decisions were taken at NATO's Wales Summit in 2014 and Warsaw Summit in 2016 that illustrated a change of consciousness and mindset among the

Allies. Both summits indicated that the Allies had arrived at a common perception of threat that saw Russia's aggression in Ukraine as having long-term consequences for transatlantic security. This revealed a common understanding of Russia's ambitions and revisionist approach in the international arena, and represented a turning point for the security of the Baltic region. Prior to Russia's aggression, several Central and West European NATO members had shown a degree of interest in normalising relations with Russia, even in the form of civil or military cooperation. From the perspective of the Baltic countries, such an approach was considered unfavourable and risky based on the national threat assessment. Nevertheless, heads of state and government meeting in Wales and Warsaw, and even more in Madrid in 2022, were able to agree on far-reaching measures to strengthen NATO's collective defence and rapid response capabilities, as well as to reinforce the central role of transatlantic relations in ensuring security, while maintaining a clear and common understanding of the threat and challenges the Alliance faces.

Although there is emerging unity among the Allies, national interests and perceptions are still at the forefront. Russia's aggression in the Ukraine, and its aggressive assertiveness in many forms, is a unifying threat that brings the NATO members together. However, assessments about how to deal with Russia differ. In this regard, the Baltic states have a slightly different perception compared with other Allies, being very sceptical of Russian military activism in the Baltic Sea and surrounding regions. The bottom line – in the perception of both political leaders and public opinion in Latvia, Lithuania and Estonia – is that Ukraine is now "fighting our war". If Putin will use any means to find success, we cannot exclude the desire to test the solidarity and unity of NATO. Consequently, the Baltic states have been among the top providers of per-capita military and financial aid to Ukraine in recent months.

From the Baltic perspective, contrary to – for example – France's position, any kind of effort to find ways to help Russia "save face" and find compromises that would satisfy the involved parties is not the right way to deal with Putin. Any show of weakness will be exploited by Russia's president, and negotiating is thus considered a manifestation of such weakness. For the Baltic states, a victory for Ukraine that includes regaining the territories inside its borders as they were in 1991 is considered the desired end result. Neither a freeze in the conflict nor the search for a compromise would contribute to international security in the long term. This, the argument goes, would only give Russia the opportunity to recover both militarily and economically and implement new expansion along the Russian border in the medium term.

Understanding the need to defend (not only) one's own country

A willingness to protect Allies and engage in conflict (if required) is an essential element of deterrence. NATO's political will to defend the Baltic region is interpreted as a readiness among the leaders of the Alliance to employ force against the threat faced by Russia and to sustain the costs and risks of those actions over time. With the deployment of an enhanced Forward Presence (eFP) in the Baltic states and Poland, this discussion became relevant in various NATO countries. It also highlighted the challenges and lack of unity among Allies, as there are still several members without a presence in any of the FP battle groups, illustrating the contrasting perceptions of both political leaders and societies in various Allied countries.

This does not imply that NATO's Article 5 has been challenged, as it remains a cornerstone of the Alliance deterrence and defence posture, and thus also the cornerstone of security of the Baltic states. However, when it comes to practical steps, opinions about NATO and related issues vary widely across the member countries. Public sentiment highlights the challenges relating to the overall willingness of a NATO member to step on an ally's soil from the very outset of a conflict or crisis. According to a survey by the Pew Research Center, when asked if their country should defend a NATO ally against a potential attack from Russia, a median of 50% of respondents across 16 NATO member states said their country should not defend an ally, compared with 38% who said their country should.[1] Public opinion in half of the NATO countries is against getting involved in the conflict with Russia. This type of research only stimulates Russia's appetite to test the Alliance's unity and solidarity. And it is this type of response that represents the main concern of the Baltic states within the context of Russia's aggression in Ukraine.

According to a survey carried out by the Institute of Land Warfare, significant negative indicators of political will within NATO exist for the following reasons:

---

1   Fagan, M., and J. Poushter (2020) "NATO seen favorably across member states". Report, Pew Research Center, 9 February. URL: https://pewrsr.ch/3G7FNmV.

---

(1) NATO lacks sufficient key leaders supporting the use of force to defend Baltic Allies;

(2) NATO's common understanding of the Russian threat to the Baltic states is questionable because of diverging threats and missions, differing perceptions of Russian actions and domestic factors;

(3) there are both positive and negative signs with regard to the availability of a commonly perceived, potentially effective solution, though NATO retains significant strength due to latent military and economic power.[2]

The willingness (or unwillingness) to protect Allies poses significant challenges in the context of collective defence. First of all, it affects the speed of decision-making. Aware of the absence of a consensus among the Allies, Russia may be able to exploit the lack of political will. By waging covert hybrid warfare, Russia may thus deter most of the Allies from engaging in the first phase of a conflict or crisis. Second, it may provide an incentive to Russia to implement a large-scale A2/AD[3] scenario. A large-scale, unexpected conventional attack could lead to the Baltic states being isolated from the rest of the Alliance. In this case, the reinforcement of Allied forces will be crucial. The involvement of the Allies will be based on the willingness of societies to protect the Baltic states. Finally, public willingness to defend Allies is particularly important in the context of new threats: cyber, strategic communications (disinformation), energy and so forth. In order to meet the challenges posed by Russia (and China), common resilience within the Alliance is of utmost importance.

The security of the Baltic states: unfinished business

The ability to adapt to an uncertain, ever-changing international security environment has been a precondition for NATO's success and development. Since the founding of NATO in 1949, the Alliance has experienced a number of internal and external shocks that have eventually come to impact its future existence. Having experienced several turbulent periods, NATO has been able to adapt and find solutions to the challenges it

---

2 Morris, Z. (Major) (2018) "The North Atlantic Treaty Organization: dubious political will to defend Baltic allies". Land Warfare Papers no. 120, Institute of Land Warfare, August, p.20–21. URL: https://www.ausa.org/sites/default/files/publications/LWP-120-The-North -Atlantic-Treaty-Organization-Dubious-Political-Will-To-Defend-Baltic-Allies.pdf.

3 Anti-Access/Area Denial.

faces. One of the most significant shocks in Europe, which also had a significant impact on NATO's adaptation process, was Russia's annexation of Crimea in 2014, which was a wake-up call for both the Alliance as a whole and each ally individually. It also highlighted gaps and weaknesses in the Alliance's perceptions, approaches and actions. Since 2014, NATO members nationally – and the Alliance as a whole – have implemented a number of adaptation processes that have strengthened its deterrence and defence posture.

As front-line states, Estonia, Latvia and Lithuania have been among the most active and vocal drivers of this adaptation process, calling on other members to significantly strengthen the Alliance's ability to face the challenges highlighted and reinforced by Russia's aggressive approach. Through the support of the Alliance, a number of important security measures have been put in place in the region contributing to the security of all three Baltic states and strengthening their defence capabilities. Although measures implemented by the Alliance have affected the balance of military power in the region, the question remains of whether these measures are sufficient enough to deter the aggressor from any kind of contingency.

Given Russia's ambition, activity and military development in the Baltic region, the engagement of the Allies and the presence of NATO plans constitute the cornerstone of the Baltic states' security. Collective security affects both national planning and public sentiment. Measures taken in recent years have fostered and strengthened awareness of the Baltic countries' ability to withstand military and nonmilitary threats. With the participation of the Allies, the desire of societies to get involved in comprehensive defence is also transforming and improving. Several measures taken by NATO have stimulated this trend.

From a military perspective, several key decisions have been taken by NATO in recent years impacting the overall deterrence and defence posture, especially regarding the Baltic states. The most important decisions reached at the 2014 Wales Summit were approval of the Readiness Action Plan and the commitment to spend at least 2% of GDP on defence by 2024. At the 2016 Warsaw Summit, the Allies agreed to enhance NATO's military presence in the eastern part of the Alliance, with four battalions in Estonia, Latvia, Lithuania and Poland on a rotational basis. The decision to transform battalion-level units into brigades was made at the Madrid Summit in 2022. As set down in the Madrid Summit Declaration, the intent is to have robust and multinational units, demonstrating the strength of the transatlantic bond and making clear that an attack on one

Ally will be met by forces from across the Alliance.[4] All previous summits and subsequent meetings of foreign and defence ministers have revealed an emerging consensus among the Allies on the continuing vulnerability in the Baltic region.

During these years, NATO Command and Control has been improved and developed in the Baltic region (with a new HQ of Multinational Division North in Ādaži, Latvia). In addition, the Baltic Air Policing mission has been enhanced, while NATO Force Integration Units have been established in all three Baltic states, among another five on NATO's eastern flank. The military Allied presence, elements of command-and-control structure and supporting civil-military mechanisms indicate several gaps and vulnerabilities that existed in the region prior to the necessary adaptation process started in 2014. This represents the unprecedented expression of solidarity enjoyed by the Baltic states in recent years.

Although there have been crucial military developments in the region, it would be a mistake to see Baltic security as a "done deal". Several interrelated aspects that will further determine the credibility of NATO's deterrence and defence posture are worth mentioning.

First, time is of the essence, especially in the Baltic region. Russia's aggression in Ukraine in 2014 stimulated the Allies to adapt and make necessary decisions that would enhance the speed of the Alliance response forces and their ability to provide an immediate military impact in a 360-degree approach. A new Very High Readiness Joint Task Force (VJTF) of around 5,000 troops within the NATO Response Force (NRF), with some elements able to deploy within 48 hours, was introduced at the Wales Summit. In 2018, NATO defence ministers agreed to the NATO Readiness Initiative – the "Four Thirties" – to ensure that NATO has 30 mechanised battalions, 30 air squadrons and 30 combat vessels ready within 30 days or less. The measures were complemented by the decision taken at the Madrid Summit to increase the NRF pool up to 300,000 troops.

Although all the measures have been a step in the right direction to increase overall readiness, they may still prove insufficient when it comes to the defence of the Baltic states. Moreover, the time it might take to authorise the Supreme Allied Commander Europe (SACEUR) to deploy the rest of the NRF creates serious problems for front-line Allies, which could be overrun by the time other Allies weigh in. In the absence of a

---

4 "Madrid Summit declaration". Press release, NATO, 29 June 2022. URL: https://www.nato.int/cps/en/natohq/official_texts_196951.htm.

consensus – which may be difficult to reach in cases where evidence supporting NATO involvement remains ambiguous – the VJTF, and with it the NRF as a whole, will remain unused. Therefore, it is of the utmost importance to further increase the pool of pre-authorised and exercised rapid response forces that could be used immediately by the SACEUR in a conventional short-notice scenario.

Second, stress-tested reinforcement of large-scale Allied forces in a contested environment is another piece of the puzzle. Russia is already able to carry out an attack at short notice that would cut off the Baltic states from the mainland of the Alliance. As warned by Lieutenant General (Ret.) Ben Hodges – former commander of the United States Army Europe – Russian and Belarusian troops could quickly connect and block the borders of Poland and Lithuania, thus isolating three NATO states from the rest of the Alliance.[5] Russia's A2/AD capabilities make the reinforcement of additional Allied forces challenging. In this context, large-scale military exercises and training, demonstrating NATO's reinforcement ability, including via the transatlantic link, are a vital element of its overall deterrence and defence posture. It is important that the Alliance has executable plans and a common understanding of how to reinforce troops with additional units and supplies in the event of military conflict. Exercises like Defender Europe 2020 could build strategic readiness by deploying a combat-credible force to and across Europe. Such exercises should provide the ability to coordinate large-scale movements with Allies and partners.

Third, NATO's post-2014 adaptation process has been largely land-based, leaving the air and maritime dimensions vulnerable. Russia has superiority in the region both in the air and at sea. Given the costs associated with the development of two dimensions, the Baltic states cannot fully respond to these challenges without a significant contribution from the Allies. One of the most topical and critical points is the collective response to air defence, especially in the context of the SSC-8 missiles developed by Russia in recent years. Investments in the air and maritime dimensions are thus critical for a credible deterrence and defence posture.

At NATO's Madrid Summit, the lack of air and maritime response capability was one of the most important aspects from the perspective of the Baltic states. The decisions taken at the summit are a step in the right direction; however, they are still not enough faced with the current

---

5 "U.S. Army commander warns of Russian blocking of Baltic defence". *Baltic Times*, November 9. URL: https://www.baltictimes.com/u_s_army_commander_warns _of_russian_blocking_of_baltic_defence/.

security challenges. As stated in the summit declaration,[6] eFP forces should be supported by elements in the air and at sea. From a purely military perspective, brigade-level units also require strengthened capabilities in other dimensions. Therefore, the Baltic states should use all diplomatic, political and military means to implement what is stated in the summit declaration. With the establishment of brigade-sized units, some air and sea support elements are expected to be provided. However, they will not be enough to fully cover needs in the region. In this context, the membership of Finland and Sweden in NATO will play an important role. With the participation of both countries in the Alliance, the Baltic Sea could become a "NATO lake". The Finnish air force and Swedish navy could then pose significant challenges to any kind of A2/AD capability possessed by Russia.

Baltic military unity: room for improvement

Historically, the positions of the Baltic states on NATO and EU security issues have been united. They have shared a common understanding of existing threats and the necessary steps to address these challenges. However, when it comes to specific elements of military doctrine or joint military procurements, actions have diverged. For instance, the idea of conscription has evolved differently in all three Baltic states. Estonia has had conscription since regaining independence in 1991, while Lithuania reintroduced it in response to Russia's illegal annexation of Crimea in 2014. In Latvia there are still discussions on how to introduce it (although there is a political consensus regarding its necessity).

In recent months there have been positive joint decisions made among the Baltic states themselves. At NATO's Madrid Summit, Estonia and Latvia signed a Letter of Intent regarding joint contracts for delivery of air defence systems. Joint procurement will allow countries to coordinate defence resources, maximise the efficiency of defence investments and promote stability and security in the region. Air defence capabilities are crucial for Latvia's military security. These systems will significantly boost Latvia's ability to take down missiles that are currently used to attack Ukrainian cities. However, this will not solve the issue completely, but is rather the first step towards the eventual goal.

As Allied contributions in the dimensions of air and sea are of particular importance, the joint endeavour of Estonia and Latvia should be

---

6   "Madrid Summit declaration", NATO, 2022.

perceived in the context of the welcome move by Spain, prior to the summit in Madrid, to supply Latvia with a ground-to-air NASAMS[7] anti-aircraft missile battery, which was deployed to Lielvārde Air Base on 26 June 2022. The aim was to provide the Latvian armed forces with necessary air defence capabilities before procurement is completed. Realising that the Baltic states will not be able to answer challenges in the air and at sea on their own, Allied involvement is especially important. At the same time, joint procurement among the Baltic states is a step in the right direction.

The ability of the Baltic states to provide a joint response to aggression that is as extensive and enduring as possible is essential for the collective deterrence and defence posture. In this context, coordinated action among the Baltic states is important. Since 2014, they have been united in their public statements and have enhanced several elements of military cooperation. All three belong to the 2% of GDP defence spending club. However, there is significant room for improvement in this cooperation: first, in joint large-scale procurement, which the Baltic states have struggled with, especially in the above-mentioned context of air defence; and second, in the need for tested and synchronised military plans. As the Baltic states could be separated from the rest of the Alliance on a potential D-day, it is important to send a signal that their actions in such an environment will be united and planned. Together the three Baltic countries can deliver a more significant counterattack than each country separately.

Summary

To summarise, the Baltic states view the existing international environment from the perspective of realpolitik. The credibility of NATO's deterrence and defence posture in the Baltic region is like a tower of Jenga blocks: if one piece is pulled out, the whole structure risks collapse. Strengthening deterrence is a perennial task as the adversary is evolving every day. Slowing the speed of adaptation to the new security situation carries the risk of stimulating the aggressor's appetite for testing the Alliance's readiness and responsiveness. The Baltic region borders with an actor that exploits its opponent's weaknesses to serve its own interests. To deter such an adversary, the Alliance must continue to strengthen its capabilities, ensure an enhanced and integrated Allied military presence,

---

7   Norwegian Advanced Surface-to-Air Missile System.

and send signals that any form of aggression will provoke a broad and rapid collective response.

Russia's aggression in Ukraine in 2022 came as a surprise or even a shock to most international actors. However, this was not entirely true of Latvia, Lithuania and Estonia. The Baltic states have often been considered "Russophobic", which suggests that calls for additional security measures in the region, implemented within the framework of transatlantic relations, would lead to escalation. Attempts to understand Russia or agree on a common threat classification and consequent adaptation measures have been a challenge for the transatlantic allies. Despite several warning signs triggered by Russia in the last two decades, only now can we talk about a "wake-up call" that has awakened most of the Allies from their "long sleep". After 24 February, the perspective shared by policymakers in the Baltic states has gained greater support among the rest of the Allies. However, some discrepancies and disagreements on how to deal with Russia still exist within the transatlantic community.

At NATO's Madrid Summit in 2022 a historic decision was made on the transformation of deployed Allied battle group units from battalion to brigade level in the Baltic states. The measures earlier adopted at the NATO summit in Warsaw in 2016, considered by Baltic states as a compromise, were the first significant step, breaking the long-standing nonescalation policy by deploying an enhanced Forward Presence in front-line states. These were the first seeds of a change in ideological mindset, which, from a military perspective, needed to be followed by further steps. The brigade is not just a numerically larger unit, but is also associated with several reinforcing elements in the context of security, the air and sea dimensions, command and control elements, and so forth.

In addition, the Allies have initiated or significantly accelerated measures to strengthen their national defence policies. For example, the change in Germany's security policy should be mentioned as a significant turning point not only for European security but also in the context of transatlantic relations in general. The historical trauma that has been present since World War II prevented Germany, as the strongest European economy, from developing a full-fledged defence capability by investing the necessary military and nonmilitary resources. This change in policy will certainly have long-term consequences, which should strengthen transatlantic relations and improve Baltic security. Germany already leads the combat unit of Allied forces deployed in Lithuania, providing the battle group with the necessary military elements and coordinating its operations to make it even more effective and able to launch a counterattack on a potential

D-day. Consequently, the change in Germany's policy greatly determines the security and defence posture in the Baltic region.

At the same time, although Russia was identified as the most significant threat to the transatlantic community in 2022, there is a diversity of opinion among the Allies as to how the international security environment is classified and understood from the perspective of military threat in general. This also greatly affects how countries see the development of the transatlantic community in security matters. Although 2022 was a turning point in strengthening the security of NATO's eastern flank, this does not necessarily mean that this strengthening is permanent, as the emphasis and challenges may change.

Strength and power are elements that the Kremlin respects. To present a credible deterrence, the Alliance needs to strengthen and demonstrate its ability to use its might if required. A demonstration of strength, which could be expressed both through large-scale exercises and the deployment of permanent Allied forces, is the best signal to the aggressor that the defence of each country – and thus of the Alliance as a whole – is being seriously planned, tested and valued. Softening and reducing positions will be perceived as a point of weakness that Russia will exploit in its own interests. Therefore, in the current security environment, the measures adopted already since 2014, including in the Baltic region, form the (minimum) foundation on which NATO's common deterrence and defence policy should be further strengthened.

Further reading

Andzans, M., and M. Vargulis (2020) *Towards #NATO2030: The Regional Perspective of the Baltic States and Poland* (Riga: Latvian Institute of International Affairs). URL: https://liia.lv/en/publications/towards-nato2030-the-regional -perspective-of-the-baltic-states-and-poland-896.

Hurt, M., M. Vargulis, Z. Liudas et al. (2023) "Baltic defence development: adding value to the defence of the Baltic Sea Region". Report, International Centre for Defence and Security, March. URL: https://icds.ee/en/baltic-defence -development-adding-value-to-the-defence-of-the-baltic-sea-region/.

Spruds, A., and M. Vargulis (2021) *Deterrence Through Adaptation: The Case Study of Latvia* (Riga: Latvian Institute of International Affairs). URL: https://liia.lv/ en/publications/deterrence-through-adaptation-the-case-study-of-latvia-950.

Håkan A. Bengtsson

13 | NATO membership decisions in Sweden and Finland during the Russo-Ukrainian War

After Russia invaded Ukraine, the security map of Northern Europe was redrawn. Within the space of two months, Sweden and Finland had jointly decided to apply for NATO membership, thereby abandoning their previous long-standing security doctrine of military neutrality. The decision reflects the seriousness of the situation in which Europe now finds itself. NATO was not even on the agenda prior to the outbreak of hostilities. It was not, however, a bolt from the blue. Although Finland and Sweden have resolutely maintained their military neutrality, cooperation between the two countries – and, since 1989, with NATO – has continuously developed. There are decisive and historically significant reasons for this new security orientation in both countries, culminating in the decision by both to make a joint application for membership of the Alliance.

Russia's invasion and the subsequent war in Ukraine mark a turning point in history, a before-and-after demarcation. For the foreseeable future we will be living in a new era of uncertainty with regard to political security. War is brutal and terrible. And the war in Ukraine is particularly brutal, entailing aggression and terror aimed indiscriminately at civilians. Towns, villages and infrastructure have been continuously bombed and reduced to ruins. The waves of refugees thus created are unimaginable and immense. This is a war that will be remembered, and which will leave its mark on us well into the future. Reports from the war in Ukraine are shocking and terrifying. Neither does there appear to be an end to the conflict in sight. Furthermore, the war has had far-reaching consequences for the wider world, leading to fundamental changes in the way defence and security are viewed in the EU in general and in the Nordic countries in particular.

The war is a blatant breach of the UN Charter and the Helsinki Accords of 1975, since the signatories had undertaken to "refrain [...] from the threat or use of force". It also breaches the Budapest Memorandum of 1994, whereby Russia, the UK and the US guaranteed Ukraine's territorial integrity within its current borders. Russia's demand for changes in the balance of power and security guarantees from the US and the rest of the Western world questions an individual country's independence and right to self-determination regarding which alliances or forums of cooperation it chooses to join. The Kremlin under President Vladimir Putin considers it has the right to determine what constitutes "part of historical Russia" and to absorb Ukraine under Russian hegemony. There is no indication that Putin intends to abandon his strategic goals or Russian imperialistic ambitions of reconquering republics that were liberated in 1989, the aim being to create a wider sphere of influence similar to that established during the postwar period as a legacy of World War II.

Russia's war in Ukraine has sent a shock wave throughout Europe and large parts of the world. In the Nordic countries, a process was initiated whereby two countries – Sweden and Finland – decided to apply for membership of NATO. The decision means both countries would abandon their well-established and long-term military neutrality. Put briefly, Sweden and Finland consider that the security situation has become particularly precarious, basing their conclusion on the explicit Russian ambition to fundamentally change the European balance of power. The historical relationship between Sweden and Finland and their geographical and strategic situation almost certainly played a decisive role in ensuring that the two Nordic countries abandoned their previous neutrality. However, their applications for NATO membership are not random occurrences. In recent years, Sweden and Finland have strengthened ties to NATO and amplified cooperation with the Alliance.

Within the framework of the Nordic Defence Cooperation (Nordefco), defence collaboration between Denmark, Finland, Iceland, Norway and Sweden is aimed at supporting the national defence capabilities of the five individual countries. At the same time, bilateral military cooperation between Sweden and Finland has developed apace, further strengthening these links. Consequently, joining NATO is not such a huge step, and nor is it a surprise that Sweden and Finland are taking it together.

Nevertheless, NATO membership was not on the agenda in either country before Putin ordered the invasion of Ukraine. Admittedly, certain parties and players had supported alignment with NATO in recent years, but the topic only gained traction due to Russia's current increasing repression and escalating external aggression.

After World War II, Sweden created a strong unilateral defence capability, with both its air force and navy having formidable capacity. By the beginning of the 1970s, Sweden was spending almost 3% of GDP on defence. After the fall of the Soviet Union, however, in keeping with many other European countries, Sweden carried out substantial disarmament, not to say demilitarisation.

Disarmament has been carried out in several stages and by both social democratic and nonsocialist governments. Defence policy in Sweden has been based on a broad cross-party consensus in which the two major parties, the Social Democrats and the Moderates (right-of-centre), have been in agreement. Although the decision to abandon conscription in 2009 was not supported by the Social Democrats, it was passed in the Swedish Parliament by the narrowest of majorities. The Swedish labour movement has historically favoured conscripted defence rather than a professional army. However, in recent years, the deteriorating security situation has resulted in increases in military spending. Since the outbreak of the war in Ukraine, Sweden has decided to increase defence spending to 2% of GNP, matching, for example, Germany and Denmark.

In contrast, Finland has maintained a greater defence capacity since 1989, presumably because of the country's historical experience with its eastern neighbour. Sweden has meanwhile decided to increase conscription. The Social Democrat defence spokesman, who was defence minister prior to the 2022 election, is now advocating the creation of a "people's defence".

Sweden's and Finland's applications for membership of NATO are due to the uncertainty caused by Russia's actions. The Arctic region and the Baltic Sea are regions of considerable strategic geopolitical importance. For some time, Russian violations of Swedish airspace have been a disturbing indication and demonstration of power. The "new normal" has entailed an increased level of unpredictability since the invasion of 24 February 2022. The new joint position of Sweden and Finland on NATO is therefore logical. Together, both countries have provided security and a neutral axis in Northern Europe since the end of World War II. Even so, the idea of forming a Nordic defence alliance, which was particularly popular among Swedish Social Democrats, was initially abandoned when Denmark and Norway signed the North Atlantic Treaty establishing NATO in 1949.

It is important to view these events in a historical context. As a consequence of the war with Russia in 1808–1809, Sweden was forced to cede Finland to Russia, and it remained part of the Russian Empire until 1917. Karl XIV Johan, the Swedish king imported from France in 1818, declared that in future Sweden would renounce any claim and would not seek to reconquer Finland. When war broke out in 1914, the nonsocialist government declared Sweden neutral, a decision which was supported by the Social Democrats. This doctrine laid the foundation for the Swedish policy of neutrality that has prevailed until the present and has secured peace for Sweden for more than 200 years. Finland has a Swedish-speaking minority and is constitutionally bilingual. Many Finns emigrated to Sweden and are a recognised national minority in Sweden. The links between the two countries remain extremely close: every new Swedish prime minister makes their first foreign visit to Helsinki.

Finland was the first to apply for NATO membership. One important reason for this is the country's geopolitical situation, with its very long border with Russia. Finland drew the immediate conclusion that Russia was no longer a reliable partner. Finland has a bitter historical experience of war with the Soviet Union; notably the Winter War of 1939–1940 and the Continuation War of 1941–1944.

The historical experiences of Finland and Sweden certainly played a decisive role in this outcome. Both countries became nonaligned after World War II, although the choices available to each country were quite different. As mentioned above, Finland had been part of Sweden until 1809, when the country became part of the tsarist Russian Empire. Liberation from Russia in 1917 was followed by a savage civil war. Stalin invaded Finland in 1939 in what was called the Winter War. When peace was concluded, Finland was forced to cede huge tracts of territory. During the Winter War, Sweden chose not to enter the war on Finland's side but provided substantial, perhaps decisive military aid. In this connection it is possible to draw a parallel with the current war in Ukraine. Swedish volunteers fought for Finland, but not in Swedish uniform. During the subsequent Continuation War, at first Finland recovered most of what it had previously ceded and conquered much of Karelia, which had been part of Russia. After Stalingrad, however, Finland was forced to retreat and sustained considerable territorial losses. In both cases the country's independence was put at risk. After 1945 the country's room for manoeuvre regarding security was limited and its independence circumscribed. Finland and the Soviet Union signed the "Agreement of Friendship, Cooperation, and Mutual Assistance" in 1948, which imposed severe restrictions on the country's room for manoeuvre – not least in the fields of foreign and security policy. The pact created a framework that circumscribed the country's freedom to act. The concept of "Finlandisation" came to imply a kind of enforced neutrality, intended to satisfy the Soviet Union's demands and interests. Leading Finnish politicians and diplomats acted with great skill to ensure Finnish independence. The treaty was renewed every ten years and was not repudiated until 1992. The fall of the Soviet Union paved the way for Finland's membership of the EU and a more intimate military cooperation with Sweden, the West and NATO.

Sweden decided not to join NATO after the end of World War II, and the idea of a Nordic defence alliance came to nothing. The Swedish standpoint as neutral may have dissuaded the Soviet Union from bullying Finland, as this might have pushed Sweden into the arms of NATO. However, in reality Sweden was not neutral since there was a considerable exchange of intelligence with the West and the US – a situation that was not officially recognised by the Swedish government.

At the beginning of the 1950s a Swedish surveillance plane was shot down by the Soviet air forces, which gave rise to diplomatic repercussions and subsequently led to volatile Swedish relations with the Soviet Union. Prior to 1809, Russia and Sweden had competed for influence with the countries in the Baltic region. In modern times, there have been a number of conflicts related to territorial borders in the Baltic. During the 1980s, relations between Sweden and the Soviet Union deteriorated in an alarming way, as Sweden was subjected to several incidences of submarine encroachment. On several occasions the Swedish fleet pursued submarines well within Swedish territorial waters, in the proximity of naval bases and installations. The Swedish navy resorted to using depth charges to force the submarines to surface. In 1982, a Soviet submarine equipped with nuclear missiles ran aground off Karlskrona, where the Swedish fleet has been stationed for centuries.

Nonalignment and neutrality reflected the image of Sweden as a country able to act independently between the political blocs during the Cold War, representing a tradition that came to be associated first and foremost with Olof Palme, the former prime minister. Although these are essential elements of the identity and pride of Swedish Social Democrats, Russia's aggression and Finland's unequivocal and prompt "yes" nevertheless prompted them to support NATO membership.

During the post-World War II period and the Cold War, Sweden positioned itself as a third force maintaining its neutrality between NATO and the Warsaw Pact. The Swedish model was viewed as a third alternative to communist dictatorship and the brutality of capitalism – at least the latter's American variety. Sweden did not join the European Economic

Community (EEC), preferring instead the European Free Trade Association (EFTA). Globally, Sweden supported alliance-free movements and struggles for national independence and democracy in former colonial countries of the Third World. Sweden also officially supported the African National Congress (ANC) in South Africa and National Liberation Front (NLF) in Vietnam. Sweden worked to defuse conflict between the two Cold War blocs and sought to provide liberation movements with an alternative to dependence on Soviet aid. It could be said that there is a correlation between the Swedish welfare model on the one side and Sweden's activities on the international stage on the other, as these evolved during the years 1945–1989 as elements of its ambition to be a neutral, alliance-free country. Sweden remained neutral and enjoyed peace for over 200 years. During the coronavirus crisis, however, critics of the Swedish pandemic strategy maintained that Sweden was "peace-damaged". This may be the case, as while Finland's decision to join NATO was made swiftly soon after the outbreak of the war in Ukraine, it took a little longer for Sweden to follow suit.

After 1989 there were adjustments in the Swedish definition of neutrality. The Swedish security doctrine became "alliance-free in time of peace, neutrality in time of war". However, this doctrine was subsequently revised in both its expression and content. Although the freedom from alliances remained intact, Sweden developed a comprehensive and increasingly complex cooperation with NATO, in particular within the "Partnership for Peace".

Immediately after the fall of the Berlin Wall, in 1992, Sweden revised the orientation of its security policy. It reaffirmed "Sweden's military non-allied status aimed at ensuring that our country could remain neutral in the event of war in our proximity". However, Sweden limited the area in which it would maintain neutrality, and also joined a number of peace-keeping missions in which Swedish soldiers were involved in combat – for example, in Afghanistan.

Sweden's security policy from 2002 noted that "having the possibility to remain neutral in the event of conflict in our vicinity has served us well". At the same time, while Sweden remained "alliance-free", it maintained that threats against its security "can best be repulsed jointly and in cooperation with other countries".

The entry of Sweden and Finland to the EU in 1995 entailed Sweden's participation in a political cooperation intended to prevent war on the European continent. The Swedish Defence Resolution of 2004 stated that it was highly unlikely "that Sweden would remain neutral in the event of armed aggression against another EU country". This logic also implied the reverse – namely, that other EU countries would respond in the same way. It was a case of solidarity for European security.

The year 2009 saw a further step in this direction. It was now emphasised that Sweden's security should be based on cooperation with other countries. Military alliances were still to be avoided, but a new security declaration stated that Sweden would not stand by passively if a neighbouring country were affected by civil unrest or military aggression. Sweden announced that it was willing to send – and receive – assistance even of a military nature. "This is based on the assumption that neutrality is not an option in the event of war in our vicinity," the declaration read. In this way, Sweden's policy of neutrality has come to be redefined step by step. As a result of Putin's war on Ukraine, the policy of nonalliance has also undergone reassessment.

At the outbreak of the war, all parties on the right of the Swedish political spectrum came out in favour of joining NATO. When the Social Democrats followed suit, the matter was settled. It was not an easy step for the Swedish labour movement to take. Historically, neutrality has enjoyed a broad consensus in Swedish politics. However, over recent years, it has primarily become a doctrine associated with social democracy. It has also been linked to the opposition to nuclear weapons – and yet now Sweden is applying to join an alliance which has such weapons in its arsenal.

Immediately after the outbreak of the war, Sweden pledged humanitarian and military aid to Ukraine. This was the first time since the Soviet invasion of Finland in 1939 that Sweden has supplied arms to another country while a conflict is in progress, which is an indication of how seriously Sweden views the situation. Uncertainty relating to the security situation brought about by the war naturally explains why Finland and Sweden have decided to join NATO and abandon their nonallied status. Once Finland took the initiative, it was not long before Sweden followed suit.

In Sweden there was pressure from the nonsocialist parties who, together with the Social Democrats, declared themselves in favour of joining NATO. Nevertheless, the applications of Sweden and Finland are not yet approved. At the time of writing, Turkey is still blocking acceptance, principally due to Sweden's position on the Kurdish question and demands that "terrorists" are extradited to Turkey. The new right-of-centre government has also declared its agreement to the placement of nuclear weapons and NATO bases in Sweden – both opposed by the Social Democrats.

There is a long tradition of cooperation among the Nordic countries. Since the 1950s there has been a common labour market, and passports were not required for Nordic citizens travelling between the Nordic countries well before the EU and Schengen. On the other hand, there has been little progress on more far-reaching political and defence cooperation.

Now, however, with the Swedish and Finnish bids to join NATO, the Nordic countries may become part of the same defensive alliance. Denmark, a founding NATO member, had declined to take part in the EU defence alliance until a recent referendum (on 1 June 2022), whereby a majority of Danes voted to enter this part of EU cooperation. With this decision, the Nordic countries are more in step with each other than ever before concerning both the EU and NATO. The final piece of the puzzle is Norway, which is closely linked to the EU through its membership of the European Economic Area (EEA) but which has refused full EU membership in two referenda (in 1972 and 1994). However, there remains a possibility that Norway will reappraise its standpoint in future. The brutal and terrifying developments in Europe have shown that war and crises can necessitate reappraisals which, only a short time before, would have seemed unthinkable. This is precisely what has happened over the last year in Sweden, Finland and Denmark.

The Nordic bloc comprises a group of highly developed and stable democratic countries. These are not only situated around the Baltic Sea but also, in a larger perspective, extend throughout the strategic Arctic region including Iceland, Greenland and the Faroe Islands (the latter two both part of the Kingdom of Denmark), and the Norwegian Svalbard archipelago.

The Nordic dimension in Northern Europe provides the opportunity for coordinated defence and greater security in a precarious time and in an insecure world. In an alarming and brutal way, the latest turn of events has transformed the conditions for the defence and security of the Nordic countries. The situation constitutes a new chapter in their history.

Further reading

Bengtsson, H. A. (2022) "The Scandinavian defence repositioning". *Progressive Post*, 9 June.

Brommesson, D. (2022) "Finland´s foreign and security policy: from bridge-building to the core of the West". Brief 5/2022, Swedish Institute of International Affairs.

Brommesson, D., A. Ekengren and A. Michalski (2022) "Sweden's foreign and security policy in a time of flux". Brief 7/2022, Swedish Institute of International Affairs.

Hultqvist, P. (2022) "Vi ska bygga ett folkförsvar" ("We will build a peoples' defence"). *Svenska Dagbladet*, 16 December.

Linde, A. (2022) "Statement of government policy in the parliamentary debate on foreign affairs, Friday 10 June 2022". Minister for Foreign Affairs Ann Linde, Government of Sweden.

Pillai, H. (2022) "A new era of Finnish foreign policy begins". Report, Centre for European Reform, 19 December 2022.

Swedish Armed Forces (2022) "Överbefälhavarens militära råd" ("The Commander-in-Chief's military advice"). FM2022-19979:13, 31 October.

Uwe Optenhögel

14 | China and Russia in the war over Ukraine: how resilient is the "unlimited" friendship?

Russian President Vladimir Putin and his circle have manoeuvred themselves and their country into a position that they had not envisaged. As things currently stand, little indicates that Putin will be able to fulfil his self-imposed mission of restoring Russia to imperial greatness within the borders of the Soviet Union. For its part, Beijing views Russia's war largely from the geopolitical perspective of a common stance against the West and NATO, rather than with regard to the actual events in Ukraine. Putin's war does, however, come at an inopportune time for China as its own development model is under pressure from all sides for the first time in decades. So far, the course of events suggests that China may be better off with a war-weakened Russia than with an imperially upgraded partner that would pose an ever-growing threat to the international system.

When Russia launched its attack on Ukraine on 24 February 2022, no political observer or military expert would have bet on the war continuing unabated one year later and that the supposedly much superior Russian army would still be stuck in the Donbas or even in retreat there – least of all, we must assume, Russian President Vladimir Putin.

However this war eventually ends, it has already unleashed dynamics with far-reaching global implications. It reinforces the deglobalisation tendencies that had been observable since the financial crisis of 2008–2009, and that were then accelerated by the Covid-19 pandemic. In geopolitical terms, new centres of power are emerging, while geo-economically, a reconfiguration of energy, production, distribution and financial systems is underway. These developments, brought about by Russia's war, challenge China's international status and its highly successful model of catch-up development. It is increasingly evident that wars involving great powers can no longer be contained regionally in a globalised world.

Putin's invasion of Ukraine, and its inherent potential to provoke chaos in the international system and the global economy, was therefore viewed by Beijing with a degree of scepticism from the outset.

The return of China and Russia to the international community

The Middle Kingdom spent decades presenting itself as a constructive member as it made its way back into the international community: neutral, committed to peace, and always ready to defend national territorial integrity and the right of peoples to self-determination, China participates in UN peacekeeping missions. China not only signed the Paris Climate Agreement, it also committed itself in its constitution to creating an ecological civilisation. A current policy document initiated by President Xi Jinping on the development strategy up to the 100th anniversary of the establishment of the People's Republic of China in 2049 states that the policy of reform and opening up will be continued and that China will work to achieve an international order that takes into account the interests of developing countries and renounces the politics of power and hegemony.

Over the same period, Russia returned to the international stage in a very different way. During the 30 years of China's unprecedented rise to become the world's largest trading power, Russia was not in a position to compete in the global economic and social arena and establish an attractive model of development. Instead, it has to a large degree remained mired at the stage of a commodity-dependent rentier economy. Against this background, Putin led Russia back into international politics, traumatised by what he considered to be the ignominious demise of the Soviet Union and frustrated by the arrogance and ignorance of an expansionist West. Starting with the modernisation of the army, he has led Russia based on the claim of being a world power. Since Putin's speech to the Munich Security Conference in 2007 at the latest, he has never missed an opportunity to support anti-Western, anti-American and antidemocratic forces. Russia has profiled itself as a military protagonist that is ready and able to engage in multiple types of intervention, including state terrorism, hybrid warfare, cyberattacks, fake news campaigns and the deployment of mercenary forces. The war of aggression in Ukraine, cloaked in the euphemism "special military operation" and in violation of international law, is the greatest adventure into which the president has plunged his country so far.

Over the past 20 years, this policy has been successively endowed with a philosophical and ideological superstructure. Right-wing nationalist ideologues such as Alexander Dugin combine pan-Slavic ideas with anti-Western and neoimperial Russian nationalism. They call for a "Russian world" (*Russkiy mir*) that relativises existing state borders and explicitly includes the diaspora, a comprehensive concept that addresses ideological, political, cultural, geopolitical and identity issues. This approach is supported by the Russian Orthodox Church, which wants to make the Russian world an outpost of Christian civilisation again. The concept of *Russkiy mir* has already been employed by Putin to legitimise Russia's annexation of Crimea. The establishment of the Russkiy Mir Foundation created an instrument to propagate the approach internationally – the Russian version of "soft power". Unfortunately, the West did not really take this doctrine seriously until the outbreak of the Ukraine war, which may be because the circle Putin draws upon is made up of conservative, anticommunist, nationalist thinkers who are largely unknown outside Russia. A BBC *Newsnight* interview with Dugin, the favoured philosopher of Putin's circle, made the Kremlin's view of the world abundantly clear: "Postmodernity shows that every so-called truth is a matter of believing. So, we believe in what we do, we believe in what we say. And that is the only way to define the truth. So, we have our special Russian truth."

From a military perspective, nothing is going to plan for Russia

Looking at the war in Ukraine as an example, it seems as if the apologists for the "special Russian truth" might no longer understand the world: hardly anything is going to plan for Russia, which has instead been confronted by a multitude of unpleasant surprises. Contrary to their expectations, the invasion has not been a blitzkrieg in which Russian troops were greeted by flower-waving Ukrainians as liberators delivering them from a government run by a drug-addled Nazi clique. Ukraine is putting up fierce, highly motivated, well-organised and so far successful resistance. The people are standing behind their elected government, and many Ukrainians are clearly prepared to fight and die for a life of freedom and self-determination. Putin's vision of a Russian world is obviously not an attractive alternative.

In military terms, the campaign has so far been something of a failure for Putin and his army, with enormous losses of men and materiel, glaring tactical and strategic mistakes by the military leadership at all levels, and major problems with morale, logistics and intelligence gathering by the services. Russian chains of command seem cumbersome and hierarchical. The military's modernisation of recent years seems to have entailed corruption on a massive scale. Putin thus has to live with the leading medium of liberal capitalism, *The Economist*, going with the leader headline: "How rotten is Russia's army?"[1] Neither his friends nor his enemies will have missed this, as his claim to be a player among the ranks of the great powers is based on the assertion that Russia possesses a highly modern, professional and powerful army. The consequences are symbolic humiliations such as the loss of the flagship of the Black Sea Fleet, the failed attempt to capture the Ukrainian capital Kyiv at the start of the war, the destruction of the strategically important Crimean Bridge and attacks on military airports that were supposed to be beyond the reach of Ukraine's weaponry. In addition, there were the recaptures of the regions around Kharkiv and Kherson in the autumn of 2022.

This turn of events was due to the strategic competence, obviously superior Western weaponry and sheer determination of the Ukrainians. In the absence of military successes on the battlefield, Russia has since the summer of 2022 turned to destroying Ukraine's strategic infrastructure with the aim of terrorising and demoralising the population. The sham referenda in the four Donbas regions were purely for home consumption. They were not recognised by foreign countries and have no military significance. The war continues, and all indications suggest that it may drag on for much longer. Against this background, the Russian side has yet to achieve any of its war aims. NATO's military leaders must be scratching their heads at this turn of events, certain that they could easily manage this opponent in a conventional war: unfortunately, however, Russia is a nuclear power.

The pressure on Putin is increasing

How the conflict is playing out is becoming increasingly problematic for Putin in terms of both domestic and foreign policy. Domestically, the progress of the war is beginning to undermine his reputation as a leader. The population has almost become accustomed to suicidal oil

---

1   *The Economist*, 30 April 2022. URL: https://www.economist.com/leaders/2022/04/30/how-rotten-is-russias-army.

executives falling out of windows. There are now about a dozen cases of business leaders who have lost their lives in mysterious circumstances. And the fact that Alexander Dugin's daughter, a journalist and ardent war supporter, could be blown up in her SUV in the middle of Moscow must have been disconcerting for the Russian public.[2] The question of how long the narrative that this is a special operation in which everything is going according to plan will continue to be believed by the Russian public is one that is increasingly being asked. The partial mobilisation in the autumn brought the war home to Russian society, even to those who had ignored it until then. The political leadership, however, is continuing to do its best to spare the children of the middle classes from Moscow and Saint Petersburg, and it is recruiting the vast majority of new troops from among ethnic minorities and rural areas.

Developments on the economic front present even more of a challenge for the regime. Although the Russian economy is proving more resilient than many in the West had anticipated, comprehensive Western sanctions are having an ever-greater impact. Despite a steep reduction in its sales of fossil fuels, significant price increases on the global market have made it possible for Russia to stabilise the rouble and its export revenues, allowing it to consolidate its state budget and continue financing the war. Imports have, however, collapsed, and hundreds of international companies have left Russia. This has particularly affected industrial sectors that have modernised in recent years, such as the oil industry and agriculture, the latter of which represents a significant export market, but it has also impacted all sectors that depend on access to foreign technology and spare parts. In the opinion of Russian economists who have moved to the West during the course of the war, the country's dependence on secondary imports has meant that this effect has been greater than the West might have anticipated.

The decisive factor will therefore be the behaviour of suppliers from countries that have not joined the sanctions. These include many important emerging countries and above all, of course, China. Russia hopes that these countries will enable it to compensate for the loss of Western technology, yet this hope seems to be dashed by foreign trade statistics, which provide no evidence of increased Russian trade with these countries. Chinese exports to Russia are falling at the same rate

---

2   "Dugin-Tochter stirbt bei Autoexplosion". *Tagesschau*, 21 August 2022. URL: https://www.tagesschau.de/ausland/asien/dugin-moskau-101.html.

as Europe's exports. In other words, the secondary sanctions are working: any company in China or elsewhere that supplies goods to Russia must expect to be targeted by sanctions. The embargo on dual-use electronic goods, which generates supply problems in arms production, is particularly impacting Russia. Western military experts think that the reason Russia is now using very few cruise missiles is because it lacks the necessary Western technology. This also applies to numerous other technologically sophisticated weapons systems. In the civilian sector, Russian aviation is beginning to cannibalise itself for the same reasons. The realisation seems to be slowly dawning that the current sanctions, in contrast to those applied after the 2014 annexation of Crimea, are more comprehensive and better monitored, and hence the disruption of supply chains will not be over in a few months and it will be impossible to substitute the missing imports in any realistic manner. This means that nobody is benefiting economically from the crisis, something that is likely to become a problem for Putin sooner or later.

China's ambivalent attitude to the war

Officially at least, China is neutral and stands for peace, and has neither supported nor condemned the war. Even so, its neutrality is clearly pro-Russian and anti-American, underlined by the fact that the state media and China's censored internet push the Kremlin's line with regard to the causes and course of the war. While there is some controversy within China over the position it should adopt vis-à-vis Russia, Beijing is not a mediator for a negotiated solution. Nevertheless, China is probably the only state that could exert influence on Putin. After a year, it is clear that China views Russia's war less in terms of the actual developments in Ukraine than from the geopolitical perspective of a common stance against the West and NATO. This view is backed up in diplomatic terms. For example, Moscow supported Beijing when US Congresswoman Nancy Pelosi, former speaker of the House, visited Taipei, although Russia had never previously been concerned about the Taiwan question.

From an economic point of view, however, the situation looks very different. For some time now, the People's Republic has been in a phase of development that has seen it switch from quantitative to qualitative growth and a greater focus on developing its domestic market. This relies to a great extent on open markets, functioning supply chains and a rules-based international order. In contrast to Russia, it is not in China's interest to destroy the existing international order.

China's successful development model is reaching its limits

The US has regarded China as a key geopolitical adversary for quite some time, even before the election of Donald Trump. From the EU's point of view, China has gone from being its largest market to being seen as a strategic rival, and the European Parliament suspended ratification of a laboriously negotiated investment agreement with China even before the war began. Given the Russian aggression in Ukraine, if the US, Europe, Japan and countries such as South Korea, Canada, Australia and New Zealand decide to prioritise their security and defence over economic and welfare issues and are prepared to make the sacrifices such a commitment would entail, this would have a negative effect on China's trade. Furthermore, the sheer scale of the recent Western sanctions, which transcend anything known before, will have far-reaching effects on the global economy. China is vulnerable in this regard, as the US, Europe and Japan are still by far the most important markets for Chinese exports. Should its market access to these countries be significantly restricted, China would need to compensate for the lost trade in other markets or its own domestic market, neither of which currently seem likely alternatives.

Not only is China suffering from a decline in its export markets, but the West is also making China's access to high-tech products more difficult. It is not only the US that has imposed sanctions on Huawei and semiconductor companies. European governments have also recently halted Chinese acquisition of cutting-edge technology. Putin's war is likewise having a negative impact on how China is viewed in the eastern parts of Central Europe. The 16+1 discussion and negotiation format established by China in 2012 with Central and Eastern European countries, which many in the EU saw as a Trojan horse, can be seen as having largely failed. Empty promises on the Chinese side and its position on Russia contradict the interests of the participating European countries.

In addition, the Belt and Road Initiative, China's prestige development policy project, is faltering. Buffeted by the aftermath of the pandemic, inflation and the impact of the Ukraine war, many countries in the Global South are struggling to repay their loans, in part due to China's self-serving lending conditions. The People's Republic seems to be driving its Silk Road partners into a debt trap. If China wants to escape a loss of reputation among countries in the Global South and prevent a series of defaults (with some $118 billion estimated to be at risk), it should not make the mistake Western lenders made in the 1980s and 1990s of rescheduling loans and letting countries bleed further. Beijing claims to offer a better model of development finance. But being the world's largest lender today, it now has the opportunity to demonstrate its ability to handle developmental challenges more responsibly than the West it frequently criticises.

Cyclical and structural problems in the domestic market

The country's domestic market faces major cyclical and structural challenges: high levels of private and public debt, an imploding real estate sector, over-indebted banks and nonfunctioning banking supervision, the continuing ageing of the population, and close to 20% youth unemployment are impacting China's growth. This is accompanied by extreme income inequality, continuing corruption, an explosion in housing costs and embryonic welfare state institutions that are not yet able to compensate for declining demand and cushion its social impact. A further factor is the ever-increasing cost of China's zero-Covid strategy. The recent lockdowns in Shanghai and Chengdu have left their mark on China's economy. The growth target of 5.5% set out in the country's economic policy had to be reduced to below 3%. It is also becoming clear that the country is not prepared for the Omicron variant and that its own vaccines are unable to compete with those of the West. Stringent enforcement of quarantine rules has revealed the political dimension of the zero-Covid strategy. The population is reacting with increasing incomprehension and opposition to the state's harshness, which is unlikely to be changed by the party's volte-face in early December and abrupt abandonment of its zero-Covid strategy. Whether the government's decision is a reaction to the growing violent unrest or to the economic costs of zero-Covid is of only secondary importance. What the new radical pragmatism shows is that the party is willing to expose a population with low vaccination rates, a comparatively ineffective national vaccine and a poorly equipped health system to the threat of unrestrained contact with the virus. The human and economic costs of this experiment remain to be seen, but it is clear that this policy is hardly likely to build confidence between the government and the people.

If we consider the Covid years together with the economic problems outlined above, it seems that the population's trust in the leadership has dipped for the first time in decades. The Chinese development compact between the people and the leadership – which states: "We (the government/party) will ensure a continuous increase in prosperity. In return, you (the people) will forego political participation and codetermination" – is apparently losing its appeal and its identity-forming power. Western economists are already predicting that China may be heading for a "Japanisation" of its economy (an allusion to Japan's two lost decades of low growth and deflation) or find itself in a middle-income trap in the foreseeable future.

Given this background, it is clear that Putin's war comes at an inopportune time. China would have preferred a quick end to the war. The campaign, which has so far been unsuccessful for Russia, has only led to an escalation of the conflict and the increasing brutality of the fighting, including terrorising and committing war crimes against the civilian population. Beijing's contradictory stance on the war is also becoming increasingly difficult to communicate internationally: supporting Russia verbally in all aspects detrimental to the West, but at the same time respecting Western sanctions and not providing Russia with any military support so far. Furthermore, China took full advantage of Putin's weakness by increasing its influence in Russia's Central Asian backyard at the SCO (Shanghai Cooperation Organisation) summit in Samarkand in September, where Xi Jinping made unmistakably clear to his "best friend" what he considers responsible great power policy to be; namely to "instil stability and positive energy in a world of chaos". Beijing has also plainly rejected Russia's threats to deploy nuclear weapons, as was recently again made clear during the German chancellor's visit to Beijing and at the G20 summit in Bali.

Putin should therefore be cautious about expecting China to help him circumvent Western sanctions openly. Tellingly, while China has signed partnership agreements with Russia, it has not formed an alliance that might entail any commitment to mutual support. Russia should be under no illusions: China has always been an exceptionally self-interested power in international politics. China is pursuing its integration into international structures with a long-term perspective, in a planned manner and against the background of its deep-rooted historical realisation that its phases of international isolation (in the 19th century and during the Cultural Revolution) were to the country's detriment and caused it to be left behind technologically. No Chinese leader can afford to seriously jeopardise the enormously successful development model just because a friendly country – plainly based on a disturbed perception of reality – has unleashed a war that it does not want or is unable to end.

Unlike Russia, China can determine for itself how it emerges from the conflict. It will analyse the sanctions against Russia and their impact. It is thoroughly monitoring the positioning of and the mood in the Global South. Here, one can observe a diplomatic race between China and the West for the dominant narrative on the war and its origins. As regards its Taiwan policy, Beijing will observe the course of the war and weigh up what risks eventual actions against the island would entail. The Russian army and its weaponry have to date been held in high esteem in Chinese security and military circles. This reputation has in all likelihood been tarnished given the developments on the battlefield. Everything indicates that China may be better off with a war-weakened Russia than with an imperially upgraded partner that would pose an ever-growing threat to the international system.

Putin is playing a high-stakes game

The Russian president and his circle have manoeuvred themselves and their country into a position that they did not envisage, and it is becoming increasingly difficult to imagine how they could extricate themselves successfully from it. The Russian leadership has largely underestimated the determination of the Western alliance. The West and Europe remain united – despite all the difficulties the repercussions of the war are causing. Sanctions are being tightened, Ukraine is being supplied with increasingly heavier weapons and NATO is about to be enlarged by Sweden and Finland, countries with excellent military capabilities and a border with Russia.

Putin pretends to be waging the war in Russia's interests. But Russia is a multiethnic state, and there are probably enough ethnic groups who already think that this is not their war. Putin is now not only risking himself and his regime but the Russian Federation as a whole. Economic pressure and military ineffectiveness have so far only led Russia to raise the stakes. From Washington to Berlin, people should not fool themselves: against the backdrop of the historical, philosophical and ideological construct of ideas to which Putin refers, the operation in Ukraine is seen as part of a much larger battle with the West and NATO for Russia's survival and for the continued existence of the "Russian world". To secure the support of its own public, the Kremlin is creating a type of endgame mood to keep open the option of employing all military means. By hardening his position in this way, Putin is removing the opportunity for himself and the Russian elites that surround him to retreat. As things currently stand, little indicates that he will be able to fulfil his self-imposed mission of restoring Russia to imperial greatness within the borders of the Soviet Union. The opposite scenario could well be the case, with Russia emerging from the conflict humiliated, weakened and diminished. This would guarantee Putin a place in the history books – as the leader who finally gambled away Russia's greatness.

Further reading

"Dossier: Russlands Krieg gegen die Ukraine und seine Folgen". Stiftung Wissenschaft und Politik website. URL: https://www.swp-berlin.org/themen/dossiers/russlands-krieg-gegen-die-ukraine.

Farrer, M. (2022) "Point of no return: crunch time as China tries to fend off property crash". *The Guardian*, 29 August 2022. URL: https://www.theguardian.com/business/2022/aug/28/crunch-time-china-tries-to-fend-off-property-crash-global-economy

Kofman, M. (2018) "Raiding and international brigandry: Russia's strategy for great power competition". *War on the Rocks*, 14 June. URL: https://warontherocks.com/2018/06/raiding-and-international-brigandry-russias-strategy-for-great-power-competition/.

Roach, S. S. (2022) "China's growth sacrifice". *Project Syndicate*, 23 Aug. URL: https://www.project-syndicate.org/commentary/three-reasons-for-china-growth-slowdown-since-2012-by-stephen-s-roach-2022-08.

Stahl, G. (2022) *China: Zukunftsmodel oder Albtraum? Europa zwischen Partnerschaft und Konfrontation* (Bonn: J. H. W. Dietz).

The Economist (2022) "Xi Jinping won't ditch Vladimir Putin, for now. China's goal in Ukraine is Western disunity and failure, more than a Russian triumph". Editorial, 15 September. URL: https://econ.st/40St0wi.

Watkins, S. (2022) "Five wars in one: the battle for Ukraine". *New Left Review*, 137, September/October.

Zizek, S. (2022) "War in a world that stands for nothing". *Project Syndicate*, 18 April. URL: https://www.project-syndicate.org/commentary/russia-ukraine-war-highlights-truths-about-global-capitalism-by-slavoj-zizek-2022-04.

Aline Burni Gomes

15 | The Russian aggression and the future of the BRICS cooperation

Against the backdrop of Russia's war in Ukraine and the West's coordinated and unified response, Brazil, India, China and South Africa have refrained from openly condemning Russia, albeit for different reasons. What can be expected now from the BRICS cooperation? Initially projected to diverge due to their heterogeneity, the members of the BRICS group have continued to work together and converge on some fronts of global politics. Pragmatism is likely to keep driving the BRICS cooperation, with China remaining its main beneficiary.

Champion of the current global liberal order, the West was caught by surprise when clear worldwide condemnation of Russia's full-scale invasion of Ukraine on 24 February 2022 did not occur, with a number of (relevant) countries in Asia, Africa and Latin America taking ambiguous stands regarding responsibility for the war and the adoption of sanctions against Russia. President Vladimir Putin sought to increase the resilience of the Russian economy before launching the attack, declaring a "friendship without limits"[1] with China's Xi Jinping at a summit in Beijing only 20 days earlier, consolidating the deepening economic and strategic partnership with China, and at the same time increasing the Russian Central Bank's international reserves. However, Russia had already long been strengthening its ties with developing countries through increased military and development cooperation, and in trade and other areas. The BRICS group has been one tool for such South–South cooperation.

---

1   "Joint Statement of the Russian Federation and the People's Republic of China on the International Relations Entering a New Era and the Global Sustainable Development". President of Russia website, 4 February 2002. URL http://en.kremlin.ru/supplement/5770.

Against the background of Western sanctions on Russia, both China and India have increased their purchases of Russian oil,[2] offered at a discount price. And yet it is not only material interests that help explain the ambiguity of the BRICS members regarding the Ukraine war. Over recent years, Brazil and India have considered it more advantageous to cultivate good relations with Moscow, Beijing and Washington simultaneously, not generating animosity with the US but as a way to counterbalance the latter. Therefore, to explain the positioning of the other BRICS countries based only on a full ideological alignment with Putin's Russia would be too simplistic and inaccurate. Instead, the BRICS stance seems to be mainly driven by pragmatic considerations of an economic, political and/or geopolitical nature.

While their arguments differ, one common trait of Russia's fellow BRICS members is their overall disinclination to explicitly condemn Russia as the aggressor or support the sanctions led by the West. Instead, the BRICS countries have taken a pragmatic approach to the conflict, trying to both maximise their advantages and question US global hegemony, while at the same time limiting the disadvantages arising as consequences of the war, such as rising energy prices and disrupted food supply chains. Participation in the BRICS cooperation over the last decade has led to proximity and built trust among the members of the club and, although not ensuring convergence on all political issues, has encouraged members to avoid creating a sense of malaise among themselves. In the present situation, none of the other BRICS states seem willing to explicitly go against Russia on the international stage.

While not the only countries to avoid adopting a clear stance on the conflict, the position of the BRICS is particularly relevant to the future of the global order and the rebalancing of power due to their strong economic relevance (particularly that of China) and fundamental ambition to reform the multilateral order beyond the Western liberal model – one of the drivers of the BRICS cooperation. On the one hand, the BRICS countries are said to be underdeveloped, having failed to deliver as much as first expected of them. On the other hand, to understand the power of the BRICS bloc and its potential, it is necessary to extrapolate a like-minded, values-based logic of the kind that unites the West; except that in the case of the BRICS, it should be understood more as a coalition based on interests and issues. Although such cooperation is not sufficient to resolve historically divisive questions, such as border disputes between

---

2   Menon, S. (2022) "Ukraine crisis: who is buying Russian oil and gas?" *BBC*, 6 December. URL: https://www.bbc.com/news/world-asia-india-60783874.

China and India, it is an important motor to promote convergence on topics of common interest and to challenge Western hegemony.

Against this background, this chapter aims to briefly discuss how the BRICS countries (except Russia) have responded to Russia's aggression against Ukraine.

What is the BRICS?

The term BRIC was first used in the financial world, coined by Goldman Sachs economist Jim O'Neill in 2001 to highlight the economic potential of Brazil, Russia, India and China in his famous paper, "Building better global economic BRICs", which predicted that "over the next ten years, the weight of the BRICs and especially China in world GDP will grow".[3] Following informal meetings from 2006, it was only in 2009 that Brazil, Russia, India and China took ownership of the term and held their first official summit in Yekaterinburg, Russia. South Africa joined the club in 2010, adding the capital "S" to make the current BRICS acronym. Initially focusing on cooperation in finance, the birth of the BRICS as a political group was marked by the 2008 international financial crisis, which sparked a crisis of legitimacy in the international financial order as a profound recession shook up developed countries, while emerging economies managed to maintain relative stability. The financial crisis was one key element not only in strengthening the narrative of multipolarisation but also in transforming the BRICS into a political grouping that attempted to develop common positions in several areas, starting with global financial governance but expanding to international security, development and other areas. Since 2009 the BRICS leaders have convened 14 formal meetings and 9 informal meetings; their combined population amounts to 3.23 billion and their combined GDP to more than $23 trillion.

Even though the BRICS emerged against the backdrop of the 2008 crisis, the economic meltdown was not the only driver. A complex combination of factors motivated the emergence of the BRICS grouping, including a clear shift in global economic power away from the West and towards the East, together with an impasse in sharing global economic decision-making power between the West and the rising East. Also contributing were violations of international rules by the US, for instance the latter's resort to violence to protect the order, as well as the West's abuse

---

3   O'Neill, J. (2011) "Building better global economic BRICs". Global Economics Paper 66, Goldman Sachs. URL: https://www.goldmansachs.com/insights/archive/archive-pdfs/build-better-brics.pdf.

and misuse of financial and diplomatic sanctions against most BRICS states and other noncompliant developing countries.[4] The BRICS cooperation has been largely interpreted as a reaction to the Western model of international liberal order, and as an attempt mainly to reform the international financial system, but also the political order, notably multilateral institutions such as the UN.

Most analysts of the BRICS have seen little potential for the group due to its political and economic heterogeneity. Economically, Russia and Brazil are big commodity exporters, whereas China is a large commodity importer. In the area of trade, China is a proponent of the Doha Round, while India is a sceptic. Politically, Brazil, India and South Africa were vibrant democracies in the 2000s, while China and Russia have a history of authoritarian governments. Among the BRICS, all except India are signatories of the Non-Proliferation Treaty (NPT). While India is believed to possess nuclear weapons, Brazil and South Africa do not. Permanent members of the UN Security Council, Russia and China are among the five countries officially recognised as holding nuclear weapons. Mohammed Nuruzzaman describes the BRICS grouping as a potential challenger but not a serious threat to the existing liberal world order due to its real ideological, political and strategic limitations[5].

However, one key unifying element that is often overlooked is precisely the global project of all four initial members of the BRICS (prior to South Africa's accession in 2010), who committed to jointly push for further reform of global financial structures at the first informal meeting of their foreign ministers on the sidelines of the UN General Assembly in 2006. Since then, all BRICS communiqués have called for reform of international structures, in particular the International Monetary Fund (IMF) and the World Bank Group, which "should move forward and be guided towards a more equitable voice and participation balance between advanced and developing countries".[6] Oliver Stuenkel considers the BRICS grouping an interesting political category precisely because of its members' voiced global ambitions, though these are vaguely defined. He further stresses that no emerging powers outside of this group have a systematic engagement in the UN Security Council.

4   Nuruzzaman, M. (2020) "Why BRICS is no threat to the post-war liberal world order". *International Studies*, 57(1): 51–66. DOI: 10.1177/0020881719884449

5   Ibid.

6   Stuenkel, O. (2020) *The BRICS and the Future of Global Order*, 2nd edition (Lanam, MD: Lexington Books).

Over time, the BRICS has become more deeply institutionalised and more closely convergent on diverse political issues. Although there is no permanent BRICS secretariat to date, two major financial initiatives have been launched: the New Development Bank (NDB) and the Contingent Reserve Arrangement (CRA). The NDB was expected to invest in sustainable development projects in Eurasia and is viewed as an alternative to the World Bank. In turn, the CRA, founded as a safety net to help member states weather financial crises, is viewed as a countermeasure to the IMF.[7]

BRICS members have gradually adopted a common stand on a host of crucial international issues. In March 2014, the BRICS countries abstained from a UN General Assembly vote on Russia's annexation of Crimea. They also directly or indirectly obstructed the US plan for regime change in Syria. During the Arab Spring, the BRICS formed a united front against Western powers to prevent a vote on resolutions likely to break the sovereignty of repressive states. They all voted for Security Council Resolution 1970, which placed sanctions on Libya. Several weeks later, however, they abstained (except for South Africa) from the decisive vote on Resolution 1973, which paved the way for NATO's military intervention. In one way or another, all the BRICS states expressed the view that NATO had overstepped the rights created by Resolution 1973 in Libya, and they feared a repeat of this pattern in Syria.[8]

In 2014 the BRICS (except Russia) signalled their opposition to Western attempts to pull Russia out of the G20. Except for Brazil, they went further: while China and South Africa blamed NATO for the conflict, India mobilised to help Russia maintain its trade ties.

Concerns raised by Western liberals that the BRICS would undermine the global liberal order have resurfaced in the context of Russia's 2022 invasion of Ukraine, with recent news emerging that other authoritarian-leaning states such as Egypt, Iran, Saudi Arabia, Turkey and Argentina have either applied or are considering applying to join the BRICS. However, for some analysts, such as Zaki Laidi,[9] the BRICS countries do not seek to form an anti-Western political coalition based on a counterproposal or radically different vision of the world, but are concerned with maintaining

---

7   Liu, M. (2016) "BRICS development: a long way to a powerful economic club and new international organization". *Pacific Review*, 29(3): 443–453. DOI: 10.1080/09512748 .2016.1154688

8   Laidi, Z. (2011) "The BRICS against the West". CERI Strategy Papers, Sciences Po. URL: https://www.sciencespo.fr/ceri/sites/sciencespo.fr.ceri/files/n11_112011.pdf.

9   Ibid.

their independence of judgement and national action in a world that is increasingly interdependent economically and socially. To some extent, the reactions of Brazil, India, China and South Africa to Russia's war on Ukraine reflect the search for greater autonomy, nonalignment and consolidation of an international position more aligned with their own self-interest. While China's "neutral" position has been leaning towards supporting Russia, it is less clear that Brazil, India and – to a lesser extent – South Africa would look for direct confrontation with the West and the US. Their stances have been mostly justified by pragmatism and the search for autonomy from the hegemonic powers, inserted within other trends characterising their foreign policies in recent decades.

Ideological convergence or pragmatism? Interpreting the BRICS response

One common feature of BRICS countries has been their alleged neutrality regarding Russia's war against Ukraine. While China has been more open about supporting Russia, India, South Africa and Brazil have tried to walk the diplomatic tightrope over the war, maintaining ambiguous positions. They have neither openly criticised Russia nor supported the Western-led sanctions, but have instead advocated negotiations to end the war and reach peace as soon as possible. Among the three resolutions adopted by the UN General Assembly in the course of 2022, the BRICS mostly abstained (see Table 15.1). China even voted against the resolution adopted on 7 April 2022 calling for the withdrawal of Russian troops from Ukrainian territory. Brazil voted in favour of two resolutions, adopted on 24 March and 12 October, but abstained from the one adopted on 7 April. Nevertheless, the government of then Brazilian President Jair Bolsonaro was ambiguous and incoherent over condemning Russia and taking clear sides. Following the invasion, then Brazilian Foreign Minister Carlos França said his country's stance was one of "impartiality", not "indifference", and that it sought peace. He further added: "Brazil's position is clear [...] We are on the side of world peace. We think we can reach that [peace] by helping to find a way out [of the war], not by taking sides."[10]

---

10 "Brazil won't take sides over Russia's invasion of Ukraine – foreign minister". *Euronews*, 9 March 2022. URL: https://www.euronews.com/2022/03/09/us-ukraine-crisis -brazil.

Table 15.1. Votes of the BRICS (except Russia) on UN General Assembly resolutions on Russia's aggression against Ukraine.

	Resolution adopted on 24 March 2022 deploring the aggression committed by Russia against Ukraine	Resolution adopted on 7 April 2022 calling for the withdrawal of Russian troops from the entire territory of Ukraine	Resolution adopted on 12 October 2022 condemning Russia's illegal referenda in regions of Ukraine and demanding reversal of its annexation declaration
Brazil	In favour	Abstention	In favour
China	Abstention	Against	Abstention
India	Abstention	Abstention	Abstention
South Africa	Abstention	Abstention	Abstention
General vote	In favour: 141 Against: 5 Abstentions: 5	In favour: 93 Against: 24 Abstentions: 58	In favour: 143 Against: 5 Abstentions: 35

Although Bolsonaro shares common characteristics with Putin – notably authoritarianism, ultranationalism, conservatism and the centrality of strongmen – what better explains Brazil's position is not this apparent ideological convergence. Two main factors account for its ambivalent stand on the war: first, Brazil's diplomatic tradition of noninterventionism and its foreign policy seeking autonomy; and second, its important trade ties with Russia. On the trade dimension, Brazil is a major commodity-exporting economy and the world's largest producer and exporter of soybeans. In 2021, Brazil exported 86 million tons of soybeans, more than two-thirds to China alone. At the same time, Brazil is also an importer of fertilisers to produce soy and other crops. Some 85% percent of its fertilisers are imported, the equivalent to 40 million tons, with Russia accounting for 23% of this. Since the end of the USSR, Russia has increased its ties with Brazil and became a significant partner. In addition to the issue of fertiliser imports, potential logistic bottlenecks and payment problems generated by the sanctions on Russia, as well as rising oil prices, have become major concerns for Brazil, especially among the agribusiness sector, one of the main supporters of Bolsonaro, who ran for reelection in October 2022.

However, even before Bolsonaro's government and the Workers' Party administrations of Luiz Inácio Lula da Silva and Dilma Rousseff, Brazilian foreign policy refrained from any unrestricted alliance with the US and aimed at preserving a degree of autonomy for Brazil in an increasingly interdependent world. Concerns over the US were driven by its excessive influence in the Latin American region, including on the domestic politics of some countries – and not always in the direction of promoting democracy and the rule of law. Rousseff resisted pressure from the US to "uninvite" Putin from the BRICS summit in Fortaleza in July 2014. Even so, despite their differences, Brazil managed to preserve cordial ties with the US and Europe. Over recent decades, the rise of competing powers such as China, as well as Russia's resurgence, has been beneficial to Brazil from the perspective of placing some limitation on the US's room for manoeuvre in Latin America. Consequently, the South American giant has developed a flexible and ambiguous international position, avoiding excessive ties with either of the great powers. This has been reflected in Brazil's stand on the Ukraine conflict, and no leading policymaker or presidential candidate – including Lula – proposed joining the West in imposing sanctions on Russia or isolating Putin diplomatically, despite Brazil's official vote for the resolution of 24 March 2022. Despite the ideological shift of Brazil's government in 2023, President Lula da Silva continues to prioritise "talks about peace" over explicit disapproval of Russia, support for sanctions or dispatch of weapons to Ukraine.[11]

The Russian attack has put India's diplomatic balancing act between Moscow and Washington under pressure, as well as threatening its security vis-à-vis China's growing power in the Indo-Pacific region. India's position has evolved since Russia's annexation of the Crimean Peninsula in 2014, when New Delhi was sympathetic to Russia and considered "all parties had legitimate interests" at stake. Before 24 February, India's proximity to Russia had been beneficial to New Delhi's national interest in terms of having a steady defence supplier and potential mediator in Sino-Indian conflicts. India and Russia have had a deep relationship for decades and Russia accounted for $5.51 billion of the $12.4 billion that India spent between 2018 and 2021 on arms imports.[12] Short-term

---

11   John, T. (2023) "Lula says Brazil is no more divided than the US as he meets Biden". *CNN*, 11 February. URL: https://edition.cnn.com/2023/02/10/americas/brazil-president-lula-interview-intl-latam/index.html.

12   Ghoshal, D., and A. Ahmed (2022) "India, world's biggest buyer of Russian arms, looks to diversify suppliers". *Reuters*, 18 May. URL: https://reut.rs/3K6LmD7.

---

economic interests also help understand India's stance towards Russia. Bilateral trade between India and Russia reached an all-time high of about $18,229 million between April and August 2022, mainly due to the upward trend in trade of oil and fertilisers. Thus one reason India does not appear to support Western sanctions against Russia is because of their impact on such oil and fertilisers trading.

However, the war has created several issues of discomfort for New Delhi, which is also likely to be negatively affected in the longer term. In order to maintain good relations with both the US and Russia, India abstained from the UN votes and only stated that it is "strongly against this conflict". It has been argued that India's ambiguous position is not a reflection of its views on values and norms in world politics, nor motivated by supporting a counternarrative against the West. The ambiguity might instead be justified to avoid any uneasiness with Russia, not only for economic interests, but also because India cannot afford another unfriendly neighbour in the region. As explained in an article in Indian magazine *Frontline*:[13]

> In the broader region, India is caught in the whirlwind of a number of geopolitical contestations: China's aggressive rise, displacing India from its traditional sphere of influence in South Asia and in the Indian Ocean region; the Taliban's return in Afghanistan, where India suddenly finds itself friendless after having invested over $3 billion in development assistance; the potential coming together of countries such as China, Pakistan, Afghanistan, Iran and Russia to fill the regional power vacuum under Chinese leadership.

Geopolitically, this convergence of risks has put India in a particularly difficult position.

The war has weakened Russia and further increased the dominance of China in Eurasia. New Delhi still relies on its US/Western alliances to counterbalance China's power. As the conflict has evolved, India has articulated its position against the war more robustly to counter criticism that it has been supportive of Russia, but it still has not held Moscow responsible for the invasion and will likely not alter its policy of importing cheap Russian energy. One of New Delhi's concerns is that if Putin is further isolated, Russia could be drawn even closer to China. India's ties with China have been strained over disputes in the Himalayas. In the event of

---

13   Jacob, H. (2022) "India offers nuanced response to changing tides of the Ukraine war". *Frontline*, 6 October. URL: https://frontline.thehindu.com/world-affairs/india-offers -nuanced-response-to-changing-tides-of-the-ukraine-war/article65958364.ece.

condemning Russia, India would end up with an additional hostile power in an already hostile neighbourhood. If it explicitly supports Russia, New Delhi would risk losing the political and diplomatic support of the US and the West vis-à-vis China. Harsh geopolitical circumstances and national interests therefore seem to better account for India's response.

China has not vocally condemned Russia's invasion of Ukraine, calling for "dialogue and a peaceful resolution" of the conflict, though implicitly supporting Russia. Economic cooperation between China and Russia has grown, and the former has profited from cheap energy supplies no longer absorbed by Europe. What seems most important for China is that Putin's war should not cause collateral damage, especially to the Chinese economy. Beijing does not have an interest in continuation of this war, and has closely observed the articulation of the West in isolating Russia. It is not to its benefit to destroy an international order that has allowed China's unprecedented economic rise and the consolidation of an allegedly successful development model.

South Africa is an example of a country in the Global South with historical attachments to the Western model based on markets and democratic values, which has nevertheless avoided directly criticising Russia. Pretoria has abstained in several UN votes condemning Russia and has also called for a negotiated settlement to bring the conflict to an end. South Africa's narrative on the Russian invasion has focused on the West's hypocrisy – its double standards on multilateralism, and the use of force to change regimes – and on framing the war as one between Russia and NATO, and thus rooted in NATO's eastward expansion. According to Elizabeth Sidiropoulos, two elements help explain South Africa's position.[14] The first is its independent and nonaligned foreign policy as a form of resistance to great power conflicts, which has been invigorated by the pressure to take sides. In addition, as part of its foreign policy tradition, South Africa has advocated for a fairer, more consistent multilateral system and is generally opposed to the adoption of unilateral sanctions against countries by the West. The second is the solidarity shown by the African National Congress (ANC) government with parties and countries that supported the national liberation struggle against apartheid and fights for independence. The BRICS, for instance, also represents an important channel of international solidarity and has

14   Sidiropoulos, E. (2022) "How do Global South politics of non-alignment and solidarity explain South Africa's position on Ukraine?" Brooking's Insitute website. URL: https://www.brookings.edu/blog/africa-in-focus/2022/08/02/how-do-global-south-politics-of-non-alignment-and-solidarity-explain-south-africas-position-on-ukraine/.

remained an important body for mutual support between its smallest African member and rising powers like China.

What to expect from the BRICS cooperation

As suggested by its positioning in the Russian war against Ukraine, the BRICS cooperation is likely to continue based on pragmatic interests, rather than ideological convergence. It has functioned as a platform to build trust and advocate for the interests of developing countries, as well as reforms in the global order, even though it has not made the member countries converge in all areas. In the context of the war, Russia has revived the BRICS out of necessity, in an attempt to keep allies and prevent full isolation on the global stage. Nevertheless, the BRICS cooperation is largely a story about the economic rise of China.

Since China has become the second greatest economic power in the world, it has seen its economic relations with the other BRICS countries grow significantly. Today, China is the primary trading partner of Brazil, India and South Africa. Therefore, although the BRICS countries seek to profit from the cooperation, China is likely to continue to be the one that gains the greatest advantage due to its economic power, rising geopolitical influence and clear antagonism to the US. This is particularly the case given that the war has weakened Russia and further strengthened China. China's GDP is more than twice as high as that of the other four BRICS combined: almost $18 trillion, compared with Brazil ($1.6 trillion), Russia ($1.8 trillion), India ($3.2 trillion) and South Africa ($400 billion).[15] Even though the Covid-19 pandemic and subsequent strict zero-Covid policy implemented by the Chinese government has put a brake on the country's economic growth, China's economy remains extremely large and the country has by now created many interdependencies around the world, including with Russia, by importing energy resources no longer absorbed by Europe.

Even if the BRICS cooperation by itself does not explain the unclear positions of Brazil, India, China and South Africa in condemning Russia's aggression, the existence of the club has fostered connections with Russia over the last decade and served to avoid creating uneasiness with Putin's regime. With the 2022 election of Lula da Silva in Brazil, whose previous governments from 2003 to 2010 played a key role in building the

---

15   Bishop, M. (2022) "The BRICS countries: where next and what impact on the global economy?" *Economic Observatory*, 20 October. URL: https://www.economicsobservatory .com/the-brics-countries-where-next-and-what-impact-on-the-global-economy.

BRICS, one can expect renewed BRICS activity as Lula has already signed an autonomous and interest-driven foreign policy. Additionally, there have been discussions about expanding the BRICS membership, which is at least to some extent about giving new impetus to the cooperation in a context where the BRICS members still hold divergent interests, development trajectories, relative levels of geo-economic significance and ability to exercise substantial influence over the international system. Indeed, the economic trajectories of the BRICS countries have been very uneven, and some analysts argue that this has limited the BRICS in forming a clear, unifying set of ideological principles or shared vision for managing the global order.[16]

Despite the advanced proposals from the BRICS to challenge the international liberal order, there are also important limitations on the bloc's ability to fundamentally change the world order, including the low degree of convergence in foreign policy goals and preferences, the lack of political and ideological unity, and the absence of a clear vision for world order commonly shared by the group members and palatable to the broader international community.

Originally an informal group of leading emerging economies in the 2000s, the BRICS have nevertheless managed to work together on a series of international issues beyond the economic dimension, despite their very different economic growth paths. They have proven their ability to overlook their differences when it suits their mutual interests. The war on Europe's doorstep is a new test for the BRICS. Their ability to cooperate despite their differences should not be underestimated.

Finally, the potential of the BRICS cannot be disentangled from the ability of the West to rebuild trust with partners across the globe and the effectiveness of the international liberal order. If the US and Europe continue to disengage from their international commitments and their relations with the developing world, or if their initiatives are only perceived as empty promises – as has been the case with the EU's Global Gateway initiative – then alternative models of development, political regimes and global order will only continue to gain prominence. In this context, the BRICS would be in a favourable position to leverage its role as voicing the concerns and defending the interests of the developing world. Therefore, part of the West's response to contain mainly China and Russia as alternative models, and by extension the multipolar international order the BRICS advocates, entails rebuilding trust and credibility with its partners

---

16   Ibid.

in Asia, Africa and Latin America. The nonaligned positions observed in the context of the current war should have been a wake-up call to Europe and the US. However, the persistent narrative of the West framing the Russo-Ukrainian War as a fight of democracy versus autocracy is not a sign that it has taken this wake-up call seriously.

Further reading

McLean, J., and L. Mpungose (2022) "BRICS and the Russia–Ukraine war: a global rebalance?" South African Institute of International Affairs website, 19 September. URL: https://saiia.org.za/research/a-global-rebalance/.

Panda, J. (2022) "What does the Russia–Ukraine war mean for India in the long term?" TRENDS Research and Advisory, website 7 December 2022; https://trendsresearch.org/insight/what-does-the-russia-ukraine-war-mean-for-india-in-the-long-term/.

Rewizorski, M. (ed.) (2015) *The European Union and the BRICS: Complex Relations in the Era of Global Governance* (Springer).

Sidiropoulos, E. (2022) "How do Global South politics of non-alignment and solidarity explain South Africa's position on Ukraine?" Brooking's Insitute website. URL: https://www.brookings.edu/blog/africa-in-focus/2022/08/02/how-do-global-south-politics-of-non-alignment-and-solidarity-explain-south-africas-position-on-ukraine/.

Stuenkel, O. (2020) *The BRICS and the Future of Global Order*, 2nd edition (Lanam, MD: Lexington Books).

Stuenkel, O. (2022) "The war in Ukraine and the emergence of the post-Western world: a view from Brazil". Institut Montaigne website, 29 September 2022. URL: https://www.institutmontaigne.org/en/analysis/war-ukraine-and-emergence-post-western-world-view-brazil.

Peter Rudolf

16 | The nuclear shadow over Ukraine and Europe: deterrence, compellence and the risk of escalation

After the end of the Cold War, nuclear deterrence had receded into the background and largely faded from public awareness.[1] This changed abruptly with Russia's war of aggression against Ukraine and President Vladimir Putin's threatening nuclear gestures in February 2022, thereby introducing an element of "strategic unpredictability".[2]

A potential nuclear crisis

Moscow's repeated nuclear signalling turned the war against Ukraine into a potential nuclear crisis – with the risk of either a deliberate or inadvertent escalation resulting from misperceptions.[3] Crises involving antagonistic nuclear powers are overshadowed by the risk of nuclear escalation. This is particularly true of the US and Russia, whose nuclear postures have not changed substantially since the end of the Cold War and the dissolution of the Soviet Union. The number of strategic nuclear warheads has been reduced, but both sides retain a substantial portion of their strategic missiles ready for prompt launch in case early warning systems report incoming enemy missiles ("launch on warning" or, as the US military prefers to say, "launch under attack"). This is intended

---

1   This essay is adapted from two earlier publications in German: *Welt im Alarmzustand – Die Wiederkehr nuklearer Abschreckung* (Bonn: Verlag J. H. W. Dietz, 2022); and "Bidens Balanceakt – die Ukraine stärken, Krieg mit Russland vermeiden" (SWP-Aktuell no. 41, Stiftung Wissenschaft und Politik, June 2022).

2   Stigler, A. L. (2022) "Strategic unpredictability: assessing the doctrine from Nixon to Putin". *Survival*, 64(3): 49–66.

3   Talmadge, C. (2022) "The Ukraine crisis is now a nuclear crisis". *Washington Post*, 27 February.

to prevent the other side from destroying one's own missiles and command and communications systems via a first strike. The fear that the other side might be tempted to launch a disarming nuclear first strike in a major crisis played an important role at the time of the US–Soviet antagonism. This "worst-case" scenario continues to shape the nuclear deterrent relationship between the US and Russia.[4]

It is no wonder that US President Joe Biden has walked a fine line while supporting Ukraine. From the outset, he made it clear that a direct military conflict between his country and Russia should be avoided, because, as he said, this would mean "World War III".[5] Uncertain of what Russia might understand as interference, the Biden administration's early line was to say yes to arms deliveries to Ukraine, to some intelligence support for the country and to comprehensive sanctions, but to strictly reject the Ukrainian request to enforce a no-fly zone and to avoid anything that might be understood as immediate involvement in the war or that might lead to direct confrontation with Russian military forces. From the outset, the Biden administration designed its support for Ukraine with an eye on a possible escalation of the war, horizontally (expansion of the war zone into NATO territory) or vertically (use of nuclear weapons). Therefore, Washington pursued a policy of incrementally increasing support for Ukraine, thereby testing Russia's reactions. It also refrained from supplying weapons that Ukraine could use to attack targets inside Russia.[6]

In this sense, one might argue that Moscow's nuclear signalling had some deterrent effect in dissuading the US and its allies from supplying all the arms Ukraine had requested. But it might not have needed this kind of signalling to remind the US of the risk of escalation. Deterring the West has not been the only effect of Russia's nuclear signalling.[7] It has also raised the fear that Moscow might at some point turn to the nuclear option in a coercive way to compel Kyiv into submission through "nuclear blackmail".[8]

---

4   Koblentz, G. D. (2014) *Strategic Stability in the Second Nuclear Age* (New York/ Washington, DC: Council on Foreign Relations), pp. 7–9.

5   Blake, A. (2022) "Why Biden and the White House keep talking about World War III". *Washington Post*, 17 March.

6   Sanger, D. E., et al. (2022) "US is reluctant as Ukraine asks to upgrade arms". *New York Times*, 18 September.

7   Horovitz, L., and A. C. Arndt (2022) "Russia's catch-all nuclear rhetoric in its war against Ukraine". SWP Comment no. 60, Stiftung Wissenschaft und Politik, October.

8   In general on this, see Bracken, P. (2017) "Blackmail under a nuclear umbrella", *War on the Rocks*, 7 February.

Should Russia turn to nuclear coercion, the US and other countries supporting Ukraine would face a dilemma. On the one hand, Moscow must be denied the benefits it might derive from using the nuclear option; that is, there must be no cessation of support for Ukraine and no pressure on Kyiv to bow to Russian demands. On the other hand, a further escalation, possibly leading to war between Russia and NATO, must be avoided.[9]

The risks of brinkmanship

Unlike those experts without political responsibility who speak of an extremely low risk of nuclear escalation, the US administration has remained concerned about the possibility that at some point Putin might raise the stakes and confront the US with difficult decisions. The US administration does not publicly speculate about what the Russian leadership might perceive as an existential threat to the state or regime that could lead to the use of nuclear weapons. However, it does not rule out the possibility that Putin – facing humiliating defeat – might seek to change the dynamics of the war with the use of tactical nuclear weapons.

US concerns seem to have risen after Putin, in September 2022, designated the red line beyond which all means of defence may be justified: namely, in the event of a threat to Russia's territorial integrity. With the incorporation of four regions of Ukraine into Russia, Putin elevated the war to a defence of Russian territory and Western support of Ukraine as an aggression directed against Russia, signalling his readiness to use all means of defence and warning that he was "not bluffing". He also reminded his audience that the US set a "precedent" by using nuclear weapons in 1945. With this statement and his decision to mobilise hundreds of thousands of soldiers, Putin seems to have narrowed his political room for manoeuvre should Russia face imminent defeat.[10]

Putin's policy basically follows the logic of what is called "brinkmanship" in classical deterrence thinking. This involves the determination to take risks in an escalating crisis, to raise the stakes and to push ahead with a process which cannot be fully controlled – in the expectation that

---

9   Betts, R. K. (2022) "Thinking about the unthinkable in Ukraine: what happens if Putin goes nuclear?" *Foreign Affairs*, 4 July.

10   Stanovaya, T. (2022) "Putin's apocalyptic end game in Ukraine: annexation and mobilization make nuclear war more likely". *Foreign Affairs*, 6 October.

---

the other side will back down.[11] Brinkmanship means "manipulating the shared risk of war" to one's own advantage, as Thomas Schelling, the conflict theorist and later Nobel laureate in economic sciences, wrote in the 1960s. But what happens when the other side also raises the stakes in this "competition in risk taking"?[12] The US government has repeatedly warned the Russian government against using nuclear weapons. President Biden stated in May 2022 that any use of Russian nuclear weapons in the Ukraine war would have "severe consequences".[13] In response to Putin rhetorically raising the stakes, the US administration sharpened the tone: there was talk of "catastrophic consequences" (National Security Advisor Jake Sullivan) and "horrific" consequences (Secretary of State Antony Blinken).[14] Publicly it is unknown what specific warnings the administration sent to the Russian government through confidential channels.

Regarding the US, one can speak of a deliberate "strategic ambiguity". However, by talking about the "catastrophic consequences" of Russia's use of nuclear weapons, the Biden administration may have manoeuvred itself into a corner, putting its own credibility on the line.[15] If Washington reacts militarily (certainly not with nuclear arms, as it would make no sense militarily or politically to violate the nuclear taboo), Putin would feel under pressure to respond if he wants to demonstrate his resolve. What would then be Russia's next step on the escalation ladder? Conventional attacks against NATO targets? A nuclear attack against NATO vessels? Or detonating a nuclear bomb over a military base in Europe to cripple it with an electromagnetic pulse? The Russian leadership seems convinced it has the better cards in the "competition in risk taking" and that the West will not risk a nuclear war over Ukraine.[16]

Following the logic of deterrence in a crisis situation, it is quite rational to run some risks and raise the stakes in order to put the burden of further

---

11   Traub, J. (2022) "The crazy logic of brinkmanship is back". *Foreign Policy*, 26 September.

12   Schelling, T. C. (1966) *Arms and Influence* (New Haven, CT: Yale University Press), quote on p. 99.

13   Biden, J. R. (2022) "What America will and will not do in Ukraine". *New York Times*, 31 May.

14   Sanger, D. E., and J. Tankersley (2022) "US warns Russia of 'catastrophic consequences' if it uses nuclear weapons". *New York Times*, 26 September.

15   Auslin, M. (2022) "The dangers of 'catastrophic consequences'". *Foreign Policy*, 21 October.

16   Sanger, D. E., A. Troianovski and J. E. Barnes (2022) "In Washington, Putin's nuclear threats stir growing alarm". *New York Times*, 1 October.

escalation on the other side. In his cost–benefit calculation, Putin would probably factor in whether the possible, but by no means certain, success of nuclear compellence or the military benefits outweigh the reputational costs to Russia of violating the nuclear taboo, especially among countries in the Global South that so far have not opposed Russia but are worried about its nuclear rhetoric. Statements by Chinese leader Xi Jinping and the G20 Bali Leaders' Declaration left no doubt that the use of nuclear weapons or the threat to use them is "opposed"[17] and widely regarded as "inadmissible".[18]

The limits of rationality

At the same time, Putin's decision to go to war against Ukraine has raised the question: is the Russian president still behaving rationally? Was the decision to launch a war of aggression against Ukraine an outgrowth of false assumptions; a completely distorted perception of the situation in Ukraine; an obsession with a threat that might emerge from Ukraine turning westward; or a misjudgement of US and European reactions? Or is Putin no longer the sharply calculating practitioner of realpolitik he once was? An opponent acting irrationally poses a fundamental problem for deterrence thinking.[19] The assumption of a rational actor consistently calculating costs and benefits, adopted from economic theory, is the "weak link" in the logic of nuclear deterrence.[20]

In economic thinking, the rationality assumption has long been challenged by behavioural economics, which incorporates psychological and

17 "The international community should [...] jointly oppose the use [of] or threats to use nuclear weapons, advocate that nuclear weapons must not be used and nuclear wars must not be fought, in order to prevent a nuclear crisis in Eurasia," Xi Jinping stated during a meeting in Beijing with German Chancellor Olaf Scholz. (Quoted by Lau, J. (2022) "No nuclear weapons over Ukraine, Chinese President Xi Jinping says, in clear message to Russia", *South China Morning Post*, 4 November.)

18 "The use or threat of use of nuclear weapons is inadmissible" (G20 Bali Leaders' Declaration, Bali, Indonesia, 15–16 November 2022).

19 Geist, E. (2022) "Is Putin irrational? What nuclear strategic theory says about deterrence of potentially irrational opponents", *RAND Blog*, 8 March; Krepinevich, A. F., Jr. (2022) "Is Putin a rational actor? How and why the Kremlin might use the bomb", *Foreign Affairs*, 22 November.

20 Knopf, J. W., A. I. Harrington and M. Pomper (2016) "Real-world nuclear decision making: using behavioral economics insights to adjust nonproliferation and deterrence policies to predictable deviations from rationality". Report on a workshop organised by the James Martin Center for Nonproliferation Studies. Center on Contemporary Conflict, January, p. 4.

neuroscientific insights into actual human decision-making behaviour. Heuristics (rules of thumb) and associated cognitive biases strongly determine thinking, as comprehensively analysed and described by Nobel Prize-winning psychologist Daniel Kahneman.[21] People tend to be more risk-tolerant when it comes to avoiding losses and more risk-averse when it comes to gains. People overestimate their own strengths; they tend to be overly optimistic and have the "illusion of control"; they tend to see the behaviour of others as an outgrowth of their character or nature; and they are not good at assessing their own behaviour and its effect on others. Doubts about rational deterrence logic are also cast by findings from neuroscience and evolutionary psychology that support research on perceptual biases and bring into focus the role of emotions in decision-making. Decisions do not (always) follow a purposive, rational weighing of possible courses of action, but are the result of an interplay of reason and emotions such as anger and fear. These are not necessarily conscious to those acting.[22]

Since the assumption of rationally acting statesmen (and women) is problematic, it cannot be taken for granted that in crises involving nuclear powers there will never be a use of nuclear weapons or a chain of nuclear escalation. No doubt, during the Cold War, mutual vulnerability in crises had a moderating effect on leaders in Washington and Moscow. But the deterrence relationship between the United States and the Soviet Union remained fraught with risks. Both sides feared that the other might consider a preemptive strike in a serious crisis. In retrospect, it seems likely that political leaders tended to underestimate the risks of nuclear weapons use, "particularly those arising from the interaction of complex warning and alert systems and the dynamics of crisis decision-making".[23] Nuclear war remains a "global catastrophic risk" whose probability and consequences defy any precise determination.[24] This is especially true of the climatic consequences, but also the

21   Kahneman, D. (2011) *Thinking, Fast and Slow* (New York: Farrar, Strauss and Giroux).

22   Thayer, B. A. (2007) "Thinking about nuclear deterrence theory: why evolutionary psychology undermines its rational actor assumptions", *Comparative Strategy*, 26(4): 311–323; Scheber, T. (2011) "Evolutionary psychology, cognitive function, and deterrence", *Comparative Strategy*, 30(5): 453–480.

23   Bennett, A. (2021) "Historical case study", in J. Scouras (ed.), *On Assessing the Risk of Nuclear War* (Laurel, MD: Johns Hopkins Applied Physics Laboratory), pp. 17–42 (quote on p. 33).

24   Scouras, J. (2019) "Nuclear war as a global catastrophic risk". *Journal of Benefit-Cost Analysis*, 10(2): 274–295.

infrastructural ones. Nuclear deterrence thinking tends to ignore these risks. Keeping them in the public consciousness, and thus strengthening the reluctance to use nuclear weapons, is more urgent than ever in the era of new great power conflicts and the return of nuclear deterrence in Europe.

The return of nuclear deterrence in Europe

Nobody can predict when and how the war in Ukraine will end. But the war has clearly exposed the conventional weakness of the Russian military. Therefore, it can be plausibly assumed that nuclear weapons will gain an even stronger role in Russia's military strategy vis-à-vis NATO than is already the case. The new confrontation in Europe will probably assume a strong nuclear dimension.[25] This might lead to a new debate within NATO about what it takes to credibly deter Russia from exploiting the threat or actual use of nuclear weapons in scenarios directly affecting the alliance. No matter how much NATO styles itself as a "nuclear alliance", the fact remains that exposed states without nuclear weapons cannot completely rule out being abandoned when the going gets tough. As a reminder, during the Cold War, the credibility problem of US-extended nuclear deterrence was a recurring issue for NATO. Among European allies, especially the Federal Republic of Germany, lingering doubts persisted about the credibility of the nuclear security guarantee – or, as it is sometimes metaphorically called, the "nuclear umbrella". Neither multinational troops along the German–German border nor thousands of American nuclear weapons deployed on West German soil could completely eliminate this concern.

Today's NATO members on the "front line" seem to be averse to articulating doubts about the credibility of US-extended nuclear deterrence. But given the widespread concern in Europe about future developments in US politics and foreign policy, Paris might find a more open audience than in the past for its standing offer to engage in a strategic dialogue on the "European dimension" of France's nuclear deterrent posture.

---

25 Koziej, S. (2022) "The Russia–Ukraine war: scenarios for Euroatlantic security". Report, Geopolitical Intelligence Services AG, 22 July. URL: https://www.gisreportsonline .com/r/euroatlantic-security/.

Further reading

Betts, R. K. (2022) "Thinking about the unthinkable in Ukraine: what happens if Putin goes nuclear?" *Foreign Affairs*, 4 July.

Horovitz, L., and A. C. Arndt (2022) "Russia's catch-all nuclear rhetoric in its war against Ukraine". SWP Comment no. 60, Stiftung Wissenschaft und Politik, October.

Krepinevich, A. F., Jr. (2022) "Is Putin a rational actor? How and why the Kremlin might use the bomb". *Foreign Affairs*, 22 November.

Stanovaya, T. (2022) "Putin's apocalyptic end game in Ukraine: annexation and mobilization make nuclear war more likely". *Foreign Affairs*, 6 October.

Traub, J. (2022) "The crazy logic of brinkmanship is back". *Foreign Policy*, 26 September.

György Mudri

17 | Disrupted food supply chains

The consequences of Russian aggression for the food industry are serious. Beyond shortages of essential items, the impact on lives is more complex. Food is being used as a bargaining chip in this war, causing severe shortages in Ukraine and disrupting the global food supply. In addition, global food prices are subject to financial speculation. This chapter focuses on some of these effects and examines possible solutions to overcome global food imbalances.

The role of Russia and Ukraine in global food supply

Wars and conflicts have been around for a long time, but in 2022 the front line came close to a neighbouring country of the EU. Moreover, Russia's aggression has affected a region with prominent status within the grain belt. This combination makes a difference. Russia and Ukraine are significant players in the global food chain, producing and exporting several commodities, including wheat, corn, sunflower oil and fertilisers.

Before the war, Russia and Ukraine accounted for a respective 10% and 3% of global wheat production on average over the preceding five years. Russia was the number one wheat exporter, accounting for 20% of global exports, while Ukraine's role was also considerable, providing 10% of global exports, ranking the country the number five global exporter. Ukraine was the third largest corn exporter and the top producer of sunflower oil globally, followed by Russia. Ukraine exported 50% of global sunflower oil, while Russia was second with a 25% share.

Russia has played a crucial role in other input markets in agriculture, being the world's top exporter of natural gas and nitrogen fertilisers, as well as, respectively, the second and third leading supplier of potassium and phosphorus fertilisers. The purchase of these articles has been partly limited due to the war, with further, indirect effects on the agricultural sector.[1]

Ukraine alone exported more than 5 million tons of grain monthly before the war, mostly to African, EU and Middle Eastern countries. Many countries, both neighbouring and further away, are dependent on these commodities. One surprising example of a direct, immediate impact caused by the outbreak of war was the shortage of cooking oil in the UK.

It is understandable that, in the event of war, agreements are important to ensure the reestablishment of supplies of key export articles. It is also important to involve third parties in the creation of such agreements. Fortunately, Moscow and Kyiv were able to agree to reestablish exports of available stocks from Ukraine (under the Istanbul agreement). Free shipping lanes from some Black Sea ports were designated, with the United Nations and Turkey playing key roles in agreeing the terms. However, such agreements often prove fragile – as seen, for example, in the Russian bombing of Odesa, one of the key cities for grain exports, a day after the signing of the Istanbul deal. Russia promised not to hit ships carrying food to the world, but it did hit key infrastructure, an act showing "Russia's total disregard for international law and commitments" (as tweeted by Josep Borrell Fontelles, the EU's foreign policy chief).

Despite the fragility of the shipping agreement, many benefit from it: Russia gets some relief from sanctions; Ukraine earns income by selling more than 20 million tons of grain; African and Middle Eastern countries receive shipments; the UN facilitates the flow of food articles; and Turkey makes money by assisting in the transport of goods.

Unfortunately, Russia has also hit civilian locations and agriculture itself during the war, destroying grain terminals, fields and export channels. Both the harvest in 2022 and sowing of crops for 2023 have suffered serious damage. This is a common though underhand military manoeuvre reminiscent of the Middle Ages. The Geneva Convention prohibits the interruption of food supplies to an occupied territory for a long period. In

---

1   "The impacts and policy implications of Russia's aggression against Ukraine on agricultural markets", Organisation for Economic Co-operation and Development website, updated 5 August 2022 (www.oecd.org/ukraine-hub/policy-responses/the-impacts-and -policy-implications-of-russia-s-aggression-against-ukraine-on-agricultural-markets -0030a4cd/); "Agricultural markets in Russia and Ukraine", Economic Research Service, US Department of Agriculture (www.ers.usda.gov/newsroom/trending-topics/agricultural -markets-in-russia-and-ukraine/).

this case there is more at stake: both the target and the aggressor are top grain producers and exporters.

This strategy not only violates international agreements and afflicts the attacked territory but has also led to volatile global supplies of food, fertiliser and energy. It has resulted in instability in certain countries of Africa and the Middle East, igniting further regional tensions and migration flows. Moreover, the strategy followed by Russia is no secret. The words of ex-president Dmitry Medvedev, cited in multiple news channels, clearly revealed Russian intentions on 1 April 2022: "Our food has proven to be our silent weapon. Quiet, but scary." Nevertheless, even the EU was forced to ease sanctions on Russian fertiliser in order to mitigate hunger in other parts of the world.

Pressure builds on the food trade

The food chain is one of the most vital parts of our lives. Besides the obvious biological value of alimentation globally, its economic weight is also considerable. The largest global economic and political players are also the largest food producers, importers and exporters.

The Covid-19 pandemic and the Russo-Ukrainian War in the grain belt quickly demonstrated the fragility of food supply. These circumstances accelerated the rise in food prices and caused distributional problems. Some elements of the situation are immediate, while some present long-term challenges. In war situations the problems are further exacerbated artificially, as food can be used for unscrupulous "hunger games" and speculation.

Pressure on the food sector has been building gradually for a while. The growing global population, changing eating habits, economic instability, speculation, climate challenges, the pandemic and war have all played their part. The sector reflects on these challenges by changing gradually, but food price rises and distributional problems happen first.

Higher food prices mean higher consumer and trade prices, and also higher revenues for many. However, price increases are not reflected equally in the food chain. In practice, the highest price boosted by global shocks is paid by consumers, due to the cumulative effects of inputs (production, energy, logistics and trade).

Distributional problems translate into particularly acute food shortages in certain regions. North African and Middle Eastern countries are especially affected by stress on food supply, but even the UK – for example – faced serious shortages of cooking oil after the war broke out.

Table 16.1. Examples from the FAO Food Price Index (FPI).

Date	FPI	Cereals	Meat	Vegetable oils
2020	98.1	103.1	95.5	99.4
Jan 2022	135.6	140.6	112.1	185.9
Mar 2022	159.7	170.1	119.3	251.8
Oct 2022	135.9	152.3	118.4	150.1

Source: https://www.fao.org/worldfoodsituation/foodpricesindex/en/. The FPI consists of the average of five commodity group prices: meat, dairy, cereals, vegetable oils and sugar.

After steadily declining for decades, world hunger has been rising since 2019, affecting over 10% of the world population. An additional 19 million people may find themselves suffering from famine in 2023, according to the OECD-FAO Agricultural Outlook 2022–2031.[2]

This means the situation with respect to food insecurity and malnutrition is worsening. It seems that the 2015 hunger situation will not be fundamentally resolved until 2030, despite efforts and commitments such as the 2030 Agenda for Sustainable Development.[3]

Prior to and parallel with the Russian aggression, the challenges have been growing harder in the production and supply of food articles, brought on by drought, floods, spring frost damage, unequal population growth, economic instability and so on.

Most of the biggest players in the global economy committed themselves to achieving better environmental conditions, in line with UN climate targets and in some cases even going beyond these goals. Unfortunately, many of these green-transitioning actions have been halted by global health problems and war. These developments are definitely not pointing in a sustainable direction.

Unfortunately, prices are not based on supply and demand alone. Some experts agree that speculation plays a massive role in the development of food prices, as can be expected in a world living largely according

2 Organisation for Economic Co-operation and Development (OECD) and Food and Agriculture Organization of the United Nations (FAO) (2022) "OECD-FAO Agricultural Outlook 2022–2031". Report, 29 June. URL: https://www.oecd-ilibrary.org/agriculture-and-food/oecd-fao-agricultural-outlook-2022-2031_f1b0b29c-en.

3 FAO, International Fund for Agricultural Development, United Nations Children's Fund, United Nations World Food Programme and World Health Organization (2022) "The state of food security and nutrition in the world 2022". Report, Rome. URL: www.fao.org/publications/sofi/2022/en/.

to capitalist principles. There are even more extreme opinions, stating for example that "the global food crisis is a consequence of commodity price speculation on Wall Street and the CME – not directly the Russian invasion of Ukraine".[4]

Disruptive outcomes

The short- and long-term effects of global disruptive circumstances on food are manifold. Food prices have been skyrocketing since the onset of the Covid-19 situation and have continuously grown since the war started. After the initial shock, there was a dramatic rise in the prices of cooking oil, grain and meat products in March 2022, and although the supply situation was somewhat remedied, prices are still higher than before.

This means that food prices were already on the rise before Russia invaded Ukraine. Supply chain problems connected to Covid-19, spikes in the prices of inputs such as fertiliser connected to rising energy prices, crop yields in light of climate change, financial speculation and economic instability have all contributed to rising prices since the beginning of 2020. The ongoing war and Russia's flouting of international commitments have only deepened these painful processes.

While price rises and food shortages are hitting the global population as a whole, the impact of such disruption differs from region to region. For example, both the EU and the US are large agricultural food producers with single markets, intervention mechanisms and various trade agreements. Everything can be bought in these markets, even though purchasing power and consumption itself may be declining. Other territories, such as certain regions of North Africa and the Middle East, are seriously suffering from food shortages. Even available commodities are further burdened with extreme logistics and speculative costs.

Main areas of intervention

It should be underlined again that higher food prices and disruption in the global food supply in the given period are the result of many factors, not limited to the Russo-Ukrainian War. Global prices are volatile, and they

---

4 Pettifor, A. (2022) "Grain inflation: starve the poor, feed the rich". *System Change*, Substack, 26 July. URL: https://annpettifor.substack.com/p/grain-inflation-starve-the-poor -feed.

swung back to more acceptable levels in the second half of 2022. In spite of this, prices remained higher for consumers and food shortages were palpable in certain regions at the end of 2022. Factors disrupting the food chain are forecast to continue.

Consequently, the situation in the food chain requires lasting action, with short- and long-term impacts.

- Constant monitoring of the food chain is needed, as well as of the effects of the war on the grain belt and input markets of the agriculture sector. With the food sector confronting many global challenges and an obvious strategy to further disrupt it, the first step is to investigate agriculture, being the level of primary production. It has long been known that existing environmental challenges make farmers' lives difficult, but this time the challenge is even greater. The effects can be mitigated in the EU or US as both have mechanisms to compensate primary producers. *Intervention in the agri-food market in all regions should be further discussed at the World Trade Organization level in situations such as these.*

- The EU and the US are able to protect and assist not only the agricultural sector but the rest of the food industry as well, in order to ensure sufficient alimentation. Faced with the neighbouring war, the European Commission and the EU member states together agreed on coordinated action to respond to the global food crisis through solidarity measures such as emergency and humanitarian relief, open trade, ensuring sustainable production and increasing global cooperation. The Commission opened Solidarity Lanes to ease grain exports and made available advance payments and a crisis reserve for member states, while allowing production on land set aside for biodiversity and easing crop rotation rules. *These actions have been only partly successful, however, and thus good practices should be collected and translated to all regions in order to mitigate hunger in such circumstances.*

- Strategies such as Farm to Fork and the European Green Deal should be revised in the EU in order to increase climate-friendly, healthy and stable food production. No agricultural country can afford to reduce production while millions are suffering malnutrition or dying of hunger. *Therefore, it is vital that EU strategies related to food production are regularly revised so that regions can maintain their activities.*

- Good agricultural and rural development practices can increase sustainable production and mitigate the impact of the war in the grain belt. *Assessment of the best practices in the field could give a boost to healthy food production, for example by evaluating the work of the European Network for Rural Development and the Common Agricultural Policy Network, the US Department of Agriculture's Best Practices or the Australian Good Agricultural Practice Programme.*

- Short-term action is needed in response to situations such as these. Some countries, for example, have introduced price caps on certain food articles for consumers. In theory, price caps on basic food articles should mitigate inflation; in practice, however, they create further problems, such as accelerating price rises of other products not affected by the capping. This leads to rising inflation, increases cross-border food shopping and results in food shortages. *Short-term actions such as price capping of food articles can be efficient if specific social layers are targeted, such as families at or below the minimum income level.*

- In many regions there is a lack of skilled workers in rural areas. There is a renewed trend of people moving to rural areas from cities – for example, due to the recent pandemic – while some urban citizens plan to engage in agriculture. However, access to land, funds and other incentives are still lacking even in developed regions. *Therefore, immediate, medium and long-term investments are needed in the creation and protection of workplaces and other opportunities in rural areas.*

- Besides the war's direct and indirect impacts on the food sector, structural problems in the food chain need to be addressed in many regions. *Ensuring structural investments – for example in smart irrigation systems or storage capacities, is a must to mitigate climate challenges and disruption caused by wars. These investments need time to be implemented and should be started immediately.*

- The grain stock produced in the grain belt is needed globally, and the Russo-Ukrainian War and other conflicts thus drastically impact the global food chain. Exports from these war zones need to be secured. Partial improvement has occurred in exports from war-affected Ukraine, such as the agreement to open Black Sea ports for food exports. However, while agreements and Solidarity Lanes have helped increase grain exports, attacks on grain shipments further deepen the conflict. *Further safe agreements on grain shipments from these regions are needed, and the Geneva Convention must be respected in order to mitigate global food crises.*

- Solidarity is essential for society. Higher food prices mean higher tax revenues for the state in many forms, such as in the form of value-added tax (VAT). VAT rates on food articles differ even among EU member states. The highest rate applied in Hungary is 27%, with some exceptions. *Governments should reduce VAT rates while ensuring that retailers do not profit from the reduction. They could use the extra profits to help the most deprived social classes and most impacted agri-food sectors.*

- Regarding tax regulation, a global tax rate on food articles would be beneficial. It would create equality on the food market, help eliminate tax fraud, and potentially ease the social impact of global disturbances such as wars or pandemics. *A major part of regulated and increasing state income would need to be spent on social infrastructure, employment and welfare.*

- Food prices react quickly in crisis situations and usually bounce back slowly to a higher level compared with their starting position. There is a complex problem behind this phenomenon. Extra profits may be realised at the private sector level, besides the government level. However, these profits are not evenly distributed. The private sector is frequently expected to contribute during a crisis, an issue which the United Nations addressed recently after the start of the war in 2022. *Such expectations are legitimate in the event that other segments of the agri-food sector are also expected to contribute. However, these contributions need to be differentiated, while ensuring that the burden on primary producers is fair.*

- Food prices can fall victim to speculation, as many analyses show. *Further research is needed to identify how big companies and markets are influencing food prices.*

- The question of household incomes and the proportion they spend on food is a complex subject, and well researched. Circumstances cannot be changed from one day to the next, and it is a socioeconomic fact that the poorer sections of society spend proportionately more of their incomes on food and energy. *The proportion of food articles in household spending is even higher in the event of global challenges, and steps should be taken to address the situation and assist social strata in need.*

- Agriculture is dependent on inputs such as fertiliser and energy. Russia is one of the largest fertiliser producers and exporters. EU farmers have been unable to access a large part of this resource due to the war, while farmers in some other regions have continued to enjoy access. In addition, there are many energy-intensive areas of agriculture, such as animal husbandry and greenhouse production. Many of these inputs or ingredients are imported by the biggest agricultural countries and represent a very large part of the costs of agricultural production. *The restoration or replacement of sources of fertiliser in the event of conflicts needs to be addressed. Other interventions might also be needed in order to eliminate bottlenecks in domestic production lines.*

- The Russo-Ukrainian War hit part of an important grain-producing region. At the same time, a very advanced agricultural sector exists in other parts of the grain belt, with room to expand. Areas for expansion include the additional involvement of new farmlands and new technologies. *Technological transfers and expansion of production are needed, while technologies need to be put into focus as part of rebuilding assistance for Ukraine.*

- Food shortages in a war zone and in the most hard-hit regions create global challenges such as famine and increasing migration. Both short- and long-term solutions are therefore needed to address tensions of this kind. *Development and humanitarian aid tools should be among the priorities of the developed countries. These tools should include technological assistance and smart technological solutions to produce more food in the developing/non-food-producing countries.*

Conclusions

As we can see, disturbances in the global food chain have both immediate and long-term effects. Immediate shortages of food articles occurred in many regions after the start of the Russian aggression in early 2022. The global population should also be prepared to face the long-term consequences of disruptive situations such as these, as production in a war zone can be destroyed for years. This is what has happened in Ukraine, where disruption of food production will remain serious in the grain belt for years to come. Some products may disappear from the market after available stocks are exhausted. Moreover, financial speculation is worsening the situation, unfortunately without any consequences. Although countries neighbouring a war zone can produce more food, in this event they may end up having to reduce the production of other important articles. In the case of the ongoing Russian aggression, countries in the grain belt can produce more food but only in limited amounts. It should also be noted that storage capacity is limited in these countries and has likewise become a challenge, not only in Ukraine but for importing countries too.

In a global situation such as that resulting from the Russian aggression against Ukraine, there is a burden of responsibility on the whole of society, including the private sector and governments. Besides holding war criminals to account in these situations, all stakeholders need to act together, and they need to act quickly. Asking for committed action from only the private sector and international financial institutions is not realistic. We must speed up action to end the "hunger games" instigated by Russian aggression and to rebuild Ukraine's food economy, as the food chain is literally one of the most vital parts of our lives.

Further reading

FAO, International Fund for Agricultural Development, United Nations Children's Fund, United Nations World Food Programme and World Health Organization (2022) "The state of food security and nutrition in the world 2022". Report, Rome. URL: www.fao.org/publications/sofi/2022/en/.

OECD and FAO (2022) "OECD-FAO agricultural outlook 2022–2031". Report, 29 June. URL: https://www.oecd-ilibrary.org/agriculture-and-food/oecd-fao -agricultural-outlook-2022-2031_f1b0b29c-en.

Pettifor, A. (2022) "Grain inflation: starve the poor, feed the rich". *System Change*, Substack, 26 July. URL: https://annpettifor.substack.com/p/grain -inflation-starve-the-poor-feed.

Savage, S., B. Brzezinski, B. Moens et al. (2022). "EU agrees to ease Russia fertilizer curbs after row, angering Ukraine". *Politico*, 15 December. URL: https:// politi.co/3U1VKAD.

Wax, E. (2022) "The world food crisis is about to get worse". *Politico*, 15 August. URL: https://politi.co/3zk19cL.

Wixforth, S., and K. Haddouti (2022). "How big companies are profiting from inflation". *International Politics and Society*, 19 December. URL: https://www.ips-journal.eu/topics/economy-and-ecology/how-big-companies-are-profiting-from-inflation-6388/.

Péter Tamás Bózsó

18 | American LNG to save Europe from Russian gas dependency

As a result of the Russian aggression against Ukraine, we are experiencing a historic shift in natural gas imports into Europe, a delinking from Russia and the entry of the US as an important source. Taking a step back for a broader perspective, we see how new technologies have enabled this shift, creating an alternative to pipeline networks that has changed the geopolitical context of this key market, opening new opportunities for the EU.

Europe set to decouple from Russian gas to punish Putin

Natural gas is not only vital for home and industrial heating but also an important input material for the chemical industry. It is critical in the production of fertiliser, cement, steel and glass. In 2021 gas also fuelled 34% of electricity generation in Europe. The adjustment of EU gas imports to the political reality will take time, and the technology of liquefied natural gas (LNG) is set to play a significant role in this shift in the import pattern.

After the Russian invasion of Ukraine, the EU decided to help Ukraine by weakening Russia's military potential. Cutting Russian oil and gas imports – as taxes on these contribute greatly to the Russian state budget – was one obvious way to punish the aggressor. Although sanctions were not applied to Russia's gas exports, Moscow has cut its exports in retaliation for European support of Ukraine. Furthermore, the terrorist attack against the Nord Stream natural gas pipelines directly delivering Russian gas to Germany has cancelled the ability of Russia to use potential renewed large-scale gas exports as a carrot. More than a year after Russian troops entered Ukraine, Moscow's natural gas exports have declined to well below half of prewar levels.

However, according to preliminary data from the Russian government, the Russian oil and gas industry grew by 28%, or $36.5 billion, in 2022. Oil production rose 2% to 535 million tons, while oil exports increased by 7%, despite Western sanctions. Nevertheless, the picture is different for Russian gas exports. Gazprom had to decrease gas production by over 20%, from 514.8 billion cubic metres in 2021 to 412.6 billion cubic metres in 2022, with a steep decline in the second half. Russia's total gas production amounted to 672 billion cubic metres in 2022, down 12%. Gazprom's exports to so-called far-abroad countries (Europe excluding the Baltics, plus Turkey and China) dived 45% from 185 billion cubic metres to about 101 billion cubic metres. Exports only increased to China. Deliveries via the Power of Siberia 1 pipeline, utilising gas fields in the Far East, went up from 10 billion cubic metres to an estimated 18 billion cubic metres.

Figure 18.1. Gazprom's exports to the so-called far-abroad countries in 2021–2022.

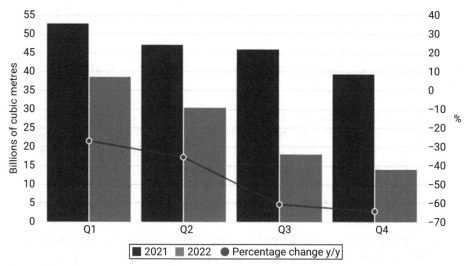

Source: Gazprom.

In the first half of 2022, Gazprom made a record profit of about $37 billion, more than it made in the previous two years combined. The Russian government exempted the company from publishing its second-half financials, due to the sanctions, but experts estimate that it only broke even.

The Power of Siberia 1 pipeline is scheduled to transport 22 billion cubic metres of gas to China in 2023. In future, Power of Siberia 2 – a pipeline connecting the West Siberian gas fields (the main source of exports to Europe) to China – may add 50 billion cubic metres to this, while Power of Siberia 3, also from the Far East, will add an additional ˒ 10 billion cubic metres. The EU purchased 155 billion cubic metres in 2021. Gazprom is also negotiating with Turkey to establish a gas hub there to reach the European market from the south.

In order to have a better understanding of ongoing processes regarding the gas market in Europe, we need to take a glimpse at a longer time horizon. Technological development is a slow process but can cause profound change in geopolitical settings. I argue that the shale gas revolution that started in the US, added to the technology of LNG, is one of the main underlying developments over the past 10–20 years that have defined the present situation in which the EU is able to diversify its supply away from Russia.

In the first year of war, the punishment inflicted on Russia's gas revenues may have failed, but the economic war is still not over as the outlook for Russia's gas exports is rather gloomy for 2023.

Development of technology: US competes with Russia for EU's gas imports

The first oil crisis, in 1973, triggered by the actions of the Organization of Petroleum Exporting Countries (OPEC), marked a shift in the balance of power in the global energy market, to the disadvantage of the US. In response, the US government reevaluated its energy policy with the aim of reducing its dependence on imports. President Richard Nixon launched Project Independence, setting a goal for the country to achieve energy self-sufficiency. However, by that time, American oil companies had largely relocated production to foreign fields, making it difficult to increase conventional domestic reserves. Meanwhile, increasing domestic demand, driven by economic growth, only heightened the country's energy dependence. After the second oil crisis in 1978, the US government began to incentivise domestic production through tax benefits aimed at nonconventional reserves such as shale gas. With government support, the first shale gas field was established in 1981 near Barnett, Texas, marking the start of the shale gas revolution.

The growth of US shale gas production can be divided into three phases: the preparation period until 2007; the surge in production until 2014; and the massive increase in production due to exports. In the pre-revolutionary period, US gas imports were expected to greatly increase. However, US domestic production rose in 2016–2017. To illustrate the main trends, we need to take a closer look at the development of natural gas production and consumption in the United States.

The US has nonconventional shale gas reserves that were not accessible with conventional technologies, but the new method of fracking was developed to exploit them. The US government actively helped boost shale gas production via tax incentives, active involvement in research and development, and setting up a friendly regulatory framework. In addition to the role of the state, the independent factor in success is a flexible and innovative corporate sector. Shale gas production is a technology- and thus capital-intensive industry. With the help of developed capital markets, the way has been opened for domestic and foreign investors to seize the profit opportunities provided by the new technology.

Figure 18.2. US natural gas consumption, dry production and net exports, 1950–2021.

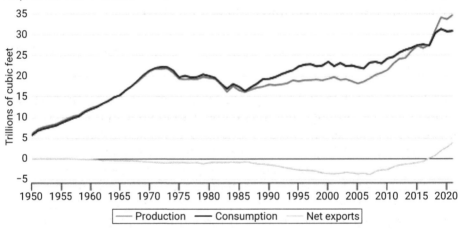

Data source: US Energy Information Administration, *Natural Gas Annual*, September 2022.

The increase in domestic natural gas production in the US presented an opportunity for exports, as the technology for liquefying natural gas was available. This technology enables the storage and transportation of gas via tankers instead of pipelines.

The commercial use of liquefied natural gas began in the 1940s with the creation of fixed storage capacities to regulate peaks in energy consumption. During high energy demand, LNG was regasified to meet the additional need. Maritime trade of LNG started in 1958, when the *Methane Pioneer*, the first ship carrying LNG, set sail from Louisiana to Britain. In Europe, Algerian gas was delivered to French and British ports starting in 1964. Many other routes followed, with the first in the Pacific running from Alaska to Japan. However, the US did not enter the LNG market until later. The development of the LNG market was driven by growing demand from both energy-poor East Asian economies (Japan, Korea and Taiwan) and European countries. During this period, the US was a net importer of LNG, until 2015.

Figure 18.3. US LNG imports and exports, 1985–2021.

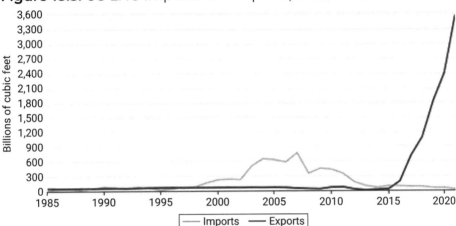

Data source: US Energy Information Administration, *Natural Gas Annual*, March 2021; data for 2021 are preliminary.

The transportation of LNG via sea requires a specialised infrastructure, needing significant investment. Initially, facilities were constructed on shorelines. However, a more flexible solution was developed in the form of the floating storage and regasification unit (FSRU), essentially a large specialised ship. Production of these started in the 2000s, while "mass" production of FSRUs (if this word can be used here) began after 2015. They offer several benefits compared with fixed regasification units, including lower costs, easier installation and the ability to be relocated.

Technological development has readjusted the geopolitical settings, as the US has gained the ability to compete with Russia for the EU's gas imports:

- the "shale revolution" made the US a significant natural gas (and oil) producer;
- LNG technology created the possibility for tanker exports via oceans and seas;
- floating LNG import terminals allow for relatively quick installation.

With the availability of huge amounts of relatively cheap gas, the United States has become a gas exporter since 2017. Its overseas exports in the form of LNG await receptive markets, the natural target for which is Europe on the other side of the Atlantic Ocean, as most extraction takes place in the eastern regions of the US. In 2022 the US became the top LNG exporter, overtaking Qatar, with Australia remaining the solid third.

The role of the US in European gas imports was already on the rise beginning from 2019, from which time Russia also delivered significant amounts.

Figure 18.4. Qatar and US tied for World's top LNG exporter.

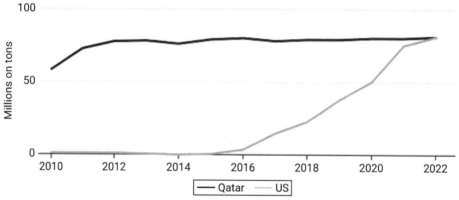

Source: BloombergNEF, Ship-Tracking Data; 2022 figures are according to ship-tracking data compiled by Bloomberg.

Russia's dependency on gas exports creates pressure to sell

Russia has been one of the largest exporters of natural gas in the world, with a significant portion of state revenues deriving from gas exports. Russia's budget has enjoyed exceptionally high revenues from oil and gas inflows. Both are taxed via mineral extraction tax and export duties. Oil and gas revenues have contributed some 36–51% of total revenues in the last 15 years. The share is on a declining trend, however, falling from 46% in 2018 to 39% in 2022, and it is set to drop to 34% in the 2023 budget plan.

Among Russian commodity exports, amounting to $491.6 billion in 2021, oil and gas products contributed 48.9%. Natural gas represented about a quarter of this contribution, as crude oil and petroleum products had a share of 36.4% of the total, and natural gas 12.5%. Of the latter, pipeline-transported gas accounted for 11% and LNG 1.5%.

Figure 18.5. Europe (EU-27 and the UK) LNG imports by source country, 2010–2021.

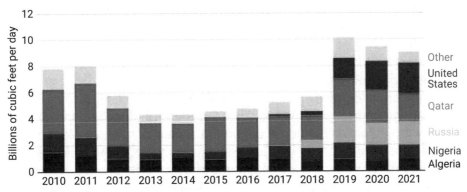

Source: Energy Information Administration.

As the Russian budget is heavily dependent on oil and gas sales, with a lack of other easily available export opportunities or internal sources for raising budget revenues, the country is under pressure to sell its hydro-carbon products. This creates a situation in which Russia is forced to sell these products at the most competitive prices – that is, cheaply – which is possible due to low production costs. The coalition sanctioning Russia is utilising this situation with the imposition of price caps on oil exports from the country.

The traditional way of exporting gas is by building pipelines, which provide the cheapest transportation cost of transfer after the initial investment in building the infrastructure. Russia enjoyed a monopoly in Eastern Europe because of its network inherited from the Soviet period and lack of feasible alternatives for importing countries.

The history of Russian gas pipelines to Europe can be traced back to the 1960s, when the Soviet Union first began exporting natural gas to Western Europe. The first major pipeline was the Yamal–Europe pipeline, which was built in the late 1980s to transport natural gas from the Soviet Union to Germany. In the 1990s Russia continued to expand its pipeline network, connecting it with several other European countries, including the Czech Republic, Slovakia and Austria. The country became one of the largest gas suppliers to Europe, supplying approximately 40% of the continent's gas needs.

Russian LNG production also started in the 1960s when the first LNG plant was built in the Soviet Union. In the following decades the country continued to develop its LNG infrastructure, with new plants and export terminals built in the 1970s and 1980s. However, it was not until the 2000s that Russia became a major player on the global LNG market. This was in part due to the growth in demand for natural gas, especially from Asia, as well as the increase in the country's own gas production. In addition, the rise of shale gas production in the US and other countries made it more difficult for Russia to maintain its dominant position on the European gas market.

In response to these challenges, Russia ramped up its LNG production and began exporting the fuel to Asia, Europe and other regions. One of the key projects was the construction of the Sakhalin-II LNG plant on the eponymous island in the Far East, which began producing LNG in 2009. This was followed by the development of other LNG projects, including the Novatek-led Yamal LNG plant in the Russian Arctic, which began production in 2017.

Russia is in many ways more dependent on gas exports to Europe than the EU is on imports from Russia, as a RAND Corporation article noted in summarising the situation in April 2022.[1]

Prelude: competing pipelines – Russian dominance

The EU's need for energy imports and the preference for cost-effective solutions have made gas imports from Russia a significant part of its energy mix. However, the EU has also explored alternative sources, especially prior to the rise of abundant US LNG. The competition among various sources has been primarily dominated by the construction of competing pipelines.

The Nabucco project: an alternative source

The availability of vast gas reserves in the Caspian Sea region offered the EU a chance to reduce its reliance on Russian gas exports and develop its own supply by building its own 1,326-kilometre pipeline from Erzurum (Turkey) to Baumgarten (Austria), baptised Nabucco in 2002. Originally

---

1 Marcinek, K. (2022) "Russia does not seem to be after Ukraine's gas reserves". *RAND Blog*, 11 April. URL: www.rand.org/blog/2022/04/russia-does-not-seem-to-be-after -ukraines-gas-reserves.html.

the intention was to purchase gas from Iran, but after US-initiated sanctions the EU shifted to Azerbaijan. Further supplies from Iraq, Turkmenistan and even Egypt were also considered. However, Azerbaijan opted for the Trans Adriatic Pipeline (TAP) in summer 2013, in which Switzerland's Axpo initially held a stake of 42.5%, Norway's Statoil 42.5%, and Germany's E.ON 15%. As this pipeline supplies the markets of Greece and Italy, it has not eased the heavy dependence of Hungary and Bulgaria on Gazprom.

The planned cost of Nabucco kept rising, hitting a bill of €10 billion compared with the TAP's €1.5 billion. A Catch-22 situation emerged as Azerbaijan would not sign any supply contract from its huge untapped Shah Deniz gas field until the viability of the Nabucco pipeline was proven, while banks would not finance the project in the absence of guaranteed supply.

Immediately after the idea of Nabucco emerged, Russia tried to prevent any competition for Gazprom by developing the rival South Stream, despite the costs and difficulties of building the pipeline. As two pipelines were competing for one source, only one could be built.

The Nord Stream projects: alternative route via transit countries

The first pipeline routes to be built that connected Russian gas fields to their main export markets in Germany and Western Europe pass through transit countries. This allows these countries to interfere in the export process, which is sensitive to political changes. To reduce this political risk, Gazprom initiated the building of Nord Stream, a direct pipeline connection to Germany through the Baltic Sea, which was also approved by the importer. A similar plan, with a lower capacity, was also developed to bypass Ukraine to the south from the Black Sea to reach Southeast and South European consumers.

This not only hurt the political influence of the transit countries, most of all Ukraine, but also their revenues, as transit fees add up to a considerable sum. Transit fee revenues of Ukraine amounted to about 2–3% of GDP in the 2010s. According to the calculations of Ukraine's gas pipeline operator, the original 2020–2024 gas transport contract signed with Gazprom, with reduced transport volume, would provide 2% of GDP. For comparison, according to the Hungarian National Bank's balance-of-payments data, Budapest received EU funds the equivalent of 3.3% of GDP on average annually in 2010–2020.

The Nord Stream project was officially announced in 2005 and the company running it set up in Switzerland in 2006. Nord Stream 1, a

1,224-kilometre subsea pair of pipelines, started operation with an annual capacity of 55 billion cubic metres in 2011.

For Germany, the economic advantages may not have been as evident as they are for Russia. However, Germany was able to secure a reliable and relatively cheap energy supply, given also that there were concerns about the durability of Ukraine's pipeline infrastructure. Meanwhile, German energy companies like E.ON that participated in the project could hope for potential involvement in the exploitation of natural gas in Siberia.

The project was repeated when Nord Stream 2 was launched in 2015. Its construction started in 2018 and was completed in 2021, doubling the original capacity.

The large-scale German–Russian cooperation project faced increasing opposition from the US. Since the early days of the Cold War, the US had seen that such economic interdependence has the potential to be used as a weapon by Russia. Parallel to the growing US gas export potential that could replace Russian deliveries, the stand of the US became stricter. In January 2019, then US President Donald Trump's ambassador to Germany, Richard Grenell, even sent threatening letters to German companies involved in the project.

According to Deutsche Welle: "the Nord Stream pipeline between Russia and Germany has caused much trans-Atlantic strife in its two-decade history. But [German Chancellor] Angela Merkel's dogged separation of trade and politics won out in the end."

The new administration of US President Joe Biden also tried everything it could to prevent the opening of the Nord Stream 2 gas pipeline, which was essentially complete at the time, and through which even more cheap Russian gas could have reached the German and West European markets. In March 2021, US Secretary of State Antony Blinken warned that all interested companies working on the project "should immediately abandon work".[2] Due to the political debates, which were reflected in delayed approval processes, and later because of the Russian aggression, Nord Stream 2 never started operation.

At the same time, the construction of pipelines bypassing the traditional gas transit routes via Ukraine and Poland continued in the south, as the Serbian section of the TurkStream pipeline was opened on 1 January 2021. In order for Hungary to receive gas from the south, a 15-kilometre pipeline had to be built on the Hungarian side, which was delivered on

---

2   Zengerle, P., T. Gardner (2021) "Democratic US senators urge Biden to speed sanctions over Nord Stream 2". *Reuters*, 23 March 2021. URL: https://reut.rs/3mdjo0x.

30 September 2021, just as the long-term Hungarian–Russian gas contract expired. In terms of capacity, it can handle the arrival of 8.5 billion cubic metres of gas to Hungary annually.

Figure 18.6. Russian gas flows to Europe, 2022 (weekly volumes).

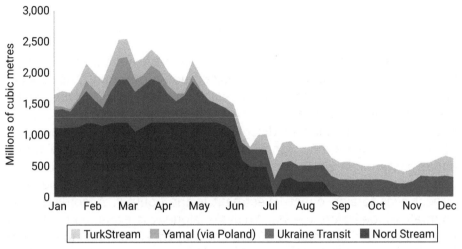

Source: Zachmann, G., G. Sgaravatti and B. McWilliams "European natural gas imports", Bruegel Datasets, accessed 23 December 2022 (https://www.bruegel.org/dataset/european-natural-gas-imports); via Center for Strategic and International Studies, Energy Security and Climate Change Program.

The political problem of Nord Stream was solved like the cutting of the Gordian knot by the – at time of writing, unattributed – terrorist attack on the pipelines on 26 September 2022. Speaking at the US Senate hearing on "Countering Russian aggression: Ukraine and beyond" on 26 January 2023, US Under Secretary of State for Political Affairs Victoria Nuland said: "Senator Cruz, like you, I am, and I think the administration is, very gratified to know that Nord Stream 2 is now, as you like to say, a hunk of metal at the bottom of the sea."

According to a source cited by the investigative journalist Seymour Hersh,[3] even before the war broke out in Ukraine, President Biden allegedly instructed American special forces, with the help of Norway, to place explosives on the pipelines near the Danish island of Bornholm during a NATO exercise, and ordered them to be detonated later.

---

3   Hersh, S. (2023) "How America took out the Nord Stream pipeline". *Seymour Hersh*, Substack, 8 February. URL: https://seymourhersh.substack.com/p/how-america-took-out-the-nord-stream.

In the wake of the terrorist attack on the Nord Stream pipelines, in January 2023, Russia started negotiations in Turkey for laying down additional pipelines to the country, establishing a gas hub there and cooperating in securing the safety of these facilities. They agreed that TurkStream alone is insufficient to cover European needs.

Shale gas fields in Ukraine: a challenge

Ukraine is among the countries in Europe that have not banned shale gas production due to environmental considerations. The country has considerable proven gas reserves. The largest such gas field is Yuzivska, which was predicted to hold the third largest deposits in Europe, of 2 trillion cubic metres. The field was discovered in the Donbas region in eastern Ukraine in 2010. Ukraine signed an agreement with Shell for exploration and exploitation in 2013, but works were derailed by fighting in the area that started the following year. The $10 billion deal could have been the largest ever foreign direct investment in the country. According to an estimate made before the war, Yuzivska alone was expected to produce up to 20 billion cubic metres of gas annually by 2030, equal to Ukraine's overall gas output in 2011.

Figure 18.7. Shale gas fields in Ukraine.

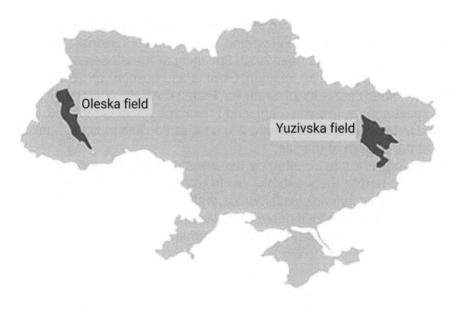

The war has made all immediate prospects for development of the field impossible. If there had been no war, then the existing pipeline network could have been used for exporting the gas to Western markets, thus replacing Russian deliveries. It is also highly possible that further gas reserves could be found in the Black Sea around Crimea, which might amount to more than 2 trillion cubic metres according to claims made in early 2012. Some 80% of Ukraine's gas reserves are located east of the Dnipro River, amounting to about 3% of Russia's total natural reserves. However, as a writer for US think tank the RAND Corporation argued in a blog article in April 2022,[4] it is unlikely that Russia started the invasion in order to acquire such gas reserves.

Present: US LNG partly replaces Russian pipeline gas in EU's imports

Russia exported some 202 billion cubic metres of natural gas through pipelines in 2021. Of this amount, some 83% was sent to Europe and Turkey, 13% to CIS countries and 4% to China. After Russia invaded Ukraine, gas deliveries were reduced in several steps. Concerning land-laid pipelines from Russia, on 10 May 2022 Ukraine rejected receipt of Russian gas at Sokhranivka, one of the border crossing points for the pipelines, and as a result the daily volume of natural gas transport via Ukraine fell by 25% to 72 million cubic metres. Two days later, Gazprom ended its shipments via the Yamal pipeline that crosses Poland. Daily shipments via Ukraine fell to 49.3 million cubic metres on 17 May, or by 50% compared with a week earlier. Via the northern sea route, Gazprom shut down Nord Stream 1 at the end of August, ostensibly for maintenance work. Nord Stream 2, which was about to be opened, never started operation and the aforementioned terrorist attack critically damaged both pipelines in the Baltic Sea on 26 September. This halted all possible gas deliveries from Russia to Germany under the Baltic Sea.

Compared with 2021, EU natural gas imports remained stable at about 337 billion cubic metres in 2022, according to preliminary data. Russia halved its exports to Europe, and the continent has turned to LNG as a replacement as non-Russian pipeline capacities are limited. The share of pipeline imports decreased from 77% in 2021 to 61% in 2022, while, in parallel, the share of LNG increased from 23% to 39%. Pipeline imports dropped nearly 20%, mainly due to the halving of Russian deliveries, in

---

4   Marcinek, K. (2022) "Russia does not seem to be after Ukraine's gas reserves".

which a key role was played by the shutdown and subsequent terrorist attack on Nord Stream 1 – which went out of service. Russia also halved gas transit via Ukraine, while flows to Poland dived 91% as the Yamal pipeline was closed in May. Russia also denied deliveries to countries with which it had payment disagreements, such as Finland. TurkStream deliveries remained stable at 12 billion cubic metres. Bulgaria was cut off, but Hungary increased its purchases.

Norway has become the largest pipeline gas supplier of the EU, with annual deliveries of approximately 70 billion cubic metres, but 5% less than in 2021. It exported more to France, Belgium and Germany – where it became the top supplier, covering 33% of their needs – but deliveries declined to the Netherlands, which increased its LNG imports. Due to the end of the Moroccan transit contract with Algeria in October 2021, North African imports fell 8% year-on-year to about 35 billion cubic metres. This left the Algeria–Morocco–Spain pipeline idle. Net imports from the UK also increased as the island country has access to large LNG receiving capacities, resulting in imports of 24 billion cubic metres, compared with a net export of some 2 billion cubic metres a year earlier. Azerbaijan increased its exports to the EU by 40% to 12 billion cubic metres. In July 2021 a memorandum of understanding was signed to double this capacity to at least 20 billion cubic metres by 2027.

Figure 18.8. EU-27 gas imports.

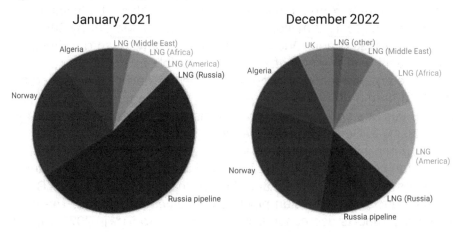

At the end of January 2023 the European Commission appointed gas-capacity trading platform Prisma to register the gas needs of EU member countries as a starting point for joint gas purchases. The Commission plans to receive orders from member countries reaching at least 15% of their storage capacities. Purchases may start in the spring of 2023.

What we can observe about Russian gas exports to Europe:

- Russian pipeline exports are confined to TurkStream and some Ukrainian transit;
- the missing volume is mostly replaced by US LNG and Norwegian sources;
- Russian LNG exports remain steady as some EU countries purchase more;
- increased Russian pipeline gas deliveries to China free American LNG to Europe.

Outlook: Global South punished by high gas prices fuelled by European demand

In response to the loss of Russian gas imports, the EU turned to other markets and consequently pushed up global prices, especially in the summer of 2022 when gas reserves were filled for the coming winter. The high prices caused problems not only to energy-intensive industries in Europe but also to poor countries that were relying on the use of gas mostly for electricity generation, such as Pakistan and Bangladesh, which suffered blackouts. Electricity in these countries is also used to fight floods and extreme heat. Suppliers even broke their LNG delivery contracts with Pakistan, paying default interest but transporting the gas to countries that paid much more.

According to the argument of Vijaya Ramachandran and Jacob Kincer, writing in *Foreign Policy*:

> Europe's rush to secure its own energy security lays bare a hypocrisy that hasn't gone unnoticed by leaders in Africa, South Asia, and elsewhere. [...] European countries insist that poor countries must not be provided with financing to build downstream gas infrastructure that could provide reliable power and economic growth. At the same time, nothing has stopped US- and EU-based multinationals from using their own capital to develop poor countries' gas reserves for export to richer nations in East Asia and Europe.

Ramachandran labels this policy "green colonialism", also referring to lobby activities led by Norway, which makes a fortune from high gas prices as a producer expanding its deliveries to Europe, for inducing the

World Bank to stop financing natural gas projects in Africa and elsewhere from 2025.

If Europe follows this policy of curbing fossil fuel projects in Africa and the South while increasingly purchasing their natural gas, then it is less surprising that its influence is diminishing in these countries, as they can turn to other powers for help. It also creates a credibility problem as to whether European countries are – as they claim – really pursuing policies of moral value, such as fighting climate change.

Furthermore, if the present fight of the West against Russia in Ukraine is really a fight between democracy and authoritarianism, then it does not look good when oil and gas-rich authoritarian states are approached and asked to increase their deliveries, even with the offer of concessions if they do so – as in the example of Venezuela and the status of "president" Guaidó. Can we cast out demons by appealing to Beelzebub?

A credibility problem is created if declared goals, such as the fight against climate change and for democracy (versus authoritarianism), do not match actual actions; solving gas demand problems in the EU might have unwanted repercussions in the South, which should be dealt with if we wish to reduce global tensions.

Further reading

Batkov, S. (2015) "Russia's silent shale gas victory in Ukraine". *Euractiv*, 2 September. URL: https://www.euractiv.com/section/energy/opinion/russia-s-silent -shale-gas-victory-in-ukraine/.

Harper, K. (2022) "Can Ukraine do without Russian gas transit fees?" *Deutsche Welle*, 28 January. URL: https://www.dw.com/en/can-ukraine-do-without -russian-gas-transit-fees/a-60552279.

Hersh, S. (2023) "How America took out the Nord Stream pipeline". *Seymour Hersh*, Substack, 8 February. URL: https://seymourhersh.substack.com/p/ how-america-took-out-the-nord-stream.

Humpert, M. (2022) "EU imports of Russian LNG soar to record highs; supply mostly from Arctic". *High North News*, 26 October. URL: https://www.highnorthnews .com/en/eu-imports-russian-lng-sore-record-highs-supply-mostly-arctic.

Marcinek, K. (2022) "Russia does not seem to be after Ukraine's gas reserves". *RAND Blog*, 11 April. URL: www.rand.org/blog/2022/04/russia-does-not-seem -to-be-after-ukraines-gas-reserves.html.

Ramachandran, V., and J. Kincer (2023) "Europe's hunger for gas leaves poor countries high and dry". *Foreign Policy*, 1 February. URL: https://foreignpolicy .com/2023/02/01/europe-energy-natural-gas-lng-russia-africa-global-south -climate/.

Sachs, J. (2023) "The war in Ukraine and the missing context and perspective". *AcTVism Munich*, 19 January. URL: www.youtube.com/watch?v=C1EwmYbK 7QA.

Stapczynski, S. (2023) "US surges to top of LNG exporter ranks on breakneck growth". *Bloomberg*, 3 January. URL: https://bloom.bg/40G3s5Z.

Sabine Schiffer

19 | Communication strategies, war propaganda and the role of the media

Although we know little about what is really going on in the war in Ukraine, since reporting consists for the most part of statements issued by official bodies, the media nevertheless also take clear positions on the war, putting forward both specific and conjectural solutions of their own.[1] The government of Ukrainian President Volodymyr Zelenskyy, a media professional, with his lobbyists, PR people and influencers, has proven particularly successful, while Russian propaganda seems rather dated in its approach; as a result, its powers of persuasion in the outside world have been decidedly limited. However, the focus of this article is on the propaganda efforts of other actors who are often ignored. This sidelining of participants, and the reduction of the conflict to a bipolar one between Russia and Ukraine, is itself an element of successful war propaganda.

Truth isn't just the first casualty of war; it dies long before that.[2] Since Russian disinformation was already on the tip of every tongue in the run-up to the attack on Ukraine and this remains the case, we will instead examine

---

1   Maurer, M. et al. (2022) "Die Qualität der Medienberichterstattung über den Ukraine-Krieg". Research for the Otto Brenner Foundation, 15 December. URL: https://www.otto -brenner-stiftung.de/sie-moechten/sich-ueber-aktuelles-informieren/detail/news/die -qualitaet-der-medienberichterstattung-ueber-den-ukraine-krieg/news-a/show/news-c/ NewsItem.

2   Morelli, A. (2004) *Die Prinzipien der Kriegspropaganda* (Springe: Dietrich zu Klampen). We need to contradict Lord Arthur Ponsonby, to whom this statement is attributed and who in 1928 listed ten principles of war propaganda in the aftermath of World War I. They are timeless and are as follows. (1) We do not want war. (2) The other side is solely responsible for the war. (3) The leader of the enemy is a devil. (4) We are fighting for a good cause. (5) The enemy is fighting with illicit weapons. (6) The enemy knowingly commits atrocities; we only do so unintentionally. (7) We suffer very few losses; the enemy's are enormous. (8) Artists and intellectuals support our cause. (9) Our cause is "sacred". (10) Those who question our propaganda are traitors.

our own side's propaganda, and above all the role of the media in democracies and in particular in the context of ubiquitous strategic communication.

We need to start by looking more closely at the terms "disinformation" and "propaganda". The second of the two may seem perplexing when applied to the public relations activities of Western governments, think tanks and allies. If we take the view of Edward Bernays – who as author of the books *Crystallizing Public Opinion* (1923) and *Propaganda* (1928) made a significant contribution to advancing PR for civilian purposes in the United States – the term "public relations" is merely a euphemism for "propaganda".[3] In the US and in English-language publications, the term "communications" is also used as a synonym for PR or "strategic communications". It is not so much public strategic communications such as that practised by companies, NGOs or even political parties that are problematic in this regard; after all, representing one's interests through communication and debate is integral to the democratic process. In terms of democratic theory, however, at least two aspects are problematic.

(1) Greater financial resources result in a greater impact in debates that are supposed to be about finding the better idea. Financially strong PR primarily lobbies to preserve the status quo that has made the lobbyists wealthy. This generally means that it promotes a conservative view, and therefore has a tendency not to advocate for creative progress.[4]

(2) Lobbying and "grey" PR – that is, PR that is covert and as low under the radar as possible – attempt to influence the public sphere and/or politics directly. This "fifth estate" should be critically investigated by the "fourth estate", since the media are seen as having a scrutinising function over all forms of power. This ideal type stands in contrast to how the media system is organised on the one hand and the particular PR focus on media relations on the other, as journalistic media are particularly valuable as vehicles for strategic messages (see below).[5]

---

3   "Happiness machines" (part 1 of the four-part documentary series *The Century of the Self*): https://www.youtube.com/watch?v=DnPmg0R1M04.

4   Schiffer, S. (2021) *Medienanalyse. Ein kritisches Lehrbuch* (Frankfurt am Main: Westend Verlag), chapter 3.

5   Leif, T., and R. Speth (eds) (2006) *Die fünfte Gewalt. Lobbyismus in Deutschland* (Wiesbaden: Springer).

The most succinct way to define "disinformation" is as "false information + intent" and it should not be projected onto the internet as a haven for fake news.[6] The more consequent fake news stories are still those that are spread by particularly credible sources, which in Germany are respected personalities and the journalistic media. Going back to what Lord Ponsonby said about propaganda, fake news in Germany is put down to mistakes, while intentionally false reports with the intention of manipulation are currently attributed to Russia alone.

If (free) media can be persuaded to disseminate strategic communication messaging, it has the advantage of being perceived by uncritical members of the public as verified and, as a result, more trustworthy. PR focuses on journalism in particular because it has the power to refine PR messages – whether intentionally or not – due to the fourth estate role typically attributed to it. It is thus particularly effective and hence bears enormous responsibility. In accordance with the principles of the press code of conduct, journalists are obliged to perform factual checks by carrying out research as an independent authority and bringing all relevant facts to light to allow opinion-forming, while PR can restrict itself to only a few facts that are useful for its communication purposes. In contrast to the strategic communication of specific interests, journalism should aim to achieve the ideal of being a neutral supplier of information to the public.

This defines the difference between PR and journalism in general terms. Turning to the specifics, let us now take a look at some key aspects of strategic communication in the war against Ukraine. As nothing but misleading propaganda is to be expected from the Russian side,[7] we will focus on attempts by Western sources to exert influence.

The boundaries of war propaganda are being crossed

Initial research findings suggest that German journalism has already moved firmly into the territory of activism.[8] According to communications

---

6   "Fake News als aktuelle Desinformation". German Federal Agency for Civic Education website, 2 May 2019. URL: https://www.bpb.de/themen/medien-journalismus/digitale -desinformation/290561/fake-news-als-aktuelle-desinformation.

7   This is why the tried and tested Enlightenment principle of "*Audiatur et altera pars*" ["May the other side also be heard"] is denigrated.

8   Prinzing, M. (2022) "Medien und die Ukraine: Grenzen zum Kriegsaktivismus scheinen fließend", *Meedia*, 17 June 2022 (https://meedia.de/2022/06/17/medien-und-die-ukraine -grenzen-zum-kriegsaktivismus-scheinen-fliessend); Eddy, K., and R. Fletcher (2022) "Perceptions of media coverage of the war in Ukraine", Reuters Institute, 15 June (https:// bit.ly/3pcsJa3).

scientist Jörg Becker, it is common for "tunnel vision" to prevail at the out-set of a crisis, but this generally begins to differentiate after around two months. The one-sidedness of the coverage about the war against Ukraine seems, however, to be more sustained – at least in the German media.[9] This does not automatically mean that the media in other countries are more critical of their governments. It could simply be that their respective governments hold different political positions than those of Germany's. In other words, the question of whether the media generally fulfil their role as the fourth estate with an inherent distrust of the authorities, or whether their function is more one of communicating official opinions, is one that would need to be thoroughly examined at an international level.

There is also a need to address the question of when a journalistic approach becomes partiality. According to German journalist Peter Welchering, a journalistic stance depends on keeping an open space for debate, promoting exchanges of views and opinion-forming, and standing up to power and attempts at censorship – but not proclaiming what "the right opinion" is or, even worse, "the only right solution". Such a biased approach was successful during the Covid-19 pandemic, but it cannot be assumed that this distinction will be successful in the current war situation, which is similarly fraught with fear. Taken as a whole, attitudes and opinions seem to be ever more frequently confused, giving rise to further activism and campaigning rather than journalistic neutrality in the form of fact-checking and presenting the facts as they currently stand.[10]

State repression on the Russian side is balanced by an increase in media repression in Ukraine too, while pro-war, pro-militarisation dis-course is subtly asserting itself in Germany:[11]

> While weapons are now referred to euphemistically as capabilities or heavy equipment, solidarity mutates into arms deliveries. Aid to Ukraine is now also understood almost exclusively in terms of materiel. The question of the danger of prolonging the killing and dying is tentatively raised on occasion, but – and in contrast to the assessments

9   Schiffer, S. (2022) "Zensur macht nur die Sowjetunion, wir selbst haben freie Medien". Interview with Jörg Becker in *Telepolis*, 24 June 2022. URL: https://www.heise.de/tp/features/Zensur-macht-nur-die-Sowjetunion-wir-selbst-haben-freie-Medien-7152051.html?seite=all.

10   Welchering, Peter (2020) "Gesinnung oder Haltung: Klärung in einer journalistischen Werte- und Erkenntnisdebatte", Journalistik (3/2020), https://journalistik.online/ausgabe-03-2020/gesinnung-oder-haltung

11   Deutschlandfunk (2022) "Umstrittenes Mediengesetz beschlossen", DLF, 14 Decem-ber 2022, https://www.deutschlandfunk.de/umstrittenes-medien-gesetz-beschlossen-104.html

of some senior military figures, who urge moderation – the focus is clearly on victory and the "annihilation of Russia", as German Foreign Minister Annalena Baerbock once put it. Anyone who speaks out against the logic of war and a spiral of escalation is quickly dismissed as a Putin troll. This is how a coherent system of war propaganda is created. As George W. Bush put it, "Anyone who is not for us (and the war) is against us."[12]

Phrases such as "special assets" as a substitute for the historically loaded term "war loan" also serve to conceal the dimension of war policy that the German government has adopted since Russian troops invaded Ukraine on 24 February 2022 and simultaneously avoid two problematic aspects. In addition to avoiding historical references to World War I, they also sidestep the problem that the decision to invest €100 billion in the Bundeswehr actually circumvents the law – namely the constitutional debt brake.

While handsomely paid spin doctors come up with strategic terms designed to put particular spins on statements, the media should be critically questioning the framing that accompanies them – in this specific case, the legitimacy of a decision, together with its strategic designation and the strategy of omitting relevant facts. A few do indeed engage in this from time to time, but these brief moments of critical inquiry are not enough to change the flow of news. In reality, Russia's attack on Ukraine is not the first war on European soil since World War II. Ignoring important facts, such as the Yugoslav Wars, was the basis for the false claim of a "turning point" (*Zeitenwende*) that German Chancellor Olaf Scholz invoked in the Bundestag on 27 February 2022 and for which he received a standing ovation. In reality, the turning point occurred in 1999, when the Bundeswehr went to war in the Balkans – for the first time since World War II and breaking with the previous credo of "No more war!" Since this initial "foreign deployment" in a NATO war and many other war missions, the Bundeswehr has been a component of global intervention forces that camouflage the martial philosophy of military involvement with euphemisms such as "stabilisation mission". While politics should be honest but is nonetheless permitted to communicate strategically, it is the sacred task of the media to expose such subtleties and to fill in any missing details.

---

12 Schiffer, S. (2022) "Von Solidaritätsmythen und Kriegslogiken: Medien im Fokus politischer Medienstrategien". *Journalistik* (2/2022). URL: https://journalistik.online/ ausgabe-2-2022/von-solidaritaetsmythen-und-kriegslogiken.

The coverage of the war in Ukraine confronts us with the almost schizophrenic situation whereby our screens are dominated by horrific images of war – which are likely to achieve their effect as they come with the bonus of authenticity, particularly as they are hastily interpreted in real time – while reference is simultaneously made to the impossibility of independently verifying them. Ultimately, it is the respective announcements of the warring parties that form the perception of the war's events. The fact that reference is repeatedly made to the inaccessibility and nonverifiability of what is reported represents progress compared with the war reporting from the Yugoslav and Iraq wars. It remains to be seen, however, whether this will allow some degree of scepticism to be maintained with regard to having certain knowledge, rather than being convinced that we know what is happening. The war in Ukraine would not be the only news story where media audiences confuse the portrayal in the media with what are in reality always far more complex facts, while not remaining open to taking on board new facts that change the picture considerably when taken into account.

Of course, it is also the case in this war, as in all others, that all sides are creating propaganda and that those sides consist of more than the two parties directly engaged in the conflict. The Ukraine Communications Support Network, headed by David Gallagher, is a relatively transparent organisation in this respect, and even has a website.[13] Nonetheless, the most successful PR is always that which is not recognised as being PR (see above), which is why we will follow its trail below.

Strategies of grey PR

Spinning represents a type of covert PR, in which the aim of coining distracting terms is, of course, to avoid them being recognised as such. As a result, it is possible to become angry about Russian state media and troll factories while at the same time talking up dictatorships like Saudi Arabia as a "stability factor in the Middle East", playing down your own country's war missions as "stabilisation missions", or even asserting that Ukraine, which had a high ranking for corruption in a variety of leaked reports before the start of the war, is now a free democracy.

While strategic wording can easily be exposed by cross-checking (linguistic substitution test), more extensively staged efforts are not so easy to recognise. One of the most established methods of grey PR is the

---

13   URL: https://iccopr.com/ukraine-communications-support-network.

setting up of grassroots movements, which is a ploy known as "astroturfing" (in joking reference to grassroots movements). In Germany, examples of astroturfing included Citizens for Technology, which was sponsored by the nuclear industry; a pro-Stuttgart 21 initiative as a counter-voice to opponents of S21; the Wortbruch in Hessen campaign against Andrea Ypsilanti when she was preparing to govern with the Left; and several other cases that the Recherche Network has looked into, some of which have been covered by NDR's ZAPP media magazine.[14] We can assume that the current approaches are not as cack-handed as they were back then, when PR agencies could be identified easily by a Denic domain query, or when the background structures were quickly uncovered via the financial trail.

In modern wars we can find NGOs that were founded or repurposed specifically for PR purposes, in order to be on the ground as an aid organisation and/or to investigate human rights violations and serve as a point of contact for responsible journalists who want to fulfil their duty to undertake basic research and fact-checking and seek a second independent source to confirm the first.[15] The Syrian Observatory for Human Rights in London has long been suspected of being such a set-up, repeatedly criticised in the media as one-sided and then used again as a source for information on war crimes in Syria.[16] A similar approach is taken with Bellingcat, a controversial forensic image service provider.[17]

14   Fuchs, C. (2008) "Atomkraft – ja, bitte!" *Die Zeit*, 17 April (https://www.zeit.de/ 2008/17/Atomlobby); Jakat, L. (2010) "Astroturfing – Geheimkampf um Botschaften im Netz", *Süddeutsche Zeitung*, 6 October (https://www.sueddeutsche.de/politik/streit -um-stuttgart-21-astroturfing-geheimkampf-um-botschaften-im-netz-1.1008550); ZAPP-Medienmagazin (2009) "Die PR-Branche und ihre Tricks", NDR (no longer online; from personal archive).

15   Becker, J. (2016) *Medien im Krieg – Krieg in den Medien* (Wiesbaden: Springer); Becker, J., and M. Beham (2008) *Operation Balkan. Werbung für Krieg und Tod* (Baden-Baden: Nomos-Verlag).

16   Kampl, M. (2012) "Beobachtungsstelle für Menschenrechte: Der Ein-Mann-Betrieb berichtet aus Syrien", *Der Standard*, 15 May (https://www.derstandard.de/story/ 1336696814431/der-ein-mann-betrieb-berichtet-aus-syrien); Tepper, A. (2017) "Wie verlässlich ist die Syrische Beobachtungsstelle für Menschenrechte?" *Deutschlandfunk*, 5 April (https://www.deutschlandfunk.de/informationen-aus-dem-krieg-wie-verlaesslich -ist-die-100.html). The BBC examines the critical debate on the White Helmets: https:// www.bbc.com/news/stories-56126016.

17   Bidder, B. (2015) "Bellingcat betreibt Kaffeesatzleserei". Interview with forensic image expert Jens Kriese, *Der Spiegel*, 3 June 2015. URL: https://www.spiegel.de/politik/ausland/ mh17-satellitenbilder-bellingcat-betreibt-kaffeesatzleserei-a-1036874.html. Verification in editorial offices plays an increasingly important role in times of leaked photos and videos, but the same applies here as everywhere else: the inputs that match your expectations must be examined just as critically as those that tally with the usual framing.

The many other strategies include guerrilla techniques, which aim to create a moment of surprise or shock with as little effort as possible, which is then picked up by others and further disseminated – first virally and then, in the best-case scenario, in the reputable media; this is something that is celebrated in the PR industry as "earned media" (that is, unpaid/gained attention). Alexander Gauland's "*Vogelschiss*" thesis in 2018 was one such targeted provocation that succeeded in attracting a good degree of attention. It corresponded to an internal Alternative for Germany (AfD) strategy paper from 2017 and factored in fierce opposition as an attention generator.[18] It corresponds exactly to the strategies used in targeted (hate) campaigns on the internet, as described by Karolin Schwarz in her book *Hate Warriors* (2020) about global right-wing extremism. These rely either on verbal provocations, horrific images that cannot be verified or particularly cute images that aim to frame those depicted as human and empathetic. Particularly popular are propaganda efforts featuring images of cats, which are also used in the Ukraine war.[19] The photos surrounding the opening of the opera in Odesa in early summer 2022 – for example in *Die Tageszeitung* under the headline "High culture in Odesa: symphonies and sirens" on 27 June 2022 – are reminiscent of a campaign by Croatia during the Yugoslav war, in which cultural marketing was used to present the country in a positive light. Jörg Becker gave the following example in an interview with the author:

> When the Croatian government launched the major Krajina offensive against Serbia, the Zagreb Symphony Orchestra was sent on a concert tour to the USA on the recommendation of a US PR agency while the offensive was taking place. What was the message being conveyed? See, Croatia is a civilised country, an interesting country with good taste and a love for old baroque music – this at a time when their guns were pounding Krajina. That's how public relations works.[20]

Images of war crimes such as those from Bucha in Ukraine are not staged, as forensic image verification confirms. Nevertheless, they say nothing about the course of events. This was something that was hotly debated among journalists on Twitter, but barely touched upon in the flow of mainstream news, with blame quickly assigned to one side.

---

18   See http://talk-republik.de/Rechtspopulismus/docs/03/AfD-Strategie-2017.pdf.

19   "Krieg mit Katzenbildern". ORF, 8 May 2022. URL: https://orf.at/stories/3263640.

20   Schiffer, S. (2022) "Zensur macht nur die Sowjetunion".

The following observation is interesting in this context: by defining a supposedly responsible party right at the outset and proclaiming this hypothesis as fact, the inevitable opposing viewpoint is also immediately declared to be the "truth" and is seen as siding with the previously – prematurely and unilaterally – accused party. Yet both are only claims of truth or hypotheses framed in a way that suggests that the truth can only be an either/or assertion. The antagonism of the two possibilities creates a restrictive framework, which supposedly pits the two camps against each other and, even more importantly, means that other possibilities are overlooked and not all alternatives are carefully investigated.[21] This fosters a bipolar restriction of discourse to a friend-or-foe format, which is very much a part of war propaganda. The same holds true for the many unasked questions about the sabotage of the Nord Stream pipelines, which – remarkably – is a topic that is barely discussed in the media.[22]

The fact-checking boom – or how to avoid fact-checking

As media analysis textbooks state, the status of fact-checking must be viewed critically,[23] as fact-checking is in reality the sort of basic research that should form part of any (investigative) research, rather than representing a genre of its own.

The dilemma confronting much fact-checking is exemplified by an example from a Deutsche Welle programme of 26 May 2022 on the topic of "hunger as a weapon".[24] The piece compares claims made by critics of this phrase with claims made by official bodies (sic), uses the latter to refute the critics' claims (sic), and goes on to address and explain some facts with regard to food exports from Ukraine. Yet the programme avoids the elephant in the room by failing to clarify the cause of hunger worldwide. The

---

21   For further information on this topic, see Schiffer, S., "Von Euphemismen, Deutungs-rahmen und Doppelstandards", in S. Kostner and S. Luft (eds) *Mit Russland. Warum Europa eine neue Entspannungspolitik braucht* (Bielefeld: transcript-Verlag) (to be published in 2023).

22   For further information on this topic, see Schiffer, S., "Medienverantwortung in Krieg und Krise", transcript of a lecture on Media Day 2022 (10 November) at the University of Innsbruck (compilation to be published in 2023; editor: Theo Hug).

23   Schiffer, S. (2021) *Medienanalyse. Ein kritisches Lehrbuch* (Frankfurt am Main: Westend-Verlag).

24   Prange de Oliveira, A. (2022) "Faktencheck: Wird Hunger als Waffe im Ukrainekrieg eingesetzt?" *Deutsche Welle*, 26 May. URL: https://www.dw.com/de/faktencheck-wird-hunger-als-waffe-im-ukrainekrieg-eingesetzt/a-61924334.

attribution by German politicians – Annalena Baerbock and Cem Özdemir in particular – of "hunger as a weapon" is now frequently applied to the war in Ukraine. These politicians are thus attributing sole responsibility for grain shortages and price increases to Russian President Vladimir Putin, but this does not stand up globally. First of all, Ukraine accounts for only around 12% of the global grain market. Second, the first shipments following the deal between Russia and Ukraine that was negotiated with the help of Turkey went to Ireland and Scandinavian countries, and many of those shipments were used in part to produce animal feed.[25] And third, the term "hunger as a weapon" has been around at least since 2001, when UN Special Rapporteur Jean Ziegler used it to express his outrage that the unjust global economic system and stock market speculation on food resulted in food crises and deaths from starvation, which was why he used the term "murder" to describe the deaths of children from starvation as a result of this situation.[26] The points he raised, which are as valid now as they were then, are obscured by such limited fact-checking as that carried out by DW.

Alongside fact-checking, reporting, commenting, and manipulative wordings and framings, there are also some fine-sounding initiatives that may well be relevant in contexts other than war reporting, among them the EU's Trusted News Initiative and NewsGuard.[27] Their objective is to assign labels to help identify which media should be believed and which should not. This is not without its problems in democracies that enshrine and uphold freedom of the media and freedom of expression in their constitutions, as the criteria and the executors are often not so explicit or impartial. First and foremost, however, the very premise of the approach poses a major problem, as there are well-thought-out and meticulously researched contributions and errors in every type of media – both mainstream and "alternative". This is something Germany's ARD is more than

25 "Proportions in per cent of Ukraine/Russian Federation, as of 2020", German Federal Statistical Office website (https://www.destatis.de/DE/Themen/Laender-Regionen/Internationales/Thema/landwirtschaft-fischerei/Ukraine-Landwirtschaft.html); "Ukraine-Frachter laden meist Tierfutter statt Brotweizen", *Der Spiegel,* 2 September 2022 (https://www.spiegel.de/wirtschaft/ukraine-frachter-laden-meist-tierfutter-statt-brotweizen-a-58d8017c-26f5-47e2-977d-68cbdc268d66); Wandler, R.(2022) "UkrainischesTierfutter", *Die Tageszeitung,* 28 November 2022 (https://taz.de/Getreideexporte-aus-der-Ukraine/!5898475).

26 "Welternährungstag: Jean Ziegler gegen Hunger als Waffe". *Swiss-Info,* 16 October 2001.URL:https://www.swissinfo.ch/ger/welternaehrungstag--jean-ziegler-gegen-hunger-als-waffe/2311720.

27 URLs: https://de.ejo-online.eu/tag/trusted-news-initiative, https://www.newsguardtech.com/de/solutions/newsguard-ratings

familiar with, as we can see if we take a look back at its coverage of the 2014 Maidan protests in Ukraine. In this particular instance, ARD's own programme advisory board attested to the fact that it had failed to report the situation accurately.[28]

It should be noted at this point that both media self-regulation and independent science have proven their worth as methods of media analysis verification. The fact that Germany's new State Media Treaty of November 2020 now puts the governmental media authorities in charge of reviewing the journalistic quality of online media not subject to self-regulation is another indication that a critical eye is required if we are not to throw the baby out with the bathwater. Fake news and hate speech are not purely an internet phenomenon, of course. They exist everywhere and must be critically examined, but those who put governmental or economically interested organisations in charge of the media must set out clear limits of influence.

Strategic communication organisations

We will confine ourselves below to two examples that directly concern Germany and Europe: the Centre for Liberal Modernity (LibMod) and the East StratCom Task Force. These case studies may serve as a stimulus to examine other influencers on media discourse.

Transatlantic think tanks and those that maintain contacts with Russia are frequently the subject of criticism.[29] German think tanks tend not to be in the spotlight as much, which is why we will have a closer look at LibMod. Founded in 2017 by the former head of the Heinrich Böll Foundation, Ralf Fücks, the think tank essentially continues to pursue a somewhat anti-Russian line that Fücks and his wife, former Green MP Marieluise Beck, have cultivated for many years.[30]

---

28   ARD Programme Advisory Committee (2014), "Resümee zur Ukraine-Berichterstattung aus Protokoll 582", report, June; Thoden, R., and S. Schiffer (eds) (2014), *Ukraine im Visier: Russlands Nachbar als Zielscheibe geostrategischer Interessen* (Frankfurt am Main: Selbrund Verlag).

29   Krüger, U. (2014) *Meinungsmacht. Der Einfluss von Eliten auf Leitmedien und Alpha-Journalisten – eine kritische Netzwerkanalyse* (Leipzig: Herbert von Halem Verlag). See implementation of the network findings in the satirical ZDF programme *Die Anstalt*, 2014.

30   The special friendship with Ukraine as an antithesis to Russia is expressed, among other places, in some of the think tank's projects, as can be seen from the website: https://libmod.de. These range from "Understanding Ukraine", "Understanding Russia", "Ostklick" and the programme "Eastern Partnership Plus" to the topics "Ecological Modernity" and "Liberal Democracy". The latter two projects are missing from the English-language website, which further emphasises the focus on Eastern Europe.

While some criticise the fact that the think tank calls itself an NGO but is financed by the state,[31] it is its media studies aspect that is of particular interest to us here. Taking a look at the membership list and, above all, the members of LibMod's executive board, it soon becomes apparent that several of the people sympathetic to this think tank's views sometimes feature as guests on talk shows without being identified as such.[32]

The "opponent analysis" in particular is a curious project given the think tank's political orientation towards Eastern Europe. LibMod claims that its analysis, which includes monthly monitoring and "studies" of individual "alternative media", is conducted with the objective of protecting democracy from its enemies. Even journalists are involved in the project, although there cannot really be "opponents'" in the journalistic sense, and there are more journalists sympathetic to LibMod than are listed on its website. They participate in monthly monitoring, while external contracts are awarded for the assessment of opponents' media. The project is funded by the "Demokratie leben!" programme of the German Federal Ministry for Family Affairs. Together with funding from the Federal Press Office, the government's press office, it is certainly questionable that state agencies are targeting the media, however bad they may be. This is a case of activism replacing independent research, with "opponent analysis" being a particularly problematic feature. It avoids the basic question of whether "alternative media" are to be seen as a symptom of restricted media discourse, or whether they represent a fractioning into separate discourse spaces, something that communication studies have criticised as "atomised public spheres" at least since the introduction of dual (public and private) broadcasting in the 1980s. No exhaustive catalogue of criteria defining what constitutes journalistic quality is employed when analysing the identified "opponents". This also overlooks the fact that an activist group is permitted to run a blog without having to meet the criteria of being a fully-fledged broadcaster. Without clearly defined criteria for democratic discourse and the limits

31   See "Staatsknete für die richtige Meinung", *Küppersbusch TV*, 2022, (https://www .youtube.com/watch?v=iZ-iEEfBGt0); Lübberding, F. (2022) "Wenn der Aktivismus zur Bekämpfung politischer Gegner staatlich subventioniert wird", *Welt*, 24 November (https:// www.welt.de/kultur/plus242119813/Zentrum-Liberale-Moderne-Wenn-politischer -Aktivismus-staatlich-subventioniert-wird.html); interview with Ralf Fücks (Centre for Liberal Modernity), *Jung & Naiv*, episode 607, 2022 (https://www.youtube.com/watch?v= CcWPrphl29Q).

32   See Appel, R. (2022) "Lügen für ½ Millionen Euro jährlich". *Beueler Extradienst*, 26 April. URL: https://extradienst.net/2022/04/26/luegen-fuer-1-2-million-euro-jaehrlich.

of discourse, this seems to leave the door open to arbitrariness, in particular since the author of this chapter was able to establish that there were qualitative empirical deficiencies in the work of the author of the first "opponent analysis".[33] Instead of following up on these indications and correcting errors, the organisation continues to use its position in the media to further the campaign it has launched. As previously mentioned, this raises the question of partiality and whether any attempt is being made to ensure impartiality, as well as the conceivable aims and benefits of pillorying media online.

The East StratCom Task Force is at least accurately named, given its focus on strategic communications, which is what the acronym in the second part of its name stands for. This initiative of the European External Action Service was founded in 2015 in the aftermath of the 2014 Ukraine crisis and was initially directed against disinformation from Islamists and China; its current focus is on Russia. What is less well known, at least among journalists trained by East StratCom to recognise Russian disinformation, is that it is a collaborative project between the EU and NATO; in other words, between a political actor and an executive military organisation without a mandate. While the EU has good reason to be concerned about the media system, it nonetheless promotes the principle of "media as market", and the question may well be asked of whether a military alliance with its own interests in Eastern Europe should be interfering in journalists' briefings on how Russia is perceived. This is particularly the case given the lack of transparent criteria and methods for precisely determining disinformation, as German journalist Eric Bonse ascertained in Brussels for the Institut für Medienverantwortung (Institute for Media Responsibility – IMV).[34]

East StratCom's own clipping on its blog (https://euvsdisinfo.eu/de/in-den-medien) represents only part of the medium's success. Press releases, blog entries and journalists' briefings are regularly reflected in reporting – always with reference to their (sole) source, such as in *Der Spiegel* of 8 March 2021 under the title "This is why Germany is the top

---

33   Schiffer, S. (2022) "Die willkommene Botschaft". *Medien, Meinungen* blog, Instituts für Medienverantwortung, 27 June. URL: https://medien-meinungen.de/2022/06/die -willkommene-botschaft.

34   Bonse, E. (2021) "Wie EU und NATO gegen Desinformation vorgehen". *Medien, Meinungen* blog, Instituts für Medienverantwortung (IMV), 7 October. URL: https://medien -meinungen.de/2021/10/wie-eu-und-nato-gegen-desinformation-vorgehen. The IMV is headed by the author of this chapter.

target for Russian fake news".[35] Similar articles appeared in almost all of the major media on the same day.

When assertions are made such as "NATO's eastward expansion poses a serious threat to Russia", "Western sanctions will cause food shortages and price increases" or "EU sanctions harm Europe more than Russia," or even "The US will benefit from the sabotage of Nord Stream," these are now automatically taken as Russian propaganda rather than contributions to a discussion aimed at checking and establishing the facts. The questioners are thus considered "Putin trolls" or, more recently in the Ukrainian view, "information terrorists".

Excluding such opinions or questions makes the possibility of negotiations as a possible course of action in the war even more unlikely than might have been expected after the first months of belligerent tunnel vision. Intentionally or not, the media play their part in this. But this ignores all the experiences gained from other wars: namely, that in the end negotiations always take place that nobody wished to conduct at the start of the war or even before it began – but they take place only after many more lives have been lost or destroyed.

Further reading

Becker, J., and M. Beham (2008) *Operation Balkan: Werbung für Krieg und Tod*, 2nd edition (Baden-Baden: Nomos-Verlag).

Bernays, E. L. (1928) *Propaganda* (New York: Horace Liveright).

Ellul, J. (1990) *Propagandes* (Paris: Economica).

Herman, E. S., and N. Chomsky (2002) *Manufacturing Consent: The Political Economy of the Mass Media* (New York: Pantheon).

Morelli, A. (2010) *Principes élémentaires de propagande de guerre: Utilisables en cas de guerre froide, chaude ou tiède* (Bruxelles: Edition Arden).

Schiffer, S. (2021) *Medienanalyse: Ein kritisches Lehrbuch* (Frankfurt am Main: Westend-Verlag).

Thoden, R., and S. Schiffer (2014) *Ukraine im Visier: Russlands Nachbar als Zielscheibe geostrategischer Interessen* (Frankfurt am Main: Selbrund-Verlag).

---

35 Bonse, E. (2021) "Fake News: Nicht Deutsche sind das Ziel, sondern Russen". *Lost in Europe*, 9 March. URL: https://lostineu.eu/ist-deutschland-das-topziel-fuer-fake-news-aus-russland.

Edward Knudsen

20 | The Ukraine war endgame: is there a way out of the ceasefire trilemma in 2023?

Over a year into Russia's invasion of Ukraine, peace still looks a distant prospect. Despite Ukrainian successes in the latter half of 2022, Russia's mobilisation and difficulties in supplying Ukraine with sufficient ammunition and equipment have left the conflict in what appears to be a prolonged stalemate. Reflecting on these military and political developments, this chapter examines potential endgames for the war in Ukraine, examining the possibility that outcomes are constrained by an irresolvable "trilemma" for the foreseeable future. Based on the constraints of this trilemma, it argues that a war of attrition may be the easiest option politically for both sides, risking a "long war by default" and all the destruction and potential escalation it entails.

Distant hopes for peace

Over a year after Russia's invasion of Ukraine, is there any viable option for peace on the horizon? Despite devastating attacks on civilian infra-structure and staggering battlefield losses, neither side looks willing to end the conflict.[1] Ukrainian President Volodymyr Zelenskyy, emboldened by increased Western support, has pledged to continue the fight, while Russian President Vladimir Putin has begun to prepare his population for a long struggle and potential further mobilisation. Ukraine's major Western backers have also pledged to support the country for "as long as it takes".[2]

Even as the war shows no sign of ending, analysts have begun fervently sketching out potential endgame scenarios, including advocating what

---

1   Santora, M., and M. Levenson (2022) "Lauding their soldiers, Putin and Zelensky signal long fight ahead". *New York Times*, 20 December. URL: https://nyti.ms/3Mf2gC8.

2   Chatterjee, P. (2022) "Ukraine war: Zelensky's visit shows neither Ukraine nor US want peace, Russia says". *BBC News*, 22 December. URL: https://bbc.in/3nKBZ50.

---

concessions, if any, Ukraine should be prepared to accept. Some of the more hawkish interlocutors favour backing Ukraine until it retakes all its previous territory, including Crimea.[3] More cautious voices point to the ongoing humanitarian disaster and the risks of escalation that a long war would bring, urging negotiations without reclamation of the 1991 borders as a prerequisite.[4] The different poles of this debate repeatedly invoke two seemingly self-evident yet ultimately contradictory points: Ukraine should have the right to determine its own fate; and the West should have the right to seek an outcome in its own interests if it is to provide crucial support for Ukraine.

Without wading into a normative debate about what Ukraine *should* accept, this chapter instead explores the tensions between different potential outcomes. Building on an article I wrote in June 2022 for *Encompass Europe*,[5] I discuss the possibility that there is a "trilemma" of potential outcomes: the idea that no potential outcome can combine alignment with EU interests, domestic acceptability in Ukraine, and military feasibility. I then discuss the possibility of what I call a "long war by default", a situation in which the domestic calculus of all parties perversely makes a lengthy, destructive conflict more politically palatable than an earlier compromise.

The war, a year on

Few observers predicted that Russia would launch a full-scale invasion of Ukraine. Even fewer thought that Ukrainian forces would still be a formidable force after a year of fighting. Despite some setbacks, Ukrainian resistance has exceeded almost all expectations, while Russia's once-vaunted military has floundered in its offensive and has even been beaten back by successful counterattacks. While early 2023 has seen slow, grinding Russian progress near Bakhmut, heavy losses and Wagner Group founder Yevgeny Prigozhin's own admission that capturing eastern Ukraine could take up to two years[6] make clear that a conclusive Russian victory in the near term is virtually impossible.

---

3   Zagorodnyuk, A. (2023) "The case for taking Crimea: why Ukraine can – and should – liberate the province". *Foreign Affairs*, 2 January. URL: https://fam.ag/3INZysQ.

4   Zubok, V. (2022) "No one would win a long war in Ukraine: the West must avoid the mistakes of World War I". *Foreign Affairs*, 21 December. URL: https://fam.ag/3M4sp6C.

5   Knudsen, E. (2022) "The Russia–Ukraine trilemma". *Encompass*, June. URL: https://encompass-europe.com/comment/the-russia-ukraine-trilemma.

6   Harding, L., and D. Sabbagh (2023) "Russia's plans to seize eastern Ukraine could take two years, says Wagner boss". *The Guardian*, 11 February. URL: https://www.theguardian.com/world/2023/feb/11/russia-eastern-ukraine-wagner-boss-yevgeny-prigozhin.

While the performance of Ukrainian forces has encouraged its embattled population and backers in the West, total victory still feels like a distant prospect. Russia's mobilisation and changing tactics have stymied further gains, while Ukraine has had to contend with ammunition shortages and a relentless aerial campaign against vital infrastructure. While Ukraine is not on the verge of collapse, neither is absolute victory imminent. Indeed, US General Mark Milley has said that Ukraine may now be in a better negotiating position militarily than it will be in the future.[7]

What do these developments mean for an eventual settlement between the Russian aggressor and Ukraine? In June 2022, in my article for *Encompass*,[8] I proposed that the tensions ahead of achieving a successful peace negotiation pose a trilemma. I argued that from the European Union's perspective, there are three important characteristics of any potential deal: alignment with EU interests; domestic acceptability in Ukraine; and military feasibility. Unfortunately, I pointed out, any given outcome at that time was likely to achieve only two of the three given objectives. The diagram illustrating this relationship appears below, with the characteristics of a given settlement at the vertices and the types of compromise on the sides of the triangle.

Why did these tensions seem irresolvable at the time? To quote from the original piece at length, I argued:

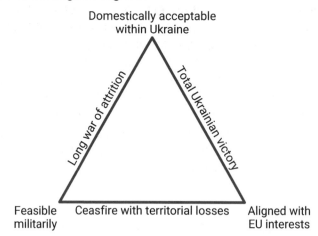

7   Liebermann, O. (2022) "Top US general argues Ukraine may be in a position of strength to negotiate Russian withdrawal". *CNN*, 16 November. URL: https://edition.cnn .com/2022/11/16/politics/milley-ukraine-strength-russia/index.html.

8   Knudsen, E. (2022) "The Russia–Ukraine trilemma".

The EU would prefer an absolute Ukrainian victory, expelling Russia, ending the war, and continuing Ukraine's process of moving closer to the West. However, even considering substantial weapons deliveries from both the US and EU and crippling sanctions on Russia, a total Ukrainian victory (of any sort) remains unlikely. As US General Stephen Twitty recently argued at the Council on Foreign Relations, "there's no way that the Ukrainians will ever have enough combat power to kick the Russians out of Ukraine". While the optimistic case that more advanced weapons may alter this battlefield reality, for now the impossibility of a complete victory leaves only two realistic options.

First, the war could settle into a long and attritional conflict. Russia's slow progress and Ukraine's increasingly formidable defensive arsenal make this stalemate scenario a distinct possibility. Moreover, domestic pressure on Zelenskyy not to accept significant territorial losses may make a simmering conflict more palatable politically, even in the face of mounting battlefield losses. This would be a difficult outcome for Europe. With dependency on gas (and proximity to many regions most affected by food shortages) still a major issue, the EU is far more susceptible to the collateral effects of the war than the US. This divergence of transatlantic interests could eventually result in political divisions, as the US would be far better suited by a protracted conflict than Europe, in spite of rising inflation.

Alternatively, Ukraine could accept a ceasefire in the near future, likely involving the loss of substantial swathes of territory. This may be in the EU's interest (especially for the countries more reliant on trade with Russia) but is unlikely to be palatable to Ukrainians. With an increasingly militarised society and many well-armed rightist groups, any resolution deemed as "appeasement" could spell the end of Zelenskyy's government. The hope of more and more advanced weapons deliveries may also make this outcome politically infeasible. This leaves Ukraine – and the West – with a dearth of acceptable options.

To summarise, at time of writing the above, total Ukrainian victory seemed militarily impossible, prolonged conflict would damage the EU's economy to an unacceptable degree, and territorial losses to Russia were deemed unacceptable to Ukraine's populace. Although the specific details of each outcome have shifted in the last half-year, many of the basic premises remain valid.

Do the constraints still apply?

Have any of these constraints substantially shifted since June 2022? On the military front, Ukrainian successes – particularly stunning advances in Kharkiv Oblast in September – may seem to have increased the prospect of absolute military success. However, despite these optimistic views, it is now unlikely that similarly dramatic gains will be possible in most of the rest of Russian-occupied Ukraine. Although often underequipped and poorly trained, Russia's 300,000-strong mobilisation has bolstered defences (where low-quality troops are more effective than in complex offensive operations). Russian forces have also dug in to key southern and eastern positions to avoid another Kharkiv-style rout.[9] The quick success of autumn 2022, which relied on a lack of Russian preparedness, is unlikely to happen again.

Russian coffers are also not being depleted as much as the West had hoped. Although the Western powers implemented unprecedented sanctions in early 2022, the Russian economy has contracted without collapsing.[10] Trade volumes with the West have shrunk dramatically, but these decreases have been compensated for by large gains in trade between Russia and countries including China, Turkey and India. Moreover, rising energy prices mean that while the *volume* of Russia–West trade is lower, the *value* is not. The recently implemented price cap on Russian oil of $60 per barrel is also unlikely to greatly reduce export revenues, as the price Russia has been charging already hovered around that level and many enforcement mechanisms lack teeth.[11]

Domestically, Ukrainians have shown few signs of giving up the fight. An October 2022 poll by the Kyiv International Institute of Sociology found that 86% of Ukrainians supported continuing the war effort and refusing negotiations, despite mounting Russian efforts to paralyse Ukraine's infrastructure.[12] Even when the trade-off for continuing the war is more bombing of cities, huge majorities in all regions opposed a negotiated end to the conflict (see Table 19.1). Similar numbers of Ukrainians also opposed any territorial concessions, according to polling conducted in

9   Hernandez, M., and J. Holder (2022) "Russia has built vast defenses across Ukraine. Will they hold?" *New York Times*, 14 December. URL: https://nyti.ms/40ZYaID.

10   Gamio, L., and A. Swanson (2022) "Russian trade boomed after invading Ukraine, providing ample war funds". *New York Times*, 30 October. URL: https://nyti.ms/40Co6UA.

11   Strupczewski, J., et al. (2022) "G7 coalition agrees $60 per barrel price cap for Russian oil". *Reuters*, 2 December. URL: https://reut.rs/3McivA7.

12   Hrushetskyi, A. (2022) "Russian shelling of Ukrainian cities: continuation of the armed struggle or transition to negotiations". Press release, Kyiv International Institute of Sociology, 24 October. URL: https://www.kiis.com.ua/?lang=eng&cat=reports&id=1151&page=1.

Table 19.1. Ukrainian views on a ceasefire to end attacks against civilian infrastructure.

	Ukraine as a whole	West	Centre	South	East
It is necessary to continue armed resistance to Russian aggression, even if shelling of Ukrainian cities continues	86	88	89	86	69
Completely agree	71	73	75	68	59
Rather agree	15	15	14	18	9
It is necessary to proceed to negotiations in order to stop the shelling of cities as soon as possible, even if this means making concessions to Russia	10	8	6	12	29
Completely agree	6	4	4	7	14
Rather agree	4	3	2	5	15
Undecided	4	5	5	2	2

Source: Kyiv International Institute of Sociology.

late December.[13] Moreover, Ukrainians overwhelming defined "victory" as recovering all territorial losses incurred since 2014, including Crimea.[14] Clearly, the Ukrainian will to fight is strong and any settlement short of absolute victory is unacceptable to the public for the foreseeable future.[15]

While Ukrainian resolve in the face of a horrific war is admirable, it poses challenges for the West. A mild winter and resourceful searches for new energy supplies have spared Europe from the worst-case scenario of gas shortages. Still, barring monumental efforts, 2023 may prove

13   "85 per cent Ukrainians oppose territorial concessions to Russia, poll reveals", *ANI News*, 4 January 2023. URL: https://www.aninews.in/news/world/europe/85-per-cent -ukrainians-oppose-territorial-concessions-to-russia-poll-reveals20230104140309/.

14   Reinhart, R. (2022) "Ukrainians support fighting until victory". Gallup website, 18 October. URL: https://news.gallup.com/poll/403133/ukrainians-support-fighting-until -victory.aspx.

15   President of Ukraine (2023) "On the one year anniversary of the full-scale invasion". Office of the President of Ukraine website, 11 February. URL: https://www.president.gov .ua/documents/742023-45789.

even worse than the previous year, with EU budgets already burdened by existing efforts to shield the population from high natural gas costs.[16]

These pressures have led many in Europe to conclude that a long war is not in their interests. Despite European Commission President Ursula von der Leyen pledging her support to Zelenskyy for "as long as it takes",[17] European citizens are somewhat less enthusiastic. Recent polling found that support for weapons deliveries is declining across Europe. Only about half of respondents now favour continuing shipments of arms, revealing a steady decline from when the same question was asked in March and June.[18] In September, this figure was only 36% in Italy, and under 50% in Germany, although still as high as 76% in Poland. In many key EU countries, awareness is growing that a long war may not serve their interests, with reports of some European leaders even pushing quietly for future peace talks.[19]

Although some important factors have shifted since June 2022 – such as Europe finding entirely new natural gas sources and Ukraine's impressive September counteroffensive – the basic tenets of the trilemma still hold up. It will be difficult for any ceasefire agreement to simultaneously satisfy alignment with EU interests, domestic acceptability in Ukraine and military feasibility. At the moment, a protracted conflict would not suit the EU for economic reasons, a ceasefire with territorial concessions would be unacceptable to most Ukrainians, and a total Ukrainian victory (including retaking Crimea) is still not militarily feasible.

Are the constraints immovable?

While the basic constraints of the trilemma still exist, this revisited trilemma argument does not imply that the constraints governing a

---

16   "How the European Union can avoid natural gas shortages in 2023". International Energy Agency website, 12 December 2022. URL: https://www.iea.org/news/how-the -european-union-can-avoid-natural-gas-shortages-in-2023.

17   Ogirenko, V. (2022) "EU to support Ukraine for 'as long as it takes' von der Leyen says". *France 24*, 15 September. URL: https://www.france24.com/en/europe/20220915 -eu-s-von-der-leyen-vows-unfaltering-support-for-ukraine-on-kyiv-visit.

18   Hoffmann, I. (2022) "Support for Ukraine is declining slightly". Bertelsmann Stiftung website, 1 December; https://www.bertelsmann-stiftung.de/en/topics/latest-news/2022/ december/support-for-ukraine-is-declining-slightly.

19   Pancevski, B., and L. Norman (2023) "NATO's biggest European members float defense pact with Ukraine". *Wall Street Journal*, 24 February. URL: https://on.wsj.com/ 3K6MCpP.

Ukraine–Russia settlement are entirely set in stone. As I argued in June 2022:[20]

Are these constraints immovable? Likely not. The situation on the battlefield may suddenly shift, sanctions may eventually cripple Russia's warmaking ability, or Zelenskyy may decide he is willing and politically able to accept territorial losses. Still, the essential logic reflects the broad outline of the current situation, one that is unlikely to change soon.

As with any war, there is always the possibility for rapid change. Recent tank deliveries from the West and discussions about sending fixed-wing aircraft show that resolve to support Ukraine is strong, especially at the elite level. Further deliveries may shift the battlefield balance significantly in Ukraine's favour. Alternatively, Ukrainian morale – which has proven durable enough even in the face of grinding winter assaults on infrastructure – could eventually weaken and become more amenable to a peace deal with territorial losses. For now, though, these shifts appear unlikely to alter the basic logic of the trilemma at any point in the near future.

Could other variables, such as Russian domestic politics, allow any room for manoeuvre? Since the war's outbreak, a sudden collapse in support at home for Putin's invasion has been the desired *deus ex machina* for those hoping for a rapid end to the war. Limited and highly publicised protests, men of military age fleeing mobilisation and other limited signs of opposition have fostered hopes that Russia may simply come to its senses and stop its brutal and destructive invasion. For now, however, such hopes look misplaced. Putin continues to poll over 80%[21] and support for the war has hardly budged, with about half "fully supporting" the war and another 30% "mostly supporting" it.[22] A further mobilisation may erode some enthusiasm for the war, but Putin has so far been effective in shifting public expectations from an easy victory in a "special operation" to a long, grinding patriotic defence of the motherland.

20   Knudsen, E. (2022) "The Russia–Ukraine trilemma".

21   "Putin's approval rating ends 2022 at 81%, boosted by support for the war in Ukraine". *BNE IntelliNews*, 2 January 2023. URL: https://www.intellinews.com/putin-s-approval -rating-ends-2022-at-81-boosted-by-support-for-the-war-in-ukraine-265628/.

22   Treisman, R. (2022) "What Russians think of the war in Ukraine, according to an independent pollster". *National Public Radio*, 18 April. URL: https://n.pr/3AVuD1B.

As a result, a "long war by default" may be the most likely outcome. With Ukraine unable to accept permanent territorial losses, Russia refusing to admit defeat and the West unwilling to force Ukraine to the negotiating table, political inertia alone may prolong the war far past the point that it benefits any of the parties involved. In this likely scenario, a long and destructive war perversely becomes the easiest path forward politically.

The political risks of a long war

Although the West is mostly insulated from the worst effects of the conflict, the political spillover poses a distinct risk to Europe. Even as transatlantic unity in the face of Russia's attack has been impressive, the seeds of greater disunity have already been sown. As the EU has scrambled to wean itself off Russian natural gas, imports of US liquefied natural gas (LNG) have soared and profits for American firms have been staggering.[23] Europe's rearmament efforts will likewise disproportionately favour the US arms industry, while the EU remains more exposed to migration flows than its ally across the Atlantic.

The transatlantic divide shows up in public opinion. Compared with roughly half of Europeans who wish to continue weapons deliveries, citizens of the US – Ukraine's main military backer – remain significantly more hawkish. About two-thirds (66%) support continued military and economic aid, according to polling conducted by the Chicago Council on Global Affairs in November.[24] On both sides of the Atlantic, elite support for Ukraine is generally more robust, but divergences in public opinion may eventually undermine transatlantic unity on opposing Russia's aggressive war, especially if a harsh winter returns to fuel-strapped Europe.

Tensions over the war's conduct have also surfaced between the US and Ukraine. The Americans have repeatedly insisted that Ukraine should not strike targets on Russian soil, making a pledge not to do so a precondition for the delivery of weapons. While this has limited Ukraine's ability to strike back at the aggressor, the loss of heavy weaponry from the West would be far more debilitating, and Ukraine has largely obeyed. Recent drone strikes on Russian territory triggered mild US condemnation, with

---

23 Stapczynski, S. (2022) "China sells U.S. LNG to Europe at a hefty profit". *Bloomberg*, 15 March. URL: https://bloom.bg/3MhTWSs.

24 Smeltz, D., C. Kafura and E. Sullivan (2022) "Growing US divide on how long to support Ukraine". Report. Chicago Council on Global Affairs, 5 December. URL: https://globalaffairs.org/research/public-opinion-survey/growing-us-divide-how-long-support-ukraine.

Ukraine walking a fine line between its desire to disrupt Russia's war effort and its need to maintain flows of Western aid.

Aside from intra-Alliance risks, the ultimate danger is of course Russian nuclear escalation. While the most panicked pronouncements about Putin's willingness to employ tactical nuclear weapons in the face of battlefield defeats seem to have been premature, every day the war continues is another day that could develop into a cataclysmic atomic exchange between great powers. High-risk, low-probability events like this are notoriously hard to calculate, but any discussion of a peace settlement in Ukraine must factor in the prospect of nuclear catastrophe.

To reiterate a point I made for *Encompass*,[25] I do not intend this piece to advocate for any particular outcome. Rather, I seek to explore the tensions between various solutions that have been suggested and to alert readers to the contradictions inherent in many proposals, ranging from "Ukraine must win" to "ceasefire now":

> This piece specifically does not advocate for any particular approach to ending the war. Rather, it intends only to shed light on the difficult choices faced in Western capitals. There's no easy way out of this conflict and arrogant proclamations of total victory or glib pronouncements that Ukraine should willingly accept substantial territorial losses ignore the material and political constraints on the ground. The sooner that our political discourse can acknowledge these tensions, the better.

Now, as then, policymakers and analysts would be wise to acknowledge the constraints that define any effort at a peace settlement. A sudden Ukrainian victory and rapid peace settlement appear equally unlikely. Instead, the default scenario of a long war looks the most likely for the foreseeable future, including all the destruction and risks of nuclear escalation that entails. European leaders should prepare themselves for this reality.

Further reading

Chatterjee, P. (2022) "Ukraine war: Zelensky's visit shows neither Ukraine nor US want peace, Russia says". *BBC News*, 22 December. URL: https://bbc.in/3nKBZ50.

Gamio, L., and A. Swanson (2022) "Russian trade boomed after invading Ukraine, providing ample war funds". *New York Times*, 30 October. URL: https://nyti.ms/40Co6UA.

---

25   Knudsen, E. (2022) "The Russia–Ukraine trilemma".

Harding, L., and D. Sabbagh (2023) "Russia's plans to seize eastern Ukraine could take two years, says Wagner boss". *The Guardian*, 11 February. URL: https://www.theguardian.com/world/2023/feb/11/russia-eastern-ukraine-wagner-boss-yevgeny-prigozhin.

Hernandez, M., and J. Holder (2022) "Russia has built vast defenses across Ukraine. Will they hold?" *New York Times*, 14 December. URL: https://nyti.ms/40ZYalD.

Hoffmann, I. (2022) "Support for Ukraine is declining slightly". Bertelsmann Stiftung website, 1 December; https://www.bertelsmann-stiftung.de/en/topics/latest-news/2022/december/support-for-ukraine-is-declining-slightly.

Hrushetskyi, A. (2022) "Russian shelling of Ukrainian cities: continuation of the armed struggle or transition to negotiations". Press release, Kyiv International Institute of Sociology, 24 October. URL: https://www.kiis.com.ua/?lang=eng&cat=reports&id=1151&page=1.

Knudsen, E. (2022) "The Russia–Ukraine trilemma". *Encompass*, June. URL: https://encompass-europe.com/comment/the-russia-ukraine-trilemma.

Liebermann, O. (2022) "Top US general argues Ukraine may be in a position of strength to negotiate Russian withdrawal". *CNN*, 16 November. URL: https://edition.cnn.com/2022/11/16/politics/milley-ukraine-strength-russia/index.html.

Ogirenko, V. (2022) "EU to support Ukraine for 'as long as it takes' von der Leyen says". *France 24*, 15 September. URL: https://www.france24.com/en/europe/20220915-eu-s-von-der-leyen-vows-unfaltering-support-for-ukraine-on-kyiv-visit.

Pancevski, B., and L. Norman (2023) "NATO's biggest European members float defense pact with Ukraine". *Wall Street Journal*, 24 February. URL: https://on.wsj.com/3K6MCpP.

President of Ukraine (2023) "On the one year anniversary of the full-scale invasion".Office of the President of Ukraine website, 11 February. URL: https://www.president.gov.ua/documents/742023-45789.

Reinhart, R. (2022) "Ukrainians support fighting until victory". Gallup website, 18 October. URL: https://news.gallup.com/poll/403133/ukrainians-support-fighting-until-victory.aspx.

Santora, M., and M. Levenson (2022) "Lauding their soldiers, Putin and Zelensky signal long fight ahead". *New York Times*, 20 December. URL: https://nyti.ms/3Mf2gC8.

Smeltz, D., C. Kafura and E. Sullivan (2022) "Growing US divide on how long to support Ukraine". Report. Chicago Council on Global Affairs, 5 December. URL: https://globalaffairs.org/research/public-opinion-survey/growing-us-divide-how-long-support-ukraine.

Stapczynski, S. (2022) "China sells U.S. LNG to Europe at a hefty profit". *Bloomberg*, 15 March. URL: https://bloom.bg/3MhTWSs.

Strupczewski, J., et al. (2022) "G7 coalition agrees $60 per barrel price cap for Russian oil". *Reuters*, 2 December. URL: https://reut.rs/3McivA7.

Treisman, R. (2022) "What Russians think of the war in Ukraine, according to an independent pollster". *National Public Radio*, 18 April. URL: https://n.pr/3AVuD1B.

Zagorodnyuk, A. (2023) "The case for taking Crimea: why Ukraine can – and should – liberate the province". *Foreign Affairs*, 2 January. URL: https://fam.ag/3lNZysQ.

Zubok, V. (2022) "No one would win a long war in Ukraine: the West must avoid the mistakes of World War I". *Foreign Affairs*, 21 December. URL: https://fam.ag/3M4sp6C.

Michael Landesmann

21 | What future for the economic reconstruction of Ukraine?

Ukraine has the potential to follow the convergence experiences of the countries of Central and Eastern Europe once the vehemence of the military conflict declines. However, this will require huge support and engagement by the European Union and other Western partners, while overcoming the institutional and political economic deficiencies that have characterised the country in the past. Much effort needs to be put into reversing the outward migration flow, making the country attractive to foreign investors, rebuilding and modernising infrastructure, and managing the necessary reorganisation of the economy both regionally and structurally.

While public attention has been and continues to be overwhelmingly devoted to the military aspect of the Russian invasion of Ukraine, there is also major concern over the viability of the Ukrainian economy to withstand the huge challenges which the conflict presents in the short, medium and long term. Ukraine's economy contracted by over 30% in 2022, inflation climbed over 20%, and the government faced dramatically falling tax revenues (by over 50%). While government spending in real terms declined significantly (apart from military and security spending), budget deficits were sizeable and only partly financed through financial support from donor countries and international institutions (with access to international financial markets no longer possible). The rest had to be covered through monetary expansion by the National Bank of Ukraine. A major problem lay in the unreliability of the commitment by donor countries (the EU in particular) to translate financing pledges into reliable financial flows in the months when the necessary expenditure (on pensions, teachers' pay, health, infrastructural repair and so forth) accrued.

For 2023, there seems to be a better-coordinated effort in place so that external financial pledges should cover actual public expenditures in time (with budgetary needs estimated at about €40 billion for the year). The financial pledges come principally from the EU, the United States, individual donor countries within the EU and outside (especially other G7 members), and principal international organisations such as the European Investment Bank (EIB), the European Bank for Reconstruction and Development (EBRD), the World Bank and the International Monetary Fund.

Apart from planning economic (and military) support for the current and next year, a number of conferences and background reports deal with the issue of longer-term reconstruction of Ukraine's economy. A very extensive set of documents was already prepared by Ukraine (the so-called National Recovery Plan) for the first conference of donor countries and institutions that took place in Lugano, Switzerland, on 4–5 July 2022.[1] This was a very comprehensive plan organised around sectoral needs over a planning period of reconstruction of ten years.[2] Apart from this report, there are also a number of other reports and studies that cover longer-term plans for reconstruction of the Ukrainian economy.[3] Themes common to all the reports include the importance of coordination among the multitude of donor entities; "ownership" of planning and implementation of sectoral programmes by Ukrainian authorities (central government and local authorities), combined with safeguards to ensure efficient and noncorrupt execution of these programmes by a supervisory body (but also transparency and involvement of Ukraine's civil society); the need to develop plans closely in line with EU accession agenda, which implies regulatory convergence and strong attention paid to intensified

---

1   Zogg, B. (2022) "Lugano conference: a first step towards Ukraine's recovery". *Security and Human Rights Monitor*, 21 July. URL: https://www.shrmonitor.org/lugano -conference-a-first-step-towards-ukraines-recovery/.

2   See National Recovery Council (2022) "Ukraine's National Recovery Plan" (https://bit .ly/410juaF). For a critical review, see Bogdan, T., M. Landesmann and R. Grieveson (2022) "Evaluation of Ukraine's National Recovery Draft Plan", WIIW Policy Note/Policy Report no. 61, Vienna Institute for International Economic Studies.

3   See Becker, T., et al. (eds) (2022) *A Blueprint for the Reconstruction of Ukraine* (London: Centre for Economic Policy Research) (https://cepr.org/publications/books-and -reports/blueprint-reconstruction-ukraine); Ganster, R., J. Kirkegaard, T. Kleine-Brockhoff et al. (2022) "Designing Ukraine's recovery in the spirit of the Marshall Plan: principles, architecture, financing, accountability – recommendations for donor countries", working paper, German Marshall Fund, September; Gorodnichenko, Y., I. Sologoub and B. W. di Mauro (eds) (2022) *Rebuilding Ukraine: Principles and Policies* (London: Centre for Economic Policy Research) (https://cepr.org/publications/books-and-reports/rebuilding -ukraine-principles-and-policies); World Bank (2022) "Ukraine: rapid damage and needs assessment", report, July.

economic integration with neighbouring EU member countries and the EU in general; the need to accompany implementation of the plan with a strong agenda of institutional reform and anticorruption, including "deoligarchisation"; and using opportunities in all the programmes to "build back better" (including important efforts towards decarbonisation and improved energy efficiency).

In the following I shall discuss the principal challenges and potential regarding the longer-term reconstruction of the Ukrainian economy.

It is possible to take both an upbeat and a pessimistic position with respect to the possibility and potential of economic reconstruction of Ukraine. I shall outline both these perspectives with respect to the outlook for Ukraine's economic development. In any event, the current military situation is such that it is impossible to predict the length or intensity of the war over the coming period and any outlook for Ukraine's economy will heavily depend on this.

On the upside: EU candidate status, convergence potential, restructuring progress achieved

Let us start with the upbeat assessment. First, the war itself has brought about a change in perspective regarding the possibility of EU accession. It will not happen overnight, but Ukraine has now been officially recognised as a candidate country for EU membership. This means that Ukraine's economic reconstruction will take place in the context of such an EU accession perspective, bringing with it pre-accession support both in financial terms and in the form of technical assistance to gradually align Ukraine's regulatory framework with the *acquis communautaire*, as well as (at least partial) inclusion in EU programmes such as the European Green Deal and intensified involvement in Trans-European Network programmes. All of these are likely to give coherence to any plans for Ukraine's economic reconstruction, while also providing significant support to improve the institutional capacity to implement such plans. The emphasis on EU accession and convergence in institutional/legal terms should provide a basis for economic stabilisation and focus efforts by the main (internal and external) actors towards this goal.

Second, the adaptation of economic structures to the new geopolitical reality already started in the aftermath of the 2014/2015 events, namely Russia's annexation of Crimea and intervention in the Donbas region, leading to substantial trade reorientation as well as the economic decline of what was once the industrial heartland of Ukraine's economy. In this sense, the impact of the 2022/2023 war means a further acceleration of the structural and regional realignment of Ukraine's economy. It also means a much weaker position for some traditional industrial sectors, specifically the iron and steel industry and metallurgy, which used to account for a major part of the country's exports. On the other hand, this has led to a much greater reliance on agriculture and the agro-food industry, which will likely enjoy further scope to strengthen its position by upgrading into processing and higher value-added segments. Moreover, the IT industry has expanded strongly and is now a major contributor to export earnings; this industry (like other service industries) offers job opportunities for highly skilled persons and thus plays an important role in catering for this segment of the labour force, thereby preventing or slowing the brain drain. Even those who have emigrated seem to keep in touch with the domestic activities of this industry, thereby contributing to its international reach.

Third, prewar Ukraine was plagued by very problematic governance structures (in particular in the areas of rule of law and corruption), as well as entrenched oligarchic power structures. There are a number of reasons why we can expect a positive break in political and economic governance structures, as the shock of the war has weakened specifically oligarchic economic interests based in the east of the country and strengthened the position of the presidency through its successful leadership role during the war. Furthermore, there will be strong involvement of international agencies (the European Commission, international financial institutions, donor countries) in monitoring use of the huge funds that are likely to flow into Ukraine to support its reconstruction after the war. It is difficult to make confident forecasts in this respect, but it is likely that both civil society and international donors will exert strong pressure to improve the situation with respect to transparency, rule of law and control of corruption. At least for some time, the spirit of mobilising national efforts to successfully move towards a path of economic, political and social renewal is likely to prevail.

Fourth, we have the track record of Central and Eastern European countries that moved towards EU accession and are examples of successful international convergence processes in income terms. There has also been improved institutional development, even though there are also examples of backsliding in a number of countries (most notably in Hungary). It can be expected that Ukraine will follow these experiences given that there is plenty of scope for gaining from intensified trade and production integration with the European economy, and from the role that international investors can play in modernising production facilities and facilitating access to markets. Given the legacies of war (destroyed infrastructure, loss of people through emigration, risk of continued military conflict), it is likely that such a convergence process will face big hurdles, especially in the initial phase. Even so, in comparison with previous "transition countries", Ukraine has the advantage of having seen the institutional and systemic changes associated with transition already take place to an important extent. After all, it is embarking on its accession process well after the shift away from a planned economy. The establishment of the DCFTA (Deep and Comprehensive Free Trade Area) furthermore speeded up regulatory convergence with the EU. The pre-accession phase – if handled well – has the potential to encourage reforms as it focuses society's interests towards achieving this goal.

On the downside: very high costs of reconstruction, demographic decline, questions over investment attractiveness

We now move to the other side of the coin, which leads to a more sober assessment of the scenario of fast and successful recovery (and restructuring) of the Ukrainian economy and polity.

First, what we consider the most important factor that might hold back economic recovery is the dramatic "demographic shock" that Ukraine has experienced. There are around 6 million internally displaced persons, plus about 7 million persons who have emigrated abroad, mostly women and children (according to December 2022 estimates). This comes on top of the demographic decline that was already apparent before the start of the current war. Ukraine had a population of over 50 million in the mid-1990s, which fell to about 42 million at the start of the war and – accounting for recent emigration – now stands at about 35 million. This decline has been due to a long-term low fertility rate (about 1.3 children per woman) and emigration due to a widening income gap with neighbouring Central and Eastern European countries (Poland in particular) before the war. Furthermore, the conflict since 2014 has led to depopulation in regions in which military conflict was most acute and in the regions close to these. The age profile of the population has deteriorated strongly, putting strong pressures on the social security (pension and health) system long into the future. Furthermore, as is common in most migration flows, the composition of migrants is biased towards the young and more highly skilled, which is likely to have a significant impact on the domestic labour force

---

(in terms of size and quality). Of course, there may be "return migration" of a significant portion of those who migrated, but the longer the military conflict lasts (and hence the integration of young families and children in host countries proceeds), the less likely this becomes. It will therefore be extremely important to initiate effective policy initiatives to attract the more highly qualified in particular to return to the country, as well as to keep in close contact with a sizeable and growing diaspora.

Second, given the experiences of other converging economies, we consider the role of foreign investors as very important in the task of restructuring and modernisation of Ukraine's economy. However, there are a number of reasons why it might be difficult to attract foreign investors at least in the medium term. First, there is the risk of continued military conflict deterring foreign investors. In this respect, we (in line with other policy analysts) strongly advocate internationally funded "risk insurance" schemes to cover some of the risks international investors and traders will encounter in Ukraine, even when a cessation of the most intense phase of the conflict has taken place. Second, Ukraine will start its recovery with a lot of destruction of its infrastructure, major damage to its housing stock and potentially a strong mismatch between regional labour needs and the availability of adequately trained workers.[4] Third, there is the issue of institutional factors that deterred foreign investment in the past (rule of law, corruption, market structures and political influence skewed towards oligarchs), and these will take time to rectify. Finally, the regions needing economic reconstruction and modernisation the most will be in (or close to) areas heavily affected by the military conflict, suffering the greatest destruction of infrastructure, most displaced persons and most risk of continued conflict, hence making them the least attractive for international investors. These regions will have to rely mostly on public investment and public support for training and education, and will need to be the most heavily covered by risk insurance schemes.

Third, quite a few studies[5] have made very high calculations of the necessary funds for economic reconstruction of Ukraine, with estimates

---

4   Anastasia, G., T. Boeri, M. Kudlyak et al. (2022) "The labour market in Ukraine: rebuild better", in Y. Gorodnichenko, I. Sologoub and B. W. di Mauro (eds) *Rebuilding Ukraine*.

5   Becker, T., et al. (eds) (2022) *A Blueprint for the Reconstruction of Ukraine*; Bogdan, T., M. Landesmann and R. Grieveson (2022) "Evaluation of Ukraine's National Recovery Draft Plan"; Ganster, R., J. Kirkegaard, T. Kleine-Brockhoff et al. (2022) "Designing Ukraine's recovery in the spirit of the Marshall Plan"; Principles, architecture, financing, accountability: Recommendations for donor countries; World Bank (2022) "Ukraine: rapid damage and needs assessment".

ranging from $450 billion to $1 trillion over about a ten-year period. The financing of these funds is far from clear at this stage as the international community (US, EU, G7) is mostly concerned with covering the most urgent budgetary needs to support current vital social and administrative services, in addition to military needs. However, some major analyses have already discussed detailed sectoral plans and priority areas of economic restructuring in Ukraine.[6] There are also proposals regarding the institutional set-up of such a reconstruction effort and how to deal with coordination of the multiplicity of donor countries and institutions. It is fair to say that we are still far from having a clear idea of the sources of financing for these massive funding needs and how problems of coordination, but also Ukrainian "ownership" of such programmes, will proceed given institutional deficiencies in the country that may persist after the war.[7]

Fourth, the experiences of the "transition countries" also showed that macroeconomic imbalances emerge in the process of economic restructuring and convergence. The economic reconstruction of Ukraine will – over a considerable period – likely be accompanied by persistent trade deficits as initially there will be very strong import demand, with domestic production (and export) capacities having taken a hit from which they will take time to recover. On top of this, the considerable inward financial flows supporting the reconstruction effort, together with significant remittances of a sizeable Ukrainian diaspora, may exert upward pressure on the Ukrainian hryvnia exchange rate, which can be detrimental for competitiveness and the building of export capacities. We have seen such developments in a range of transition countries, particularly in the Balkans, which have experienced long-term balance-of-payments problems. It will be difficult to counter these pressures without a special focus on supporting the tradable sector (such as efforts to support integration into cross-border production networks through regionally differentiated industrial policy measures including infrastructure, training, foreign direct investment support, and so on), measures to avoid domestic real

6   Gorodnichenko, Y., I. Sologoub and B. W. di Mauro (eds) (2022) *Rebuilding Ukraine*; Bogdan, T. (2023) "Public expenditure policy for post-war reconstruction of Ukraine", mimeo, to be included in the forthcoming *Report on The Economic Reconstruction of Ukraine*, Vienna Institute for International Economic Studies.

7   There are already institutional initiatives in this direction, as well as sets of detailed proposals. See, for example, Eichengreen, B., and V. Rashkovan (2022) "How to organise aid", in Y. Gorodnichenko, I. Sologoub and B. W. di Mauro (eds) *Rebuilding Ukraine*.

estate booms and channelling remittance flows at least in part towards investment and business start-ups.

Finally, the speed and the very commitment to Ukraine's EU accession are far from settled. The example of the terribly protracted process of EU integration of the Western Balkans (let alone Turkey) should be a warning sign, with respect also to the political repercussions such long delays and indecision of EU partners can cause in candidate countries. The pre-accession phase can (as the track record of previous accessions shows) be a successful time of institutional reform and economic convergence provided credible milestones are set and consistency in conditionality and timelines is maintained. It will also be important in the pre-accession phase that new schemes of fast integration into major EU programmes (regional and industrial policy, educational exchange and research collaboration, trans-border infrastructure development, the Green Deal) are developed and offered so that Ukraine (like other candidate countries) can – from the perspective of integration into such schemes – be considered a "quasi-EU member" country even when it still has candidate status.

Further reading

Anastasia, G., T. Boeri, M. Kudlyak et al. (2022) "The labour market in Ukraine: rebuild better", in Y. Gorodnichenko, I. Sologoub and B. W. di Mauro (eds) *Rebuilding Ukraine: Principles and Policies* (London: Centre for Economic Policy Research).

Becker, T., et al. (eds) (2022) *A Blueprint for the Reconstruction of Ukraine* (London: Centre for Economic Policy Research). URL: https://cepr.org/publications/books-and-reports/blueprint-reconstruction-ukraine.

Bogdan, T. (2023) "Public expenditure policy for post-war reconstruction of Ukraine". Mimeo, to be included in the forthcoming *Report on The Economic Reconstruction of Ukraine*, Vienna Institute for International Economic Studies.

Bogdan, T., M. Landesmann and R. Grieveson (2022) "Evaluation of Ukraine's National Recovery Draft Plan". WIIW Policy Note/Policy Report no. 61, Vienna Institute for International Economic Studies.

Eichengreen, B., and V. Rashkovan (2022) "How to organise aid", in Y. Gorodnichenko, I. Sologoub and B. W. di Mauro (eds) *Rebuilding Ukraine: Principles and Policies* (London: Centre for Economic Policy Research).

Ganster, R., J. Kirkegaard, T. Kleine-Brockhoff et al. (2022) "Designing Ukraine's recovery in the spirit of the Marshall Plan: principles, architecture, financing, accountability – recommendations for donor countries". Working paper, German Marshall Fund, September.

Gorodnichenko, Y., I. Sologoub and B. W. di Mauro (eds) (2022) *Rebuilding Ukraine: Principles and Policies* (London: Centre for Economic Policy Research). URL: https://cepr.org/publications/books-and-reports/rebuilding -ukraine-principles-and-policies.

National Recovery Council (2022) "Ukraine's National Recovery Plan". URL: https://bit.ly/410juaF.

World Bank (2022) "Ukraine: rapid damage and needs assessment". Report, July.

Glossary: war and politics, people, topography, weapons

The information in this chapter and the next covers the period up to 26 February 2023. The following abbreviations are used in both.

AT: Austria or Austrian
CY: Cyprus or Cypriot
DK: Denmark or Danish
EN: England or English
FI: Finland or Finnish
GE: Georgia or Georgian
IL: Israel or Israeli
IT: Italy or Italian
PL: Poland or Polish
RO: Romania or Romanian
SE: Sweden or Swedish
TR: Turkey or Turkish
UK: United Kingdom
US: United States
WW: World War

CN: China or Chinese
DE: Germany or German
EL: Greece or Greek
EU: European Union
FR: France or French
HU: Hungary or Hungarian
IN: India or Indian
MD: Moldova or Moldovan
PM: Prime Minister
RU: Russia or Russian
SK: Slovakia or Slovak
UA: Ukraine or Ukrainian
UN: United Nations
USSR: Union of Soviet Socialist Republics

War and politics

Appeasement   The act of giving the opposing side, in an argument or war, an advantage that they have demanded in order to prevent further conflict. Classic example: UK PM Neville Chamberlain appeasing Hitler at the Munich Conference (September 1938), allowing Germany to take the territory of the Sudetenland from Czechoslovakia, and by this averting war for a while and encouraging Hitler to look East rather than West.

Armistice   A formal agreement between two countries or groups at war to stop fighting for a particular time, especially to talk about possible peace (although a formal peace treaty may not necessarily follow quickly, e.g. as on the Korean peninsula).

Autonomous Crimean Republic (ACR)   Administrative definition introduced in a 1991 referendum (on 20 January); capital city Simferopol; official languages: UA, RU and Crimean Tatar.

Azot   Factory in Severodonetsk, the third largest producer of ammonia in Ukraine, and one of Europe's largest chemical companies producing nitrogen fertilisers. Location of fights between RU and UA forces in June 2022.

Azov Regiment   Volunteer paramilitary militia founded in May 2014 under the command of Andriy Biletsky to fight separatist forces (supported by RU) in the Donbas War, with a far-right ethnonationalist ideological orientation and a major role in the eventually unsuccessful defence of Mariupol against RU invasion.

Azovstal   Metallurgical Combine Azovstal iron and steel works, established in 1930 (during first five-year plan of the USSR), a metallurgical facility located in Mariupol; location of fierce battles between UA and RU forces in May 2022.

Batkivshchyna   Major political party in UA after its foundation in 1999, mainly popular in central, northern and western UA. Main leader Yulia Tymoshenko. Associated with the European People's Party. Had its own battalion in the war in Donbas.

Belovezh Accords   Agreement signed by leaders of RU, UA and Belarus in 1991, agreeing to abolish the USSR and committing to principles including self-determination, human rights, territorial integrity and freedom of movement. (With this treaty, RU explicitly forfeited any claim to Crimea in favour of UA.)

Berkut   Special riot police of UA, formed in 1992, used for violent suppression of Euromaidan protests. After it was disbanded (25 February 2014), many Berkut officers fled to Crimea, Donbas or RU.

Budapest Memorandum   A series of political assurances agreed in 1994 at the conference of the OSCE whereby the signatory states committed to respect the independence, sovereignty and existing borders of Ukraine, which in exchange abandoned nuclear weapons. The meaning of the security assurances was deliberately left ambiguous. (Full title: "Memorandum on security assurances in connection with Ukraine's accession to the Treaty on the Non-proliferation of Nuclear Weapons". Signed by RU, UA, UK, US.)

Burisma Holdings   An oil and natural gas company founded in 2002, based in Kyiv but registered in Cyprus, owned by M. Zlochevsky. US President Joe Biden's son Hunter joined it in 2014 as a board member – around the same time his father was vice president of the US, responsible for US–UA relations – and held the position for five years (Trump claimed this amounted to a conflict of interests).

Carthaginian peace   Brutal conditions imposed on the defeated combatant with the intention of permanently crippling the losing side. Arguably, it was the case after WWI, contributing to German revanchism and eventually paving the way to WWII.

Casus belli An event, action or condition that justifies or allegedly justifies a war or conflict. It can be real or manufactured (e.g. in the case of the invasion of Iraq in 2003). In the current conflict: UA's aspiration for NATO membership, oppression of RU-speaking minority especially in East, government's reliance on "Nazis", alleged preparations for UA offensive against separatist Donbas region.

Ceasefire A temporary stoppage of a war in which each side agrees with the other to suspend aggressive actions. It may be followed by a peace treaty, but may also remain the main framework for coexistence for a longer period.

Chauvinism Unreasonable belief in the superiority or dominance of one's own group or people, who are seen as strong and virtuous, while others are considered weak, unworthy or inferior. Originates from post-Napoleonic France.

Civil war A war between organised groups within the same state (or country), also called an intrastate war. Examples: US (1861–1865), Russia (1918–1920), Ethiopia (2020). Typically, they last longer than interstate wars. A conflict can be called a civil war even if one or more parties are supported by external actors (e.g. the Spanish Civil War).

Cold war Open yet restricted rivalry between great powers or even superpowers entailing an arms race and economic as well as propaganda warfare, but refraining from open and direct military clashes (except for proxy wars).

Collective Security Treaty Organization (CSTO) Military alliance established by RU in 1992, with some but not all members of the former USSR; not including UA.

Cossacks Predominantly East Slavic Orthodox Christian (but originally Turkic) people living in the steppes of UA and RU. The original meaning of the word is free man, vagabond or fortune seeker. They were a seminomadic and semimilitarised people, particularly noted for holding democratic traditions.

Crimean sovereignty Established at the time of the dissolution of the USSR through a 1991 referendum. Nearly 84% of registered voters participated in this referendum, and 93% voted for it. (The result was recognised by the Supreme Soviet of the UA Soviet Socialist Republic.)

Crimean Tatars Turkic ethnic group and nation who are an indigenous people of Crimea, and constituted the majority of Crimea's population until the mid-19th century. After WWII most of them were deported to Central Asia. In 1989 the USSR Supreme Soviet declared their removal inhuman and illegal.

Cyberwarfare Actions by a nation-state, international organisation or civilians to attack and attempt to damage another nation's computers or information networks through, for example, computer viruses or denial-of-service attacks.

Decolonisation of Russia A maximalist programme of some Western actors that in practice would mean the breakup of the Russian Federation along ethnic, national or religious lines, with reference to the outcome of WWI, when the German and Ottoman empires and Austria-Hungary were destroyed; and

WWII, after which the British and French empires, at least formally, were dissolved.

Defenders Day Commemoration honouring the UA armed forces, from 2015 held on a day matching the foundation date of the Nazi-backed UA Insurgent Army (replacing the "Defender of the Fatherland Day" on 23 February, which originated from the USSR).

Donetsk People's Republic (DPR) Separatist statelet in Donbas (2014–2022), backed by RU, which claims the entirety of Donetsk Oblast within the historical Donbas region.

Economic warfare Use of economic means against a country in order to weaken its economy, including cases in which the purpose is to reduce the political or military power of the adversary. Means can include trade embargoes, boycotts, sanctions (including sanctions on a third party), tariff discrimination, freezing of capital assets, suspension of aid, prohibition of investment and other capital flows, and expropriation.

Escalation A drift towards greater engagement, risks or costs. In a military context: moving from low- to high-intensity conflict. E.g. the Vietnam War (1960s) started through escalation rather than at one specific point in time.

Ethnic cleansing The attempt to create ethnically homogeneous geographic areas through the deportation or forced displacement of persons belonging to particular ethnic groups (minorities).

Ethnonationalism Understandings and forms of nationalism that regard ethnicity and ethnicities as core components of conceptions and experiences of the "nation" (and of a nation-state). In scholarly literature, ethnic nationalism is usually contrasted with civic nationalism, and in practice it often leads to the suppression of linguistic pluralism and regional autonomies, forced assimilation or even ethnic cleansing.

EU Association Agreement A legally binding act to establish trade-centred cooperation; in the case of UA, prepared by the European Commission and UA government in 2013 but in the end abandoned by then President Viktor Yanukovych under pressure from RU, and apparently in hope of a more favourable offer from RU. With commercial parts only, ratified by both sides in 2014 after regime change in Kyiv.

EU candidate status Granted to UA (together with MD) in June 2022 by European Council; does not necessarily lead to actual membership in the EU (see example of TR).

Euromaidan Mass protest movement sparked by the Ukrainian government's sudden decision not to sign the EU–UA Association Agreement, eventually leading to civil unrest, clashes with security forces and the removal of President Yanukovych from office.

European Bank for Reconstruction and Development (EBRD) Multilateral bank launched in 1991 to finance the economic transition of the formerly centrally planned economies, including the former Soviet republics. It provides loans and investments and manages donor funds (e.g. funds to ensure safety around the Chernobyl nuclear plant).

European family Emotional categorisation used by EU officials in 2022 to signal togetherness with UA fighting for its independence (carrying no legal significance).

European Political Community (EPC) Proposal by FR President Macron ahead of the June 2022 meeting of the European Council, reviving the concept of a confederation that would be geographically wider than the EU and could include the Western Balkans and countries with membership aspirations in the East, but also the UK, Switzerland and EEA members. The first EPC meeting was held in Prague (on 6 October).

Genocide The deliberate and systematic destruction of a group of people because of their ethnicity, nationality, religion or race. RU and UA mutually accused each other of it (RU before and UA during the war). Since the 2022 RU invasion, it has become more common to refer to the Holodomor as genocide.

Gerasimov doctrine A supposed plan for combined psychological, political, subversive and military operations (hybrid warfare) to destabilise the West, first outlined in a 2013 speech by Valery Gerasimov delivered to an RU military conference, which was subsequently published in a journal called the *Military-Industrial Courier*.

Ghost of Kyiv A fictitious UA ace pilot (scoring a number of aerial victories in the skies over UA's capital city by shooting down RU fighter jets), who is actually a composite image of pilots of the 40th Tactical Aviation Brigade.

Holodomor A period of severe starvation in UA in the early 1930s; largely a consequence of forced industrialisation and collectivisation of agriculture during the first five-year plan (*Pyatiletka*) of the USSR, with victims in the range of millions (with actual numbers disputed among historians). Just like Ireland's Great Famine (1845–1849) or the Bengal famine (1943), it can be considered a man-made disaster.

Hybrid warfare Actions that blend conventional warfare, irregular warfare and cyberwarfare with other influencing methods, such as fake news, diplomacy, lawfare and foreign electoral intervention.

Imperialism State policy and practice to extend power and dominance geographically, especially by direct territorial acquisition or by gaining political and economic control of other areas. It always involves the use of power, whether military or economic or in some subtler form, and is considered morally reprehensible.

Intermediate-Range Nuclear Forces (INF) Treaty Signed in December 1987 by the US and USSR, it limited both sides from fielding both "short-range" and "intermediate-range" land-based ballistic missiles, cruise missiles and missile launchers that could be used to house either nuclear or conventional payloads. The US withdrawal in 2019 represented a step that would allow nuclear deployments in Central and Eastern Europe and around the RU periphery in Asia.

Internationalised civil war   A conflict involving organised violence on two or more sides within a sovereign state, in which foreign elements play a major role in instigating, prolonging or exacerbating the struggle.

Irredentism   A policy built around the wish to recover lost territory and restore a country within a preexisting geography, with territories formerly belonging to it (e.g. DE and HU in 1930s, Serbia and RU in recent decades).

"It's done"   Text message from UK PM Liz Truss to US Secretary of State Antony Blinken after the explosions damaging the Nord Stream gas pipelines.

Jingoism   Advocacy of a belligerent foreign policy, with the use of threats or actual force, driven by extreme patriotism, nationalism or chauvinism, usually without appreciation of the costs and consequences of international conflict.

Kerch Bridge   Bridge over the Kerch Strait, built in 2016–2018 at a cost of $4 billion, becoming the longest bridge in Europe, a symbol of Crimea's reunification with RU. (Project originally proposed by the British to Tsar Nicholas II, who could not follow up due to WWI.) It was damaged by explosions in October 2022.

Little green men   Popular name for masked RU soldiers in unmarked green army uniforms and carrying modern RU military weapons and equipment, who appeared in Crimea before annexation, with allusion to stereotypical portrayal of extraterrestrials. RU media referred to the same group with the euphemism "polite people".

Luhansk People's Republic (LPR)   Separatist statelet in Donbas (2014–2022), backed by RU, which claims the entirety of Luhansk Oblast within the historical Donbas region.

Minsk I   The Trilateral Contact Group (TCG) and the leaders of two pro-Russian separatist regions (DPR and LPR) agreed a 12-point ceasefire deal in the Belarusian capital in September 2014. Its provisions included prisoner exchanges, deliveries of humanitarian aid and the withdrawal of heavy weapons.

Minsk II   The TCG and the leaders of DPR and LPR signed a 13-point agreement in February 2015, facilitated by the leaders of France and Germany; never fully implemented.

Misappropriation of Ukrainian state funds (MSF)   Sanctions (restrictive measures, including freezing and recovery of assets) introduced by the EU in 2014, and renewed on a yearly basis against a number of individuals identified as responsible for the misappropriation of UA state funds or for the abuse of office causing a loss to UA public funds.

Mobilisation   The action of a country or its government preparing and organising troops for active service. The mobilisation ordered by Putin in autumn 2022, intended to add 300,000 soldiers to the RU military, triggered an exodus of hundreds of thousands of young men.

Mozart Group   Private security company operating in UA during the 2022 RU invasion, composed of Western volunteers with military experience, providing military training, civilian evacuations and rescue, and humanitarian aid distribution; named to counter the RU private military organisation Wagner. Led by Andrew Milburn (US).

New European Security Order   RU President Dmitry Medvedev's proposal in 2009 for a legally binding treaty that would de facto codify NATO's current borders, restore RU influence in the "near abroad", and establish "rules of the game" to maintain peace and stability in Europe (published on the Kremlin website on the 20th anniversary of the fall of the Berlin Wall).

New START   Treaty between the US and RU, signed in 2010 in Prague by Presidents Obama and Medvedev, aiming at the reduction of strategic offensive arms, calling for halving the number of strategic nuclear missile launchers and a new inspection and verification regime. On 21 February 2023, RU suspended its participation in the treaty.

No-fly zone   Also known as an air exclusion zone (AEZ), a territory or area established by a military power over which certain aircraft are not permitted to fly. Demanded by the UA government in the early phase of the 2022 war, but denied by Western supporters with reference to the risk of escalation (possibly to WWIII).

Nord Stream (1 and 2)   Underwater natural gas pipelines built by Gazprom (RU) with the purpose of export to Western Europe (without crossing either UA or PL) since 1997, despite occasional US objections. Blown up in September 2022 (in an alleged act of sabotage ordered by Joe Biden, according to investigations by veteran US journalist Seymour Hersh in January 2023).

Normandy Format   An informal forum set up by French, German, Russian and Ukrainian diplomats in June 2014, aimed at diffusing tensions between RU and UA, named after the venue of the first high-level meeting where leaders from the four countries sat together informally during the commemoration of the 70th anniversary of the Allied landings along beaches there.

North Atlantic Treaty Organization (NATO)   A military organisation of collective defence formed in 1949, including North American and European countries. After the Cold War, it opened up to some former adversaries and went beyond its original defensive mission (see wars in Western Balkans, Afghanistan and Libya).

Oligarch   Extremely rich and powerful businessman (or other person); one of the few people who rule or influence leaders in an oligarchy based on their economic power. E.g. RU oligarchs: Roman Abramovich, Vladimir Potanin,

Alisher Usmanov, Oleg Deripaska; and UA oligarchs: Rinat Akhmetov, Viktor Pinchuk, Ihor Kolomoyskyi, Henadiy Boholyubov, Yuriy Kosiuk.

Orange Revolution   A series of protests and political events that took place in UA from late November 2004 to January 2005, in the immediate aftermath of the run-off vote in the 2004 presidential election, which was claimed to be marred by massive corruption, voter intimidation and electoral fraud.

Organization for Security and Co-operation in Europe (OSCE)   The world's largest regional security-oriented intergovernmental organisation, with observer status at the United Nations. Its mandate includes arms control, promotion of human rights, freedom of the press, and free and fair elections. Established in 1994 (replacing the CSCE).

Orthodox Church of Ukraine   An autocephalous Eastern Orthodox church whose canonical territory is Ukraine (founded 15 December 2018).

Our Ukraine   Centre-right political party of UA, formed in 2005, supported mainly in north and west of the country. Backed President Viktor Yushchenko; de facto phased out after 2013.

Party of Regions   Formed in 1997, was major political force in UA, especially in 2006–2010 period, with strongest support in eastern and southern counties. Russophile, Eurosceptic catch-all party, replaced in 2016 by the Opposition Bloc. Main figure: Viktor Yanukovych.

Peace treaty   A legal agreement between two or more hostile parties (usually countries or governments) formally ending a state of war between those parties. Since WWII, and especially since the end of the Cold War, international conflicts rarely end with peace treaties (as the lines between a state of war and a state of peace have become more blurred).

People's Front   UA nationalist and conservative party launched by Arseniy Yatseniuk and Oleksandr Turchynov in September 2014, with a political and a military council (the latter including leading commanders of the territorial defence battalions).

Pereiaslav Agreement   Ceremonial pledge of allegiance by Cossacks to the Tsar of Russia (1654) undertaken by the *rada* (council) of the Cossack army, which ultimately led to the transfer of the UA lands east of the Dnieper River from PL to RU control.

Pravy Sektor (Right Sector)   Right-wing to far-right, UA nationalist organisation. It originated in November 2013 as a right-wing, paramilitary confederation of several radical nationalist organisations at the Euromaidan revolt in Kyiv, where its street fighters participated in clashes with riot police.

Propaganda war   Targeting distorted or outright false information at an audience whose behaviour in relation to a conflict matters and could change (affecting the overall dynamics of war); usually comes with false moralising and a strongly biased presentation of history, and aims at building support for antagonism, hatred or belligerence.

Proxy war   A war instigated by a major power that does not itself become involved in open conflict. The relationship between the external actor and the belligerent can take the form of funding, military training, delivering light and heavy weapons, or other forms of material assistance that help the belligerent party sustain its war effort.

Rasputitsa   A season without roads; or a reference to road conditions during such a period (in spring or autumn). A topic of speculation about the dynamics of the RU–UA war in autumn 2022.

Reconstruction   An act (or period) of rebuilding, repairing or reassembling (a country) after a war or major shock; does not necessarily restore prewar conditions.

Refugees   Persons who have been forced to leave their country to escape war, persecution or natural disaster. By August 2022, over 6.6 million refugees had left UA (and a comparable number of persons were internally displaced within UA).

Reparation   The action of making amends for a wrong one has done, by providing payment or other assistance to those who have been wronged. Reckless demands for reparation can sow the seeds of the next conflict (as after WWI).

Revanchism   A policy of seeking to retaliate, especially to recover lost territory; focusing on revenge against a foreign adversary with military means, or on restoration of status or authority (see for example FR against DE before WWI, and DE against FR after WWI).

Revolution of Dignity   Propagandistic name for the events in Kyiv in February 2014, when the president of UA was evicted from his office by force following the violent culmination of the Euromaidan protests.

Rules-Based International Order (RBIO)   An imaginary arrangement of global affairs that is supposed to have existed before this expression started to be widely used, which is exactly the time when the RBIO came under attack, or was perceived to be in crisis, in particular in connection with the more assertive foreign policies of RU and CN.

Russian Orthodox Church (ROC)   Also known as the Moscow Patriarchate, the largest autocephalous Eastern Orthodox Christian church, originating from the Kyivan Rus. Reformed by Peter I, and oppressed at the time of the USSR. It claims exclusive jurisdiction over the Eastern Orthodox Christians, irrespective of their ethnic background, who reside in the former member republics of the USSR, excluding GE.

Russification   Also called Russianisation, is a form of cultural assimilation in which non-Russians, whether involuntarily or voluntarily, give up their culture and language in favour of the RU culture and the RU language. Pushed within the RU empire under Alexander III and after, and within USSR from the 1930s onwards, with varying intensity.

Russophobia   Intense fear, dislike or often irrational hatred of Russia, RU people or RU policy (or the former Soviet Union). In extreme versions, questioning the legitimacy of the existence of the Russian Federation (as a multiethnic state that is also a military great power).

Sanctions   Measures taken by countries to restrict trade and official contact with a country that has broken international law or committed a grave provocation, or companies and individuals associated with an adversary. Sanctions are tools of economic warfare that also damage those who impose them, and they may not influence actions in the military theatre in the short term.

Separatism   The advocacy or practice of separation of a certain group of people from a larger body on the basis of ethnicity, religion or gender, aiming at independence or autonomy.

Servant of the People   Liberal, pro-European political party in UA formed in late 2017; name alluding to a popular television show that made Volodymyr Zelenskyy famous.

Siloviki   RU expression to designate "people of force" or "strongmen", emerging as leading political figures from circles of the army, police, security and intelligence (examples: Sergei Ivanov, Igor Sechin, Sergei Shoigu, Nikolai Patrushev and Vladimir Putin himself).

"*Slava Ukrayini!*"   Meaning: "Glory to Ukraine!" UA greeting originating in 1920. Together with its response, "*Heroyam Slava!*" ("Glory to the Heroes!"), it became very popular in the 1940s and 1950s when the OUN/UPA partisan movement swept across most of UA. In 2022 it became an international slogan to express solidarity with the UA defensive war effort.

Special military operation   Euphemism introduced by RU President Vladimir Putin to avoid calling the invasion of UA a war (for reasons of international law as well as domestic politics).

Steinmeier Formula   Attempt in 2016 by then DE foreign minister to ensure implementation of Minsk II by calling for elections to be held in the separatist-held territories under UA legislation and the supervision of the OSCE; rejected by radical UA nationalists.

Svoboda   UA ultranationalist political party, formed in 1995, led by Oleh Tyahnybok since 2004.

The   Determiner, not supposed to be used before the country name Ukraine (since it would reflect RU etymology, suggesting that the country in question is a border region of another state).

Total war   A war without restrictions in terms of the weapons used, the territory or combatants involved, or the objectives pursued, especially one in which the accepted rules of war are disregarded.

Trilateral Contact Group (TCG)   A format established by RU, UA and the OSCE for peaceful settlement of the situation in eastern UA.

Ukrainian language   East Slavic language, using a version of the Cyrillic alphabet in written form. In 2018, 68% of Ukrainians considered UA their mother tongue, but only 50% spoke it at home, and only 39% used it at work.

Unconditional surrender   A surrender in which no guarantees are given to the surrendering party. It is often demanded with the threat of complete destruction, extermination or annihilation. Demand for it puts psychological pressure on a weaker (or weakening) adversary, but it may also prolong hostilities.

Verkhovna Rada   The unicameral parliament of UA (official name: Supreme Council of Ukraine).

Volhynia massacre   Actions of the UA Insurgent Army (UPA) in 1943 leading to the killing of about 100,000 PL people in the Volhynia region, under Nazi occupation; one of the major examples of violent ethnic cleansing (genocide according to some, especially in PL) in the 20th century (subject of a 2016 PL film drama).

Wagner Group   RU mercenary organisation, established in 2014, believed to be owned or financed by Yevgeny Prigozhin, which has been active across the world, and in 2022–2023 in the RU–UA war (in the battle for Bakhmut in particular).

War aims   A set of issues a government or nation entering war wishes to resolve. Traditionally, a clear statement of war aims has been essential to establish that a cause was just.

War crimes   In international law, serious violations of the laws or customs of war as defined by international customary law and international treaties; subject to systematic studies and prosecution efforts since the US Civil War and especially WWI. The Geneva Conventions (1949) are the main reference point for judging actions and framing legal initiatives.

War of aggression   A military conflict waged without the justification of self-defence, usually for territorial gain and subjugation (also called a war of conquest).

War of attrition   A prolonged period of conflict during which each side seeks to gradually wear down the other by a series of small-scale actions.

War of dissolution   Intense military activity accompanying the breakup of an empire or a federal state, typically entailing territorial disputes and ethnic cleansing (e.g. post-Yugoslav wars in the 1990s or post-Soviet wars since 1991).

War of movement   Warfare taking place in open country, whereby military operations are not restricted by extensive defensive obstacles and can become rather dynamic.

Westsplaining   A pejorative term (adopted mainly by academics from Central and Eastern Europe) that represents criticism of the Western world's sociopolitical views of Central and Eastern Europe, primarily for interpreting

East–West relations in a global context and thus often downplaying or ignoring the concerns of RU's neighbours.

World War III   A hypothetical global conflict, possibly with the deployment of nuclear weapons and with devastating effects comparable to the 20th century world wars or going even beyond those. Very few explicitly advocate WWIII, but the need to avoid it often appears in various warnings against the escalation of conflicts, including the RU–UA war.

Z   Enigmatic symbol used by the RU army for forces involved in the invasion of UA in 2022.

Zeitenwende   DE expression introduced by Chancellor Olaf Scholz to describe the fundamental shift in policy triggered by the RU aggression against UA, including a massive increase in defence spending and the securitisation of international economic relations.

People

Note: UA and RU names are without patronymics.

Abramovich, Roman (1966–)   RU businessman (in metal and other industries); owner of Chelsea football club, which he sold after the invasion of UA; sanctioned by Western countries; attended peace negotiations in TR.

Akhmetov, Rinat (1966–)   Richest oligarch in UA, with major interests in steel industry, which was largely destroyed during the war. In 2021, President Zelenskyy accused him of staging a coup. In June 2022 he filed a lawsuit against RU at the European Court of Human Rights.

Bandera, Stepan (1909–1959)   UA nationalist leader before and during WWII. His movement collaborated with the Nazis, including in murdering Jews and Poles. He was assassinated (by the KGB) in Germany, where he lived after WWII.

Bennett, Naftali (1972–)   Israeli politician, former PM (2021–2022), who tried to broker a truce between RU and UA shortly after the 2022 invasion, allegedly undermined by the West.

Biden, Hunter (1970–)   US attorney, second son of President Joe Biden. Has had extensive business engagements in CN and UA (including the Burisma company, where he earned CA$80,000 monthly); a 2022 film (*My Son Hunter*) was produced about him, starring Laurence Fox.

Brink, Bridget (1970–)   US career diplomat, ambassador in Kyiv from 2022, confirmed unanimously by the US Senate on 18 May; served previously in Belgrade, Tbilisi and Bratislava.

Burns, William J. (1956–)   US diplomat, ambassador to RU (2005–2008), Deputy Secretary of State (2011–2014), CIA Director in the Biden administration.

Catherine the Great, or Catherine II (1729–96) German-born RU empress, listed among enlightened absolutists (supported arts and the education of women). She extended RU territory to Crimea and participated in partitions of PL.

Dolgorukiy, Yuri (1099–1157) Rurikid prince, founder of Moscow; curbed the privileges of the landowning boyar class in Rostov-Suzdal; fought for the control of Kyiv, where he was presumably poisoned by local boyars, sparking the anti-Suzdalian uprising in Kyiv.

Dugin, Alexander (1962–) Postmodernist philosopher, political analyst and strategist, ideologue of Eurasianism; believed to have intellectual influence over Putin; sanctioned by US in 2015; lost his daughter to assassination in Moscow in August 2022.

Dvornikov, Aleksandr (1961–) RU military leader, main commander of invasion forces in UA (April–June 2022); commanded the RU military intervention in Syria (2015); described as a "blood and soil nationalist".

Gerasimov, Valery (1955–) RU army general, Chief of the General Staff of the RU armed forces and first deputy defence minister (since 2012); author of "hybrid warfare" doctrine. He became overall commander of the UA campaign in January 2023.

Haines, Avril (1969–) US lawyer, Director of National Intelligence in the Biden administration.

Kadyrov, Ramzan (1976–) Chechen leader (warlord and Head of Republic); appeared in Mariupol with his fighters participating in the siege; criticised RU army in September after setbacks.

Kerpatenko, Yurii (1976–2022) Conductor of the Mykola Kulish Kherson Music and Drama Theatre, the Kherson Regional Philharmonic and the Gileya Chamber Orchestra; spoke out against RU occupation until he was murdered by occupying RU forces in his home.

Khmelnytsky, Bohdan (1595–1657) UA military commander, educated in PL and served in PL army. As Hetman of the Zaporozhian Host, he led revolt against PL rule, directed Cossacks to take an oath of allegiance to RU tsar and died when trying to conclude a treaty with SE.

Khrushchev, Nikita (1894–1971) Communist politician, grew up as son of a coal miner (in Donbas); head of the UA party organisation in the years before and after WWII; de facto leader of the Soviet Union after the death of Stalin (1953–1964); transferred Crimea from RU to UA in 1954.

Kirill or Cyril (1946–) RU Patriarch, studied theology in Leningrad, became head of the RU Orthodox Church in 2009; considered to be a close Putin ally, lauded the invasion of UA, but excluded from anti-RU sanctions at the request of HU Prime Minister Viktor Orbán in June 2022.

Klitschko, Vitali (1981–)   Professional boxer, politician, mayor of Kyiv (2014–).

Kolomoyskyi, Ihor (1963–)   UA oligarch, supported Yushchenko and Tymoshenko, and in 2014–2016 served as governor of Dnipro Region. He is among the main funders of Jewish causes in UA, and considered to be Zelenskyy's main original backer. Holds IL and CY passports, and was accused of money laundering by US.

Kravchuk, Leonid (1934–2022)   President of UA (1991–1994), originally a teacher of political economy.

Kuchma, Leonid (1938–)   President of Ukraine (1994–2005), originally a mechanical engineer.

Kuleba, Dmytro (1981–)   UA politician, diplomat, foreign minister (2020–); communications specialist; actively participated in the Euromaidan protest.

Kusyuk, Sergey (1966–)   Berkut commander, fled to RU, serves in RU police (wanted in UA).

Lavrov, Sergey (1950–)   RU diplomat, foreign minister (2004–). Worked at UN HQ for 15 years.

Makhno, Nestor (1889–1934)   UA anarchist, organiser of peasant and worker movement. He fought occupying Germans at the end of WWI, then took part in RU Civil War in shaky alliance with Bolsheviks. Following imprisonment in PL, died in FR emigration.

Mazepa, Ivan (1639–1709)   Ruthenian military, political and civic leader who served as Hetman of the Zaporizhian Host (1687–1708). Turned against Peter I and sided with SE, and died in emigration shortly after. His figure inspired Eugene Delacroix, Victor Hugo, Franz Liszt and Peter Tchaikovsky.

McCain, John (1936–2018)   US right-wing politician, Vietnam War veteran, Republican senator (1987–2018), failed presidential candidate (2008); stoked UA nationalism and violence against separatists in the Donbas.

Medvedchuk, Viktor (1954–)   Lawyer, business oligarch and politician, chairman of the pro-RU organisation Ukrainian Choice (2018–2022). Considered Putin's main ally in UA, he was put under arrest in April 2022.

Medvedev, Dmitry (1965–)   Former RU resident (2008–2012) and PM (2012–2020); deputy chair of RU Security Council (2020–); considered to be more liberal than Putin before his presidency, but notorious for extreme chauvinistic statements during 2022 war.

Melnyk, Andriy (1975–)   Diplomat, lawyer, ambassador to Germany (2014–2022); leading voice in UA propaganda war against DE; replaced on 9 July.

Meshkov, Yuri (1945–2019)   UA politician and leader of the pro-RU movement in Crimea; served as the only President of Crimea (1994–1995); deported to RU in 1995 and 2011.

Milburn, Andrew (1963–)   Retired US Marine colonel. He was born in Hong Kong and grew up in UK; served 31 years in US Marine Corps. He created and leads the Mozart Group, comprising special operations veterans in 2022 war.

Murashko, Danylo (1998–2023)   Pilot of UA air force, killed in action on 27 January 2023, after destroying about 70 RU armoured vehicles, more than 80 cars and about 30 fuel tanks, and killing about 600 RU soldiers in fights; posthumously awarded title of "Hero of Ukraine".

Nuland, Victoria (1961–)   US diplomat, Under Secretary of State for Political Affairs (2021–), State Department spokesperson (2011–2013); in 2013–2017 responsible for European and Eurasian Affairs in the State Department; remembered for a leaked phone call with Ambassador Geoffrey Pyatt ("f-ck the EU"). Spouse of neoconservative theorist Robert Kagan.

Patrushev, Nikolai (1951–)   RU politician, security and intelligence officer, leading figure among *siloviki*, head of the FSB (1999–2008), and secretary of the RU Security Council (2008–).

Peskov, Dmitry (1967–)   RU diplomat (served in TR) and press secretary of President Putin (2012–). Sanctioned by EU, US and UK after the RU invasion of UA.

Peter the Great, or Peter I (1672–1725)   Monarch who ruled RU for 43 years, modernised it and made it a European power. He was raised in an atmosphere open to progressive influences from the West, founded Saint Petersburg and made it RU capital city. Invoked by Putin to frame the 2022 war against UA.

Pinchuk, Viktor (1960–)   UA oligarch, earned doctorate in industrial engineering in Dnipro; became pipe and railway wheel manufacturer; son-in-law of former UA President Kuchma. He provided financial support to the UA army and civilians at the time of war.

Podolyak, Mykhailo (1972–)   Politician, journalist and negotiator. He was deported from Belarus in 2004. In 2022, serving as chief adviser to UA President Zelenskyy.

Poroshenko, Petro (1965–)   Businessman, former president of Ukraine (2014–2019). Previously played roles in both Party of Regions and Our Ukraine, including as foreign minister (2009–2010). Signed Minsk agreements and in 2016 appeared in Panama Papers.

Potemkin, Grigory (1739–1791)   RU military leader and statesman, governor-general of Russia's new southern provinces under Catherine II, founder of Kherson and Sevastopol. His name is preserved in the title of a film by Sergei Eisenstein and the famous steps in Odesa. His remains were removed from St Catherine's Cathedral by RU troops before their evacuation from Kherson.

Putin, Vladimir (1952–)   President of the RU Federation; twice PM (before and in between presidential cycles); originally an intelligence officer, including in the former GDR.

Radakin, Tony (1965–)   UK Admiral, Chief of the Defence Staff (since 2021).

Ratushniy, Roman (1997–2022)   Euromaidan activist, subsequently environmentalist and civic campaigner, killed during fights against RU forces at Izyum (on 9 June 2022).

Reznikov, Oleksii (1966–)   UA lawyer, businessman, deputy PM for the reintegration of the temporarily occupied territories (2020–2021), defence minister (2021–2023).

Shevchenko, Taras (1814–1861)   UA poet, writer, artist, public and political figure, folklorist and ethnographer, advocated UA independence, also known as Kobzar Taras. Main UA university in Kyiv named after him.

Shmyhal, Denys (1975–)   UA entrepreneur and politician, prime minister (2020–).

Shoigu, Sergei (1955–)   RU Minister of Defence (2012–), ex-minister for emergency situations (1991–2012); signed deal on grain exports with UA in July 2022.

Steinmeier, Frank-Walter (1956–)   DE Social Democratic politician, head of state (2017–); twice foreign minister previously; known for his efforts to preserve peace between UA and RU. His visit to Kyiv was called off by UA government in April 2022.

Stoltenberg, Jens (1959–)   Norwegian centre-left politician, son of former defence and foreign minister Thorvald Stoltenberg; serving since 2014 as the 13th Secretary General of NATO (previously twice PM of Norway). His appointment as governor of central bank of Norway was announced in February 2022, but the transfer was postponed due to UA war.

Sullivan, Jake (1976–)   US political analyst, national security adviser in the Biden administration.

Surovikin, Sergei (1966–)   RU general, commander of aerospace forces, also known as "General Armageddon" for brutality displayed in Syria. He was leading the war on UA from September until December 2022 (after which he became deputy to Gerasimov).

Trytek, Piotr (1971–)   PL major general, appointed in October 2022 to lead the EU mission for training UA troops. Previously served in Iraq and Afghanistan, was commander of 11th Lubuska Armoured Cavalry Division.

Turchynov, Oleksandr (1964–)   Politician, economist, screenwriter, Baptist minister, acting UA president in Spring 2014, acting PM in 2010, Director of the Security Service in 2005.

Tyahnybok, Oleh (1968–)   Lviv-born doctor, far-right politician, leader of Svoboda party, considered to be neo-Nazi and anti-Semitic (fights against "Muscovite-Jewish mafia", in his own words); voted Person of the Year in 2012 by readers of UA's leading news magazine (*Korrespondent*).

Tymoshenko, Yulia (1960–)   Engineer and economist, successful but controversial businesswoman in gas industry, PM of Ukraine (in 2005 and again in

2007–2010), co-leader of the Orange Revolution, recognisable by her crown of braids.

Vadatursky, Oleksiy (1947–2022)   Grain tycoon, one of the richest businessmen in UA, killed by a rocket attack against Mykolaiv on 31 July, together with his wife.

Von der Leyen, Ursula (1958–)   European Commission president (since 2019); previously DE CDU politician, minister holding various portfolios in coalition governments led by Angela Merkel.

Yanukovych, Viktor (1950–)   Transport manager, governor of Donetsk Oblast (1997–2002); president of Ukraine (2010-2014), PM before and after the Orange Revolution; deposed from presidential office by Revolution of Dignity.

Yaroslav the Wise (980–1054)   Grand Prince of Kyiv from 1019 until his death; also Prince of Novgorod on three occasions. He promoted the spread of Christianity in the Kyivan state and fortified Kyiv (including building Golden Gate).

Yatsenyuk, Arseniy (1974–)   Economist, lawyer, politician, PM of Ukraine (2014–2016). Previously served as economy minister, foreign minister, and chairman of the parliament.

Yovanovitch, Marie Louise "Masha" (1958–)   Canadian-American former diplomat, recalled from her posting in Kyiv before the end of her term. She was accused by lawyer Rudy Giuliani of trying to undermine President Trump and blocking efforts to investigate Democrats such as former vice president Joe Biden.

Yushchenko, Viktor (1954–)   President of Ukraine (2005–2010), co-leader of the Orange Revolution (2004–2005); known for disfigured face due to poison attack (most likely by RU agents).

Zaluzhnyi, Valerii (1973–)   UA four-star general, Commander in Chief of the armed forces (since 2021). Rumoured as a possible replacement for Zelenskyy in August 2022.

Zelenskyy, Volodymyr (1978–)   Comedian, actor, president of UA (2019–). Unpopular before the RU invasion, widely supported afterwards. Compared to Churchill. His Jewish origins are often mentioned as evidence of UA not being dominated by Nazis, contrary to RU propaganda.

Zlochevsky, Mykola (1966–)   UA oil and natural gas businessman, politician, oligarch. Minister of Ecology and Natural Resources (2010–2012), Deputy Secretary of National Security and Defence Council (2012–2014), co-founder of largest UA oil and natural gas company Burisma Holdings; targeted by UK Serious Fraud Office (2014–2018), reportedly lives in Monaco.

Topography

Azov Sea   A sea in Eastern Europe connected to the Black Sea by the Kerch Strait, and sometimes regarded as a northern extension of the Black Sea, fed by the Don and Kuban rivers.

Bakhmut   UA city in Donetsk Oblast but outside DPR, on Bakhmutka River; target of RU offensive efforts (including by Wagner Group) in autumn 2022 and following winter.

Balaklava   A settlement on the Crimean Peninsula, on the south side of Sevastopol, known for the disastrous Charge of the Light Brigade during the Crimean War (1854).

Black Sea   A marginal Mediterranean sea of the Atlantic Ocean lying between Europe and Asia, bounded by Bulgaria, Georgia, Romania, Russia, Turkey and Ukraine.

Bornholm   DK island in the Baltic Sea between SE and PL. Sabotage against the Nord Stream gas pipelines took place close to its shores in September 2022.

Bucha   A small town northwest of Kyiv, close to Hostomel Airport, venue of atrocities committed by RU soldiers during the first phase of the war in March 2022.

Chernobyl   Site of nuclear power plant in northern UA, venue of 1986 disaster. Occupied by RU forces in the early phase of the war.

Crimea   A peninsula situated along the north coast of the Black Sea (population 2.4 million, made up mostly of ethnic Russians with significant Ukrainian and Crimean Tatar minorities, among others). Seized from Ottoman Empire by RU in late 18th century, defended in 1850s against allied invasion, transferred to UA while in USSR (1954).

Debaltseve   A city in Donetsk Oblast, venue of major battle in 2015 (victory of separatist forces).

Dnieper, or Dnipro   A major river cutting UA into western and eastern halves, rising near Smolensk, RU, before flowing through Belarus and UA into the Black Sea. It is the longest river in UA and Belarus, and the fourth longest river in Europe.

Dniester   Third longest river in UA; rising close to the PL border, and marking much of the border between UA and MD, discharging into the Black Sea (south of Odesa).

Donbas   Historical, cultural and economic region in southeast UA, rich in minerals, comprising Donetsk and Luhansk counties (oblasts), with significant RU-speaking population; venue of civil war since 2014; name abbreviated from Donets Basin. It became incorporated into UA when the USSR was formed.

Donets   Fourth longest river in UA, feeding into the Don River (in RU territory).

Donetsk   Eastern UA city, capital and administrative centre of Donetsk Oblast, which is UA's most populous county (and DPR). Originally called Yuzovka (Hughesovka), and later Stalin and Stalino (1921–1964).

Galicia   A region of East-Central Europe, north of the Carpathian Mountains. A former province of AT, it now forms part of southeastern PL and western UA. Not to be confused with a Spanish region with the same name.

Hostomel   A city in Bucha Raion, Kyiv Oblast, northwest of the UA capital city of Kyiv, mainly known for Hostomel Airport (or Antonov Airport), a major international cargo facility, site of an intense battle at the time of the RU invasion in February 2022.

Irpin   A town and river west of Kyiv, with a history of protecting Kyiv in various wars. UA forces blew up its dam to flood the area and prevent the RU advance on Kyiv in February 2022.

Izyum   Eastern UA city on the Donets River in Kharkiv Oblast, under RU occupation from 1 April until 10 September 2022.

Kerch Strait   A strait connecting the Black Sea (south) and the Azov Sea (north), separating the Kerch Peninsula of Crimea in the west from the Taman Peninsula of Krasnodar Krai (RU) in the east. It is 3.1 to 15 kilometres wide, and up to 18 metres deep.

Kharkiv   A major city in northeast UA, which the RU army tried but failed to conquer in spring 2022.

Kherson   Southern UA city on Dnieper River, occupied by RU army shortly after the start of the 2022 invasion, later liberated by UA forces in November 2022.

Kramatorsk   Eastern UA city in western part of the Donbas, maintained under UA central government control after 2015; centre of administration of Kyiv-controlled part of Donetsk Oblast.

Kyiv   UA capital city in the north of the country, built on the Dnieper River, centre of state since late ninth century. Population around 3 million (before 2022 war). Was "Hero City" of USSR.

Luhansk   Eastern UA city, capital and administrative centre of Luhansk Oblast (and LPR).

Lviv   Western UA city, founded in mid-13th century; main centre of historic Galicia, with Polish, Jewish and Austro-Hungarian traditions. It never was part of RU or UA until WWII, and appeared as strong base of UA nationalism (obtaining derogatory nickname *Banderstadt*). Temporary seat of various embassies in spring 2022.

Lyman   Formerly Krasnyi Lyman from 1925–2016; city in Donetsk region of UA, important railway junction; occupied by RU forces from May until October 2022; UA authorities found two mass graves there after liberation.

Mariupol   Eastern UA industrial (Azovstal) and port city, originally founded by Greeks. Carries military importance for invading RU army to create land corridor between Donbas and Crimea.

Mykolaiv   A city in southern UA, located on Southern Bug river, with access to Black Sea; administrative centre of Mykolaiv Oblast; with observatory (founded in 1821) and Museum of Shipbuilding. In 2022 functioned as block preventing RU forces moving towards Odesa and served as base for UA forces fighting to retake Kherson.

North Crimean Canal   A land improvement canal for irrigation and watering of Kherson Oblast and the Crimean Peninsula, built in 1961–1975, providing 85% of the freshwater needs of Crimea. Blockage from 2014 caused economic and environmental damage, and RU forces blew up the NCC dam in February 2022.

Odesa   Third most populous UA city, major Black Sea port and cultural centre. Was "Hero City" of USSR. Saw violent clashes in 2014, and was hit by rocket attacks in 2022.

Oskil   South-flowing river in RU and eastern UA (with major reservoir in Kharkiv Oblast); reached by UA forces after September 2022 counteroffensive east of Kharkiv.

Pereiaslav   A town in central UA, regimental city of UA Cossacks from 16th century, venue of controversial agreement in 1654. Home of Jewish community since 17th century, and saw a number of pogroms. Hosts over 20 museums.

Poltava   East-central UA city, venue of 1709 battle (Peter I defeating SE army).

Przewodów   PL village close to UA border, hit by UA-fired missile in November 2022 (causing death of two civilians).

Ruthenia   Originally a medieval Latin name for the Kyivan Rus and the Kingdom of Galicia-Volhynia; since early modern times mostly associated with the Ruthenian lands of the PL crown and the Cossack Hetmanate. AT officials from 1770s until 1918 maintained this name for lands inhabited by Ukrainians in the Kingdom of Galicia and Lodomeria, overlapping with contemporary western UA.

Sevastopol   A city with major military harbour on the west side of Crimea. Was "Hero City" of USSR.

Severodonetsk   A major eastern UA industrial city in Donbas, invaded by RU forces in May–June 2022.

Snake Island   A small island of strategic importance belonging to UA, located in the Black Sea near the Danube Delta. The RU navy seized it shortly after the 2022 invasion, but lost it by the end of June.

Southern Bug An 806-kilometre-long river beginning in western UA and moving downstream, in a southeasterly direction, reaching the Black Sea below Mykolaiv. (Not to be confused with the Western Bug that flows from UA to PL.)

Transcarpathia Geographical and historical region; part of HU for about a millennium, then joined to the newly established Czechoslovakia after WWI (as Subcarpathian Ruthenia); annexed by HU in 1938–1939 and finally incorporated into UA after WWII.

Transnistria A narrow strip of land between the Dniester River and the UA–MD border; officially called the Pridnestrovian Moldavian Republic (PMR); an unrecognised breakaway state that is internationally recognised as part of MD but controlled by RU, which stations a small army unit there.

Volhynia A historic region in Central and Eastern Europe without clearly defined borders, between southeastern PL, southwestern Belarus and western UA; name preserved in "Volhynia massacre" by UA nationalists.

Zaporizhzhia A city on the Dnieper River in southeast UA, historically a Cossack base. Location of Europe's largest nuclear power plant (at nearby town of Enerhodar); venue of intense fighting and fire in March 2022 and subsequent controversies.

Weapons

Abrams (M1) US main battle tank with 1500 HP gas turbine engine and 120 mm cannon, designed by Chrysler Defense (now General Dynamics Land Systems), named after US army General Creighton Williams Abrams, Jr. In service since 1980; a decision about donating a small number to UA was announced in January 2023.

AGM-88 HARM A tactical, air-to-surface antiradiation missile designed to home in on electronic transmissions coming from surface-to-air radar systems; originally developed by Texas Instruments, it was used against RU air defence systems in eastern UA.

AMX-10 RC FR armoured fighting vehicle (light combat tank) manufactured by Nexter Systems, with 105 mm cannon and two machine guns; donation to UA announced in January 2023.

Archer FH77BW L52 Mobile artillery system developed by Swedish company Bofors, with 35–50 km range, offered to UA in 2023.

ATACMS US missile with minimum 300 km firing range; 13 feet long, GPS aided, in service since 1991 Persian Gulf War; a single firing costs $1 million. Produced by Lockheed Martin. Demanded by UA but US refused to provide.

Avenger US-made air defence system, provided to UA for protection from Iranian drones in 2022.

Bayraktar TB2   TR-made "cheap but lethal" military drone, with cameras on board, can remain airborne for 27 hours; deployed in Donbas in 2021, and turned out to be most valuable for UA in first phase of the war in 2022 by bringing precision air-strike capabilities.

BAZ-5921   Wheeled amphibious vehicle of load capacity 7 tons capable of travelling on all categories of roads, designed in USSR in late 1960s.

BM-21 Grad   Self-propelled 122 mm multiple rocket launcher designed in the USSR.

BMP   RU amphibious tracked armoured infantry fighting vehicle; EL and SK donated to UA.

Bradley   Tracked armoured fighting vehicle platform of the US, developed by FMC Corporation and manufactured by BAE Systems Land & Armaments; named after US General Omar Bradley. US announced donation to UA in January 2023.

BTR   RU amphibious armoured personnel carrier, used since 1980s.

Bushmaster   Australian-built lightly armoured infantry mobility vehicle; its role is to provide protected mobility transport (or protected troop lift capability), with infantry dismounting from the vehicle before going into action.

Caesar   Long-range, self-propelled howitzer, donated to UA by FR.

Challenger 2   A third-generation UK main battle tank, in service with the armies of the UK and Oman. It was designed and built by Vickers Defence Systems, now known as BAE Systems Land & Armaments (8.3 m length, 120 mm cannon).

Dirty bomb   A radiological weapon that combines radioactive material with conventional explosives (e.g. a mix of explosives, such as dynamite, with radioactive powder or pellets).

F-16   US single-engine multirole combat aircraft, produced by Lockheed Martin, demanded by UA since January 2023, but denied by both US and UK.

Gepard   All-weather antiaircraft gun, developed in the 1960s, supplied by DE to UA.

GMLRS   US missile (six can be loaded in one HIMARS), $160,000 cost of firing.

HARMs   High-speed Anti-Radiation Missiles.

Harpoon   All-weather, over-the-horizon, antiship missile developed and manufactured by McDonnell Douglas (now Boeing Defense, Space & Security), supplied to UA by DK.

HIMARS   Multiple launch rocket system (High Mobility Artillery Rocket System) with 70–80 km range; donated to UA by US, becoming a game changer in summer 2022 (even though the most powerful version was not provided);

particularly effective against ammunition depots and distant infrastructure (e.g. bridges).

Howitzer   A short gun for firing shells on high trajectories at low velocities.

Hypersonic weapon   One that can travel at hypersonic speed, i.e. 5–25 times faster than sound (1 to 5 miles per second). Apart from the US and RU, CN, IN and Iran can build these.

IRIS-T   Medium-range infrared homing missile, designed to protect cities, available in both air-to-air and ground defence surface-to-air variants; provided to UA by DE from autumn 2022.

Iskander   Short-range RU ballistic missile (9K720) with precision to hit targets 500 km away, carrying up to 800 kg explosives; 310 mile range, both GPS and inertial guidance, cost $3 million, 2006–2008.

Javelin   US antitank missile, effective within 2 km range, destroys tanks from the top. UA received them from US already before 2022; played major role against invading RU tank columns in early phase of war in 2022.

Kinzhal   RU hypersonic, nuclear-capable, air-to-surface missile with 2,000 km range, travels at more than five times the speed of sound.

KRAB, or AHS KRAB   A 155 mm NATO-compatible, self-propelled tracked gun-howitzer designed in Poland by Huta Stalowa Wola (HSW).

Leclerc   A third-generation FR main battle tank developed and manufactured by Nexter Systems. It is 9.8 m long, has a 120 mm cannon, and was named in honour of Marshal Philippe Leclerc de Hauteclocque. Used in the Yemeni civil war, delivery to UA floated in January 2023.

Leopard   A main battle tank designed by Porsche and manufactured by Krauss-Maffei in West Germany, first entering service in 1965, with 105 mm cannon (weaker than T72).

Leopard 2   A third-generation, 10 m long main battle tank originally developed by Krauss-Maffei in the 1970s for the West German army. It entered service in 1979 and succeeded the earlier Leopard 1 as the main battle tank of the West German army. Requested by UA government, and donated in 2023 by DE and other European governments.

M113   US armoured personnel carrier, an all-terrain vehicle used since the Vietnam War; provided to UA, used – for example – in the Kharkiv counteroffensive.

M270 MLRS   US-produced armoured, self-propelled multiple-launch rocket system with 80 km range, firing two rounds per minute. First delivered to the US army in 1982.

M777   Long-range howitzer provided to UA by US and Canada.

M982 Excalibur   A 155 mm, 48 kg extended-range guided (with GPS) artillery shell developed in the US; first used in Iraq in 2007.

Malloy   UK heavy-lift drone (T150) transporting medical, food and ammunition supplies.

Marder   DE armoured personnel carrier, supplied to UA by DE in 2023.

Mastiff   Armoured vehicle, resistant to landmines; UK donated 120 to UA in 2022.

Mi-8   Originally USSR war helicopter (medium size, twin-turbine); used by both RU and UA.

Mi-26   Soviet/RU heavy transport helicopter with 800 km range (first launched in 1977).

MiG   Originally USSR warplane; US rejected PL transfer of them to UA.

MIM-23 HAWK   US-made medium-range surface-to-air missile, provided to UA by Spain in December 2022.

NASAMS   National Advanced Surface-to-Air Missile Systems.

NLAW   Next Generation Light Anti-Tank Weapon: an SE/UK-produced portable system used by a single operator, with armour-piercing warhead, effective in 20–800 m range.

OTR-21 Tochka   RU missile, with 43 mile range and passive radar, entered service in 1976. Each cost around $300,000.

Pantsir   Medium-range surface-to-air missile and antiaircraft artillery systems, manufactured by Ulyanovsk Mechanical Plant.

Panzerfaust 3   Portable shoulder-fired antitank weapon from DE, supplied to UA.

Patriot   Surface-to-air missile system manufactured by Raytheon; US and a few other countries promised to provide to UA in December 2023 after RU rocket campaign against UA cities.

Phosphorus bombs   Used by RU to produce large amount of smoke and burning of targets.

PM M1910   A heavy machine gun used by the Imperial RU army during WWI, RU Civil War and WWII. Later, the gun saw service in the Korean War and the Vietnam War, and some have been spotted in the recent war in Donbas (UA).

PRSM   The most advanced rocket artillery to be developed by the US.

PzH2000 (Panzerhaubitze 2000)   DE 155 mm self-propelled howitzer developed by Krauss-Maffei Wegmann and Rheinmetall in the 1980s and 1990s for the DE army.

RAAM   Remote Anti-Armour Mine.

RIM-7 Sea Sparrow   US ship-borne short-range antiaircraft and antimissile weapon system, primarily intended for defence against antiship missiles, provided to UA by US.

RM-70 Vampire   Multiple rocket launcher with up to 20 km firing range, designed and manufactured in the Czech Republic by Excalibur Army.

Sarmat (RS-28)   An RU liquid-fuelled, MIRV-equipped super-heavy intercontinental ballistic missile produced since 2009, also known as "Satan II".

Shahed-136   A very small, simple, low- and slow-flying UCAV (drone), originating from Iran, used by RU since October 2022.

Starstreak   UK semiautomatic air defence system with 7 km range (UK donated seven to UA).

Stinger   US surface-to-air missile, up to 8 km range, used in Soviet–Afghan and Iraq–Iran wars. US gave around 1,500 to UA to prevent air superiority by RU (also supplied by NL).

Stormer HVM   Mobile platform for Starstreak missiles, with 640 km range.

Stryker   Eight-wheeled US combat vehicle, produced by General Dynamics Land Systems–Canada; donation to UA announced in January 2023.

Sukhoi   Originally USSR, single-seat, twin-engine jet aircraft, used by both RU and UA in the 2022 war (Su-25).

Switchblade   US drone, effective against tanks; ten sent by US to UA in 2022.

T-72   Battle tank introduced in Soviet army in 1970s, with 125 mm cannon; replacing T-34 and T-55. PL and CZ provided some to UA in 2022.

TOS-1 Buratino   A Soviet multiple rocket launcher (220 mm 30-barrel or 24-barrel) capable of using thermobaric warheads, mounted on a T-72 tank chassis.

UCAVs   Unmanned combat aerial vehicles.

Vacuum bombs   Also called thermobaric weapons; a particularly brutal bomb filled with an explosive and chemical mix, causing supersonic blast waves on explosion.

Zuni   127 mm unguided aircraft rockets developed by the Hunter-Douglas Division of Bridgeport Brass Company and deployed by US and FR, offered to UA in January 2023.

Timeline: Ukrainian history and the first year of the Russia–Ukraine war

882	State of Kyivan Rus established by Viking Prince Oleg
988	Vladimir I, pagan prince of Novgorod and grand prince of Kyiv, accepts the Orthodox Christian faith and is baptised in the Crimean city of Chersonesus
1037	Construction of Golden Gate and Saint Sophia Cathedral begins in Kyiv under Grand Prince Yaroslav the Wise
1157	Yuri Dolgorukiy dies in Kyiv (followed by the expulsion of his son Andrei Bogoliubsky)
1253	Daniel of Galicia forms Kingdom of Ruthenia after destruction of Kyiv by Mongols
1385–1386	Union of Krewo creates Polish-Lithuanian state, including much of today's UA
1579	Polish-Lithuanian Commonwealth incorporates most Ruthenian lands, codified in the Union of Lublin
1648–1657	Khmelnytsky Uprising (Cossack–Polish War) against PL domination
1654	Pereiaslav Agreement (ceremonial pledge of allegiance by Cossacks to RU Tsar)
1709	Battle of Poltava; RU defeats SE (end of Great Northern War)
1763	Catherine II's decree banning teaching in UA in Kyiv-Mohyla Academy
1775	Zaporizhian Sich destroyed by RU forces, Cossack self-government liquidated; closing of UA schools at the offices of the Cossack regiment
1787	RU Empress Catherine II visits newly acquired Crimea (ahead of further RU–TR wars)

1795	Scottish-born industrialist Charles Gascoigne launches metal industry in Luhansk
1804	According to a special decree in the RU empire, all UA language schools are banned, leading to the degradation of the UA population
1847	T. Shevchenko arrested and exiled
1848	Spring of Nations; Supreme Ruthenian Council created and declares that Galician Ruthenians are part of the bigger UA nation. The Council adopts the yellow and blue flag (Flag of Ukraine), hoisted for the first time over Lviv Town Hall.
1853–1856	Crimean War: RU vs TR/EN/FR (results in weakening RU influence in Europe)
1859	Ministry of Religion and Science of Austria-Hungary attempts to replace UA Cyrillic alphabet with Latin in Eastern Galicia and Bukovina
1863	RU interior minister bans publications and instruction in UA language (decree remains in force until 1905)
1868	Welshman John Hughes wins concession from RU government to set up a metallurgy plant in a town named after himself (Yuzovka), today's Donetsk
1869	Introduction of the PL language as the official language of education and of the administration of PL Eastern Galicia (today's western UA)
1905	First RU Revolution, crew of Black Sea battleship Potemkin rebel against officers
1917–1921	Ukrainian–Soviet war (part of broader civil war)
28 Dec 1922	USSR created, with UA becoming one of founding members (with Donbas incorporated into Ukrainian Soviet Socialist Republic)
1924	Law of the Republic of PL on limiting the use of UA language in administration, judiciary, education
1930	Organisation of UA Nationalists (OUN) begins sabotage actions (in PL)
1932–1934	Great UA famine ("Holodomor")
1939–1941	Southeast PL integrated into UA, within USSR, after Molotov–Ribbentrop Pact

1941–1944	OUN, led by Stepan Bandera, collaborates with Nazis (killing Jews and Poles)
1945	WWII ends, southeast PL transferred to Ukraine (within USSR)
1954	USSR transfers Crimea from Russia to Ukraine, following death of Stalin, in honour of the 300th anniversary of the Pereiaslav Agreement
1965	Arrests and show trials of UA "sixtiers" (anti-Stalinist intellectuals)
1986	Nuclear explosion at Chernobyl power plant, major disaster resulting from design flaws and negligence (contributing to the demise of the Soviet Union)
Jul 1990	New UA parliament (Verkhovna Rada) declares independence from USSR
Jan 1991	The Crimean regional government decides to hold its own referendum on restoring the autonomy of Crimea
4 Sep 1991	The Supreme Soviet of the now Autonomous Crimean Republic (ACR) proclaims the region's sovereignty, adding that it intends to create a sovereign democratic state *within* UA
8 Dec 1991	Leaders of RU, UA and Belarus sign the Belovezh Accords in Viskuli (Belarus) to end the USSR and lay the foundations for future relations
31 Dec 1991	Dissolution of the USSR; Commonwealth of Independent States (CIS) formed with UA as a founding member, which, however, did not ratify the CIS Charter
1993	UA becomes associate member of Economic Union of the CIS amid hyperinflation
1994	Budapest Memorandum (UA given vague security guarantees by great powers)
16–17 Mar 1995	UA President Kuchma, after consulting with RU President Boris Yeltsin and receiving his support, sends UA special forces to arrest the Crimean government. Pro-RU Crimean leader Yuri Meshkov deported to RU.
1996	The hryvnia replaces the coupon as national currency
1997	RU and UA sign Partition Treaty, establishing two independent national fleets and dividing armaments and bases between them

21 Oct 1998	Constitution of the Autonomous Republic of Crimea enters into force, defining the legal framework of the ARC within the UA state
2002	NATO-Russia Council established for handling security issues and joint projects
2003	RU threatens to seize the UA island of Tuzla in the Azov Sea by force (violating UA territorial integrity)
2004	Viktor Yushchenko poisoned with dioxin during presidential campaign; Viktor Yanukovych wins but election appears to have been rigged
2005	Orange Revolution; Yushchenko installed as president (and Tymoshenko as PM)
2006	Constitutional reform enhancing the powers of the UA prime minister
20 Jul 2006	A joint UA–US military exercise is cancelled, following anti-NATO protests on the Crimean Peninsula (Feodosia)
Apr 2008	Bucharest NATO summit considers UA and GE membership ("open door" policy)
16 May 2008	UA becomes 152nd member of the World Trade Organization (WTO)
18–19 May 2008	EBRD Annual General Meeting held in Kyiv
Autumn 2008	UA quickly and heavily affected by global financial crisis, turns to IMF for loan
Jan 2009	Gazprom stops gas deliveries to UA, triggering crisis of supply for two weeks
24 Aug 2009	Anti-UA demonstrations held in Crimea by ethnic RU residents
29 Nov 2009	RU President Medvedev proposes "New European Security Order"
2010	Yanukovych elected UA president, plans for NATO membership shelved. Outgoing President Yushchenko awards Bandera the status of "Hero of Ukraine", sparking protests from PL and Israel (status withdrawn in 2011).
21 Apr 2010	Kharkiv Pact: lease of Sevastopol to RU extended to 2042
5 Feb 2011	New START treaty between US and RU enters into force

Jun 2011	Missile cruiser USS *Monterey* (carrying Aegis Ballistic Missile Defence System) enters Black Sea to attend the Sea Breeze 2011 UA–US naval exercise; criticised by Moscow
7 Jul 2011	Meshkov in press conference calls for a referendum on restoring the Constitution of Crimea (1992 version), which actually declared Crimea a sovereign state
Oct 2011	Former UA PM Tymoshenko sentenced to seven years imprisonment
8 Nov 2011	Nord Stream 1 inaugurated by DE Chancellor Angela Merkel, RU President Dmitry Medvedev, FR PM François Fillon and NL PM Mark Rutte, together with EU Energy Commissioner Günther Oettinger, at a ceremony held in Lubmin
7 Feb 2012	Kivalov–Kolesnichenko Law adopted, giving the status of regional language to RU and other minority languages
Jun 2012	UA co-hosts (with PL) UEFA European Football Championship
2013	EU Association Agreement completed but President Yanukovych does not sign it
Nov 2013	"Euromaidan" protest begins against Yanukovych and for EU association in Kyiv
13 Dec 2013	John McCain meets Yatsenyuk and far-right Tyahnybok in Kyiv, speaks to crowd
4 Feb 2014	Conversation of Victoria Nuland with Ambassador Pyatt appears on Youtube (including proposition for Yatsenyuk to lead government and "f-ck the EU" rant)
Feb 2014	European foreign ministers mediate a compromise between government and demonstrators, involving a unity government and early elections
22 Feb 2014	Yanukovych leaves Kyiv (Oleksandr Turchynov becomes interim president)
23 Feb 2014	Kivalov–Kolesnichenko language law abolished by Verkhovna Rada (decision not signed by the interim president)
Mar 2014	Russia invades and annexes Crimea (after referendum); condemned by West
5 Mar 2014	EU launches sanctions in connection with misappropriation of state funds in UA

21 Mar 2014	PM Yatsenyuk, Herman van Rompuy and José Manuel Barroso sign the core chapters of the EU Association Agreement in Brussels
Apr 2014	Separatist forces declare independence in the Donbas region (DPR and LPR)
2 May 2014	Fascist riot in Odesa leaves about 50 people dead and hundreds injured
25 May 2014	Billionaire Petro Poroshenko wins presidential election
17 Jul 2014	Malaysia Airlines Flight 17 from Amsterdam to Kuala Lumpur shot down with RU-made Buk missile while flying over eastern UA. All 283 passengers and 15 crew killed.
Sep 2014	Minsk I agreement (Minsk Protocol); ceasefire breaks down shortly after
Jan 2015	Battle of Debaltseve (DPR separatist forces recapture city from UA army)
Feb 2015	Minsk II agreement signed (but civil war continues for subsequent years)
14 Oct 2015	Defenders Day celebrated for first time on new date
Dec 2015	Bank of Russia issues a new 100 rouble banknote featuring images of Crimea. RU cyberattack hits Kyiv's power grid and causes major blackout.
1 Jan 2016	Entry into force of the EU–Ukraine free trade area
6 Apr 2016	Dutch referendum voters overwhelmingly reject (by 61% majority with 32% turnout) closer EU links to UA (EU–UA partnership deal)
Jul 2016	NATO summit in Warsaw, NATO-Ukraine Commission endorses Comprehensive Assistance Package (CAP), boosting NATO's assistance for UA, and standing by 2008 pledge that UA and GE "will be members"
31 Dec 2016	US senators John McCain, Lindsey Graham and Amy Klobuchar visit front-line UA armed forces and call for tougher actions against RU (for allegedly interfering with US elections), promising generous material support
28 Sep 2017	New UA law on education enters into force, as a key instrument for modernising UA's education system and bringing it up to EU standards, but triggering protest due to the potentially negative effect on minority languages

Oct 2017	RU cyberattack hits key UA infrastructure, including National Bank and power grid
Feb 2018	UA Constitutional Court rules (after delays) that Kivalov–Kolesnichenko law is unconstitutional
15 May 2018	Inauguration of the 19 km Kerch Bridge by Putin, leading the first ever convoy from mainland RU into Crimea (an industrial and cultural show of force)
Jan 2019	Independence of the Orthodox Church of Ukraine from the Russian Orthodox Church formally recognised
Feb 2019	Membership of EU and NATO enshrined as goals in preamble of UA Basic Law
21 Apr 2019	Comedian Volodymyr Zelenskyy wins presidential election on platform to reduce power of oligarchs and find negotiated solution in Donbas instead of war
25 Apr 2019	Verkhovna Rada passes language law promoted by outgoing president Poroshenko
May 2019	Donald Trump recalls US ambassador in Kyiv, Marie Yovanovitch
25 Jul 2019	Trump–Zelenskyy phone call (discussing military aid and Burisma gas company)
2 Aug 2019	US withdrawal from INF Treaty, after accusing RU of noncompliance
1 Oct 2019	UA government agrees to Steinmeier Formula to create peace in Donbas
Feb 2020	Hardliner Vladislav Surkov replaced by Putin with UA-born RU official Dmitry Kozak, to be in charge of managing Moscow's relations with UA
Mar 2020	UA goes into first lockdown to curb Covid-19 pandemic; economy enters recession
Spring 2021	RU army begins concentration of forces close to UA border
Jun 2020	IMF approves a $5 billion stand-by agreement to help UA stave off default during a pandemic-induced recession
16 Jun 2021	Putin–Biden summit in Geneva over UA question
1 Jul 2021	New UA law on agriculture; land would be available for sale to individuals and to legal entities beginning in 2024. The World Bank supports the creation of a "fair and transparent farmland market" with $200 million in loans.

12 Jul 2021	Putin publishes 7,000-word essay, "On the historical unity of Russians and Ukrainians", denying existence of UA and Belarus as independent nations
23 Aug 2021	Zelenskyy launches multilateral "Crimea Platform" initiative
27 Aug 2021	US President Joe Biden authorises $60 million in largely defensive weapons to be sent to UA
1 Sep 2021	UA President Zelenskyy visits US President Biden in Washington
12 Oct 2021	(23rd) EU–UA summit in Kyiv (with Charles Michel and Ursula von der Leyen)
Nov 2021	US Director of National Intelligence Avril Haines briefs NATO allies in Brussels about RU preparations for full-scale invasion of UA
7 Dec 2021	Putin–Biden two-hour virtual summit discussing war and potential sanctions
9–10 Dec 2021	Two-day online "Summit for Democracy" organised by US President Joe Biden
16 Dec 2021	NATO Secretary General Stoltenberg welcomes UA President Zelenskyy to NATO Headquarters in Brussels
Late Dec 2021	President Biden authorises further $200 million in weapons to be drawn from US inventories for UA
23 Dec 2021	Gerasimov discusses regional security issues with his UK counterpart Radakin
Jan 2022	Jake Sullivan sets up regular process at White House to steer information war, helping to thwart RU plans and propaganda
12 Jan 2021	CIA Director William Burns flies to Kyiv and explains RU plans to Zelenskyy, who refuses idea of moving to Lviv and creating panic
16 Jan 2022	New legal provision on the use of the UA language enters into force, criticised by Venice Commission (for lacking right balance between state and minority languages)
19 Jan 2022	Blinken goes to Kyiv, meets Zelenskyy and Kuleba, trying to convince them about moving to Lviv and ensuring continuous functioning of government
	President Biden in Washington publicly speaks about RU plans, hinting at "minor incursion" not prompting same severe response as full-scale invasion

22 Jan 2022	Vice Admiral Kay-Achim Schönbach (chief of DE navy) resigns after saying that Putin "deserves respect" and UA will never win back annexed Crimea (at livestreamed event in IN)
26 Jan 2022	US presents a written response to RU security demands, repeating a commitment to NATO's "open-door" policy while offering a "principled and pragmatic evaluation" of RU concerns (Putin considers it insufficient two days later)
4 Feb 2022	Putin meets China's President Xi Jinping in Beijing, forming united front
18–20 Feb 2022	Munich Security Conference, Zelenskyy attending
21 Feb 2022	RU parliament recognises DPR and LPR (Moscow abandons Minsk process)
24 Feb 2022	Russian forces invade UA (from east, south and north, including from Belarus)
28 Feb 2022	UA government applies for EU membership (followed by MD and GE)
28 Feb 2022	First round of RU–UA peace talks in Gomel region (Belarus), followed up in March
2 Mar 2022	RU forces enter Kherson and surround Mariupol
	UN General Assembly resolution demands end to RU offensive against UA, reaffirms UA sovereignty, independence and territorial integrity (141 out of 193 countries vote in favour)
9 Mar 2022	IMF executive board approves $1.4 billion in Emergency Financing Support to UA
11 Mar 2022	EU heads of state and government issue Versailles Declaration, calling on member states to strengthen defence spending, investment, research and coordination
15 Mar 2022	President Zelenskyy states UA would not join NATO any time soon. Right-wing PMs of PL, Czech Republic and Slovenia visit Kyiv to show support.
24–26 Mar 2022	US President Joe Biden visits Europe, offers liquefied gas deliveries and, in speech in PL, alludes to removal of RU President Putin (point withdrawn day after)
25 Mar 2022	Pope Francis consecrates both UA and RU as "a spiritual act of trust"
29 Mar 2022	RU forces start withdrawing from Kyiv area after failed siege of UA capital city

30 Mar 2022	RU–UA peace talks in TR conclude, without getting closer to ceasefire
3 Apr 2022	Pictures of civilian victims massacred by RU soldiers start to emerge from Bucha
8 Apr 2022	President of the European Commission Ursula von der Leyen and HR/VP Josep Borrell travel to Kyiv to show unwavering support
12 Apr 2022	DE President Steinmeier's proposed trip to Kyiv rejected by UA leadership
14 Apr 2022	Sinking of warship *Moskva*, flagship of Russia's Black Sea Fleet
24 Apr 2022	US Secretary of State Antony Blinken and Secretary of Defence Lloyd Austin meet Zelenskyy in Kyiv (visit only announced after the fact)
26 Apr 2022	UA military donor conference convened by US at Ramstein Air Base in DE
28 Apr 2022	UN Secretary-General António Guterres visits UA (including Irpin and Bucha, venues of alleged RU atrocities) after holding talks with Putin in Moscow
4 May 2022	RU airstrike against Mariupol theatre inflicts death toll of around 600
15 May 2022	UA's Kalush Orchestra wins 2022 Eurovision Song Contest
18 May 2022	SE and FI apply for NATO membership
19 May 2022	US Senate overwhelmingly approves $40 billion in new aid for UA
	In a Freudian slip, former US President George W. Bush mixes up invasion of UA with "unjustified and brutal" invasion of Iraq
20 May 2022	RU declares victory at Azovstal plant, ending two-month battle for Mariupol
1 Jun 2022	US decides to send HIMARS to UA under condition they are not to be used against targets in RU. DE Chancellor Olaf Scholz announces delivery of modern surface-to-air missiles to protect cities from Russian air attacks.
7 Jun 2022	World Bank announces $1.49 billion additional financial support, bringing the value of support package to $4 billion (and reaching $16 billion since independence)

16 Jun 2022	FR President Macron, DE Chancellor Scholz, IT PM Draghi (with RO President Iohannis) visit Kyiv and declare further support for UA
23 Jun 2022	European Council turns UA and MD (but not GE) into EU membership candidates
25 Jun 2022	UA forces start evacuation of Severodonetsk, ending fierce defence effort
1 Jul 2022	NATO concludes three-day summit in Madrid; leaders reiterate unwavering support for UA's independence, sovereignty and territorial integrity
4–5 Jul 2022	UA Recovery Conference in Lugano, Switzerland, discussing reconstruction, with UA PM Denys Shmyhal
9 Jul 2022	President Zelenskyy recalls several ambassadors, including Andriy Melnyk from DE
16 Jul 2022	RU–UA–TR–UN agreement on grain exports (followed by RU strikes on Odesa)
19 Jul 2022	New UA labour law curtailing workers' and trade unions' rights enters into force
26 Jul 2022	Wife of UA president, Olena Zelenska, appears on front page of *Vogue* fashion magazine, inviting international controversy
4 Aug 2022	Amnesty International claims UA army tactics endanger civilians (criticised by many)
9 Aug 2022	Series of explosions at Saki Air Base (Crimea) destroy RU war planes, cause panic
18 Aug 2022	UN chief Guterres and TR President Erdoğan meet President Zelenskyy in Lviv to discuss grain and the situation around Zaporizhzhia nuclear power plant
20 Aug 2022	Car bomb kills Darya Dugina, daughter of RU philosopher A. Dugin, near Moscow
24 Aug 2022	On UA Independence Day: Zelenskyy awards Order of Liberty to former UK PM Boris Johnson in Kyiv; UN chief Guterres laments "sad and tragic milestone"
8 Sep 2022	Long-awaited UA counteroffensive for regaining Kherson, with moderate success
9–10 Sep 2022	As part of a major counteroffensive, UA forces recapture parts of Kharkiv Oblast, including cities Kupiansk and Izyum

14 Sep 2022	Von der Leyen focuses her State of the Union speech on supporting UA war effort, with wife of UA president present in Strasbourg; receives Order of Yaroslav the Wise, 1st class, the day after from Zelenskyy in Kyiv
21 Sep 2022	Putin orders a partial military mobilisation (the first large-scale military mobilisation since WWII) and expresses support for the staged referenda (as precursors to annexation of UA territories)
23 Sep 2022	Four RU-occupied regions (Luhansk, Donetsk, Zaporizhzhia and Kherson) hold referenda to join RU. Western leaders including US President Joe Biden and DE Chancellor Olaf Scholz refer to them as shams.
27 Sep 2022	More than 1,600 RU propaganda accounts taken down by Facebook
	Undersea blasts rupture the Nord Stream 1 and 2 pipelines, leading to huge methane leaks. Former PL foreign minister Radosław Sikorski thanks US on Twitter. Case subsequently considered to be sabotage of disputed origin.
28 Sep 2022	US announces $1.1 billion military aid package to UA (including 18 HIMARS with ammunition and 150 Humvees)
29 Sep 2022	FI announces closure of its borders to RU citizens in response to security threats linked to RU mobilisation
30 Sep 2022	Putin announces four new regions of RU Federation. In response, Zelenskyy requests NATO membership for his country.
1 Oct 2022	UA forces arrive in Lyman; Chechen leader Ramzan Kadyrov calls for drastic measures
8 Oct 2022	Explosion causes damage to Kerch Bridge, supposedly marking Putin's birthday (on 7 October); described by Zelenskyy adviser Podolyak as "the beginning"
10 Oct 2022	RU retaliates for Kerch Bridge attack: 84 cruise missiles and 24 drones hit civilian targets; US replies by offering more powerful weapons
17 Oct 2022	RU forces kill musician Yuri Kerpatenko in his Kherson home for refusing to play music in RU-organised event
19 Oct 2022	Putin signs a decree on the introduction of martial law in the Donetsk, Kherson, Luhansk and Zaporizhzhia regions, recently annexed from UA

26 Oct 2022	RU starts recruiting members of the Afghan National Army Commando Corps, i.e. soldiers previously trained by US Navy SEALs and British armed forces
28 Oct 2022	EU appoints PL General Piotr Trytek to lead its training mission for UA troops
29 Oct 2022	RU suspends grain deal following UA drone attack on Sevastopol (but restores it a few days later)
31 Oct 2022	RU forces launch more than 30 missiles at energy infrastructure in Kyiv and other regions
11 Nov 2022	UA forces enter Kherson after rapid evacuation by RU forces – a major UA victory
15 Nov 2022	Large-scale rocket campaign against UA cities, destroying power infrastructure and causing severe shortages of electricity and water
	UA-fired missile strikes PL village of Przewodów, killing two civilians. PL army put on alert. Zelenskyy calls for strong response against RU until origin of missile revealed. Stoltenberg declares that ultimately RU is to be blamed.
15–16 Nov 2022	G20 meeting of world leaders in Bali. Putin does not attend; Zelenskyy through online intervention sets out conditions for negotiations (including RU forces leaving entire territory of UA, including Crimea).
17 Nov 2022	Three defendants (two RU and one UA citizen) sentenced to life by Netherlands court for downing flight MH17 in 2014
23 Nov 2022	Symbolic decision by the EP declaring RU a "state sponsor of terrorism" for the way RU has systematically attacked civilians and committed war crimes; also calls for more sanctions
30 Nov 2022	DE parliament (Bundestag) approves resolution labelling the 1930s UA famine ("Holodomor") as genocide
2 Dec 2022	Zelenskyy signs decree approving a proposal by the National Security and Defence Council to ban RU-affiliated religious groups and impose sanctions on a number of pro-Moscow bishops
13 Dec 2022	International conference "Standing with the Ukrainian People" in Paris
	UA Verkhovna Rada adopts the law "On National Minorities (Communities) of UA" in its second reading, inviting further criticism

14 Dec 2022	European Parliament's 2022 Sakharov Prize handed to representatives of the "brave people of Ukraine"
19 Dec 2022	Putin visits Belarus; announcing new joint manoeuvres with Belarus President Alexander Lukashenko, raising fears of new attack against Kyiv from north
20 Dec 2022	Zelenskyy visits the front-line city Bakhmut in the Donbas
21 Dec 2022	Zelenskyy lands in Washington: meeting with President Biden and speech to Congress; thanks US for support and demands more weapons (as investment in democracy)
25 Dec 2022	Archbishop of Canterbury and Pope Francis call for end to war in UA
1 Jan 2023	UA armed forces commander Zaluzhnyi tweets picture with Bandera image, causing international scandal (especially in PL)
11 Jan 2023	RU Defence Ministry announces replacement of Surovikin with Gerasimov as head of UA campaign
14 Jan 2023	RU rocket shot down by UA air defence falls on housing block in Dnipro, leading to resignation of Oleksiy Arestovych, presidential adviser, who told the truth about it to the media
18 Jan 2023	Helicopter crash outside Kyiv kills UA interior minister and other officials
20 Jan 2023	Contact group in Ramstein announce further support for UA defence needs
22–24 Jan 2023	Several high-level UA public officials sacked for corruption
23 Jan 2023	US–DE announcements about delivering battle tanks to UA (including Leopards), following appointment of new defence minister in DE
2 Feb 2022	Zelenskyy welcomes von der Leyen and a number of EU commissioners in Kyiv
8–9 Feb 2023	Zelenskyy visits London, Paris and Brussels, speaks at UK and EU parliaments, demands fighter jets from Western countries
10 Feb 2023	Large-scale RU missile attacks on UA territory (allegedly also violating RO and MD air space)
20 Feb 2023	Joe Biden pays unexpected visit to Kyiv, bringing further $0.5 billion in financial aid

21 Feb 2023	Putin speech to Duma repeats usual tropes about origins of war (blames war on West), threatens boosting nuclear armaments
23 Feb 2023	On the eve of invasion anniversary, 141 members of UN endorse resolution to end the war (calling for a "just and lasting" peace). Seven oppose (including RU and Belarus); CN, IN and South Africa among major abstentions.
24 Feb 2023	Anniversary of RU invasion. Demonstrations in solidarity with UA all over Europe. Leopard tanks from PL arrive in UA; RU halts pipeline oil supply to PL. CN presents "peace plan". European Commission bans TikTok from official devices.

About the editors and authors

LÁSZLÓ ANDOR

Secretary general of FEPS, visiting professor at the ULB (Brussels); previously EU commissioner for employment, social affairs and inclusion (2010–2014), and before that executive director at the European Bank for Reconstruction and Development (EBRD).

ENRIQUE BARÓN CRESPO

Economist and lawyer; president of the FEPS Scientific Council. Formerly president of the European Parliament (1989–1992), and before that Spanish minister for transport, tourism and communication (1982–1985).

HANS-PETER BARTELS

President of Germany's Society for Security Policy (Gesellschaft für Sicherheitspolitik – GSP). Previously, SPD member of the Bundestag from 1998 to 2015, most recently as chair of the Defence Committee. Parliamentary Commissioner for the Armed Forces from 2015 to 2020.

HÅKAN A. BENGTSSON

CEO of Arenagruppen; works on economics, working life, democracy and the welfare state. Arena is a progressive, nonpartisan think tank based in Stockholm, Sweden.

IRENEUSZ BIL

Chair of the Aleksander Kwaśniewski Foundation Amicus Europae, previously assistant professor at the World Economy Research Institute of Warsaw School of Economics; member of the FEPS Scientific Council.

PÉTER TAMÁS BÓZSÓ

Economist, PhD student (University of Pécs), previously policy analyst at GKI Economic Research Ltd.

ALINE BURNI GOMES

Advisor (politics and policy) at the Tony Blair Institute for Global Change (Brussels), previously policy analyst at FEPS.

BOHDAN FERENS

Political scientist, founder of the Social Democratic Platform of Ukraine.

ANDRÉ W. M. GERRITS

Professor of international studies and global politics at the Institute for History of the Faculty of Humanities, Leiden University; member of the FEPS Scientific Council.

CHRISTOS KATSIOULIS

Heads the Friedrich-Ebert-Stiftung (FES) Regional Office for Cooperation and Peace in Europe, located in Vienna. Previously, director of the FES offices in Brussels, London and Athens.

EDWARD KNUDSEN

Doctoral researcher in international relations at the University of Oxford, previously research associate for the Dahrendorf Forum and affiliate research fellow at the Jacques Delors Centre (Berlin).

ANDRIY KORNIYCHUK

Policy analyst at FEPS, previously head of the "Europe and International Politics" programme at the Heinrich-Böll-Stiftung (Warsaw).

REINHARD KRUMM

Head of the Friedrich-Ebert-Stiftung (FES) Regional Office for the Baltic States (Riga); lecturer in Eastern European history at Regensburg University; previously, set up and directed the FES Regional Office for Cooperation and Peace in Europe (Vienna); in the nineties, correspondent of the magazine *Der Spiegel* in Moscow.

KERSTEN LAHL

Lieutenant general out of service of the German Bundeswehr, afterwards president of the Federal Academy for Security Policy.

MICHAEL LANDESMANN

Senior research associate at the Vienna Institute for International Economic Studies (WIIW) and professor of economics at the Johannes Kepler University (Linz). Previously Scientific Director of the WIIW (1996–2016).

GYÖRGY MUDRI

Expert in agriculture and rural development, previously policy officer at the European Commission and advisor at the European Parliament as well as the US Department of Agriculture.

UWE OPTENHÖGEL

Vice-president of FEPS; political analyst and publisher; previously network coordinator of ENoP (European Network of Political Foundations, Brussels) and International Director of the Friedrich-Ebert-Stiftung (Bonn/Berlin).

ANDRÁS RÁCZ

Senior research fellow at the Center for Order and Governance in Eastern Europe, Russia, and Central Asia of the German Council on Foreign Relations (DGAP). In addition, he is senior lecturer at Corvinus University in Budapest.

PETER RUDOLF

Senior fellow, Research Division "The Americas", SWP, Berlin; previously lecturer at the Free University of Berlin; member of the Board of the International Politics Section of the German Political Science Association (DVPW).

SABINE SCHIFFER

Head of the Institute for Responsible Media (IMV, Berlin); senior lecturer at the University of Applied Sciences for Media, Communications and Economics (HMKW, Frankfurt).

OLE SPILLNER

Research assistant on foreign policy in the Director's Office, German Council on Foreign Relations (DGAP).

JACK THOMPSON

Lecturer in American studies, University of Amsterdam.

MĀRTIŅŠ VARGULIS

Deputy director at the Latvian Institute of International Affairs and lecturer at Rīga Stradiņš University; former Head of Division at the Ministry of Defence of Latvia and diplomat at NATO.

GUNTRAM WOLFF

CEO of the German Council on Foreign Relations (DGAP) and Otto-Wolff-Director of its Research Institute. Previously director of Bruegel (Brussels).

YULIYA YURCHENKO

Senior lecturer in political economy at the Department of Accountancy, Finance, and Economics at the University of Greenwich, UK; editor for *Capital and Class* and *Global Political Economy* and vice-chair of the Critical Political Economy Research Network (European Sociological Association).